1-16.73.

CASS LIBRARY OF AFRICAN STUDIES

SOUTH AFRICAN STUDIES

No. 4

General Editors :

ANTHONY ATMORE
School of Oriental and African Studies

SHULA MARKS
Institute of Commonwealth Studies

STANLEY TRAPIDO
Lecturer in the Politics of New States, Oxford University

NATIVE LABOUR IN
SOUTH AFRICA

NATIVE LABOUR IN
SOUTH AFRICA

by

Sheila T. van der Horst

FRANK CASS & CO. LTD.
1971

Published by
FRANK CASS AND COMPANY LIMITED
67 Great Russell Street, London WC1B 3BT
by arrangement with Oxford University Press, London

| First edition | 1942 |
| New impression | 1971 |

ISBN 0 7146 1781 4

Printed in Great Britain by Clarke, Doble & Brendon Ltd.
Plymouth and London

PREFACE

SOUTH AFRICA offers fruitful material for the study of the political and economic problems that arise from the contact of different races and cultures. Race relations have been in the forefront of South Africa's political life ever since the first European settlement in 1652, and have been an important determinant of economic development. At the same time economic factors have helped to form the South African attitudes towards racial questions as well as the Government's racial policy. Foremost among the economic forces has been the desire of European colonists and officials to make use of the indigenous labour supply. This desire continues to-day, but it has come into conflict with the desire of the politically dominant section of the community to create a privileged economic position for all Europeans.

Contact between different peoples of different cultures has resulted in a network of measures imposed by law and custom. In this study I have traced the growth of the use of Native labour and analysed the economic significance of the measures affecting it. I have not been concerned with the rights and wrongs of 'Native policy', but have confined myself to some of its economic repercussions.

In recent years much attention has been given throughout the world to the duties and obligations of colonizing Powers. The problem of reconciling the vested interests of European settlers, the local rights of indigenous peoples, and the welfare of the rest of the world has been much discussed; and in particular the principle of European trusteeship on behalf of dependent African peoples has been widely canvassed and accepted.

In South Africa this principle is fairly generally professed. It is, however, interpreted in very different ways. There is no doubt that the majority of Europeans regard the relation as a permanent one. They do not contemplate the day when their wards will grow out of their dependent state and become full citizens. A small minority regard trusteeship as a temporary phase, during which an unenfranchised and largely illiterate people should be educated for citizenship: equality of opportunity is their goal. Another small minority hope for the eventual separation of Africans and Europeans and the creation of independent communities. They regard complete segregation as the most hopeful solution of present problems, and would even sacrifice all economic co-operation in an attempt to avoid the political and economic discrimination of a caste system.

The principle of trusteeship, as usually conceived in South

Africa, does not demand that the trustee should always place the interests of the ward first. Indeed, it is generally interpreted as involving some benefit for the trustee in return for each special benefit for the African community. Measures which limit the Natives' opportunities and protect European interests are frequently justified as a *quid pro quo* for the reservation of land for Native occupation. As the Natives have progressed, attempts have been made to restrict the opportunities open to them, in order to prevent them from competing with Europeans. Yet many of the barriers that confront the Native population are not malevolently conceived. They are the result of misunderstanding as much as of fear and distrust. Some are fairly generally believed to benefit the Native population as well as the European and Coloured. Thus, restricting the right of Natives to seek work in urban areas is thought to be the most effective method of raising urban standards of living. The misuse of resources and the strangling of economic development are overlooked, for it is not realized that the benefits are confined to a privileged few.

Fortunately, there seems to be a reawakening of the knowledge that the welfare of the Europeans is bound up with that of the Natives. Social services for Natives, including educational facilities, are slowly being increased. Commercial men and manufacturers are becoming increasingly aware that the Native population offers a potential market for their goods and that an undernourished people with low productivity cannot provide a good market. Mine managements, European miners, and farmers know that their incomes are dependent on the maintenance and increase of the supply of Native labour. Nevertheless an avowed policy of economic and political segregation has been officially adopted and there have been increasing attempts to implement it by confining Natives to certain defined spheres.

What of the future? Will the European inhabitants of South Africa attempt to bolster up and perpetuate an economic and social system based on racial privileges and discrimination? I hope this book will provide a background useful to those who contemplate a better future for South Africans of all colours and races.

There are many friends whom I should like to thank for their help. In the first place, Dr. H. M. Robertson of the University of Capetown suggested that I should undertake this study, and has been most generous of his time and knowledge throughout the course of the work. I have found it impracticable to make continual reference in the text to my debt to his researches into the economic history of South Africa and to the guidance he has given me.

The greater part of my material was presented as a thesis to the University of London, where Professor Arnold Plant, formerly Professor of Commerce at the University of Capetown, was my supervisor of studies at the London School of Economics. Without his encouragement in the early stages and constant help in the final drafting this book would never have been completed. I owe more than I can express to his teaching and inspiration.

The University of Capetown, and especially Professor R. Leslie of the Department of Economics, gave me my early training and the opportunity to carry out this study. Parts of the manuscript were discussed with Professor I. Schapera and his Seminar on African Problems, which included among its members Dr. J. S. Marais, Mr. G. F. Thirlby, Dr. H. J. Simons, and Professors A. H. Murray and W. T. Baxter, all of whom contributed valuable criticism and advice. I should also like to acknowledge my debt to the works and criticism of Professor W. H. Hutt.

Senator the Hon. J. D. Rheinallt Jones, Adviser to the South African Institute of Race Relations, Mrs. Rheinallt Jones, and other officials of the Institute have given me the benefit of their wide knowledge of Native affairs. Numerous Government officials, private individuals, and firms have assisted me by supplying information. The South African Public Library, the libraries of the London School of Economics, the Royal Empire Society, the University of Capetown, and the Transvaal Chamber of Mines were rich sources of material and their staffs most helpful.

I am also very grateful to the South African Council for Educational and Social Research,[1] and to the University of Capetown for generous grants towards the cost of preparing and publishing this book; and to Dr. Audrey Richards for seeing it through the press amid all the difficulties and delays arising from war conditions.

Finally, I should like to thank my father for his interest and my husband for his unfailing encouragement and help.

S. T. VAN DER HORST

CAPETOWN
September 1941

[1] The South African Council for Educational and Social Research is not necessarily to be understood as approving by virtue of its grant any of the statements made or views expressed in this publication.

CONTENTS

PART I

ECONOMIC CONTACT BETWEEN EUROPEANS AND NATIVES BEFORE 1870

PART II
THE IMPACT OF THE DIAMOND AND GOLD DISCOVERIES UPON THE MARKET FOR NATIVE LABOUR, 1870–1899

PART I
ECONOMIC CONTACT
BETWEEN EUROPEANS AND NATIVES
BEFORE 1870

CHAPTER I
INTRODUCTORY

A. DEFENCE IS OF GREATER IMPORTANCE THAN OPULENCE

THROUGHOUT almost three centuries of contact between European settlers and the indigenous peoples of Southern Africa the governing authorities have been confronted with the problem of deciding what measure of economic co-operation should be encouraged, or, indeed, permitted. Co-operation, which is required for economic development, means closer contact, and closer contact might spell danger—danger of military clashes, threats to privileged standards of living. Segregation might avert the dangers, but at what cost? Opulence or defence? The choice which Adam Smith emphasized in his *Inquiry into the Nature and Causes of the Wealth of Nations*[1] has been an ever-present dilemma in South Africa. Indeed, while the public men of Europe were appraising at their leisure the first edition of his treatise, the European community at the Cape of Good Hope were improvising, in the urgent stress of frontier contact, a demonstration of his thesis.

In simple societies, argued Adam Smith, every man tends to provide his own defence: the emergence of the specialized profession of the soldier waits upon the complex division of labour of an advanced economic community. In all states of society men have had to be prepared to defend themselves; the means and expense of defence have varied according to the nature of the society. Among nations of hunters, Adam Smith observed, every man is a warrior as well as a hunter. Among pastoralists the whole nation or tribe easily takes to the field to defend its herds and flocks. Where agriculture is practised the situation changes; the whole people can no longer take the field together; the old men, the women, and the children, at least, must remain to take care of the farms. Yet, even at this stage, in which all are accustomed to a hardy outdoor life, it is easy for men to turn to warfare and, as long as expeditions do not interfere with seed-time or harvest, warfare need not greatly interrupt everyday life nor require a special class of warriors. Such was his thesis.

And current events in South Africa supported it. In his time, on the northern and eastern outskirts of the Dutch East India Company's settlement at the Cape of Good Hope, the European

---

[1] Book V—'Of the Revenue of the Sovereign or Commonwealth.' Chapter I, Part I, 'Of the Expense of Defence.'

cattle farmers were driving the nomadic Bushmen from their
hunting grounds and encountering the advance guard of the South-
eastern Bantu. The Bushmen were warrior-hunters. Both
Europeans and Bantu grew crops in addition to cattle-farming
and hunting; both turned readily to the defence of herds and
homes and preferred to go campaigning when the crops were
gathered in. The frontier farmers certainly belonged to that state
of society which has little foreign commerce and few manufactures
beside 'those coarse and household ones which almost every family
prepares for its own use', and in which every man is either a
warrior or easily becomes such.[1]

The peoples of South Africa looked to their defence. And to
them also, as to Adam Smith, defence was of greater importance
than opulence.

While *The Wealth of Nations* was being read for the first time
in Europe, Van Plettenberg, Governor of the Cape, was making
his way to the outlying eastern districts of the Company's territory, impelled by news of repeated Bushmen raids and of contact
with the Bantu. His attempted solution of the problem of contact
was to separate by agreement. In parleys with minor Bantu chiefs
it was agreed that the Fish River should be the boundary of the
colony. For the next fifty years this twisting, often dry stream-bed
with thickly wooded banks was expected to separate White and
Black.

Defence, then, is the keynote of the early policy of the Dutch
East India Company towards the Bantu. It continued with the
Bantu the policy which it had traditionally pursued with the
Hottentots. At first the Company had forbidden the free burghers
to have any dealings with the Hottentots, fearing that contact
would lead to conflict, and that conflict would bring, not merely
unwanted military expenditure, but also an interruption of the
all-important cattle trade. The policy of non-intercourse was
abandoned only after epidemic disease had destroyed the cohesion
of the Hottentot tribes and diminished the importance of Hottentot
cattle supplies. During the eighteenth century, in like manner,
trade with the Bantu was repeatedly forbidden, and when contact
became more frequent an attempt was made to draw a definite
dividing line.

The policy of non-intercourse was destined to fail with the
Bantu, as it had with the Hottentots. Yet although it could not
be enforced in the outlying districts of the colony, it remained the
official policy of the Company until the end of its rule. The same
policy was continued by the British on their occupation of the
Cape, and considerations of defence dominated the scene for

[1] Adam Smith, *The Wealth of Nations*. Cannan's ed. II, p. 188.

another fifty years. Non-intercourse was, however, progressively relaxed, for purposes of trade, for missionary endeavour, to admit supplies of Native labour. There were many who thought that defence and opulence might be reconciled as closer economic co-operation between Black and White led to a realization of the benefits of peace. But ultimately considerations of defence triumphed in the gradual annexation of the Native areas to the east of the Cape of Good Hope. Not until these had come under the administration of the British Crown did the pursuit of opulence finally take precedence over the search for security.

B. THE ECONOMIC SETTING AT THE TIME OF CONTACT

(i) The European Farming Economy

Towards the end of the eighteenth century when the European colonists first came into continuous contact with the Bantu, the colony stretched some five hundred miles eastward of Capetown and three hundred miles northward.

When the British occupied the Cape, in 1795, the European colonists numbered between sixteen and twenty thousand. Nearly two-thirds lived in the western districts of Capetown and Stellenbosch. In Capetown itself and the immediate vicinity the population depended on visiting ships; prospering when many ships called and sinking into depression when visits were few. But outside Capetown many, even in the fairly accessible western districts, had for long been largely self-sufficient on their corn and wine estates. On the larger estates there were sometimes as many as a hundred people, if the landholders and their families, their Hottentot herdsmen, and their slaves were all included,[1] and yet relatively little, of their produce might be sold. The burghers grew vegetables, corn, and wine for sale, but the local market was small and easily flooded, overseas markets were too distant, costs of production were high, and the Company's monopolistic policy and restrictions on trade hindered the development of a farming community dependent upon exchange.

Farther east the difficulty of transport made commercial agriculture unprofitable even where other natural conditions were favourable. The cattle farmers who spread farther and farther afield had small inducement to grow more crops than they needed for their own use. Many had no fixed homes, but lived a roving life in their tented wagons, roaming with their flocks and herds

---

[1] 'Many of the Boers possess two hundred or three hundred oxen, one hundred, one hundred and fifty or more cows, two thousand to three thousand sheep, forty or fifty horses, twenty, thirty or more bond slaves and a large estate.' O. F. Mentzel, *Life at the Cape in the Mid-Eighteenth Century*. Van Riebeeck Society, II, p. 39.

in search of fresh grazing. Others built simple houses of mud-bricks and thatch; but there were some good houses and irrigated lands even in the far Sneeuberg to the north of Graaff Reinet with its handful of mud-coloured cottages.

The life of the frontier farmers was simple and hardy. To the food provided by their flocks, herds, hunting, and uncertain gardening they usually added coffee, sugar, and rice. To obtain these, and also ammunition, guns, and cloth, they traded their cattle and fat-tailed sheep, salted butter, and home-made soap. Self-reliance was necessary and, far removed from the Company's officials, they learned to fend for themselves and to furnish their own defence.[1] Later they were to resent bitterly the imposition of authority.

The Company was quite unable to control or follow up the eastward expansion of the colonists. The journey to the Fish River took a month by ox-wagon, and it was not until 1786 that an official was stationed east of Swellendam. It was these pioneer pastoral farmers and cattle graziers who met Xhosa clans, the advance guard of the South-eastern Bantu.

The Bantu whom they encountered were pushing west from Natal. They had already driven off the Bushmen and displaced and partially absorbed the Hottentots as far west as the Bushman's River. They were primarily a cattle-keeping people with agriculture as an important sideline. If they were to continue their mode of life, land was as essential for them as it was for the Europeans. Both required more and more land as population increased. The European cattle farmer's traditional requirement, approved by the Company, was not less than three thousand morgen[2] of grazing land for a man and his family. The Bantu clans, more numerous, if more modest in their *per caput* requirements, also needed extensive grazing grounds.

To avoid friction the Company tried to apply to the Bantu the original official policy of non-intercourse. Proclamations forbidding intercourse were repeatedly issued, and finally the Fish River, no formidable barrier, was fixed upon as the boundary between Black and White. But Bantu clans were already settled to the west of it, and in spite of 'Kaffir Wars', Xhosa cattle grazed alongside those of the Zuurveld cattle farmers, and Xhosa tribesmen entered into the service of Europeans. Even in 1778 some

[1] On this see J. Barrow, *An Account of Travels into the Interior of Southern Africa*, 1804, especially Vol. II, Chap. VI. M. H. C. Lichtenstein, *Travels in Southern Africa in the Years* 1803, 1804, 1805 *and* 1806. Ven Riebeeck Society, X, pp. 452–70, XI, pp. 1–28. Report of Lieutenant-Colonel Collins, 'Supplement to the Relation of a Journey into the Country of the Bosjemen and Caffre People.' G. M. Theal, *Records of the Cape Colony*, Vol. VII, pp. 33 et seq.
[2] 1 morgen = 2·12 British acres.

Bantu were, in fact, within the Colony, and no mere demarcation of frontiers could expel them.

(ii) The Labour Situation

The Europeans who encountered the Bantu were accustomed to the institution of slavery, but they were not themselves large slave-owners. In the eastern districts a few herdsmen, a wagon-driver, a *voorloper*,[1] some domestic servants, and perhaps some field-hands would suffice even the richer farmers. Moreover, by the latter part of the eighteenth century Hottentots were largely employed in these occupations. They were both cheaper and probably more suitable as herdsmen than imported slaves, for the Hottentots were accustomed both to the conditions of the country and to the care of cattle.

When the Dutch East India Company established its provision station at the Cape of Good Hope, the Hottentots had been living in scattered groups along the coast from Walfisch Bay in South-west Africa to the Kei River in the east, and were later also met inland north of the Orange River.[2] At first they had not proved an amenable source of labour. They could not be induced to work regularly, and the Directors of the Company refused to allow their enslavement. Indeed, strict instructions were given that they were to be treated kindly, for the Company wished to remain on friendly terms with them in order that they might supply the station with fresh meat.

The Bushmen who had roamed, hunted, and raided between the more or less settled headquarters of the Hottentots were almost unapproachable and were an improbable source of labour. Unlike the Hottentots, they were never absorbed into the colonial community as servants, but during the eighteenth and nineteenth centuries they were shot down and largely exterminated.[3] For they hunted the cattle, which had displaced the game on their accustomed hunting grounds, and the colonists found them intractable and their poisoned arrows dangerous.

The failure of the local inhabitants to provide an immediate supply of labour had been met largely by the importation of slaves. Slavery was already fairly established in the Company's East Indian possessions at the time of the settlement of the Cape,[4] and for a hundred and fifty years, until 1807, when the slave trade

---

[1] *Voorloper* is the name of the person, usually a small Native or Coloured boy, who leads a span (team) of oxen.
[2] I. Schapera, *The Khoisan Peoples of South Africa*, p. 43.
[3]. On the extermination of the Bushmen see J. S. Marais, *The Cape Coloured People*, pp. 13–31.
[4] W. Blommaert, *Het Invoeren van de Slavernij aan die Kaap*. Argief-Jaarboek vir Suid-Afrikaanse Geskiedenis. Part I., p. 3 et seq.

to British possessions was terminated, slaves were continually imported into the colony from Madagascar, Mozambique, India, and the East Indies. Throughout the eighteenth century slaves outnumbered the European colonists, their number rising from under fifteen hundred in 1700 to twenty-six thousand at the end of the century. They were principally owned by the Company and the wealthier burghers, and were employed in the homesteads and vineyards and on the cornlands in the vicinity of Capetown, Stellenbosch, and the Berg River valley. In the western districts they were the porters, field-labourers, masons, herdsmen, wagon-drivers, and domestic servants.[1] But in the pastoral east, slaves were never so plentiful. At the end of the century 80 per cent. of the twenty-six thousand slaves in the colony were in the districts of Capetown and Stellenbosch, and there were less than a thousand in Graaff Reinet, the most easterly district.[2]

In the early years of the settlement some of the free burghers had employed European servants, but their numbers were always few and slavery soon led to the growth among the European colonists of a prejudice against employment in manual work, which prevented them from readily becoming labourers.[3] Land was so easily acquired under the Company that every European who wanted his own farm was able to get one. There was always this alternative to working on another's land. By the middle of the century the more accessible and desirable areas had been taken up (in cattle runs of three thousand morgen or more); nevertheless, although there might be landless Europeans hunting and grazing their herds on the outskirts of the colony, every man regarded himself as his own master, and there were almost certainly few European employees outside the ranks of the Company's servants.

In the eastern districts, Hottentots worked for the European farmers. Indeed, in the latter part of the century the majority of the Hottentots were already dispossessed of their land and were either in the service of the farmers, or simply living on land which had come under European control. Only in a few mountain kloofs did some clans survive in semi-independence. Many of those termed 'Hottentots' were of mixed blood, for throughout

---

[1] H. Dehérain, *Le Cap de Bonne-Espérance au XVIIe Siècle.* Chap. VI. *The Reports of Chavonnes and his Council, and of Van Imhoff, on the Cape.* Van Riebeeck Society, I, pp. 88, 93, 97.

[2] J. Barrow, op. cit., II, p. 378.

[3] As early as 1743 van Imhoff reported on the Cape: 'Having imported slaves every common or ordinary European becomes a gentleman and prefers to be served than to serve. We have in addition the fact that the majority of the farmers in this Colony are not farmers in the real sense of the word, but owners of plantations, and that many of them consider it a shame to work with their own hands.'—Van Riebeeck Society, op. cit., I, p. 136.

the colony, but particularly in the west, they were already merging with the slaves and with Europeans to form the racial group now known as 'Cape Coloured'.

For more than fifty years after the Bantu had come into permanent contact with the European colonists they were to be of little importance in the labour market. They were regarded chiefly as an external problem, while the internal problem of the supply of labour was primarily concerned with the Hottentot community, particularly after the abolition of the slave trade in 1807, which put an end to the possibility of satisfying the demand for labour by the importation of slaves. At this time the labour situation in the western districts of the Cape was altering radically, for the end of the slave trade forced the western colonists back upon the indigenous labour supply. In the eastern districts the colonists were less directly affected, for they had owned comparatively few slaves. Nevertheless, they too were to feel the effects of the humanitarian movement because the growing interest of missionaries and others in the position of slaves, and of 'free' people of colour, forced the British Administration to direct its attention to the Hottentot people.

Under the Company's rule the legal status of the Hottentots had been frankly ambiguous. The practice of making the children of male slaves and Hottentot women serve an involuntary 'apprenticeship' had been recognized,[1] but the rights and duties of the so-called 'free' Hottentots were undefined and the weakness of the administration prevented it from protecting Hottentot servants from exacting employers.[2]

From 1809 onwards, however, the British Administration issued a series of proclamations to define the status of the Hottentots, both to protect them against such abuses as the withholding of wages, and to encourage them to take service with the European colonists. To achieve the latter object they were ordered to have a 'fixed place of abode' registered with the landdrost. Their legal right to acquire land, if compliance with the law involved that step, was doubtful; and in any case they had not the means. To prevent vagrancy the pass system was elaborated. Although they had the right to move unless they were bound by contract, they had to obtain a certificate or 'pass' if they wanted to move from one farm or administrative district to another. Contracts of service, however, were to be registered. Later laws in 1812 and 1819 reintroduced the apprenticeship system on the ground that

---

[1] On the Cape practice of forced apprenticeship, cf. P. J. Venter, 'Die Inboekstelsel' *Die Huisgenoot*, June 1st, 1934.
[2] On this see G. M. Theal, op. cit., Vol. VII, p. 33. M. L. Hodgson, 'The Hottentots in South Africa to 1828'. *South African Journal of Science*, 1924, Vol. XXI, pp. 594 et seq. J. S. Marais, op. cit., pp. 109–14.

Hottentot children were being neglected. The Act of 1812 allowed landdrosts to apprentice for ten years, to suitable farmers, children who had been maintained until their eighth year. That of 1819 empowered landdrosts to apprentice orphans and deserted children.

The administration of the Hottentot Code, as it was called, was in the hands of the local officials—the landdrosts and field-cornets. Under the Company the landdrosts had been salaried officials in charge of the huge administrative areas into which the Colony had been divided. In 1778, when the colony extended over some five hundred miles from west to east and three hundred from south to north, there were only three administrative divisions, namely, Capetown, Stellenbosch, and Swellendam. The district of Stellenbosch stretched from near Capetown in a north-easterly direction to the upper Fish River, a distance of about four hundred miles, while its northern limit was not defined. Not until 1786 was Graaff Reinet made a separate district with its own landdrost. Later, in 1804, Tulbagh was separated from Stellenbosch and Uitenhage from Graaff Reinet. The field-cornets were officials appointed from among the local residents. They were farmers of influence in their locality, and their duties were not dissimilar from those of a justice of the peace: to keep the peace, settle petty quarrels, take the census, and make known the laws. Commissioner De Mist had reorganized local government during the period of Batavian rule (1803–6), and the system continued under the British administration.

Landdrosts were few and far between. Consequently, the administration of the Hottentot Code lay first with the local field-cornet, who would himself be a farmer. Under these circumstances the complaints of the missionaries that the law, which definitely placed the Hottentot in an inferior position, was administered in favour of the masters were probably not without foundation.

The missionaries were gathering landless Hottentots into 'institutions', in reality Hottentot 'reserves', wherever they could. Naturally they took an interest in the treatment the Hottentots received. Equally naturally, the colonists, sometimes supported by official opinion,[1] complained that the institutions drained off their labour. The missionaries agitated for the reform of the Hottentot Code and, headed by the redoubtable Dr. Philip, came to demand complete equality for Hottentots.

In 1828 the famous 50th Ordinance 'for improving the condition

---

[1] G. M. Theal, op. cit., IX, p. 350. W. M. MacMillan, 'The Frontier and the Kaffir Wars, 1792–1836'. *Cambridge History of the British Empire*, Vol. VIII, p. 299. E. A. Walker, *A History of South Africa*, p. 155.

of Hottentots and other free persons of colour at the Cape' was promulgated. All the former discriminating laws, including the pass system, were swept away. It was explicitly stated that Hottentots might own land. The apprenticeship system was reformed and, although children might still be apprenticed, with their parents' consent, they could not be bound for more than seven years, and employers could no longer claim the right to bind children on the ground that they had maintained them.

The freeing of the Hottentots caused much dissatisfaction in Cape Colony. There were loud complaints that they roamed the country, thieving as they went. However, attempts to introduce fresh restrictions failed, a severe draft Vagrancy Ordinance being disallowed in 1834 by the Secretary of State for the Colonies.[1] Finally, in 1841, any attempt to differentiate in law between European and Hottentot disappeared with the proclamation of a Masters and Servants law which made no mention of race.[2]

Thus the British Administration, confronted on the one hand by the scarcity of labour, which was aggravated by the abolition of the slave trade, and on the other by the agitation of missionaries against the subjection of the Hottentot population, was compelled to recognize the inevitability of treating them as an integral part of the Colonial community. Towards the Bantu the British were for fifty years to try to continue the traditional policy of separation.

[1] On this see W. M. MacMillan, *The Cape Colour Question*, Chap. XVI.
[2] Ibid., pp. 255–7.

CHAPTER II

THE GROWTH OF ECONOMIC CO-OPERA-TION IN THE CAPE COLONY, 1806–1870

A. THE POLITICAL SETTING: THE ABANDONMENT OF THE POLICY OF SEGREGATION

THE Company had never been able to control or even keep pace with the eastward expansion of its cattle farmers. It had not the means to enforce its edicts in the distant eastern districts, nor even to keep in touch with developments there.[1] The British Administration had more resources behind it than the Company, and in 1812 a vigorous attempt was made to clear the Xhosa clans from the Zuurveld and to make the Fish River a real dividing-line between Black and White.

From the beginning, however, the anxiety to get labour complicated the problem of frontier relations. The European farmers wanted Bantu grazing lands, but they also wanted some Bantu labour. When, in 1812, this attempt to enforce segregation was made it was reported that 'the farmers were very reluctant to lose their servants, although they wished the kraals to be removed from the Zuurveldt'.[2]

The policy of non-intercourse was to be modified quite soon. No doubt in response to local pressure, trade was allowed at specified times and places. 'Kaffir Fairs' were permitted first in 1817, twice yearly at Grahamstown, and later weekly at Fort Willshire. After 1830 traders were given a more general permission to enter Native territories. Thus trading was allowed to extend despite another 'war' on the frontier (1818–19), and an official attempt, after 1819, to keep empty a neutral belt between the Fish River and the Keiskamma.[3]

In 1828 there was further modification of the policy of non-intercourse. In that year the important 49th Ordinance was promulgated. This ordinance marks the abandoning of the official policy of segregation on the frontier. Natives henceforward

[1] In 1809 Lieutenant-Colonel Collins, who was sent on a tour to investigate conditions on the frontier, reported: 'I have been led to think that a great portion of the miseries that have fallen to the lot both of the aborigines and the colonists of Southern Africa since they have had relations with each other, have proceeded from the ignorance of government with respect both to the events that have occurred in the remote districts and to the existing state of them.' Theal, op. cit., Vol. VII, p. 33.
[2] Paper 50 of 1835, p. 174. Quoted H. M. Robertson, '150 Years of Economic Contact between Black and White.' *South African Journal of Economics*, Vol. II, No. 4, December 1934, p. 409.
[3] Ibid., p. 410.

were admitted to the Colony, but only for work. The British were not yet prepared to undertake the administration of Native tribes.

The ordinance repealed the proclamations of 1797, 1812, 1817, and 1820 forbidding intercourse, and introduced a pass system to control the admission of Natives belonging to tribes beyond the frontier. Natives entering the Colony to seek work were to obtain written passes from the landdrost or a field-cornet of the district which they first entered. Contracts of service were also regulated and were not to exceed one month unless they were entered into before a public officer, when they might be for twelve months. Children were not to be detained, under penalty of a fine of 20s.; but abandoned children might be apprenticed, boys until they were eighteen years old, girls until sixteen.[1]

Frontier conditions remained troubled. Both Europeans and Bantu were continually seeking new grazing grounds, and conflict over the right to land was inevitable when the two groups met. The 'Kaffir Wars' on the eastern frontier during the late eighteenth century and first half of the nineteenth were essentially a struggle for land; a struggle in which the Bantu were to be pushed back and back until it was finally realized that conquest and expulsion provided no ultimate solution, but were the cause of further unrest. The Bantu were advancing because of pressure from behind. To repulse that advance inevitably increased the pressure and intensified the conflict.

Cattle-raiding and counter-raiding precipitated and fomented hostilities where men on both sides of the frontier went armed and prepared to defend themselves, but the fundamental cause of the continual disputes was the right to use the land.

The British Administration attempted to introduce law and order on the frontier, but it could not provide security. The European frontiersmen objected to being subjected to restraint when they were still inadequately protected and there was much dissatisfaction. In 1834-5 a particularly serious war brought

[1] Ordinance No. 49 of 1828 was suspended in 1829 because Natives were believed to be entering the Colony not to seek work but for hostile purposes. But subsequently Natives appear to have been permitted to enter the Colony.

In 1830 the Governor of the Cape Colony reported that he had given some of the Native chiefs 'the prospect of Caffres being again permitted to enter the service of the colonists, the chief of their tribe giving them passes, and being held responsible for their good conduct'.—Sir G. L. Cole to Sir George Murray. Brit. Parl. Paper 252 of 1835, p. 53.

In 1837 an ordinance was passed which provided for the summary arrest and trial of 'foreigners' who were without passes or wandering 'without any certain occupation or honest means of livelihood'. If under contract of service they were to be returned to their masters, otherwise they were to be contracted, with their consent, 'in the manner directed by Ordinance No. 49 (of 1828), or expelled from the Colony'. Ordinance No. 2 of 1837. See below, p. 15.

matters to a head. The farmers hoped that they would obtain additional land as a result of the war, but although the Xhosa tribes were defeated their lands were not annexed and distributed among the Europeans. After the war many of the farmers from the eastern districts began to move off northwards to look outside the Colony for farms free both from frontier trouble and from interfering officialdom. The Great Trek had begun.

Within the Cape Colony defence continued to dominate policy. Armed Natives were forbidden to enter the Colony and European patrols to enter Native territory. Europeans were also warned that if they entered they might be expelled by the chiefs. The administration was still attempting to maintain a policy of separation; but the policy was considerably modified. Government agents were appointed to reside with the tribes to use their influence with them; to assist in settling disputes over straying or stolen cattle, for the recovery of which elaborate rules were drawn up; and to grant passes to Natives desiring to enter the Colony to seek work.

This attempt to regulate frontier relations was destined to fail. The Bantu tribesmen were not sufficiently under control to make it practicable. Neither side had the means to police the frontier effectively. There was recurrent friction, and finally another outbreak (the War of the Axe 1846-7) caused Sir Harry Smith to abandon the attempt at separation along the old frontier. He annexed the country as far as the Kei River. The long-disputed area between the Fish River and the Keiskamma River was added to the Colony as the district of Victoria East. A separate Imperial dependency, British Kaffraria, was created between the Keiskamma and Kei Rivers. In these new territories a deliberate attempt was now made to introduce western civilization among the Natives, in the hope that annexation and civilization would prove a less expensive means of achieving security on the frontier.

Rapid progress was not, however, possible. Hostilities broke out once more (1850-53) before much could be done to put the new policy into operation, and the breakdown of the power of the Xhosa, following upon the tragic cattle-killing episode of 1856-7,[1] was perhaps more effective in removing the preoccupation with frontier defence than the introduction of this new policy.

Despite unrest and recurrent hostilities Natives were being increasingly employed on farms.[2] In 1844, Mr. Fynn, official Agent with the Thembu, wrote:

'No description of servants, or such an abundant supply—could be so well suited to the wants of the frontier farmers. The colonists

[1] See below, p. 23.
[2] See W. M. MacMillan, *Bantu, Boer and Briton*, pp. 245-6. *The Cape Colour Question*, pp. 252-5. H. M. Robertson, op. cit., p. 411.

are materially benefited and many a Native in times of need is saved from famishing.'[1]

Natives were only admitted for work, passes being issued by the official Agents with the tribes beyond the frontier, and also by the field-cornets and justices of the peace within the Colony. The Natives from beyond the frontier were considered to be a real danger, and in 1837 an ordinance 'for the more effectual prevention of Crimes against Life and Property within the Colony' elaborated the conditions under which they might enter and remain within the Colony.[2] If unwilling to work, they were to be removed beyond its limits and were not to return under penalty of imprisonment.

The colonial government had no desire to have unemployed Natives wandering or settling within its borders. The Reverend C. Casalis reports that at this time the Governor, Sir Benjamin D'Urban, commanded the Basuto who had sought refuge in the Colony to return to their own country. Internecine Native warfare had caused them to disperse:

> Stripped of everything, and weary of war, they desired nothing better than to repair their fortunes by the labour of their hands, and from the first showed themselves tractable, and even grateful to those who received them; while the latter welcomed with delight skilful shepherds and excellent workmen, who were satisfied with very humble remuneration.[3]

Later, apparently, they gathered together and formed 'large communities from the banks of the Orange River to Algoa Bay'.[4] It was refugees such as these that the anxious Governor wished to expel.

Nearer at hand, too, the frontier wars were reducing the land available for the 'hostile tribes'. For, even where European settlement did not take place, room was made for the friendly Fingo only at the expense of other tribes. Many of the Fingo had fled from Natal during the Chaka wars and they occupied a servile position among the Xhosa and Thembu. After the war of 1834–5 the Governor allowed them to enter the Colony and settled some sixteen thousand of them in the district of Peddie between the Fish and the Keiskamma Rivers, where they were to form a bulwark against the Thembu and Xhosa tribes. In 1846 they assisted the Colonial Government in the War of the Axe, and as a reward were given additional land in Victoria East. The

---

[1] Quoted MacMillan, *Bantu, Boer and Briton*, p. 246.
[2] Ordinance 2 of 1837.
[3] J. E. Casalis, *The Basutos; or, Twenty-three Years in South Africa* (1861), p. 71.
[4] Ibid.

same process was to be repeated in British Kaffraria and later in the Transkei itself.

The repeated reduction of the land available for the 'hostile tribes' demanded readjustment which took the form of their going out to work for Europeans. The colonists were eager for their services, but the Natives were still a military danger and even after the annexation of British Kaffraria restrictions on movement were retained. They were not to disappear until there was no longer need for defence. In the 1850's defence and opulence had still to be reconciled.

B. THE POLICY OF ASSIMILATION

One of the main determinants of the supply of Bantu labour available to European colonists in South Africa has long been the nature of the policy adopted in different places and at different periods in regard to the maintenance, disposition, and size of Native reserves and locations. It certainly appears to have been so as early as the middle of the nineteenth century.

Whenever an attempt has been made to draw a line and separate Native and European, the extent to which Native labourers are available and may be used has depended upon their ability and willingness to undertake the journey; and upon the willingness of the Europeans to allow them to cross the line. Such was the case before 1848. Some trade had been carried on and, as we have seen, Native labourers had been allowed to enter the Colony; but they were regarded as 'foreigners', temporary visitors who were useful while they worked, but whose rightful place was outside.

Only the Fingo were accepted as belonging to the Colony. Since as early as 1835, when they had been established around Fort Peddie on land allotted to them on a tribal basis, they had gone out to work for Europeans. After the War of the Axe of 1846–7, the Government acquired the land between the Fish and the Keiskamma Rivers in which the Fingo were settled. When, thereafter, the land surrounding their locations was bought by Europeans the Fingo formed a readily accessible labour supply.

The presence of small blocks of Natives in proximity to potential European employers removes the hindrance which distance imposes on the supply of labour. The Natives have more ability and willingness to work, for they need not stay so long away from home. At the same time it is easier for farmers to select labourers, and those whose needs can be met by workers living nearby find their proximity an advantage.

As early as 1849 the Imperial Government was considering such matters. In that year the Secretary of State for the Colonies,

Earl Grey,[1] wrote to Sir Harry Smith, deliberately rejecting the policy of separation and suggesting that, in Natal, permanent locations should be established with sufficient intervals between them for the spread of European settlements, in order that 'each European emigrant would thus have it in his power to draw supplies of labour from the location in his more immediate proximity'.[2]

In embarking upon the policy of introducing European settlers into Victoria East and later into British Kaffraria, the administration was in fact creating what were to become in part pools of labour, even though at the time the predominant motive was to achieve security by breaking up the cohesion of the tribes and by introducing European ideas and institutions.

The ultimate aim in view was probably broadly what to-day would be called a policy of assimilation. Sir George Grey's opening address to the Colonial Parliament in 1855 may be accepted as a declaration of his policy. The Natives were, he said, to become

a part of ourselves, with a common faith and common interests, useful servants, consumers of our goods, contributors to our revenue; in short, a source of strength and wealth for this Colony, such as Providence designed them to be.[3]

The necessity for defence was still, however, a brake on co-operation, and the incorporation of the Natives into the economic life of the Colony did not take place suddenly. Natives were to be encouraged to become 'useful servants', but fear remained potent and restricted co-operation. Before 'our present unconquered and apparently irreclaimable foes' could become trustworthy servants they must be taught to recognize common interests.[4] With this ultimate goal in mind the policy of assimilation was set on foot, both in the Colony and in British Kaffraria. In Kaffraria it was financed by the Imperial Government in the hope that the introduction of British institutions would end the frontier wars which had proved so costly.

In 1854 Sir George Grey had come to the Cape as Governor and High Commissioner for South Africa. Fresh from his success in pacifying the Maoris in New Zealand, he had immediately determined to follow up the policy inaugurated by Sir Harry

[1] Earl Grey was Secretary of State for War and Colonies, 1846–Feb. 1852, and is not to be confused with Sir George Grey, Governor of the Cape and High Commissioner of South Africa, Dec. 1854–Aug. 1861.
[2] *Parl. Papers*, 1850, XXXVIII [1292], Cape, Natal Corresp. 1849–1850, p. 118.
[3] Minutes of Legislative Council, A. 1, 1855, p. 2.
[4] Grey to Secretary of State, Dec. 22nd, 1854. *Further Papers re Kafir Tribes*, 1855, p. 38.

3

Smith in 1848. He deliberately set out to 'civilize' the Natives
and outlined his proposals in a dispatch written within a few weeks
of his arrival in the Colony.

> 'The plan', he wrote, 'I propose to pursue with a view to the
> general adjustment of these questions [frontier policy] is, to attempt
> to gain an influence over all the tribes included between the present
> north-eastern boundary of this colony and Natal, by employing
> them upon public works, which will tend to open up their country;
> by establishing institutions for the education of their children, and
> the relief of their sick; by introducing among them institutions of
> a civil character suited to their present condition; and by these and
> other like means to attempt to win them to civilization and Chris-
> tianity, and thus to change by degrees our present unconquered
> and apparently irreclaimable foes into friends who may have common
> interests with ourselves.'[1]

Thus his policy was to be developed along a number of lines.
In addition, he adopted the expedient of settling blocks of
Europeans among the Native tribes.

In British Kaffraria public works were started immediately.[2]
To open up the country, roads were begun, intended to be useful
in times of war as well as of peace. To improve Native agriculture, irrigation furrows were projected. The public works
were also used to encourage the Natives to develop European
wants. To this end payment was made both in money and
rations. Meat, corn, coffee, sugar, and tobacco were issued to
workers.[3]

In view of a common present-day attitude in South Africa
which regards the training and careful organization of Native
labour as waste of time, it is interesting to note that an attempt
was made to grade the labourers in order to offer an incentive
for increased efficiency and to reward those who remained on the
works for long periods.

The Natives employed were divided into three classes, one
man in sixteen being a first-class man or overseer, with pay of
1s. per day and rations; one man out of every eight was a second-
class man at 9d. per day and rations; the remainder received 6d.
a day and rations.[4] Under these conditions no difficulty was
found in attracting 'any number of Kaffir workmen'. The difficulty lay rather in finding and financing suitable work. By the

[1] *Parl. Papers*, 1854–5, XXXVIII [1969]. *Further Papers re Kafir Tribes*,
1855, p. 38. Grey to Secretary of State.
[2] In April 1855. *Parl. Papers*, 1857, Sess. 1, X [2202]. *Further Papers re
Kafir Tribes*, p. 11.
[3] *Parl. Papers*, 1856, XLII [2096]. *Further Papers re Kafir Tribes*, 1856,
p. 9. Sir George Grey to Secretary of State.
[4] Ibid.

end of 1855 over nine hundred men had been employed, the average number on the works having been about five hundred and fifty.[1] According to Mr Charles Brownlee, Commissioner with the Gaika (Ngqika),[2] the system of classes was a success, for 'those who are in the first and second class have never left, and others remain on the works in the hope of making themselves eligible for promotion'.[3]

The public works in British Kaffraria were destined to be short-lived, and there is little further information concerning their progress or the results achieved. Road parties began to break up in August 1856, in anticipation of 'the cattle-killing',[4] and after that calamity the Administration was fully occupied with the direct relief of distress. Moreover, the grant of £40,000 per annum which Sir George Grey received to finance his policy in the three years, 1856–8, was afterwards reduced to £20,000 and later withdrawn.[5]

Stimulating a demand for European goods through gifts was another means towards introducing western civilization, ploughs especially being presented to the chiefs when requests were made.[6] The wearing of European clothes was encouraged on the public works,[7] and the wearing of 'decent clothing' enforced in King-williamstown.[8] Among the European goods introduced was money. Money wages were paid on the public works and, to accustom the Natives to its use, fines were levied, payable in money.[9] Further, when taxation was enforced it became obligatory for taxpayers to obtain it. Money was also the only article universally acceptable to Europeans. The Natives appear quickly to have appreciated its value for these purposes.

Trade was encouraged by the removal of restrictions. The results probably went further than anticipated, for by 1866, according to Holden, the Natives were 'surrounded' by traders who gave credit on the most liberal terms, and consequently wagons, oxen, and cattle were frequently sold up to meet debts.[10] Thus Native indebtedness to local traders, which is to-day such

[1] *Parl. Papers*, 1857, op. cit. [2202], p. 11.
[2] A section of the Xhosa tribe. They lived in British Kaffraria.
[3] *Parl. Papers*, 1856 [2096], op. cit., p. 36.
[4] *Parl. Papers*, 1857–8, XL [2352], p. 10. On the effects of the 'cattle-killing', see below, p. 23 et seq.
[5] G. 17, 1859. For the reasons for the reduction and withdrawal of the grant, see footnote, p. 24, n. 3.
[6] *Parl. Papers*, 1856, op. cit. [2096], p. 3.
[7] *Parl. Papers*, 1857, Sess. 1, X [2202], p. 12.
[8] See *Transactions of Literary and Historical Society of Quebec*, 1871, p. 5, for an account of how one Native clad in the full glory of a scarlet military coat was to his disgust fined for being indecently clad.
[9] *Parl. Papers*, 1856, op. cit. [2096], p. 16.
[10] W. C. Holden, *The Past and Future of the Kaffir Races* (1866), p. 413.

an important force leading Natives to seek work in European areas, began to cause remark as long ago as the 1860's.

Missionaries, already a powerful influence spreading Western European ideas and commodities, were encouraged and assisted. Missionaries had entered Kaffraria in 1820,[1] and by 1823 there were four among the Gaika. In 1824 the famous mission school Lovedale had been founded. Wars had interrupted the work of the missionaries, but stations that had been destroyed were rebuilt. The introduction of European ideas continued, and was carried far beyond the colonial frontiers. As early as 1812 a mission station had been established at Kuruman, far beyond the northern limits of the Colony. The first mission across the Kei had been founded at Butterworth in 1827, and in the early 'thirties Casalis and other French missionaries had set up their stations in Basutoland at the invitation of Moshesh, and were now firmly established as friends and advisers of the people and the great chief himself. By 1850 the Wesleyans had at least twenty-five stations in the Eastern Province and Kaffraria.[2] The London Missionary Society, the Free and United Presbyterian Churches of Scotland, the Berlin Missionary Society, and the Moravian Church were also at work in Kaffraria.[3]

Like the Government officials, missionaries encouraged the use of European goods. Clothing in particular was often insisted upon, at least for church-going. They also encouraged the construction of square stone houses in place of circular huts and introduced such luxuries as tea and sugar.[4]

Sir George Grey assisted the missionaries by providing funds from the Imperial grant for the construction and maintenance of schools, especially schools designed to teach the Natives trades, such as carpentry, printing, and bookbinding. Four were started in the Colony and Grey announced his willingness to subsidize

[1] C. Brownlee, *Reminiscences of Kafir Life and History, and other Papers* (1896), p. 371.
[2] The Wesleyans did not distinguish between mission and colonial work. J. du Plessis, *Christian Missions in South Africa*, p. 259.
[3] J. du Plessis, op. cit., pp. 184, 257–9, 284–6, 344. Maclean, *Compendium of Kafir Laws and Customs* (1858), p. 139.
[4] cf. J. E. Casalis, op. cit., p. 111: 'The Christian women dress on a Sunday much as our villagers do; but they seem to understand that a handkerchief, worn as a turban, suits their dark complexion and rustic nature infinitely better than a bonnet or a cap; the men prefer a paletot to a jacket, and a frock to a tail-coat, which latter they consider as supremely ridiculous; the greater number still prefer arraying themselves in their cloaks of skins, and the Missionaries are not over-exacting in this particular.' C. Brownlee, op. cit., pp. 372–3: 'As the Natives came under the influence of the teaching of the missionaries, they at once abandoned red clay, and sought to cover themselves with European clothing; and thus, and in proportion to the spread of missionary influence, the desire for articles of European manufacture grew and spread, and I think will well satisfy this meeting that to the missionaries mainly we owe the great revenue now derived from the native trade.'

similar institutions even beyond the frontier. Special subsidies were later (1861) to be given to such schools within the Colony by the Cape Government and, after annexation, to be extended to those in British Kaffraria.[1]

To wean the Natives from consulting witch doctors, a hospital was established at Kingwilliamstown.

Another aspect of Sir George Grey's policy was the issue of individual title deeds to land. His object was to give the Natives a vested interest in the soil in order that, 'possessing property of their own, and a stake in the country', they might prove more amenable.[2]

An additional reason for the survey of Native reserves and the division of the arable land into fixed allotments, for which title deeds were to be granted, was the scarcity of land, which was already causing concern in the Fingo locations in the frontier districts. Several locations were surveyed, but with few exceptions the Natives failed to take up their title deeds. This was due to the heavy survey fees, which the Natives had to meet, to the fact that many of the surveyed lots were not suitable for cultivation, and, finally, to the Natives' failure to appreciate the legal importance of a title deed.[3]

The results of this attempt to prevent overcrowding and stimulate agriculture proved disappointing, probably partly because many people appear to have over-estimated the stimulus which the issue of individual title deeds would give.[4] The reason is to be found in a common under-estimate of the degree of security under Bantu systems of land tenure. The tribal system of land tenure of the Bantu was that the land was held in trust by the chief of each tribe. It was one of his duties to allocate it among his people, the detailed allocation usually being performed by the sub-chiefs and headmen. The chief had the right to expropriate, 'eat up', individuals. However, it was not usually politic for him to abuse his position and arbitrarily dispossess his subjects; for he depended for his power and wealth to a considerable extent on the goodwill of his people. Public opinion could exercise pressure, as it was always possible for a tribe to split up and the tribesmen follow a more popular leader, a proceeding which occurred not infrequently. In practice, therefore, individuals had considerable security of tenure, as is shown by the fact that once land had been allocated, cleared, and cultivated, it could

[1] G. 7, 1856, pp. 2–5. A. 1, 1855, pp. 4–5. C. T. Loram, *The Education of the South African Native*, pp. 49–50.
[2] A. 1, 1855, p. 2.
[3] A. 1, 1861, p. 2. (Cape) *Blue Book on Native Affairs*, 1882, A. 52, p. 8. U.G. 42, 1922, p. 1.
[4] cf. W. C. Holden, op. cit., pp. 427–30.

be claimed by the original cultivator, even although it might have been left untilled for years.[1]

The advantages of security of tenure have also often been stressed without regard for Native methods of agriculture. For instance, some advocates of the grant of title deeds to arable allotments have forgotten that cultivation must be shifted periodically in a system of agriculture such as that of the Bantu, who did not practise rotation of crops or scientific fertilizing.[2]

Nevertheless, the Native system of land tenure hindered agricultural progress; principally because it was the practice for the cattle of a group to graze together and to be turned into the garden plots in the autumn after the mealie and millet crops had been gathered in. The result was that it was impossible for an enterprising cultivator to grow winter crops such as wheat. Fencing, however, was as necessary as individual title. It was soon found that the survey of locations did not lead automatically to the hoped-for improvements.[3]

Finally, one of the most important aspects of the Grey policy, and one that probably had the most immediate results, was the introduction of European settlers among the Natives of British Kaffraria. As we have seen, Grey planned to extend European influence to the tribes beyond the frontier as far as the boundary of Natal, in order that 'our ultimate frontier defence would be a fertile and populous country, filled with a large population, partly European, partly native'.[4]

After its annexation in 1847 those parts of Victoria East not set aside as Fingo locations had been occupied by Europeans. This process was repeated. At the end of the next 'war', 1850–53, European settlers were introduced into British Kaffraria. They received free grants of land under a system of 'military tenure' designed to strengthen the frontier. The Fingo were again given additional land, this time in the Kingwilliamstown division of British Kaffraria, while the 'rebellious clans' were thrust back. The Gaika forfeited six hundred square miles of territory, including the fertile Amatola basin. Moreover, the land on which they were now settled was admittedly inadequate to support them. To the north the Thembu also lost much of their land, which became the district of Queenstown; parts of the tribe were, however, gathered together in the Indwe Reserve or, as it was more usually called, the Tambookie location, the present district

[1] cf. *The Bantu-Speaking Tribes of South Africa*. (Ed. I. Schapera), p. 157.
[2] On this see Memorandum by S. H. Fazan. *Kenya Land Commission*, 1934, Vol. I.
[3] (Cape) *Blue Book on Native Affairs*, G. 2, 1885, p. 36; G. 6, 1888, p. 33; G. 3, 1889, p. 29.
[4] A. 1, 1855, p. 2.

of Glen Grey. European colonists were settled in the emptied country and soon formed a flourishing community.[1]

Further redistribution of land followed the tragic cattle-killing of 1856–7, which broke up many Xhosa and Thembu clans. Obeying the commands of Native prophets, the Xhosa and some of the Thembu ate up, destroyed, or sold, cattle and grain in readiness for the day on which their ancestors were to return and, united, would sweep into the sea the Europeans and all who had not listened to the message.[2]

The Fingo were told that there was no message for them, and so were spared the consequences of this stupendous folly. In British Kaffraria some 200,000 cattle were destroyed and 25,000 Natives, chiefly women, children, and the aged were estimated to have died.[3] No one knows how many died east of the Kei River. In British Kaffraria the survivors were fed by the Government and by private charity. Many were sent into the Colony to take service; others dispersed among the Thembu, Pondo, and those of their own people who had not killed their cattle. According to contemporary estimates the Native population of British Kaffraria was reduced, at least temporarily, from 105,000 to 37,000.[4]

The locations of British Kaffraria were almost depopulated, and bands of robbers infested the countryside. To restore order, the vacant parts of the territory were filled up with colonial farmers, with German legionaries and, when these latter failed as farmers and drifted away, with German peasant immigrants. The Gcaleka Chief Kreli and those of his tribe who had not dispersed were expelled from their country between the Kei and the Bashee Rivers, and for a time this territory was kept empty by patrols of the Frontier Mounted Police.[5]

The self-destruction of the Xhosa helped Grey to carry out his policy, for it finally broke their military strength and enabled him to fill up the emptied and confiscated reserves with European settlers. It was his policy to continue the intermingling of European and Native settlement across the Kei River. Britain, however, was still opposed to increasing her commitments in Southern Africa and his successor was given definite instructions that British dominion was not to extend beyond that river.

Further annexation was to be undertaken, not by Britain but

[1] cf. J. Noble, *Descriptive Handbook of the Cape Colony* (1875), pp. 207–8.
[2] *Parl. Papers*, 1857–8, XL [2352]. *Further Papers re Kafir Tribes.* Grey to Secretary of State (Labouchere), March 6th, 1857.
[3] C. Brownlee, op. cit., p. 170.
[4] G. 5, 1858, p. 6.
[5] F. Brownlee, *Transkeian Native Territories: Historical Records*, p. 5; *Select Committee on Kafir Labourers*, A. 4, 1859, p. 11.

by the Cape Colony. Except in minor instances, following revolt, it was not to lead to the appropriation of land by Europeans, but to the administration of Native territories.

Apart from the large increase in the European occupation of British Kaffraria, the cattle-killing resulted in changes in the distribution of land among the Native tribes; and the Fingo, as usual, gained. In 1858 a mixed body of Thembu, Fingo, Dlambe, and even some of the rebellious Gcaleka were settled around Idutywa in the Gcaleka territory. On their expulsion Kreli and his followers had congregated on the banks of the Bashee River and cast longing eyes at their former territory.[1] In 1864 they were allowed to return to the seaboard portion, a thousand square miles in extent and about one-third of what they had lost. Next to them some forty thousand Fingo were settled in the district now known as Fingoland, and Thembu from the Queenstown district occupied the remainder of the old Gcaleka country.

The Fingo had multiplied rapidly, by immigration as well as natural increase, for the South-eastern Bantu had been outflanked. European settlement in Natal had increased and in the Orange Free State Europeans were pushing back the Basuto. Pressure on the tribes was increasing and squeezing out all who could find a friendly reception in the Colony.

> 'They come in from Kafirland and Natal, and squat down in the locations; and that has been going on for years. Not more than one-fourth of them there now are the original Fingoes or their descendants,'

Commandant Currie of the Frontier Mounted Police told a Select Committee in 1859.[2] The grants of additional land which they received were always at the expense of other tribes and did nothing to solve the general problem of the growing scarcity of land in the border districts.

C. THE ECONOMIC CONSEQUENCES OF CONTACT BETWEEN EUROPEAN AND NATIVE

It would be easy to lay too much stress on the effects of the Grey policy which we have just been describing. Funds were limited. Not without reason, the Imperial grant was reduced in 1859 and withdrawn in 1864.[3] Consequently public works and trade schools languished or were closed down.

---

[1] *Select Committee on Kafir Labourers*, A. 4, 1859, p. 11, q. 73.

[2] Ibid., p. 6.

[3] When Grey inaugurated his Kaffrarian policy he estimated that it would cost £45,000 per annum, of which £40,000 would at first have to be supplied by the Imperial authorities. He then considered that after three years the Imperial grant might be reduced annually and that after eight or ten years no

Moreover, in some respects the new policy merely accelerated existing tendencies. Before the introduction of the policy of assimilation, and before the Native territories began to be taken under European administrative control, traders and missionaries had already been introducing and spreading Western European goods and ideas. The official realization that contact had become permanent and the consequent determination to 'civilize' the Bantu probably served simply to hasten the process.

The effects of the intermingling of Europeans and Native settlement and of the imposition of European government were many-sided. The mode of living of the Natives, who had combined agricultural and pastoral subsistence farming, had to be modified. For one thing, it required more land than was now available. But, in the Cape Colony, the contact with Europeans tended for other reasons also to break down the former self-sufficiency. New wants were awakened and new obligations, notably taxation, imposed. All these developments necessitated change, the abandonment of that condition of self-sufficiency in which each household[1] had produced the greater part of its own requirements. In the old Bantu culture there had been little exchange within the tribe and almost none beyond it.

At the same time new opportunities for satisfying wants and obligations became available. During the forties and fifties of the last century the economic activity of the Colony was developing rapidly. Foremost among the reasons for the remarkable increase in trade which took place was the spread of commercial wool-farming, more especially in the eastern and north-eastern districts of the Colony, where, with the improvement of roads and shipping facilities farmers were now able to produce a saleable article at a profit for export. The commercial wool-farmer thus began to replace the old largely self-sufficient cattle-farmer. All the wool

further assistance would be required. (*Parl. Papers*, 1854–5, XXXVIII [1969]. *Further Papers re Kaffir Tribes*, p. 38.) In practice he used the grant for general purposes, among other things in an attempt to settle German legionaries on the land. This disregard of official instructions and cavalier treatment of official requests for information increased the official displeasure aroused by his policy for establishing a federation of the South African colonies and states, which led to his temporary recall (*Parl. Papers*, 1860, XLV [216]. 'Copies of extracts of all Correspondence which has taken place between the Colonial Office and the Governor, Sir George Grey, respecting his recall from the Cape of Good Hope, and his subsequent reappointment to the Government of that Colony.') The reduction and final abolition of the Imperial grant was in accordance with his first request and does not appear to have been unreasonable.

[1] 'Within the tribe the outstanding social unit is the household, a group consisting typically of a man with his wife or wives and dependent children, together with any other relatives or unrelated dependants who may be attached to him, but composed frequently of other combinations of close relatives.'— A. Winifred Hoernle, 'Social Organization,' *Bantu-Speaking Tribes of South Africa* (ed. I. Schapera), p. 69.

produced in South Africa was exported. Consequently wool exports provide an index of the development of the region. Those through Port Elizabeth rose from £6 million in 1852 to £15 million in 1857. The main sources were Graaff Reinet, Colesberg Somerset, Middelburg, Richmond, and the Orange Free State.[1] At this time the total wool export through colonial ports was £19 million.[2]

Stimulated by the increasing number of commercial farmers, towns began to grow, both at the coast and inland. The growth of towns led to a greater opportunity for internal exchange, and the further construction of roads.

All these developments resulted in a rise in the demand for labour. It was required on farms, and also for building roads; for building houses in the towns; and for general work, both in the inland towns and at the ports. The Imperial Government wished to meet the demand by the transportation of convicts in 1849, but in spite of the scarcity of labour, the colonists bitterly opposed the plan, and the British authorities had to abandon it. Local convicts and free European labourers, imported at Government expense, were employed to construct the roads. During the 'forties nearly 4,300 labourers, mechanics, and domestic servants were imported.[3] The assisted immigration scheme of 1857, under which nine thousand immigrants from Europe were introduced between 1858 and 1862,[4] is also a reflection of the increase in the demand for labour.

The possibility of extending the use of Native labour was also canvassed. In the eastern districts of the Colony the Fingo were already working for Europeans on farms and on the roads, and the authorities now began to employ men of other tribes. In 1856 one of the road engineers at Port Elizabeth reported:

> There has been difficulty in getting labourers at reasonable wages fit for road making; and so many new works now commencing here, will, I fear, induce all to leave, as they cannot be expected to remain at a lower rate of wages, living under canvas and separated from their families. The Fingoes lately employed I look upon as just better than none, and they can certainly keep the large stones off the roads. I look forward to the Kafirs[5] being

---

[1] G. 22, 1858, p. 2; Official report on survey of trade between Port Elizabeth and Graaff Reinet quoted, I. Murray: *Early Railway Development in the Cape Colony* (unpublished thesis, University of Capetown).

[2] A. 1, 1860, p. 6.   [3] E. A. Walker, op. cit., pp. 248–50.

[4] Ibid. footnote, p. 303; cf. also Robertson, 'The Cape of Good Hope and Systematic Colonization', *South African Journal of Economics*, Vol. V, No. 4, Dec. 1937, pp. 381 et seq.

[5] Kafir, sometimes spelt Kaffir, Kaffer, Kaffre or Caffre, is the Arabic for infidel. It was applied by the Arabs to all non-Mohammedans including, presumably, the Bantu tribes of Southern Africa. In the nineteenth century in South Africa the term was usually applied by Europeans to the Xhosa tribe of the South-eastern Bantu (Nguni tribes), sometimes other tribes such as the Thembu, Pondo, and Zulu were included.

employed, as suggested by the Board, hoping to find them better workmen.[1]

'Kaffirs' were also employed on the unskilled work, 'burning charcoal for the forge, treading mortar, carrying water', in connexion with the first church built in British Kaffraria, the Trinity Church at Kingwilliamstown.[2] But taking the Colony as a whole, throughout the century, farming remained the main field of employment for Natives, just as it was the principal occupation of the Europeans.

There were new opportunities for the sale of produce, but it was principally as farm-labourers that the Bantu entered the European economy. Europeans had appropriated much of the land in the more accessible districts, and the difficulties of transport in the more remote areas,[3] where more land was available, forced them to rely chiefly on selling their labour. The European colonists welcomed them as labourers; the traders welcomed them as suppliers and customers.

The Fingo in particular were quick to adapt themselves to the new conditions. They were favourably situated for growing and selling produce and soon were trading wool, wheat, beans, oats, potatoes, and pumpkins. According to local officials, the people of the Peddie Fingo locations, which covered an area of some three hundred and fifty square miles and in 1865 had a population of thirteen thousand, sold within a year, three hundred and fifty bushels of corn; seventeen thousand pounds of wool; and 'cattle, sheep, goats, and poultry without number'. The people of the Victoria Fingo location, which then had an area of fifteen thousand morgen and a population of five thousand, produced and sold corn and thirty-two thousand pounds of wool. Those of Healdtown and the Fort Beaufort commonage sold a 'great quantity of grain', not much wool, and a few livestock. To the north-east the inhabitants of the Tambookie and Wittebergen locations (the present districts of Glen Grey and Herschel) also sold grain and wool to Europeans.[4]

In many cases, however, the restricted area of ground, the difficulty of transport, and failure to adopt more effective methods of cultivation meant that labour was all the Bantu were able to sell. From their introduction into the Colony in 1835 the Fingo had gone out to work for the European farmers. They worked as

[1] G. 18, 1856, p. 17.
[2] F. Fleming, *Kaffraria and its Inhabitants* (1853), p. 43. The skilled work, the masonry and stone-cutting, of what was reported to be a solid and substantial building, was done by the European soldiers.
[3] On the difficulties of transport even to-day, see W. M. MacMillan, *Complex South Africa*, pp. 145–6.
[4] (Cape) *Commission on Native Affairs*, 1865, Appendix No. 1, *passim*.

shearers, reapers, general labourers, herdsmen, wagon-drivers, and domestic servants. The importance of their services was such that in 1854 Mr. Calderwood reported that 'the crops of Lower Albany . . . must have, to a considerable extent, perished without the labour of the Fingoes'.[1] Some of the Xhosa and Thembu also entered the Colony as labourers, but their reputation as cattle thieves made the colonists less ready to welcome them, although the farmers were glad to have their labour.[2]

In 1857, as we have seen, the cattle-killing sent a flood of starving Xhosa and Thembu into the Colony. Many thousands had for the first time in their lives to work outside the family or, perhaps, tribal group in order to obtain food. Between thirty-three and thirty-four thousand were estimated to have taken service under Europeans in the Colony by 1858.[3] From January 1 to April 30, 1857, some five thousand Natives were indentured to European applicants for Native labourers.[4]

By 1865 Natives were going out to work from all the locations within the Colony. At this time one-third of the inhabitants of the Peddie locations were reported to be in service. In the Fingo location at Healdtown, according to the Rev. G. Schreiner, many had 'almost to depend on service for a livelihood', because the arable allotments were only four acres, which was far too little to support them, especially as the commonage was too small. Those who went into service were employed on all kinds of work in the towns of Grahamstown, Port Elizabeth, Beaufort, Adelaide, Bedford, and Somerset, and also by the English and Dutch farmers. At this time the Tambookie location was described as 'the labour market for the upper (northern) districts', and from six to nine hundred persons were reported to go into service every year. Natives from the Wittebergen location, too, were in service in the Colony from Port Elizabeth to Beaufort West.[5]

Not much information is available as to wage-rates at this time. The average wage-rates of the refugees who were indentured after the cattle-killing are given in the official return as: for men, five shillings per month and food; for boys over fourteen years, two shillings and sixpence per month and food; for women and for girls over fourteen, two shillings per month and food. These rates were probably lower than was usual, for some reduction in the rate was surely necessary in order to absorb this exceptional supply of labour.

[1] G. 7, 1856, para. 11.
[2] cf. H. M. Robertson, '150 Years of Economic Contact', op. cit., p. 417; *Select Committee on Kaffir Tribes*, 1851 (Paper 635 of 1851), pp. 1625–6.
[3] G. 17, 1859, p. 5.
[4] See table, p. 31.
[5] (Cape) *Commission on Native Affairs*, 1865 Appendix No. 1.

Whether or not these rates were typical in 1857, by 1865, according to returns collected from magistrates, superintendents of Native locations, and farmers, wages were considerably higher. On farms where cash wages were paid for men they ranged from seven shillings and sixpence to twelve shillings a month; with rations, chiefly mealies with meat once or twice a week, in addition. Old clothes were also often given as the reward for good service. Daily labourers in the Peddie district, probably reapers and shearers, were reported to earn ninepence a day. Women received from three to eight shillings a month—the most common wage being five shillings a month—and rations were also supplied.[1]

Wages were, however, often paid in stock, particularly in the upper districts, which were remote from markets and where consequently cash was scarce. In this case payment would usually be for a year's service and take the form, for a man, of a young cow, a cow and a calf, or a mare; the value being from three to six pounds. A woman would receive a calf or four to six sheep for a year's service.

In the towns and villages wages appear to have been somewhat higher. The usual wages for men being from fifteen shillings to two pounds per month. Storemen and wool-packers might receive up to three pounds per month.[2]

D. OFFICIAL RESTRICTIONS ON THE MOBILITY OF NATIVE LABOUR

Although Natives were going out to work for Europeans in increasing numbers their movements were hampered by restrictions. This was particularly true in British Kaffraria (which had been annexed at the end of 1847 in an attempt to solve the perpetual frontier unrest). Defence had still to be considered. On this account and also for administrative reasons martial law controlled the movements of Natives until late in the 'fifties. Nevertheless, arrangements were made to permit labourers to enter the Colony.

In 1853 the Chief Commissioner[3] of British Kaffraria issued a circular to the Special Magistrates who administered the territory:

'I am not desirous', he wrote, 'that any native be permitted to enter the colony, except on special application made by the colonists—

---

[1] Two contemporary investigations into wages on farms in some of the eastern divisions of the Cape Province indicate that cash wages in some of these districts have changed little since the 1860's. See below, p. 281.

[2] (Cape) *Commission on Native Affairs*, 1865. Appendices Nos. 1 and 2.

[3] The title of the head of the Kaffrarian administration was later changed to Lieutenant-Governor.

or when, from urgent circumstances, it may appear to you desirable to grant applications made direct from natives; and I am of opinion, that the plea of visiting friends, or even relatives, ought never to be entertained—as in most cases such applications are merely made with the view of obtaining presents from industrious people who have saved property in the colony, or possibly for political intrigue.'[1]

This system must have given rise to dissatisfaction for, in 1856, 'in order that native labour might be more readily obtained by those requiring it', each of the magistrates residing with the various Xhosa and Fingo clans in British Kaffraria was directed to keep a register of all Native applicants for service. A central office for the registration of Natives was also established at Kingwilliamstown. Farmers within the Colony desiring to engage Native labourers were required to apply either to the central office or to the nearest magistrate with any particular tribe. In their application they were required to state the kind of labour they wanted and the terms both of wages and length of service, and whether wives, or wives and families, might accompany labourers.[2]

In short, the Special Magistrates added the management of labour bureaux to their already multifarious duties. As a result of the cattle-killing, they drafted thousands of labourers into the Colony.

The Colonial Government, while wishing to secure the services of these refugees for the European population within the Colony, was at the same time alarmed lest the influx should lead to disorder. To control the immigration no less than six Acts of Parliament were passed within a period of twelve months.[3]

In view of present efforts to control the movement of Natives and to regulate the flow of Native labour to the towns and farms of South Africa, the content and operation of these laws and regulations is of great interest. Apart from their efforts as temporary palliatives, they provided no final solution of the problem of controlling and supervising the movements of Natives, or of preventing crime. They were frequently amended and finally were repealed, fell into disuse, or ceased to apply.

Of the three most important of these Acts one made it an offence, under penalty of up to twelve months' imprisonment with hard labour, to enter the Colony without a pass.[4] It also imposed a penalty of up to six months' imprisonment with hard labour on 'Kafirs or other Native Foreigners' who were found with expired passes or in a place not specified on their passes.

[1] G. 39, 1857, p. 3.   [2] Ibid.
[3] Acts Nos. 22, 23, 24, 26 and 27 of 1857, and Act No. 1 of 1858.
[4] Act No. 23 of 1857: 'An Act for more effectually preventing Kafirs from entering the Colony without passes.' Repealed by Act No. 22 of 1867.

...Divisions to which such Indentures have been made, and the average rate of Wages; also the number of applications made for Kafir Servants, now standing over; and the Divisions these applications have been made from.[1]

Divisions	Kafirs registered					Average rate of wages each per month				Applications standing over				
	Adults		Minors		Total Souls	Adults		Boys over 14 yrs.	Girls over 14 yrs.	Adults		Minors		Total
	Males	Females	Males	Females		Males	Females			Males	Females	Males	Females	
Albany	215	166	142	144	667	Five shillings and food	Two shillings and food	Two shillings and sixpence and food	Two shillings and food	21	20	25	15	81
Victoria	198	166	141	179	684					0	1	18	3	22
Beaufort	154	145	112	119	530					1	1	11	0	13
Uitenhage	16	19	17	19	71					8	5	6	0	19
Port Elizabeth	3	2	0	2	7									
Queen's Town	176	96	101	82	455					19	19	25	15	78
Somerset East	486	399	365	354	1,604					0	0	4	3	7
Cradock	81	69	55	60	265									
Graaff Reinet	6	8	6	7	27									
Albert	27	24	25	27	103									
Sent from Central Office to Resident Magistrate														
Grahamstown	111	123	119	131	484									
Beaufort	32	28	24	29	113									
Somerset	14	17	17	17	65									
Bathurst	9	4	2	3	18									

Sent to Resident Magistrate, Graham's Town, by order of His Excellency the High Commissioner for service in the Colony. These people were forwarded through the Resident Magistrate of these respective districts, on application from sundry persons.

JOHN MACLEAN, Chief Commissioner.
RICHARD TAYLOR, Resident Magistrate.

[1] G 39, 1857, p. 2.

Another Act, usually known as the Kafir Employment Act, regulated the terms upon which 'Natives of Kafirland and other Native Foreigners' might obtain employment within the Colony.[1] It laid down that no contract of service was to be effective unless it was attested before a resident magistrate or 'other appointed functionary'. Contracts were to be for a maximum period of five years and, by an amendment introduced in the following year, for a minimum of one year.[2]

Colonists wanting to engage Native servants had to apply to the magistrate of their district. Passes to enable 'Native Foreigners' to take service, and passes for 'temporary lawful purposes', might be granted by Government officials. Such passes were to be valid only until a labourer had entered into his first contract of service, when a new pass, valid for the period of contract and for fourteen days after its completion, had to be issued. In other respects the colonial Masters and Servants Law was to apply.

The third Act relieved the Fingo from the disabilities imposed on other Natives by these measures. Its somewhat quaint and certainly illuminating official description reads: 'An Act for preventing Colonial Fingoes, and certain other Subjects of Her Majesty, from being mistaken for Kafirs, and thereby harassed and aggrieved.'

Provision was made in this third Act for the issue of 'certificates of Citizenship' to the Fingo and certain other Natives settled and domiciled within the Colony, and such persons were not required to carry passes.[3] The Thembu (Tambookies) of the Queenstown district were not to receive such certificates unless the Governor specially authorized their issue, but were required to carry passes in the same way and under the same penalties as 'Native Foreigners'. Under the 'Kafir Employment Act' certificates of citizenship might be issued to 'Native Foreigners' who had been in employment for five years, and who had not been sentenced to more than three months' imprisonment.

By 1864 the Xhosa and Thembu clans were rehabilitated in some degree after the effects of the 'cattle-killing', and were once more congregating in Kaffraria. It was in this year also that the Imperial authorities refused to sanction the extension of British

[1] Act No. 27 of 1857: 'An Act for regulating the Terms upon which Natives of Kafirland and other Native Foreigners may obtain employment in this Colony.'

[2] Act No. 1 of 1858. Repealed by Act No. 22 of 1867.

[3] In 1855 Mr. Calderwood had severely criticized the pass system which was operating in Victoria East, on the ground that it caused the Fingo much inconvenience and irritation. They often lived at a great distance from the superintendent and had therefore to spend much time in securing their passes. Further, the system was not in his view effective for the prevention or detection of crime, for which purpose he advocated a more effective police force. G. 7, 1855, p. 14.

dominion and settlement east of the Kei River, and allowed Kreli and his Gcaleka to return to that part of the territory which lay between the Kei and the Bashee Rivers, that is, to the border of British Kaffraria. Within the Colony and British Kaffraria there had been frequent complaints that the certificates of citizenship were abused and used to cloak cattle- and sheep-stealing.[1]

These circumstances led to the tightening up of the pass laws and to the issue of special regulations. Current certificates of citizenship were withdrawn and in future they were to be reissued annually under more stringent conditions.[2]

The provisions of the Kafir Employment Act were reinforced by regulations specifying the officials in British Kaffraria who might issue passes: some eight in all, including the Lieutenant-Governor and his Secretary, were enumerated.

Colonists desiring the services of 'Native Foreigners' had to apply in writing to the magistrates of the district in which they themselves resided; no passes were to be issued except on the application of the colonial magistrate of the district in which the Native was to be employed. Natives travelling to employment had to proceed from magistracy to magistracy, getting their passes endorsed at each stage of the journey. Contracts, as before, were to be attested by resident magistrates only.[3]

These various measures greatly hampered the flow of labour to the Colony. There was complete unanimity between farmers and Native administrators on this point. In 1865, acting on requests from the Legislative Council and the House of Assembly, the Governor appointed a commission to inquire into 'the relations of the Colony with the Native Tribes residing within and upon its borders'.[4] The commission collected much valuable evidence and, although unable to draft a report in the time at its disposal, it issued a memorandum which stated that the whole system of passes and contracts required revision and was a great inconvenience to both Natives and employers.[5]

Complaints about the system had poured in from all sides. The Superintendent of the Tyumie Crown Reserve had reported that there was little employment in Kaffraria and the Natives could not enter the Colony to look for work. The Civil Commissioner at Aliwal North reported that the Natives objected to

[1] *Select Committee on Kafir Labourers*, A. 4, 1859, p. 1.
[2] Act 17 of 1864.   [3] Government Notice 320, 1864.
[4] *Cape Gazette*, October 7th, 1864: 'To make enquiry and report upon the number of Fingoes and other native foreigners located within the Colony, their means of livelihood, and the progress made by them in civilization, the several Native Laws and Customs affecting them and their Property, the sufficiency or otherwise of the Superintendence and Government of these people and generally upon native affairs in this Colony.'
[5] (Cape) *Commission on Native Affairs*, 1865, p. xxv.

long contracts and that, when it was explained to them that under the 1858 Act they must contract for service for twelve months if they entered the Colony, many turned back, although they had already travelled a long way. From Richmond the Rev. C. W. Southey complained that the year's contract was a grievance both to the Mantatees and the farmers. The Mantatees were principally employed in making dams and stone kraals, and it was frequently most convenient to both sides that a group should work for a short period. Six or eight might contract to work for a cow or a mare, and want to go back when the work was finished; while the farmer, on his part, might not be able to continue to employ the whole gang for the minimum period of a year.[1]

The farmers objected to having to register contracts of service before magistrates who were often many miles distant, and some recommended that contracts should be registered by field-cornets or justices of the peace. They did not comment on the effect of the pass system on the supply of labour, but only on its efficacy in preventing stock-theft, and what they stressed was the need for more stringent regulations regarding the moving of stock by Natives.[2]

Regulation of the movement of stock had in due time to be improved through other machinery, for within the Colony and British Kaffraria the pass system was soon to disappear. In 1866 British Kaffraria was incorporated in the Colony, and in the following year the pass laws were revised. The laws and regulations of 1857–64 were for the most part repealed and a single Act substituted which required 'Native Foreigners' entering the Colony to be provided with passes.[3] 'Native Foreigners' were defined as 'any member of any tribe, other than a Fingo, of which the principal chief shall live beyond the borders of the Colony'. The effect was that, thenceforward, as the different Transkeian territories were annexed the pass law ceased to be applicable to their inhabitants once they had entered the Colony.

E. THE APPLICATION OF THE MASTERS AND SERVANTS LAW TO NATIVES

Act No. 22 of 1867, which relaxed the pass regulations, contained another important provision. It repealed the so-called 'Kafir Employment Act' of 1857 (amended 1858) which had prescribed minimum and maximum terms of service for Native Foreigners. Henceforth, in the Cape Colony, contracts of service between Europeans and all Natives, 'Foreigners' as well as the

---

[1] Ibid., Appendix No. 1, p. 47.   [2] Ibid., Appendix No. 2.
[3] Act No. 22 of 1867.

Fingo and other special groups, were to be governed by the ordinary colonial law of master and servant.

To understand the significance of this change, we must look back to the Masters, Servants, and Apprentices Ordinance of 1841. This Ordinance had brought to an end any attempt to differentiate in law between Hottentot and European. It had also provided that oral contracts, which had been restricted to one month by Ordinance 50 of 1828, might be binding for twelve months. Written and attested contracts had in 1841 been made compulsory only for contracts of more than twelve months, and they had not been permissible for periods longer than three years.

In 1856 the Colonial Parliament had repealed this Ordinance and passed the Masters and Servants Act,[1] which, with minor amendments, is still operative to-day. This law was based on the 1841 Ordinance and, like it, was to serve as the basis of similar laws in other parts of South Africa. 1737282

The most striking feature of the Masters and Servants Law is that it attaches criminal liability to the breach of certain civil contracts. The justification for special legislation to control the relations of masters and servants was that it had been easy for masters, on the one hand, to misrepresent terms of service and for servants, on the other, to evade, by desertion, the obligations they had undertaken. Disputes continually arose in these circumstances and contracts were difficult to enforce when one party had no possessions from which damages, the sanction for contracts under civil law, could be claimed.

The Masters and Servants Law made servants, and masters, liable to prosecution by the Crown for breaches of contract, such as desertion, disobedience, wilful breach of duty, absence without leave on the part of the servant, and, on the part of the master, the withholding of wages or failure to supply food. The Cape Act of 1856, following the terms of the Ordinance of 1841, restricted oral contracts to periods of one year, but the period for which written contracts might be made was raised from three to five years. The conditions under which children might be apprenticed either as agricultural or domestic servants, or to learn skilled trades, were also specified. The Act was wide, generally defining the duties and obligations of masters and servants. For instance, it laid down the procedure to be adopted as regards the termination of contracts in the event of the bankruptcy of the master or his removal beyond the frontier; the position of a female servant who married while under contract of service; and the position of the wife and children of a male servant. In the last

[1] Act No. 15 of 1856: 'To Amend the Laws regulating the relative Rights and Duties of Masters, Servants and Apprentices.'

case the master was to have no claim on the services of such dependents unless this had been especially arranged.

The statute was designed to protect both masters and servants. The former were to be protected principally by the provision making breach of contract a crime. Servants, on the other hand, were also in some respects placed in a privileged position. The Act provided, for instance, that unless other arrangements had been specified, servants hired to reside on the premises of employers were to be provided with food and lodging. In case of sickness, servants were to receive full wages during the first month of incapacity, and all other benefits during the second. Only at the end of two months could the master cancel the contract. Under this Act the statutory servant was thus in a better position than an employee under the common law, for in the event of illness the latter could claim wages only for the period actually worked. In the case of proved assault by a master the contract might be terminated if the servant desired.

In practice the law was not to work to the satisfaction of either masters or servants. Frequent amendments[1] are an indication of its inadequacy. Similar laws in other parts of South Africa proved equally unsatisfactory. The Natal Native Affairs Commission of 1881–2 considered that the law was bound to be unsatisfactory and that employers did not find it an effective means of enforcing discipline. It said: 'The general feeling, we think, is that which appears to be the sensible one—that as a general rule a servant who has to be brought before a magistrate to be made to work or to be civil had better be got rid of.'[2] In the Cape there were numerous complaints from employers who wanted the terms of the Act stiffened in favour of the masters.

The effects of such legislation on the labour market depend in part on its content and administration and in part on the opinions of all parties affected concerning its probable consequences. If masters consider that it reduces the cost of enforcing contracts it will for this reason stimulate their demand for statutory servants. If, on the other hand, they consider the obligations imposed on them to be onerous it will operate to reduce their demand for such labour. Similarly, if employees consider the terms which regulate service in the specified occupations to be onerous, the law will reduce the supply of labour to these occupations; and, conversely, if the terms are regarded as favourable, the supply will be stimulated.

With regard to racial discrimination, the Cape Masters and

[1] Act No. 15 of 1856 was amended by: Act No. 18 of 1873; Act No. 28 of 1874; Act No. 7 of 1875; Act No. 8 of 1889; Act No. 30 of 1889; Act No. 24 of 1895; Act No. 40 of 1895.

[2] *Natal Native Affairs Commission*, 1881–2, p. 10, para. 31.

Servants Act did not, and still does not, differentiate between races, and this precedent was to be followed in the Transvaal (1880). But it was not followed in the Orange Free State (1904), nor in Natal,[1] where, although the Masters and Servants Ordinance of 1850 had not differentiated between races, a special Masters and Servants (Native) Act[2] was passed in 1894.

It is a difficult matter to assess the general effect of these laws. The effect on different classes of servant has differed. Under the earlier statutes, the Natal Ordinance of 1850, the Cape Act of 1856, and the Transvaal Ordinance of 1880, a servant was defined as

> any person employed for hire, wages or other remuneration to per-form any handicraft or any other bodily labour in agriculture or manufactures or in domestic service, or as a boatman, porter or other occupation of a like nature.

The Clay-Martin-Mills report of the Economic and Wage Commission (1925), when discussing Masters and Servants laws, states that this definition was evidently designed to exclude occupations in which Europeans were generally employed. It said:

> In 1856 there could have been no question of differential legisla-tion for white and black in a subject of this kind, and no attempt was made to apply the Statute specifically to the one and to exclude the other. But the sole justification for it was, of course, the con-tract between civilized masters and raw natives as their servants. . . .
>
> The definition of 'servant' which is common to the Statutes, was evidently designed to exclude occupations ordinarily followed by white employees and to restrict the Act, as far as possible, to Natives and coloured.[3]

It is doubtful whether the Commissioners achieved a proper balance in this judgment. For instance, they overlooked the discrimination involved in the 'Kafir Employment Act' of 1857 which, as amended in 1858, made special provision concerning the period of service and registration of contracts of 'Native Foreigners', which definition included even the majority of the Natives living in the district of Queenstown within the Colony. Such Natives only fell under the general Masters and Servants law in respect of matters not specifically regulated by the 'Kafir Employment Act'. The pass system then operating is also an example, on a closely related subject, of differential legislation.

Further, there is no doubt that the Masters and Servants laws were in part intended to control and enforce contracts with

---

[1] The chief statutes are the Cape Act No. 15 of 1856; Natal Ordinance No. 20 of 1850; Transvaal Law No. 13 of 1880; Orange Free State, Ordinance No. 7 of 1904.

[2] Act No. 40 of 1894.

[3] *Economic and Wage Commission* (1925). U.G. 14, 1926, para. 60.

European servants, particularly those who were at this time being imported from Europe, often at considerable expense to their employers. In this connexion it is significant that the Cape Masters and Servants Act repealed and replaced an Act for 'Encouraging the Importation of European Labourers into the Colony'. In Natal the original Masters and Servants Ordinance of 1850, which had provided that contracts made outside Natal were not valid within the Colony unless they had been attested by a Government official, was amended in 1855 to make valid contracts made in writing in Europe.

That the application of these laws has been narrowed in practice is evident from the trend of court interpretations. For instance, giving judgment in 1903, Sir James Rose-Innes, who was then Chief Justice of the Transvaal, said:

> 'The legislature has, under certain circumstances, attached criminal consequences to the breach of what is essentially a civil contract; the Masters and Servants law must, therefore, be very strictly construed. When it is sought to subject any person to the penalties of the law he should receive the benefit of any doubt that may exist as to its application to his case.'[1]

This narrowing of the law and the actual use made of it, combined with the fact that most of the occupations subject to it are in fact carried on by non-Europeans, has inevitably meant that the penal sanction has been invoked chiefly in disputes between European masters and non-European servants. A feeling that the law discriminates against them has grown up amongst Natives. To what extent, if any, the actual supply of Native labour to occupations which fall under these laws has been affected can remain only a matter for conjecture, but there can hardly be any doubt that the prevalence of this belief has materially affected the psychological attitude of Natives towards work under European supervision, and especially to those occupations in which employers most frequently invoke these laws.

F. THE ECONOMIC CONDITION OF THE CAPE COLONY IN THE 1860's

By 1867, in which year Natives were granted the same legal status as people of other races, the Cape Colony extended from the Atlantic coast eastwards to the Kei River. Its eastern frontier ran northward along the Kei and White Kei Rivers to the Stormbergen and followed those mountains north-east to the Orange River, the northern boundary. North of the Orange River were the Voortrekker Republics. In 1852 and 1854 Britain had withdrawn, by agreement, first from her claim to jurisdiction over the

[1] Innes, C.J., in *Clay* v. *Rex* (1903) T.S. 482.

Voortrekkers beyond the Vaal River, and then from her brief attempt to govern the country between the Orange and the Vaal Rivers.

In 1865, when the first census was taken in the Cape Colony, the total population was almost half a million. The European population was a hundred and eighty-one thousand. More than half the population and 42 per cent. of the Europeans lived in the eastern districts. The three most easterly of the colonial divisions—Peddie, Victoria East, and Queenstown—had a European population of six thousand, although, with the exception of a few missionaries and traders, they had only been occupied by Europeans after the wars and disturbances of 1846–7 and 1850–3. In British Kaffraria,[1] according to the official returns for 1865, there were sixty-two thousand Natives and nearly three thousand Europeans.

Three-quarters of the occupied population of the Cape Colony was recorded as engaged in farming; only one-eighth in industrial occupations, such as building, carpentry, coach- and wagon-making, harness- and shoe-making; and less than one-sixteenth in trade and transport.

In the western districts, where as yet very few Natives were employed, the Cape Coloured people, descendants of slaves, Hottentots and Europeans, continued to do much of the manual work, both skilled and unskilled. Many of the slaves, particularly the Malays, had been skilled artisans, and after they were liberated (1834–8) they and their descendants continued to work as builders, bricklayers, masons, painters, glaziers, saddlers, and harness-makers, boot and shoemakers, carpenters, cabinet-makers, coach-builders, wagon-makers, wheelwrights, and in other miscellaneous trades. In 1865, when considerable numbers of European skilled and unskilled labourers had already been imported, the Coloured builders, bricklayers and masons, painters and glaziers, and tailors still outnumbered the European; whereas in the eastern divisions there were many more European workers than Coloured (including Native) in these occupations.[2]

[1] Now known as the Ciskei.
[2] Census of the Cape of Good Hope, 1865 (G. 20, 1866). Table VII, p. 133.

| | Western Divisions | | Eastern Divisions | |
	White	Coloured	White	Coloured
Builders, bricklayers, and masons	506	763	665	224
Carpenters, joiners, and cabinet-makers	937	317	668	82
Painters and glaziers	106	157	114	19
Coachbuilders, wagon-makers and wheelwrights	476	189	305	35
Tailors	156	316	153	41

Of the different types of farming, grain production predominated in the west; sheep- and cattle-farming in the east.[1] Wool production, as we have seen, had increased rapidly in the 'fifties, especially in the east of the Colony. Wool was the leading export. By 1865 there were 8,370,000 wooled sheep in the Colony, of which 6,126,000 were in the eastern districts. In spite of a fall in the price of Cape wool in the 'sixties and a prolonged drought, wool exports continued to increase in quantity and value, but the increase was less rapid than it had been in the 'fifties.[2] Since the middle of the nineteenth century wool has remained the most important farm export product of South Africa.

During the 'sixties the value of hides and skins exported also continued to rise, while the export of ostrich feathers increased rapidly. The domestic rearing of ostriches began in the district of Oudtshoorn about 1860,[3] yet for the years 1865–9 the average value of the ostrich feathers exported was £342,000, and was second only to that of wool.[4] On the other hand, the export of wine declined.

Grain was cultivated, chiefly wheat, barley, oats, and, in the eastern districts, maize, but except in specially favourable years, it was grown only for local consumption and was not generally exported; indeed, in years of exceptional drought wheat was imported. In 1875 Mr. Noble was to record that in the more remote districts, such as the north-eastern border divisions of Wodehouse, Albert, and Aliwal North, the prohibitive cost of land carriage discouraged the raising of corn beyond the immediate requirements of the inhabitants.

The nature of the Colony's exports indicates the importance of pastoral farming. Manufacturing was confined almost exclusively to working up raw materials for local consumption, such

[1] Ibid.

Farmers:

	Western Districts				Eastern Districts			
	White		Coloured		White		Coloured	
	Male	Female	Male	Female	Male	Female	Male	Female
Corn	7,173	38	810	3	2,753	19	3,660	10
Sheep and Cattle	3,904	18	590	5	7,842	79	1,160	15
Wine	1,151	2	8	—	121	4	7	—
Gardeners (Market)	138	2	61	2	125	7	31	1

[2] Average value of wool exports through Colonial ports—*Official Year Book*, No. 6, 1910–22, p. 706:

			£1000's
1850–4	.	.	384
1855–9	.	.	968
1860–4	.	.	1,509
1865–9	.	.	1,802

[3] J. Noble, op. cit., p. 265.   [4] *Official Year Book* No. 6, 1910–22, p. 706.

as milling, furniture-making, and leather working, and to naturally sheltered industries, such as building. Other manufactured goods, for instance, textiles, machinery, and tools, were imported. Thus the increase in foreign trade[1] is an indication that the colonists were acquiring a wider range of supplies. The increase in trade was not confined to the European colonists, for, as we have seen, within the Native areas, and especially within those of the Cape Colony, new products were being raised and new wants satisfied through the exchange of produce and the sale of labour. The use of European tools and clothes was increasing and commodities, such as tea and sugar, were additions to customary diet.

[1] Value of imports and exports through Cape of Good Hope ports 1845–69, in averages of five years:

	Imports £	Exports £
1845–9	1,109,443	512,718
1850–54	1,602,797	778,184
1855–9	2,095,155	1,639,240
1860–64	2,560,846	2,165,965
1865–9	2,073,255	2,371,541

Ibid., p. 705.

CHAPTER III

THE GROWTH OF ECONOMIC CO-OPERA-TION IN NATAL AND THE VOOR-TREKKER REPUBLICS, 1835–1870

A. THE POLITICAL SETTING

IN the Cape Colony the problems arising out of contact with the Bantu had been met by a policy designed to assimilate them into the European economy. The ultimate end was equality for White and Black. This policy of equality, which had been introduced in 1828 when the Hottentots had been freed from their position of semi-serfdom, was one of the causes of the Great Trek. The trek from the Colony was to some extent a northward continuation of the eastward dispersion which had been going on for more than a century, and which changed direction when the Bantu were encountered in the Fish River district. But the Great Trek was more than a mere continuation and acceleration of this drift. The men and women who left the Colony from 1835 onwards were antagonistic to the British policy. They left with the avowed intention of looking for farms in more spacious areas where they would be free from British interference and able to 'preserve proper relations between master and servant'.[1]

First in Natal and later in the northern Republics they were to be free for a time to go their own way. What they had wanted were extensive farms where their cattle and sheep could graze unmolested by thieving 'kaffirs'. They also wanted a certain limited amount of labour to look after their flocks and herds, to till what little land they cultivated, and to help with domestic work.

In Natal they proposed to meet their wants by appropriating the land and decreeing that each farm[2] might retain five Native families. The remainder of the Natives were to be removed south into what is now Pondoland, or north into Zululand. The Voortrekkers, like the British at this time, had no desire to undertake the administration or control of large numbers of Natives. Indeed, it would have been quite impossible for them to attempt it, for they had not the resources to organize an effective system of administration for their own government.

---

[1] Piet Retief's Manifesto, *Grahamstown Journal*, 2 Feb. 1837; G. W. Eybers, *Select Constitutional Documents*, p. 143. cf. Walker, *History*, pp. 202–10; *The Great Trek*, Chap. 3.

[2] The Trekkers who arrived in Natal before December 1839 were to receive two farms each. These would usually be situated one in the upland districts and one, for winter grazing, in the lower-lying warmer regions.

Their plans did not commend themselves to the Governor of the Cape. Fear of the disturbances on the eastern frontier of the Cape Colony which the proposed removal of large numbers of Natives was expected to cause, prompted him to annex Natal in 1843. After the British annexation, the majority of the Trekkers withdrew and rejoined those who had stayed on the Highveld and had by now dispersed north of the Orange and Vaal Rivers.

British policy towards the problems evoked by the northern migration was to alternate between that of intervention and withdrawal until in 1868 Britain was finally to intervene and annex Basutoland. The dominant reason for this annexation, as for the previous additions to British territory in Southern Africa, was the necessity for protecting the colonial frontiers and for achieving within them security from Native unrest.

From their arrival in the Orange Free State the Trekkers had coveted the fertile cornlands in the Caledon River valley occupied by the Bantu and half-caste tribes. By 1867, after years of disagreement and fighting over the right to occupy and use these lands, the chief resistance, that of the Basuto, was broken. The Orange Free State then proposed to annex the greater part of the arable land. To prevent this dismemberment, and the consequent dispersal of the Basuto among the colonial and Transkeian tribes, the Imperial Government was persuaded to authorize the annexation of Basutoland to the Crown.[1]

In Natal, Native policy under the British régime was to take a somewhat different line from that followed during the same period in the Cape Colony. The circumstances were different. After the Trekkers had withdrawn, British immigrants were introduced, and, especially at first, their mode of life differed from that of the stock farmers of the Cape frontier. The immigrants to Natal were introduced to grow cotton on small allotments of twenty acres. They were not intended to be pastoral farmers. Consequently their demand for labour was different from that in the eastern Cape. They wanted regular agricultural labourers, not the herdsmen, reapers, and shearers required by the Cape frontiersmen.

This difference, together with the attempt of the settlers to direct policy, and the desire of the Imperial authorities to reconcile the interests of the Natives with those of the British immigrants, invests the history of Natal in this period with a special interest.

The attempt on the one hand to protect the Natives' interests was to lead to the reservation of land for their use. The attempt on the other hand to meet the European colonists' demand for

[1] On this see: C. W. de Kiewiet, *British Colonial Policy and the South African Republics*, Chap. XIV; E. A. Walker, op. cit. Chap. X.

labour was to result in various devices calculated to induce the Natives to become farm-labourers, such as the remission of their hut tax, and the attempt to limit the right of Natives to occupy land outside Native locations. Further, it led to the importation of indentured Indian labourers.

North of the Orange River there was at this time no ordered government. Different groups of the Voortrekkers established small republics, but personal jealousies and loyalties caused dissension and sometimes strife even within the individual republics. In 1848 Great Britain intervened and annexed the territory lying between the Orange and Vaal Rivers and the Drakensberg, which was then named the Orange River Sovereignty. Great Britain withdrew in 1854. Thereafter the European settlers who remained in this area retained a unified government, but they were too fully occupied in the struggle with the Basuto to evolve a considered Native policy.

North of the Vaal River a united state was not to emerge until the 'eighties. After 1849 there was a loose union of the Republics and a central legislative body, the United Volksraad. But, whatever laws might be passed, administration was in the hands of local officials, the field-cornets and kommandants, who were themselves farmers. They had no means, beyond their individual prestige, of maintaining authority, for there were no police to enforce law and order. In many parts of the Republics the position of the Europeans was precarious and their attitude towards the Natives depended on their strength. Nevertheless, except in the Zoutpansberg, from which district the Europeans were to be compelled to withdraw during the 'sixties, the land throughout most of the present Orange Free State and Transvaal passed into the ownership of the Europeans. In many cases its Native occupants were required to render tribute in the form of labour.

B. NATAL

(i) The Economic Setting

The immediate cause of the annexation of Natal was that the Governor of the Cape Colony and the Colonial Office feared the results of the Natal Volksraad's policy of driving large numbers of Natives towards the Cape frontier. The country had at first appeared to be sparsely populated, for its inhabitants had been slain, or concentrated into the Zulu impis, or had dispersed and taken refuge during the wars of Chaka and Dingaan in 'baboon country' in the hills and mountains. After the defeat of Dingaan by the Trekkers in 1838 the original occupants began to return, together with refugees from other parts. The result was that the

British Administration was faced with the same problem that had confronted the Volksraad of dealing with an unexpectedly large Native population.

It decided to meet the situation by establishing locations, or reserves, for the Native population. In 1846 a Location Commission was appointed which set aside eight locations with a total area of 1,168,000 acres. It further recommended that a 'model mechanical school' be established in each location, that missions and schools be encouraged, and roads built. The setting aside of this land for Native occupation was to cause much criticism from the European settlers. Nevertheless it was maintained, and the Natives were secured in their right to it when in 1864 the Natal Native Trust was established.

People in England during the hungry 'forties looked to the colonies for an outlet for the poor. The first cotton famine was at the same time stimulating the search for new sources of supply. The fertile semi-tropical coastal belt of Natal appeared very suitable for the production of cotton, and two immigration schemes were organized by private promoters for this purpose. The first introduced only thirty-five poor German families, less than two hundred persons in all. The second scheme, organized by Byrne, introduced during the years 1849 to 1851 some four thousand five hundred people, who came chiefly from England and Scotland.

Both schemes failed to profit their promoters, but they are nevertheless important in that they introduced into Natal a class which expected to make a living by commercial agriculture.

The immigration failed in its design to establish a cotton-growing settlement. At the time the lack of an 'adequate' supply of Native labour was much stressed as a cause of failure,[1] but there were many other reasons. Few of the European immigrants were, in fact, accustomed to agricultural labour. It had been supposed that the Native population would provide an abundant supply of labour. Moreover, none of the settlers were accustomed to the semi-tropical conditions of the coastal belt. Further, the twenty-acre allotments were too small, and although additional land was made available, those who remained on it had a hard struggle. More than half the immigrants did not even take up their titles to land. Some started practising the trades and callings for which they had been trained, a few bought land for themselves, and many left the Colony.[2] They were inexperienced and without sufficient resources. Moreover, such cotton as they produced did not suit existing machines, nor did it appear likely to be sufficient in quantity to warrant their alteration.

[1] W. C. Holden, *History of Natal* (1855), p. 307.
[2] *Parl. Papers*, 1854–5, XXXVI [1919], paras. 130, 186.

(ii) The Demand for Labour—The Demand of the Colonists and the Official Attitude

Where cotton failed, sugar-cane was soon substituted, and in due time it was to flourish. But the commercial production of sugar, like that of cotton, required a sure supply of labour, and labour was not immediately forthcoming. The colonists did not fail to complain. The reluctance of the Natives to work for them, the colonists said, was due chiefly to two causes: the natural indolence of the men, who lived in polygamy, leaving their wives to earn sufficient food to support them; and the large locations which enabled them to continue this mode of life.

These views were not unchallenged. In 1852 the Lieutenant-Governor of Natal appointed a commission to inquire generally into the system of governing the Natives and 'the causes of the want of labour, and the remedies applicable to ensure labour'. Although the bulk of the evidence emphasized the scarcity of reliable Native labour, witnesses, such as the chief Native administrator, Shepstone, and magistrates in the Native locations, questioned both the reluctance of the Natives to work for Europeans and the ability of the European colonists to employ at a profit the Native labour which they were so constantly demanding. Mr. Peppercorne, Magistrate of the Impafana Location, bluntly said:

'I do not hesitate to question the fact of there being any real difficulty in obtaining native labour, except in individual cases, arising from individual causes. I believe that any amount of native labour may be procured at five shillings per month, by rational treatment of the natives. But I very much question the ability of the white population to employ, profitably to themselves, an amount of native labour commensurate with the annual value of even one-fourth of the native tax: say to the extent of £2,000 per annum . . .'[1]

He argued that if the Natives had been able to obtain employment for money wages they would much prefer to obtain the money necessary for paying their taxes in that way than by the alternative means of selling their cattle,[2] but he considered the landowners in Natal[3] were 'neither in a condition to employ English, nor any large amount of Kafir labour, for money wages, although they may be desirous of employing them without wages'.[4]

Concerning the supply of labour, Mr. Peppercorne also gave

[1] Natal Native Affairs Commission, 1852-4, *Proceedings*, VI, p. 4.
[2] Ibid, p. 4.
[3] A few years later it was estimated that Natal had a population of 6,550 Europeans (3,600 of British descent and 2,250 of Dutch) and 102,000 natives. H. Hall: *Manual of South African Geography* (1859), pp. 47, 48.
[4] Natal Native Affairs Commission, 1852-4, *Proceedings*, VI, p. 6.

evidence, showing that the Natives were actually performing all the unskilled work of the colony:

> 'It would', he said, 'be very difficult to contemplate any kind of product of labour, except skilled labour, which does not involve that of the Kafir in this district. On a farm he does almost everything. He herds the cattle, milks the cows, churns the butter, loads it on the wagon, the oxen of which he inspans, and leads. He cuts wood, and thatch, he digs sluits, and makes bricks, and reaps the harvest; and, in the house, invariably cooks. There is little that I ever see a farmer do, but ride about the country. In the town, there are some familiar cases in which Kafir labour is employed to a ridiculous extent: for in what quarter of the globe would male adults be found performing the offices of nurses to infants and children, or as laundresses of female apparel. These docile achievements are certainly not very congruous with their manly habits, nor compatible with the character given them of blood-thirsty savages.'[1]

The reason for their performing these many tasks was 'anxiety to obtain wages to pay for their father's and mother's kraal, and save their cattle'.[2] He pointed out that the Native hut tax would absorb the whole annual increase in their cattle if it were not partially met from wages.

He was not the only one to hold these views. The ex-magistrate of the Umvoti Location said that in his district he had heard few complaints about the lack of labour and that as far as his knowledge went the Europeans were usually well supplied. Further:

> 'I beg to remark', he continued, 'that on the sugar estates of Mr. Morewood, I have myself seen the natives in considerable numbers requesting employment from him, and he has informed me that he can, at any time, procure a superabundance of labour.'[3]

With regard to the complaint of the colonists, echoed in the Report of the Commission, that the system of large locations 'dried up the source whence an abundant and continuous supply of Kafir labour for wages might be procured',[4] Shepstone maintained that the locations in existence could not support two-thirds of the Native population; for the capability of a location to provide a means of livelihood could not be judged from its extent, and a large proportion of the country included in several of the existing locations was, he said, not capable of being inhabited at all.[5]

The attitude of the Imperial authorities and of their representative in Natal, the Lieutenant-Governor, was one of compromise

[1] Natal Native Affairs Commission, 1852–4, *Proceedings*, IV, p. 6.
[2] Ibid., IV, p. 6.
[3] Ibid., VI, pp. 48, 49, ev. J. Cleghorn, Magistrate, Umvoti Location, 1850–52.
[4] Ibid., *Report*, p. 9.
[5] Ibid., *Proceedings*, I, p. 69.

between the extreme demands of the settlers and complete non-intervention in the Native mode of life. After its annexation there had been some hesitation as to whether Natal should be retained by Britain. The decision to retain was avowedly made in the supposed interests of the Natives. Outlining future policy with regard to Natal to the new High Commissioner for South Africa, the Secretary for War and Colonies, Earl Grey, wrote:

'The civilization and improvement of the inhabitants of this part of Africa are, then, the main objects to which I look from the maintenance of this Colony.'[1]

It was hoped, however, at the same time, that Natal would become a market for British manufactures, and, more important still, that it would not be an expense to the British taxpayer. On grounds of expense it was not possible to pursue the policy which had been adopted in the Cape Colony and British Kaffraria, and which had there necessitated the Imperial grant secured by Sir George Grey.[2]

In Natal the Natives in the locations were left largely to themselves. They were, however, taxed—hut tax at the rate of seven shillings a hut being collected for the first time in 1849,[3] and the Imperial authorities also took an interest in the question of the supply of Native labour. In general the view was taken that it was both necessary and desirable that the Natives should become accustomed to going out to work for Europeans. This attitude is clearly expressed by Earl Grey in a dispatch written in 1849:

'I conceive', he wrote, 'that it would be difficult or impossible to assign to the natives such locations of an extent sufficient for their support as a pastoral people depending mainly for support on their flocks and herds. I regard it, on the contrary, as desirable that these people should be placed in circumstances in which they should find regular industry necessary for their subsistence.'[4]

This attitude was maintained. In 1854 the Lieutenant-Governor reported with satisfaction that increased acquaintance with each other's language and habits, and in some places the efforts of the magistrates, were 'gradually bringing about a greater desire on the part of the natives to assist the farmers'. The true remedy for the lack of labour was, however, 'only to be found in a better

---

[1] *Parl. Papers*, 1847–8, XLII [980], p. 94, Corresp. *re* settlement of Natal, 1844–6, p. 94, Grey to Pottinger.

[2] Ibid., p. 94; cf. Earl Grey's comments on Location Commission's Report, pp. 137–41.

[3] *Parl. Papers re* settlement of Natal, 1851, p. 17, T. Shepstone to Hon. Sec. to Government of Natal, Aug. 20, 1850.

[4] *Parl. Papers*, 1850, XXXVIII [1292], Cape, Natal Corresp., 1849–50, p. 198.

system of native government, which shall render the Kafir more dependent on his own labour for his subsistence'.[1]

That could only mean the withdrawal of some existing means of livelihood. Indeed, taxation, which would increase the pressure causing the Natives to go out to work, was officially regarded as a convenient lever for 'civilizing' them. In 1866 the Lieutenant-Governor proposed that the hut tax be increased from seven to eleven shillings, additional Native taxation being 'highly desirable, as bearing upon questions of policy connected with their moral and social advancement'.[2]

Although the Imperial authorities were anxious for the Natives to develop 'regular habits of industry', they were not prepared to sanction all the schemes for increasing the supply of labour put forward by the colonists. Forced labour was employed on the roads and other public works, the chiefs ordering out men at the request of the Resident Magistrates. But the Imperial authorities would not allow direct compulsion to be used to obtain labour for private individuals. On the ground that it might develop into 'an engine for imposing forced labour', a colonial law was disallowed in 1871.[3]

(iii) The Supply of Native Labour and the Formulation of a Labour Policy

Many schemes for increasing the supply of labour were canvassed by the colonists, the two principal being the break-up of the large locations and an increase in Native taxation. The Report of the Commission of 1852-4, which completely ignored the evidence of such men as Shepstone and the other Native administrators, recommended both these measures. It considered that the large rugged locations should be broken up and a board 'comprising some experienced settlers' should be appointed to select smaller new locations each about twenty-five thousand acres in extent. The Commissioners recommended that such locations be situated evenly throughout the colony in order to give all the colonists a convenient reservoir from which to draw labour. By limiting the size of the locations they hoped to force the Natives out to work for Europeans. Further, they recommended an increase in the annual hut tax, and suggested that Native labourers living on farms should be exempt from the whole tax.

The first of these recommendations was not carried out.

---

[1] *Parl. Papers*, 1854-5 [1919], p. 217.

[2] Government House Documents, 101, 1866. Natal and Imperial Blue Book 321, No. 4, quoted C. Axelson: *The History of Taxation in Natal prior to Union* (unpublished thesis, Natal University College).

[3] *Natal Government Gazette*, 1871, p. 45.

Shepstone, for one, considered it unnecessary. Other devices for increasing the supply of labour were adopted. In the first place, to prevent Natives from continuing subsistence farming on Crown and European-owned land, an attempt was made to limit the number of Natives who might reside there. In 1855 an ordinance was promulgated, designed to stop Natives from 'squatting' without licence on such land—a practice which (according to the preamble to the ordinance) had been carried on

> to such an extent as seriously to annoy and injure the agricultural population, and to endanger the peace and security of the District;

and which (in the official view) was,

> at the same time, injurious to the true interests of the Natives themselves, by fostering a desultory mode of culture of the soil, opposed to their application to civilized agriculture, and to regular industry.[1]

The ordinance provided that the owner or occupier of any land on which more than three Native families resided should make an annual return giving particulars of the number of such Natives and the nature of his agreement with them. It was not actively administered and large numbers of Natives continued to live on Crown- and European-owned land.[2]

Two years later, in 1857, following the recommendation of the Commission of 1852–4, Natives resident upon European-owned farms who were in the employment of the occupier were made exempt from the hut tax. To encourage 'civilization', Natives living in 'houses of European construction' who had only one wife and otherwise conformed to 'civilized usages' were also exempt.[3] This measure, according to the opinion of a conference of magistrates, did not increase the supply of labour to farmers, and they recommended its repeal. It was not, however, to be altered until 1875, when the hut tax was raised to fourteen shillings per hut and the huts of farm-labourers were no longer to be exempt from the tax.

Efforts were also made to increase the supply of Native labour from the country to the north of Zululand by regulating the conditions under which such labour might be introduced.[4] Organized attempts to recruit and introduce such labour were not, however, successful. In spite of the dangers of travelling through the territory of hostile tribes, the Natives chose to

[1] 'Ordinance to prevent the unlicensed Squatting, and to regulate the Occupation of Land by the Natives.' Ordinance No. 2 of 1855.

[2] *Natal Legislative Council, Votes and Proceedings*, 1863, pp. 59, 61; *Natal Government Gazette*, 1962, pp. 3, 191; idem, 1873, p. 301; *Natal Native Affairs Commission*, 1881–2, para. 24.

[3] Law 6 of 1857.   [4] Law 13 of 1859.

come out in small parties and seek work for themselves rather than to engage themselves for long terms to unknown masters.[1]

In addition to these measures to increase the labour supply from African sources, indentured labour was imported from India. The possibility of using convict or coolie labour had been mentioned by witnesses before the Commission of 1852–4, but no one had advocated this course, nor was it recommended by the Commissioners. Sir George Grey, however, had seen the results of the use of indentured labour in the cane-fields of Mauritius, and, when visiting Natal in 1855, he approved the suggestion put forward by some of the colonists that Natal should try to obtain Indian labourers, and immediately reported to the Secretary of State that

> One measure which would greatly tend to promote the wealth and security of that Colony, and render it of value and importance to Great Britain, would be to encourage the introduction of coolie labourers from India.[2]

He also wrote to India to see if arrangements could be made for the importation of Indian labourers. He hoped that it would be a temporary expedient only, and that the increase in the market for their goods, which would result from the development of the colony, would encourage the Natives to adopt the much-lauded habits of regular work and free the planters from dependence upon imported labour.[3]

His hopes were not to be fulfilled. The Natal Natives did not take readily to work on the sugar plantations, and the planters continued to find Indian indentured labour more suitable. The Indian labourers were indentured for five years' service at wages of ten shillings per month in addition to food, quarters, medical attention, and the cost of importation. The introduction of Indian labourers began in 1860, but was discontinued in 1866 because the demand for such labourers had temporarily ceased, principally as a result of the severe depression of 1864–8. Nevertheless, by 1872, when importation had not yet been resumed, there were estimated to be in Natal some 5,000 Indians (3,684 males and 1,709 females).[4]

At first the Indians were employed chiefly on the sugar plantations and the colonists' demand for Native labour did not cease

[1] *Natal Government Gazette*, 1863, p. 372; *Natal Legislative Council Sessional Papers*, 1874, p. 2.
[2] *Cape of Good Hope, Votes and Proceedings of the House of Assembly*, 1857, Appendix 2. Correspondence between Sir George Grey and the Secretary of State for the Colonies, p. 31.
[3] Ibid.
[4] *Natal Legislative Council, Votes and Proceedings*, 1872, Report of Coolie Commission, p. 21.

as a result of the introduction of Indian labour. In 1863 Lieutenant-Governor Scott reported that there was a great demand
for steady labour and that the wages of Native labourers had risen
from five shillings to ten shillings a month in the previous six
years.[1] During the following years complaints of the scarcity of
Native labour and petitions for the Government to take action to
increase the supply were in abeyance owing to the industrial
depression, but by 1868 they were revived, together with applications for Indian indentured labourers.[2] Renewed efforts were
soon to be made to meet both requests.

Meanwhile, in the early 'sixties, the Lieutenant-Governor,
Scott, turned his attention[3] to the conditions under which the
Natives of Natal occupied the reserves set aside for them by the
Location Commission of 1846. Shepstone, the chief Native
administrator, who for thirty years guided and administered Native
policy in Natal, had long been complaining that the uncertainty
of the Natives concerning their continued occupation of the
locations in which they had been placed hindered improvements
in agriculture.[4] The colonists in Natal were still very much
opposed to the system of large locations, on the old ground that
they enabled the Natives to make a living without going out to
work for Europeans.

Scott now proposed that tribal titles to the land in the locations
be granted, to give security of tenure. His reasons for advocating
tribal titles were that the Natives were not capable of benefiting
from individual titles; that individual tenure was not suited to
their method of pastoral farming; and that much of the location
land was rugged and broken, and therefore not suitable for division
into arable allotments. Tribal tenure, according to his plan, was
to lead to individual tenure as the Natives became able to benefit
from it.[5] A storm of protest from the colonists greeted these
proposals. The Legislative Council countered by advocating the
grant to Natives of individual titles to land, a scheme which Scott
condemned:

'In one word,' he wrote, 'I pronounce the suggestion of the
Council to be impracticable; and an impossible plan, as a substitute

[1] Public Record Office, London, C/O 179/66, No. 10699.
[2] *Natal Legislative Council, Votes and Proceedings*, 1868, p. 75; 1869, p. 82.
[3] After 1857 Natal was governed by a Lieutenant-Governor and an official
Executive Council, responsible to the Imperial government in Britain, and a
Legislative Council, partly elected (twelve members) and partly nominated
(four members). Laws had to receive the assent of the Imperial authorities.
Consequently it was possible for the Lieutenant-Governor successfully to
oppose colonial opinion.
[4] Natal Native Affairs Commission, 1852–4, *Proceedings*, I, p. 69.
[5] *Parl. Papers*, 1862, XXXVI [293], Natal, Corresp., 1861–2, p. 10.

for a practical one, is merely to retard or prevent any scheme being undertaken.'[1]

Both Shepstone and Scott considered that the suggestion of the Legislative Council was put forward to delay the issue to Natives of any titles to land. Some colonists, however, canvassed the grant of unrestricted individual title on the ground that it would lead Natives to sell their land and that consequently they would be forced permanently into the labour market.[2]

In spite of the protests of the colonists and the Legislative Council, which even petitioned for the recall of the Governor, in 1864 the Natal Native Trust was constituted under Royal Letters Patent. The Lieutenant-Governor and the Executive Council were the Trustees, and the Trust had power to hold land within the Colony of Natal and to administer and dispose of it for the benefit of the Natives.[3]

Thus were the Natives of Natal secured in possession of their locations.

C. THE VOORTREKKER REPUBLICS

The Economic Setting: Methods of obtaining Native Labour

In 1837 those Voortrekkers who remained behind when the main body crossed the Drakensberg and descended into Natal, defeated Mzilikazi, the most powerful Native chief on the Highveld. After his defeat, Mzilikazi withdrew across the Limpopo with his followers and settled in Matabeleland, now a part of Southern Rhodesia. He had broken away and fled from Chaka in the 1820's, and had already defeated and scattered the tribes which had previously inhabited the regions which are now the Transvaal and Orange Free State. Consequently, as in Natal, the Voortrekkers found the plains of the interior sparsely populated. The remnants of many of the tribes which had suffered from Mzilikazi's raids were glad to seek the protection of the Trekkers' guns, and the Trekkers, for their part, were disposed to make alliances with the more powerful chiefs. Gradually, however, they appropriated practically all land throughout the territory to the north of the Orange and Vaal Rivers. They based their claims on conquest or on agreements by which Native chiefs ceded undefined rights of occupation, or, again, individual farmers simply had tracts of land registered in their names irrespective of Native occupation.

[1] Ibid., p. 7.
[2] Colonial Office, 176/62/10978, Natal: Letter from John Sanderson to C. F. Fortescue, 9 Dec., 1861, enclosing some newspaper cuttings.
[3] Letters Patent. Natal Native Trust, quoted H. Rogers: *Native Administration in the Union of South Africa*, Appendix F, pp. 282–3.

In these different ways whole Native tribes became resident upon European-owned land where for the most part they continued to live much in the same manner as before the advent of the Europeans. Most Native tribes were, however, required to render labour service to the European farmers. This labour was demanded as a tribute to their conquerors, in return for release from subjection to Mzilikazi; or, finally, from newcomers, as payment for the right to settle in territory claimed by the Europeans.[1] Apart from the labour tax (as this forced labour has been called) and the introduction of wagons and guns, the Voortrekkers did not bring much that was new to the Natives. Their economic life was that of a predominantly pastoral people and was not essentially very different from that to which the Natives were accustomed. For the farmers who crossed the Orange River to settle in the lands beyond took with them their flocks and herds, wagons, guns, Bibles, and what little else they could load on their wagons. The conditions under which they lived for many years were simple. Beside their cattle, sheep, and land, their material possessions were few. What they could not produce for themselves they bought from itinerant traders, but there was little trade, and what there was took the form of barter.

The villages established by the Voortrekkers were very small and provided only a very limited market for farm products.[2] In 1852 Bloemfontein, which was then the largest village north of the Orange River, had about seventy houses and a population of some three hundred persons. According to Sir George Clerk, who was sent in 1853 as Special Commissioner to 'adjust' the affairs of the Orange River Sovereignty (which had been annexed by Britain in 1848), the population of Bloemfontein depended for its livelihood upon the British garrison. Smithfield, at this time the second village of the Sovereignty, had forty-two houses and a population of two hundred. The colonial markets were far away and the cost of transport made the sale of most products unprofitable.

The farmers sent cattle and wool to the Cape[3] or Natal,[4] but the journey from Capetown to Bloemfontein took two months by ox-wagon, and that from Port Elizabeth six weeks. Under such

[1] On this see J. A. I. Agar-Hamilton, *The Native Policy of the Voortrekkers*, Chap. X.
[2] It was customary for a farmer to have an allotment in a village in addition to his farm. Where houses were erected on such allotments they were usually only occasionally occupied, principally when the European inhabitants of the district gathered together for 'Nachtmaal', the periodic gatherings which took place when Holy Communion was celebrated.
[3] *Parl. Papers*, 1854, XLIII [1758]. Corresp. *re* Orange River Territory, pp. 28, 29.
[4] *Natal Blue Book*, 1861, p. 292.

conditions trade could not flourish. We have little information as to its amount. In 1853 Sir George Clerk reported that the annual wool export was estimated at from three thousand to ten thousand bales of unwashed wool, but that no returns were kept.

The population in this territory was very scattered. Men and their livestock needed water, and springs were scarce and rain infrequent. 'Often,' said Sir George Clerk, 'for ten miles together or more, no human being, white or black, is to be anywhere seen.' The land had been appropriated in huge tracts. In 1852, when the European population of the Orange River Sovereignty was estimated to be between 8,000 and 15,000 souls, the total number of grants of land was 1,265, their average extent 9,000 acres. One hundred and thirty-nine British proprietors, many of them officials, owned on the average 18,000 acres apiece. Much of this land was held for speculative purposes and was unoccupied. According to Sir George Clerk:

> The term 'farm' is here commonly misapplied to these extensive possessions which, however, having generally been obtained for the sole purpose of sales, are in many instances quite unoccupied. Where occupied, the estimate of the extent of cultivation on each, formed from my own observation and corroborated by the opinion of the chief surveyor, does not exceed a single acre. The remainder, or eight million five hundred and thirty-two thousand, two hundred and thirty-six (8,532,236) acres is owned by the Dutch settlers, who are for the most part farmers and occupiers. These reside in their long established homesteads, with somewhat more cultivation near the spring, and owning herds of cattle, sheep, and horses. Their grants average about eight thousand (8,000) acres.'[1]

North of the Sovereignty the farmers were even farther from markets and life still more isolated and primitive. Cattle or sheep might be driven to the colonial markets, but there was little or no sale for agricultural products.

Some twenty years later, in 1878, Anthony Trollope, during his journey through the Transvaal, was to find difficulty in buying forage for his horses even along the main routes. Describing conditions as he travelled by horse and cart, he wrote:

> 'Perhaps three or four times in a day a Boer's farm would be seen from the roadside, distinguished by a small group of trees, generally weeping willows. This would look like a small oasis in a huge desert. Round the house or on one side of it, there would be from six to a dozen acres of land ploughed, with probably a small orchard and sometimes an attempt at a kitchen garden. There would, too, be some ditching and draining and perhaps some slight arrangement for irrigation. . . . When questioned, the farmer

---

[1] *Parl. Papers*, 1854, XLIII [1758] op. cit. pp. 27, 28.

invariably declared that it would not pay him to extend his agriculture, as he had no labour on which to depend and no market to which he could carry his wheat.'[1]

It has been estimated that the European population north of the Vaal River was about twenty-five thousand persons in 1854.[2] The demand for labour cannot have been very great. Herdsmen, shepherds, and wagon-drivers were required; field-labourers to tend what little land was cultivated; domestic servants; and occasionally additional labourers for building simple houses and churches.

The number of Natives living within and on the borders of the Republics was large in comparison with the scattered European families. In 1852, Sir George Clerk reported that there were some ninety-seven thousand Natives and cross-breeds in the Orange River Sovereignty, which lay between the Orange and Vaal Rivers and the Drakensbergen. This estimate included the Basuto (sixty thousand) and the Griquas (two thousand five hundred), who lived to the south of the Vaal River.[3] Less information is available of the number of Natives in the territory north of the Vaal. Thirty years later, in 1881, the Royal Commission on the settlement of the Transvaal,[4] estimated that the Native population of the South African Republic was in the neighbourhood of a million: five hundred thousand in the northern and eastern districts of Zoutpansberg, Lydenburg, Wakkerstroom, and Utrecht, and five hundred thousand within or near the western border.

In spite of this large Native population the Voortrekkers resorted to compulsion in order to obtain a part of their comparatively small labour requirements. In addition to engaging voluntary labourers for wages, which were generally paid in livestock, farmers secured servants through the labour tax, and through the system of 'apprenticeship'. The voluntary labourers frequently worked as herdsmen, the usual payment for a year's service being a cow, or a cow and calf.[5] This was approximately the same remuneration as was usual at this time in the Cape Colony in those districts in which payment was made in livestock. The labour tax seems to have been used chiefly to obtain field workers.[6] According to regulations made in 1850 by the United

[1] A. Trollope, *South Africa*, 1878, Vol. II, p. 21.
[2] E. A. Walker, op. cit., p. 352, footnote 4.
[3] *Parl. Papers*, 1854, XLIII [1758] op. cit., p. 25.
[4] *Parl. Papers*, 1882, XLVIII [C. 3114], Report of Transvaal Royal Commission, pp. 18, 19. This Commission arranged the terms of the Convention of Pretoria, which restored the independence of the Transvaal in 1881. Britain had annexed the Transvaal in 1877.
[5] D. Livingstone, *Missionary Travels and Researches in South Africa* (1857), p. 26; C. A. Payton, *The Diamond Diggings* (1871), p. 137.
[6] D. Livingstone, op. cit., p. 26.

Volksraad, labourers obtained in this way were to be distributed among the farmers by the field-cornets. Individual Natives were to give fourteen days free service. Obviously discontinuous labour of this kind would have been unsuitable for responsible work, such as herding cattle and sheep. Labour was also obtained by 'apprenticing' Native children. According to a codifying law (1851) orphan children might be apprenticed to employers until they were twenty-five years old. Apprentices were to be registered with the landdrosts, the administrative and judicial officials in charge of large districts.

Both the labour tax and the system of 'apprenticeship' were liable to abuse. Missionaries and others complained that compulsory labour was exacted in the guise of the labour tax, and that Native children were kidnapped and sold into 'apprenticeship'.[1] There is little doubt that there was foundation for these allegations; for there was no effective administration to enforce the laws which were supposed to govern these practices. There were no regular police; and the local officials were themselves primarily farmers with the same interests and sympathies as their European neighbours. The traffic in apprentices was officially frowned upon, but effective steps were not taken to suppress such a useful source of labour.[2]

The labour tax was a system of forced labour levied on dependent tribes. Money taxation, such as that levied in Natal and the Cape Colony, would have been impracticable in the Republics, for money was scarcely used even by the Europeans. Labour service was probably the most convenient form of taxation for both Natives and Europeans. The objection to the principle of the labour tax is that it was forced labour used not for public but for private purposes; that is, it was taxation levied on the Natives for the benefit of individual European farmers. In practice it may well have led to arbitrary demands for unpaid labour.

The abuse of the labour tax and of apprenticeship attracted much attention at the time. In Britain influential philanthropists decried these practices as 'virtual slavery', frequently forgetting that in Europe, too, the system of apprenticeship had been widely

[1] Livingstone, op. cit., pp. 26, 33; *Parl. Papers*, 1868–9, XLIII [4141], Corresp. *re* alleged Kidnapping and Enslaving of Young Africans by people of the Transvaal Republic, pp. 1–9, 24, 38, 50–54.

[2] According to an account in the semi-official Transvaal newspaper, *De Republikein*, 'whole wagon loads' of children were 'continually being hawked about the country', several men making a regular trade of buying children from Natives who obtained them by kidnapping or in raids upon tribes. The writer commented: 'We are not sanguine enough to hope that it will be entirely suppressed; the want of household labour which this system principally supplies is so great that we can scarcely expect to see it altogether relinquished, but we do hope that some strong and continued measures may materially decrease it.'— *Parl. Papers*, 1868–9, XLIII [4141], op. cit., p. 3.

used as a means of obtaining cheap labour and that the misuse of the system had not been effectively checked until well into the nineteenth century. The allegations of the philanthropists were politically important because slavery was not permitted by the agreements which Britain had made when she withdrew her claim to sovereignty north of the Orange and Vaal Rivers. Consequently they could be used as a pretext for intervention in the affairs of the Republics. Perhaps on this account these methods of obtaining labour attracted more attention than was warranted by their quantitative significance in the labour market. Very little information is available as to their numerical importance.[1]

[1] On the Voortrekkers' methods of obtaining labour, see Agar-Hamilton, op. cit., especially Chaps. IX and X.

On British policy towards the Transvaal at this time see also de Kiewiet, op. cit., Chap. XVI.

PART II

THE IMPACT OF THE DIAMOND AND GOLD DISCOVERIES UPON THE MARKET FOR NATIVE LABOUR, 1870–1899

CHAPTER IV

INTRODUCTORY

THE first ninety years of continuous contact between Europeans and Bantu in South Africa had seen the policy of segregation abandoned in favour of that of co-operation. The next thirty years were to see a widespread increase in the desire of Europeans to use the services of African Natives. During this period diamonds and gold were discovered, and the discoveries were exploited. The development of mining, first in the Griqua territory, and later on the Witwatersrand, led to a general rise in the demand for labour and to far-reaching changes in the South African economy.

The development of mining in the remote interior of South Africa provides an interesting illustration of the effects on the surrounding economy of the emergence of a new and important consuming centre.[1] The diamond-fields, in the first period, and subsequently the diamond-mines of Kimberley and the gold-mines of the Witwatersrand, constituted new consuming centres of quite unparalleled significance in the interior of South Africa. The first emphasis must be placed upon this aspect of their impact on the South African economy. The output of the mines was sold abroad and did not compete with the products of existing South African industries. The proceeds from the sales of the mines, in so far as they were spent in South Africa, provided a net addition to the existing demand for South African goods and services.

Almost from the beginning the repercussions on the South African economy were twofold. On the one hand, the purchasing power made available by the sale of diamonds and gold stimulated such local industries as were able to provide for the wants of the mines and of the towns dependent on them. On the other hand, the mining of diamonds and gold led to a widespread rise in the costs of local suppliers of goods and services. Diamond and gold production competed directly for the factors of production, and stimulated other local industries with the same indirect effect.

[1] It exemplifies, in fact, the theoretical problem with which von Thunen concerned himself from 1826 onwards in his study 'Der Isolierte Staat'. Von Thunen's theory was principally concerned with the appropriate location of different types of farming. Assuming that a consuming centre, for example a great city, lay in the centre of a fertile plain, he showed that the territorial distribution of agricultural and pastoral production would be determined by the cost of transportation. As the distance from the market increased the farmer would produce commodities which, relative to their value, involved ever lower transportation cost; and, in general the farmer would resort to increasingly extensive methods of production.

The development of the diamond-fields came first. Within ten years from the discovery of diamonds in Griqualand West, the diamond-fields had a population, including both Europeans and non-Europeans, of some thirty thousand. This sudden concentration of population, many of them of an adventurous and carefree disposition, gave rise to a new and complex market in an arid and sparsely populated region more than five hundred miles from Capetown and nearly four hundred from Port Elizabeth.

The immediate reaction was on the transport system of the country. Henceforth, for thirty years, it was to be organized primarily to serve the mines, first the diamond-mines in Griqualand West, and later the gold-mines of the Witwatersrand. When diamonds were discovered there were only some sixty-five miles of railway in South Africa, sixty-three in the Cape Colony, with Capetown as the terminus, and two at Durban in Natal. Consequently, for a time the diamond diggings were dependent for their supplies upon road transport, which in South Africa meant the mule- or horse-drawn cart or wagonette for express passengers, and the slow, lumbering ox-wagon for more leisurely passengers, and for goods.

The traffic to the interior led to the growth of towns and villages at the ports, at the colonial railhead, Wellington, and at the habitual halting-places and junctions along the main routes to the fields. A large part of the new demand was for machinery and other manufactured goods, which had to be imported.

With the growth of the diamond diggings the Governments of the Cape Colony and Natal took over the existing railways, which had been constructed and operated by private companies. Both Governments began to construct lines to connect their ports with the diggings, and by 1884, within fifteen years from the first systematic prospecting, no less than 1,620 miles of railway had been constructed in South Africa. By that date the ports of Capetown and Port Elizabeth were both linked by rail with Kimberley.

Farmers quickly responded to the new market in the interior. Kimberley provides an illustration of the abstract case postulated by von Thunen in his *Der Isolierte Staat*; but the geographical features were naturally not identical with the homogeneous condition that he postulated. The plain upon which Kimberley came into being was not uniformly fertile. Moreover, the improvement of roads and later the coming of the railways destroyed the uniformity of transport costs in every direction. A large part of the stores required were necessarily the product of towns, and of overseas towns at that, so that communications with the ports were the first to be developed. In other respects the analysis of von Thunen is apposite.

Farming was stimulated on all sides. To the south, the Karroo stretched for hundreds of miles. Its scanty rainfall and vegetation of desert shrub made it suitable for grazing sheep, but, without irrigation, little else could be produced. To the west and north was the equally arid thorn country of Bechuanaland, giving place north-east of Kimberley to the often drought-stricken but nevertheless somewhat better-watered grass-covered plains of the Orange Free State, the 'middleveld'. Cattle could be grazed in all this country, and in the neighbourhood of springs agriculture could be carried on. Farther east, in the Caledon valley, on the border of the Free State and Basutoland, more agriculture was possible and maize and wheat flourished.

The stock farmers of the Orange Free State began to grow agricultural products as a sideline. Anthony Trollope commented, after his South African journey of 1878, on the readiness of the Free State sheep-farmer, in contrast to the Australian, to grow and take to market agricultural produce.[1] The strong incentive of Kimberley was effective.

Farther afield, also, farming responded to the new markets. Agricultural production, however, continued to be profitable only in the neighbourhood of towns, or where railways reduced the cost of transport. In most of the South African Republic and in the more remote districts of the Cape Colony and Natal, crops were still grown only for domestic purposes. But pastoral farming was stimulated throughout the country, for the demand for oxen,

[1] 'I travelled from the Diamond fields to Bloemfontein and thence through Smithfield to the Orange River at Aliwal North. I also made a short excursion from Bloemfontein. In this way I did not see the best district of the country, which is that which was taken from the Basutos—where the town of Ladybrand now is—which is good agricultural land, capable of being sown and reaped without artificial irrigation. The normal Dutch farmer of the Republic, such as I saw him, depends chiefly upon his flocks, which are very small as compared with those in Australia—three or four thousand sheep being a respectable pastoral undertaking for one man. He deals in agriculture also, not largely, but much more generally than his Australian brother. In Australia the squatter usually despises agriculture, looking upon it as the fitting employment for a little free-selector—who is but a mean fellow in his estimation. The flour to be consumed by himself and his men he buys. He grows no more than he will use about his place for his own cattle. And as his horses are not often corn-fed a very few acres of ploughed land suffices for his purpose. The Dutch patriarch makes his own bread from the wheat he has himself produced. The bread is not white, but it is so sweet that I am inclined to say I have never eaten better. And he sells his produce—anything which he can grow and does not eat himself. The Australian woolgrower sells nothing but wool. The Dutch Boer will send peas twenty miles to market, and will sell a bundle of forage—hay made out of unripened oats or barley—to anyone who will call at his place and ask for it.

'A strong Boer will have thirty, forty, or perhaps fifty acres of cultivated land round his house—including his garden.' A. Trollope, op. cit., Vol. II, pp. 235–6.

particularly for transport purposes, first for the diamond-fields, and later for the gold-fields, led to their price trebling within a few years. The price of sheep for meat and breeding purposes also doubled. And as a result stock farming flourished.[1]

The mines, and the expanding industries which served them, competed for the factors of production, for land, for capital, and for labour. Complaints about the scarcity of labour became widespread, particularly in the coastal colonies where the construction of railways and harbours and the needs of the growing towns competed with the farmers in the market for Native labour. In Natal the Government renewed the efforts which it had already made to increase the labour supply by limiting the right of Natives to occupy land outside their reserves, by taxation, and by the importation of Indian indentured labourers. In the Cape Colony, which was granted responsible government in 1872, attempts were made to promote the supply of Native labour by legislative and other administrative action of one kind and another. The South African Republic tried to meet its own labour needs by intercepting Natives who were making their way to work on the diamond-fields.

During the early 'eighties there was a temporary lull in the rise in the demand for labour. It was a passing phase, for the gold discoveries on the Witwatersrand soon augmented the complaints of scarcity of labour and the attempts to increase the supply, which characterized the 'seventies. Between 1881 and 1886, however, South Africa, together with other countries, experienced the 'Great Depression' of the 'eighties. In the 'seventies in South Africa development had been rapid. At the end of the decade there had been heavy military expenditure by the Imperial authorities in the Cape Colony, where there had been Native insurrection within the Colony and warfare on the eastern and northern frontiers; in Natal, in connexion with the Zulu war of 1878–9; and in the Transvaal, where campaigns were conducted first against the Native chief Sekukuni, and later against the European burghers. The cessation of military expenditure and the retrocession, by the British, of the recently annexed Transvaal and the failure of many of the recently floated diamond-mining companies, combined to upset confidence and precipitated in South Africa the depression of the 'eighties.[2]

In Natal, Native wages fell, and while the number of unemployed Europeans in Pietermaritzburg caused remark,[3] Native labour was

[1] J. Noble, op. cit., pp. 261, 273.
[2] G. T. Amphlett, *History of the Standard Bank of South Africa, Ltd.*, pp. 88 seq.
[3] *Natal Blue Book*, 1884, Supplement B, p. 5. Report of the Resident Magistrate of Pietermaritzburg: 'The leading feature of last year's records is

fairly generally, for almost the only time on record, reported to be 'cheap and plentiful'.[1] In the Cape Colony, also, Natives had difficulty in finding employment at customary rates, both on the farms and in the towns.[2]

Soon, however, the demand for labour began to rise once more as a result of the discovery of the Witwatersrand gold deposits. The impact of the development of gold-mining on the South African economy was similar in nature to that of the diamond-fields, but it was even more far-reaching in its repercussions. A new consuming centre arose in the interior and soon surpassed Kimberley in size and activity. To meet its wants, transport facilities were once more improvised and extended. The ports, through which many supplies came, continued to grow and farming again prospered. Consequently the demand for labour rose. It was wanted for all types of work on the mines, in the towns, and on the farms, and efforts to increase the supply of Native labour redoubled.

It is the purpose of the chapters that follow to examine the nature and extent of these events in so far as they affected the market for Native labour.

the mass of unemployed European labour, which is concentrated in the City and infests our streets.'

[1] *Natal Blue Book*, 1883: G.G., pp. 11, 19; 1894, C., p. 5; B, pp. 19, 20, 26, 29; 1896, C., p. 6; B., pp. 6, 8.
[2] (Cape) *Blue Book on Native Affairs*, G. 3, 1884, p. 171; G. 2, 1885, pp. 61, 122; cf. G. 5, 1886, p. 13: Report from East London: 'To meet the distress amongst the people the Great Kei road was promptly undertaken and those who were actually without food at once took employment on it. The bulk of the people, however, refused the terms offered by the Government, but no direct assistance was given to any of them.'

CHAPTER V

DIAMOND PRODUCTION, 1870–1899

A. THE EARLY DIGGINGS, 1869–1874

(i) Technique and the Demand for Labour

IN 1867 it became known for the first time that diamonds were to be found in South Africa. Within fifteen years, according to official statistics, diamonds to the value of £32,000,000 had been exported.[1] By the 'eighties the annual export of diamonds alone exceeded the average annual value of the total exports of the two British colonies and the Republics in the decade before the discovery of diamonds.[2]

To help to obtain this wealth African Natives were induced to work. The diamond diggings provided the first large concentrated demand for Native labour in South Africa. The early diggers individually were not, however, large-scale employers.

Although the first identification of a diamond had been made in 1867, and there had been subsequent finds along the banks of the Orange and Vaal Rivers, it was not until towards the end of the year 1869 that the search for diamonds became systematic. In March 1869 the stone weighing 83½ carats, which became known as the Star of South Africa, was found on a farm in Griqualand. Thereafter the search became more intensive, and towards the end of 1869 the treatment and sifting of the river gravel was begun on the Vaal River.[3] By July 1870 there were some five hundred diggers at Klipdrift (now the village of Barkly West) about four hundred miles north-east of Capetown, and some thirty or forty more at Hebron, three hours, by horse and cart, farther up the river.[4] Soon the river diggings extended some eighty miles, and it was estimated that there were ten thousand diggers, white and black, either in the string of camps which were established along the river or in roving parties of prospectors.[5]

[1] *Official Year Book*, No. 4, 1910–20, p. 702.
[2] According to official returns the average value of the diamond export was:

1865–7	£5,000	1880–84	£3,417,000
1870–74	£1,027,000	1885–89	£3,717,000
1875–9	£1,905,000		

The average value of all exports through Cape and Natal ports in the period 1860–70 had been:

| 1860–64 | £2,319,000 | 1865–70 | £2,626,000 |

Ibid.
[3] Ibid., pp. 600–601.
[4] *Parl. Papers*, 1871, XLVII, C. 459. Corresp. *re* Affairs of S. Africa, *Argus* Correspondent, Klipdrift, 15 July, 1870.
[5] F. Gardner Williams, *The Diamond Mines of South Africa*, p. 158. Morton, *South African Diamond Fields*: a paper read on 13 March, 1877, at a meeting of the American Geographical Society, p. 11.

On the river diggings the method of diamond-digging employed was that of the 'placer miner'. It was the only technique which had hitherto been known. Mixed gravel and sand were taken from the river-bed to the banks and there dumped in heaps or troughs.

> Then the gravel was washed in cradles, with two or three screens of perforated iron, or zinc, or wire mesh, set to form partitions with discharge holes so graduated that the larger stones were held above the upper coarser screen . . . the cradle was more or less expertly rocked. . . . The worthless stones in the upper part of the cradle were then picked and scooped out by hand and thrown away, while the concentrate was taken out carefully and carried to the sorting table, an ordinary deal stand, or any level wooden or iron structure; or to a flat stone. Here the deposit was spread out thinly and sorted over inch by inch with a short scraper of hoop iron, or any other thin strip, while the appearance of a diamond was more or less keenly watched for.[1]

Most of the early diggers were without any experience of mining. They were drawn from every type of occupation. Farmers, storekeepers, clerks, and men from the professions, all flocked to the diggings. The discovery of diamonds had come at the end of a period of severe depression and many who had become impoverished sought to restore their fortunes. A few of the diggers had had previous experience of alluvial mining in Australia, but most had had none at all. At first the search for diamonds was not very profitable. In July 1870 the *Argus* correspondent, who visited the river diggings, reported that few had 'done really well and paid expenses and had something over'.[2]

In these circumstances the diggers were not able to employ much labour, and in 1869-70 the ordinary digger rarely had more than two or three Native labourers and many had none.[3]

By the end of 1871 the four big diamond-bearing 'pipes', which became the De Beers, Kimberley, Dutoitspan, and Bultfontein mines, had been discovered. These deposits of diamond-bearing ground or 'kimberlite' are believed to be of volcanic origin. They consist of cylindrical pipes extending to unknown depths. Their surface area varied. The 'pipe' at the New Rush, which became the famous Kimberley mine, was nine acres in extent at the surface and was divided into 460 claims, each thirty Cape feet square. At the De Beers diggings there were 620 claims of the same size, at Bultfontein 1,067, and at Dutoitspan 1,441.[4] The diamond-bearing ground was of three kinds: on the surface the

---

[1] F. Gardner Williams, op. cit., p. 148.

[2] *Parl. Papers*, 1871, XLVII, C. 459, op. cit.

[3] *Transvaal Labour Commission*, Evidence, [Cd. 1897], 1904, q. 3752, ev. F. Ingle.

[4] A. Trollope, op. cit., Vol. II, pp. 171, 174.

yellow ground' was found extending to a depth of sixty or seventy feet, below it is the 'blue ground', which merges gradually into the 'true kimberlite', which has so far been found only at the bottom of the deepest of the mines. In the early days there was great uncertainty as to the depth of the diamond-bearing ground, consequently many diggers abandoned their claims when the nature of the ground changed.

On both the river and the dry diggings, as the new diamond-fields were called, claims had to be registered with elected Diggers' Committees, which settled any disputes that arose. Until 1874 no one was allowed to hold more than two claims. At first the technique employed was similar to that on the river diggings, except that before 1874 the diamond-bearing ground was not washed. The ground was extracted by open quarrying, and, to enable claims to be worked independently, long roadways fifteen feet wide were left unquarried, each claim-holder sacrificing seven and a half feet of ground on two sides of his claim. As the diamond-bearing ground was extracted the holes deepened and it had to be hoisted in buckets and carried by cart or wheelbarrow to the 'floors', level pieces of ground near the claims. If the hard 'blue ground' was left exposed it disintegrated without further crushing. Sometimes this method was used, but, more often, it was broken down mechanically with pick and shovel, for the diggers had little capital and wanted quick returns. The crumbled ground was then sifted and the diamonds sorted out.[1]

The dry-diggings soon surpassed the river-diggings, both in the production of diamonds and the number of diggers and labourers attracted. Gardner Williams considers that there may have been as many as fifty thousand people on the diamond-fields at the height of the diamond rush.[2]

Native labourers assisted the Europeans in all types of manual work. They dug and shovelled in the claims, hauled up the blue ground, wheeled it to the floors, broke it down, scraped it over, and sorted out the diamonds.[3]

(ii) Terms and Conditions of Work; Recruitment, Supply, and Sources of Native Labour

In the early days, searching for diamonds was clearly a gamble. Moreover, the diggers commonly believed that high prizes were to be won. They were accordingly prepared if necessary to offer high wages for assistance. The first non-European labour was brought to the diggings by the farmers and the colonists, who

---

[1] Morton, op. cit., pp. 17–23; F. Gardner Williams, op. cit., p. 236.
[2] F. Gardner Williams, op. cit., p. 194.   [3] Ibid., p. 152.

brought their servants with them. Soon, once the news spread of the articles which could be obtained at the diggings, Natives began to come to the diggings of their own accord. Additional supplies of labour were obtained by colonists and traders who went into the interior and shepherded batches of Natives to the diggings.[1]

According to one of the pioneers, Mr. Ingle,

> By the end of 1870, a good many of those natives who had been at work in 1869, had reached their homes with the good things, in the shape of brass and copper wire, etc., that had resulted from their immense adventure, and straggling parties of twos and threes began to come from all directions, all being readily engaged by the miners, and beginning to bargain for their wages before engaging themselves.[2]

Wages at first were commonly ten shillings per month, and Natives from the interior would work for possibly three months before returning with goods such as brass, copper or iron wire, knives and hatchets. At first the Native labourers spent almost all the money they received, taking money away only as a curiosity.

Their purchases soon became more varied.[3] Guns were imported and sold to Natives. They proved a most effective incentive; for when the Native chiefs found that guns could be obtained at the diamond diggings, they sent their tribesmen out to arm themselves.

There can be no doubt about the importance of the gun trade and the influence of Native chiefs in promoting the supply of labour in the 'seventies.[4] Both in the north-east of the South African Republic and in Basutoland, Europeans were attempting to impose their authority over that of the chiefs, who had learnt that guns were necessary for effective resistance. Describing the diamond diggings in the 'seventies, Morton said:

> 'These natives have been pouring in crowds into the diamond fields for seven years, at the rate of 30,000 a year; each gang of from thirty to forty men, after a journey on foot of often 1,000 miles, during which many of them die from starvation and cold, remaining

[1] J. Angove, *In the Early Days: Reminiscences of Pioneer Life on the South African Diamond Fields*, p. 59; C. A. Payton, *The Diamond Diggings of South Africa* (1872) pp. 43, 139.

[2] *Transvaal Labour Commission*, loc. cit.

[3] Ibid., qq. 3752, 3836, ev. F. Ingle.

[4] When Sir Henry Barkly, Governor of the Cape Colony and High Commissioner for South Africa, visited the diamond fields in 1872, a deputation of diggers impressed him with the importance of the traffic in guns as a means of obtaining labour. The diggers feared lest the complaints of the neighbouring Republics about the sale of guns to Natives should lead to its prohibition. They said that sufficient labour to work the diamond deposits would not be obtained if the supplying of guns to Natives were stopped. J. Matthews, *Incwadi Yami* (1887), p. 278.

On the trade in guns at Kimberley see also J. Angove, op. cit., pp. 60–62; [Cd. 1897], 1904, op. cit., q. 3832, ev. F. Ingle.

and working only just long enough to supply each member with gun
and ammunition, i.e. about three months—and then returning to
their land. They carry back no money, but simply a gun, and they
come for nothing else.

'The English Government permits the sale of guns to them
indiscriminately; and it is a well-established fact that 300,000 have
been thus disposed of.

'These natives declared war upon the Transvaal Government
a few months ago; and we now see what all this preparation
meant. . . .'[1]

Making due allowance for exaggeration, the gist of this report
is confirmed from the Transvaal, whence Aylward, who in 1876
took part in the campaign against Sekukuni's tribe, reported that

Secocoeni and his people are not to be confounded with utterly
uncultivated and entirely barbarous savages. Many of them, as I
have said elsewhere, are well acquainted with the use of breeches
and breechloaders. Nearly all of them have worked on the diamond
fields.[2]

From Aliwal North it was reported in 1873 that the arming of
Natives at the diamond-fields was continuing, that numbers had
passed through with arms and ammunition, and that some men
even had two guns.[3]

The magistrates in Basutoland were convinced that the desire
for guns was inspired by the chiefs, who were finding that their
power was being undermined by the European administration, and
therefore encouraged their tribesmen to get arms and ammunition.[4]
Thus one magistrate reported:

There is no doubt that the mania to become possessed of a gun
and ammunition by every Basuto who goes to the railway works or
diamond fields was suggested by the chief as a means of hold upon
the people. Had they urged the introduction of money and stock
by the returning labourers it would have been generally adopted.
The feeling of 'Divine Right' of chiefs is as strong as ever, however
much they respect the Government; possession of a gun is reassuring
to the timid, suspicious, native mind.[5]

Other tribesmen, also, were sent by their chiefs to arm themselves at the diamond-fields. If we can rely upon the tribal

---

[1] Morton, op. cit., p. 15.
[2] A. Aylward, *Transvaal of To-day* (1878), p. 142.
[3] (Cape) *Blue Book on Native Affairs*, G. 27, 1874, p. 9.
[4] The attempt which was made in 1880 to force the Basuto to surrender their
much-prized guns was the immediate cause of an insurrection, which was not
finally suppressed for three years and ended in the British Government relieving
the Cape Colony of the responsibility of administering Basutoland.
[5] (Cape) *Blue Book on Native Affairs*, G. 12, 1877, p. 4 (Report of Resident
Magistrate).
  cf. ibid., G. 21, 1875, pp. 7, 9, 10; G. 16, 1876, pp. 4, 8.

history of the Bakxatla, a Bechuanaland tribe, as recounted from one generation to the next, men were sent down by the chief with instructions to earn eight pounds each, with which they were to buy guns and ammunition.[1]

Guns were an important incentive, but they did not remain the only one. Other wants developed and, when the trade in guns was stopped, although the labour supply diminished the fall was not acute.[2] Chiefs continued to use their influence to send labourers to the diamond-fields; one motive, no doubt, being the premiums which many accepted for sending their tribesmen down.[3] Some chiefs also increased their revenues by levying taxes on returning labourers.

Wages on the dry diggings soon rose. The usual rate when diamond-digging began had been ten shillings a month. By 1871 it was thirty shillings a month for efficient labourers, in addition to rations. Rations usually consisted of mealie meal, which cost about fifteen to twenty shillings a month for each boy; meat once or twice a week, 'the coarsest and cheapest that could be had', bullocks' heads and 'plucks' being commonly provided; some 'Boer' tobacco; and on Saturday nights a tot of 'Cape Smoke', as the crude colonial wine spirit which was supplied was called. The cost of the latter items was altogether about eighteenpence a head each week.[4] By 1874 the usual rate of wages, excluding rations, was ten shillings a week. Wages were paid in coin, as the Natives were reluctant to accept notes. The result was a constant drain of specie which had continually to be imported.

Describing in 1871 the non-European labourers at the dry diggings, Payton wrote:

> The immense demand for labour, created by the rapid growth of the diamond diggings, and the splendid wages given, have attracted to our camps thousands of Natives belonging to all the tribes around and a long way north of the Vaal River. Kafirs, Korannas, Hottentots, of every colour from pale sickly yellow to polished ebony, swarm at the Fields.
>
> Formerly the 'up-country' Kafirs used to contract with the Boers and other farmers for a year's services, at the end of which time they considered themselves well rewarded with a cow, value 31s. or 41s.; now good 'boys' are freely paid on the diggings 30s. per month and fed well into the bargain.[5]

---

[1] Information supplied by Professor I. Schapera from material collected among the Bakxatla.

[2] *Transvaal Labour Commission*, Evidence [Cd. 1897], 1904, q. 3833, ev. F. Ingle.

[3] (Cape) *Select Committee on Labour Market*, 1879, p. 59, ev. A. G. Watermeyer.

[4] J. Angove, op. cit., p. 59.   [5] C. A. Payton, op. cit., p. 137.

As the diggers established more permanent quarters their Native labourers were housed in [tents or lean-to shelters under such supervision as the diggers chose to exercise.[1]

The concentration of large numbers of prospectors and labourers made some form of organization necessary. At a mass meeting at Klipdrift, on the Vaal River, a 'Diggers' Committee' was elected to make regulations for the recognition of claims and the working of these diggings.[2] It was here that it was agreed that claims should be thirty Cape feet square. This Committee had also controlled relations between diggers and Natives and settled the disputes which arose. Apparently the Committee's task was no light one; it met every evening. It was, however, according to contemporary accounts, most effective in maintaining order.[3]

Similar committees were established at the dry diggings,[4] and continued to function after the annexation by Britain in 1871 of the diamond-fields of Griqualand West. At the Kimberley diggings, the Kimberley Mining Board replaced the original 'Diggers' Committee'. It framed rules and regulations, many of which, such as those concerning masters and servants, were incorporated in official proclamations and ordinances. The Board itself continued to regulate such matters as the draining of the diggings and the removal of fallen reef which became necessary as the diamond-bearing ground was extracted.[5]

The original Diggers' Committees were not much troubled by questions of principle and equity and did not adopt the policy, introduced into the Cape Colony by the British administration, of allowing people of all races equal legal rights. Under the rules of the Diggers' Committees, Natives had not been permitted to hold claims, but, after the British annexation of Griqualand West, this prohibition was withdrawn and Natives and other non-Europeans were permitted to take out licences to hold claims on the same terms as Europeans.[6]

There were immediate complaints from European diggers that

[1] Morton, op. cit., p. 23. F. Gardner Williams, op. cit., p. 258.

[2] F. Gardner Williams, op. cit., p. 146.

[3] In 1871 the *Argus* correspondent wrote: 'I cannot close this letter without referring to the general order and decency which prevail. I have seen very little drunkenness, and certainly no rowdyism. One can go about in the evening without the chance of being bothered or molested. This is in a great measure owing to the early arrangement of rules. 'The Mutual Protection Committee consider all relations and disputes between the natives and the diggers, and sit every evening.'
Parl. Papers, 1871, XLVII [C. 459], op. cit.

[4] C. A. Payton records the 'Rules and Regulations of the Dorstfontein (Dutoitspan) Diggings', and says that regulations on the other diggings were similar. Payton, op. cit., pp. 19–20.

[5] F. Gardner Williams, op. cit., p. 236.

[6] Proclamation No. 71 of 1871, which appeared with the proclamation of annexation; *Cape Diamond Mining Commission*, 1882.

the theft of diamonds had in consequence increased.[1] Nevertheless in the following year the High Commissioner of South Africa cancelled a proclamation, which the local Commissioners of Griqualand West had issued, preventing Natives and other coloured persons from holding digging licences.[2] At the same time, however, a proclamation was issued governing the relations between masters and servants. It closely followed the rules drafted by a Diggers' Committee.[3] This law replaced and supplemented parts of the Cape Masters and Servants Act, which had in 1871 been made applicable by proclamation to Griqualand West.[4] It was designed to meet the special circumstances that had arisen as a result of the congregating of a large Native population at the diamond diggings, and particularly to prevent labourers from stealing diamonds. Although it did not discriminate between European and non-European servants, whether Natives or half-caste, it was in practice invoked, according to the Civil Commissioner of Kimberley, only in the case of non-European servants.[5]

The Griqualand West Masters and Servants Law provided that contracts, whether oral or written, for periods longer than one month, should be registered with official registrars, the employer on registration being charged a fee of one shilling. For their protection servants were to be provided with a 'certificate' stating the terms of their contract; while to safeguard employers from desertion and from the theft of diamonds, servants were required to have these 'certificates' endorsed by their masters on the completion of contracts. Moreover, they were required to obtain a pass, for which a fee of one shilling was charged, before leaving the diamond-fields. Officers were required to demand the production of endorsed 'certificates' before issuing such passes.

Further, claim-holders were given the right to search their servants' persons and property without warrant, and diamonds found in the possession of servants were presumed to be the property of the master unless the contrary were proved. Severe statutory penalties for the theft of diamonds by servants were laid

---

[1] *Cape Diamond Mining Commission*, 1882.

[2] Proclamation No. 49 of 1872, sg. 23 July 1872 by local Commissioners. Cancelled by Proclamation No. 14 of 1872, sg. 10 August 1872 by Sir Henry Barkly, High Commissioner of South Africa.

[3] Proclamation No. 18 of 1872, sg. August 27th, 1872, by Sir Henry Barkly, High Commissioner of South Africa.

[4] Proclamation No. 68 of 1871.

[5] 'The Masters and Servants Laws in Griqualand West, in so far as they differ from those in the Cape Colony, were enacted in the early days of the diamond industry, and were necessarily somewhat severe upon the servant. . . . Though the law makes no distinction between European and native servants many of its provisions are applied exclusively to the latter, it being felt that if attempted to be put in force against Europeans they would not be tolerated.'

(Cape) *Blue Book on Native Affairs*, G. 2, 1883, Appendix, p. 4.

down, the maximum penalties being imprisonment with or without hard labour for a period not exceeding one year, in addition to which lashes, not exceeding fifty, might be inflicted.

The law also provided that no one should be registered as the holder of a claim or part of a claim unless he produced a certificate from a magistrate or justice of the peace especially authorized by the Governor to grant them, to the effect that he was 'a person of good character and a fit and proper person to be so registered'. As only registered claim-holders were entitled to 'win and find diamonds' on proclaimed diggings, it is possible that this provision might have been so applied as to exclude Natives, and other non-Europeans, from holding claims. If it was administered in this way the exclusion was not absolute, for there were some 'native[1] diggers' (presumably claim-holders) on the alluvial diggings at Barkly West.[2]

Some discrimination between Natives and Europeans was allowed by law even under the British administration, for, in 1871, the sale of liquor to Native servants was prohibited without their masters' written order.[3]

In practice it was quite impossible to administer effectively either this law or the provisions of the Masters and Servants Law regarding the registration of contracts and the pass system. There were continual complaints about the sale of liquor to Natives; and there is no doubt that, in contrast to early accounts of the river diggings, there was much drunkenness among them at the dry diggings.[4] At first, as we have seen, a 'tot' of the potent 'Cape Smoke' was a regular part of a labourer's rations; by the early 'eighties there were many complaints of Natives being incapacitated for work through drink.

From the numerous complaints it would appear that the Masters and Servants Law was equally defective in achieving its purpose of preventing desertion and the theft of diamonds. It was reported that not more than half the servants whose contracts should, according to the law, have been registered, were in fact registered.[5] Moreover, the Registrar of Natives himself said that a 'vast number' of Natives left the fields without passes.[6]

[1] At this time the term 'native' was not usually confined to the Bantu, as is now customary in South Africa. It was often used to describe all non-Europeans.
[2] See below, p. 81.
[3] Proclamation No. 64, 5 Dec. 1871, 'Government Notice imposing Penalty for Sale of Liquor to Native Servants without Masters' Written Order.'
[4] See below, p. 83.   [5] Morton, op. cit., p. 15.
[6] (Cape) Blue Book on Native Affairs, G. 5, 1886, p. 28. The Civil Commissioner of Kimberley estimated that at least 30,000 Natives left the diamond fields in 1882, and reported that only 12,000 obtained return passes.
Ibid., G. 2, 1883, Appendix, p. 3. The Registrar of Natives, North Beaconsfield, reported that a comparatively small number of natives secured passes when leaving the diamond fields. Ibid., G. 3, 1884, p. 25.

Although, according to contemporary accounts, the diamond diggings were not rough and lawless for Europeans, as mining camps go,[1] the conditions under which Native labourers lived and worked must have seemed strange, compared with life in the kraal.

Living conditions were reported to be poor and the death-rate high. Sanitary arrangements were defective in spite of Government regulations and, according to the Registrar of Natives, this, together with the 'want of cleanliness at the compounds', was responsible for the high mortality.[2] Nevertheless, those who survived appear to have improved in physique. The difference in the appearance of Natives coming to the fields in a starving condition and those leaving was remarked on by several observers.[3]

Conditions and wages were sufficiently attractive to induce many Natives to come to the diggings without the intervention of European agents. In the early days a popular master would be kept supplied with labour because his 'boys', on their return home after a few months' work, would send their relatives and friends to him.

To supplement the labour which found its own way to the diggings, colonists and traders would go into the interior and bring down gangs of Natives. Labour touts would also go out along the roads and simply collect into parties the Natives they found making their way to the diggings. A fee of one pound was charged by these suppliers of Native labourers, the Natives usually contracting for three months' service. Contracts, however, were often broken. Large numbers of Natives frequently absconded; the Natives who came to the diamond-fields were for the most part quite unaccustomed to regular employment. According to

---

[1] Describing the diamond fields in 1876, Morton (p. 16) said, 'Dress suit and society paraphernalia are indispensable. . . . An abundant supply of negro labour allows men of education and capital to engage in the occupation of "digging". This word must therefore be dissociated from the conventional idea of roughness and lawlessness.'

[2] The number of deaths in 1882 was reported to be 639, the causes being: dysentery, 107; fever, 85; natural causes, 74; pneumonia, 229; typhoid fever, 18; miscellaneous, 126.

(Cape) *Blue Book on Native Affairs*, G. 2, 1883, Appendix, p. 5. See H. Sauer, *Ex Africa*, pp. 66–92, for an account of an outbreak of smallpox in the compounds in 1883 and of attempts to suppress knowledge of it. The Inspector of Diamond Mines in his report for 1883 said that this outbreak 'had one excellent result: the question of cleanliness throughout the community became a subject requiring the most earnest alteration, and the filthy Kaffir compounds of the mining companies were at last cleaned and made less unwholesome.' Quoted G. 11, 1890, p. 17.

[3] e.g. Sir Bartle Frere stated that there was great physical improvement in the Natives while at the diamond diggings, and that it was possible on the roads to pick out those going and those returning. Bartle Frere, 'Laws affecting the relations between Civilized and Savage Life', *Journal of the Anthropological Institute*, Vol. XI, 1882, pp. 315–54.

Payton (p. 137), it was desirable for an employer to have a written contract because, he said, 'it impresses the Kafir', but it was not always effective.

Morton (p. 14) graphically described the arrival of gangs of Natives. He writes:

> A stream of foot passengers lines the side-walks, while along the centre of the streets crowds of naked negroes, often singing their weird songs, go to and fro from their work. Or perhaps, a gang of 'raw' natives, just down thousands of miles from the countries to the North, dusty, thin as skeletons, foot-sore, dirty and strange with barbaric utensil and ornament, thread their way along, hooted at, and pelted with dirt and stones by their initiated countrymen. This reception of the neophyte is of daily occurrence, and the ear can readily follow the direction pursued by the entering band by listening for the succession of derisive yells which greet it at each step of its progress.

Agents obviously served a useful purpose in shepherding such gangs to employers who wanted labour.

Official attempts were also made to increase the supply of Native labour. In 1877 the Administration of Griqualand West dispatched an agent to go as far north as Matabeleland (now part of Southern Rhodesia) to open up new sources of supply and to induce the Native chiefs to protect and assist labourers who were making their way to the diamond-fields.[1] A few years later, in 1880, when the Basuto left Kimberley to take part in the War of Disarmament in Basutoland, their employers made representations to Sir Owen Lanyon, Administrator of the recently annexed Transvaal.[2] The result was an 'accession of 12,000 labourers'.[3] It is, perhaps, relevant to note in this connexion that at this time the British administration attempted to impose and collect a hut tax of ten shillings per hut throughout the Transvaal.

The diamond diggings quickly drew labour from far afield. In the 'seventies, most of the Natives are reported to have come from 'the interior'. In 1874, for instance, the Lieutenant-Governor reported that 'the great bulk' of the Native labourers came from 'the interior northward of the South African Republic', and comparatively few from British Basutoland and Natal.[4] He was, however, attempting to refute the allegation that Natives from the latter territories were being armed at the diamond-fields, and

---

[1] *Parl. Papers*, 1878–9, L. 11 [C.2220]. Further correspondence *re* affairs of South Africa, pp. 35, 41, 72, 78–9.

[2] Britain annexed the Transvaal in 1877. The independence of the Transvaal was restored in 1881 in terms of the Convention of Pretoria.

[3] (Cape) *Blue Book on Native Affairs*, G. 20, 1881, p. 130.

[4] Lieutenant-Governor Southey in a despatch dated Kimberley, 11 April, 1874. Quoted J. W. Matthews, op. cit., p. 278.

so may have belittled the supply from these sources. Morton (p. 15), however, who had no such reason for bias, was of the same opinion.

> 'The native labourer', he said, 'comes mostly from a region of teeming population, between 16° and 22° of south latitude—that is to say, from the country between the Zambesi and Limpopo rivers, beyond the northern borders of the Transvaal Republic.'

It has been estimated that by 1874 ten thousand Natives were employed at the diggings.[1] The number employed seems to have continued to be round about ten thousand until the end of the 'eighties, although there were very considerable temporary fluctuations.

Individual Natives would remain at the diggings for from three to five months, long enough to earn sufficient to buy a gun, costing from £5 to £7 10s., and ammunition, or whatever else they might fancy.[2]

B. CONCENTRATION AND AMALGAMATION, 1874–1899

(i) *The New Technique and the Demand for Labour*

After 1874 the method and organization of winning diamonds changed rapidly. As more and more ground was extracted the diggings became deeper and the open quarrying of hundreds of small claims became impossible. The narrow roadways which were maintained at ground-level across the ever-deepening pit inevitably collapsed and could not be built up again. Consequently, a system of aerial ropeways for hoisting the 'blue ground' from the individual claims to the edges of the great pits was evolved. But although one of the difficulties of independent working was thus overcome, falls of reef, which buried the blue ground, and the accumulation of water in the pits, made some co-operation between claim-holders essential.

In 1874 the prohibition on 'claim-blocking', that is, the holding of more than two claims, was relaxed, and one person was permitted to hold up to ten claims.[3] Two years later, in 1876, even this limitation was withdrawn and the consolidation and amalgamation of claims could thereafter proceed unchecked by legal restriction.[4]

---

[1] *Transvaal Labour Commission*, Evidence [Cd. 1897], 1904, q. 3831, ev. F. Ingle.

[2] J. Angove, op. cit., p. 60.

[3] Ordinance No. 10 of 1874. Schedule, Section I, 18. This ordinance also made provision for the allocation of claims on new public diggings. After the prospector's or discoverer's claims had been selected and marked off, a government official was to allot claims (thirty feet square) to certificated miners, or their agents, in the order in which the claims had been marked out.

[4] Ordinance No. 12 of 1876.

By this time the influx of Europeans had fallen off and the shifting body of prospectors dropped to the number that could find employment in the mines and dependent towns.[1] The day of the small independent digger employing his two or three labourers was over.[2] Diggers began to form small companies, for the technique of diamond-digging was changing. In 1874 horse-whims came into use for hoisting up the blue ground. At the same time washing-machines were introduced for breaking down the blue ground. The following year the first steam-engine was brought to the diamond-fields. The introduction of machinery had been delayed by several factors. The cost of transport from the coast was high, being thirty pounds per ton from Port Elizabeth. The scarcity of fuel in the neighbourhood made the cost of raising steam prohibitive, for within a few years every tree within miles had been chopped down and used. Moreover, uncertainty as to the depth of the diamond-bearing rock made the introduction of fixed plant inexpedient.

During the later 'seventies and 'eighties falls of reef were frequent. At one pit after another the surface of claims was buried and working restricted. This led to the development of shaft-sinking and underground mining, which began in 1882 in the Kimberley pit. At this time the open pit had reached the depth of four hundred feet. By the end of 1887 open quarrying had also proved quite impracticable at De Beers and Dutoitspan. Finally, two years later, almost all the pit bottoms at Bultfontein were buried by fallen reef.[3] The persistent falls of reef caused the smaller proprietors to sell their claims and move off, many of them to prospect for gold beyond the Vaal River.

Underground mining led to further concentration, both because it required more capital, and because tunnelling by rival companies resulted in frequent disputes, which could most easily be settled by amalgamation. At the end of 1885 there were still ninety-eight separate holdings in the four diggings. By 1888 Rhodes had secured unified control of the Kimberley and De Beers mines,[4] and shortly afterwards arrangements were made for controlling production at Dutoitspan and Bultfontein. Henceforward

[1] F. Gardner Williams, op. cit., p. 261.

[2] Describing conditions at the Kimberley diggings in 1876, Morton wrote (p. 28): 'In spite of his confidence, there are influences at work which are crowding out the small capitalist from the fields. The increasing depth, crumbling reef, inflowing water are fast multiplying the expenses of working. The great bugbear of the diggers is the word 'company', but even now small proprietorships are becoming merged in large aggregations of claims, and the next phase of mining operations must undoubtedly be that of several large and competing companies, or perhaps a single one controlling the whole mine.'

[3] F. Gardner Williams, op. cit., pp. 236, 244.

[4] Ibid., p. 278.

De Beers Consolidated Mines Ltd. was to dominate the South African diamond industry.

The change in the technique of mining and the concentration of employers into larger units led to changes in the nature of the demand for Native labour. Under the early technique Natives had worked alongside their European employers, often doing the same kind of work. By 1876 diggers were working on a larger scale, and at the Kimberley diggings the average digger was employing a gang of about twenty Natives and a European overseer. Ten of the Natives would work at the claim, loosening, shovelling out, and hoisting up the blue ground. The other ten would work at the 'compound', the enclosure where each digger had his house, washing-machine, well, tents for his labourers, and his 'floor', the hard piece of ground on which the blue ground was broken down, pulverized, and sorted.[1]

As underground mining displaced open quarrying, the nature of the work changed somewhat. Skilled miners were required to direct operations, and mining became organized on the basis of Native manual labourers supervised by more or less skilled European miners, mechanics, and overseers.[2] Natives continued to do the greater part of the manual work and they added rock drilling to their other accomplishments.

The proportion of European to Native workers appears to have varied considerably during the 'eighties, both at the different diggings and at different times. According to the reports of the Inspectors of Mines, the proportion of European to Native workers varied between one to three and one to eleven. But methods of mining were changing and work was frequently interrupted by reef falls, so that it is impossible to draw definite conclusions from the figures available. There is no doubt, however, that after the general adoption of underground mining, the proportion of European to Native labour was much lower than it had been during the first few years after the discovery of diamonds.

(ii) Wages and Conditions of Work and Recruitment

In the 'seventies and early 'eighties the wage-rates of Native labourers were very sensitive to fluctuations in the supply of and the demand for labour. They varied considerably.[3] On at least

---

[1] Morton, op. cit., pp. 20-23.

[2] In his report for the year 1882 the Assistant Inspector of Machinery said: 'I estimate that probably not one half of the engine-drivers, boiler attendants, etc., employed at these mines would pass muster for such employment in England.'—Quoted *Report of Inspector of Diamond Mines*, G: 11, 1890, p 7.

[3] *Parl. Papers* [C. 2220], 1879, Further Correspondence *re* affairs of South Africa, p. 64. Report of the Commission upon the Griqualand West Labour Question (1876).

two occasions the supply was reduced by warfare. The demand
was likewise restricted from time to time as the result of falls of
reef, which interrupted work. Later, as underground mining
developed and amalgamation proceeded, the demand for labour
was reduced; partly because the new methods required less labour
than the old, and partly because De Beers Consolidated adopted
from the beginning the policy of regulating production in accordance with the market price of diamonds. The desire to regulate
the market was, even more than the anxiety to reduce costs, the
actuating motive in achieving final amalgamation.

In the 'seventies, on occasions when the supply of Native labour
fell off, wages rose as high as twenty or even thirty shillings a
week.[1] Ten shillings a week with rations in addition was, however,
the more usual wage.[2] When, in June and July of 1880, some
four thousand Basuto labourers left the diamond-fields to take
part in the Basuto War of Disarmament, the works as a result
were 'almost at a standstill', and wage-rates shot up.[3] Subsequently, when additional labour was obtained from the north,
wages fell; but not to the former level. In 1881 and 1882 wage-
rates were reported to range from fifteen shillings, and food, to
thirty shillings a week.[4]

From about this time wage-rates appear to have become more
stable. At the same time, probably as the result of the formation
of companies, the practice of employers providing their Native
labourers with food was abandoned. Wage-rates at the different
mines are recorded in the reports of the Inspectors of Mines
between 1882 and 1889. The wages of Native labourers during
that period were from fifteen to thirty shillings a week, twenty-five
shillings being the most common wage reported. In addition to
this cash wage, lodging was provided, and in most cases, firewood,
but food was no longer supplied. Many companies employed
Natives as drillers, paying them according to the amount of
drilling they did. They earned from twenty to thirty shillings a
week. Some reports show wages to have been lower at the
Dutoitspan and Bultfontein than at the Kimberley and De Beers
mines.[5] Underground mining was further developed in the latter,
and probably required more efficient labour; which would explain
this difference in wage-rates.

On such river diggings as were still worked in the 'eighties,

[1] A. Trollope, op. cit., Vol. II, p. 182. Parl. Papers [C. 2220], 1879, op. cit.,
p. 41.
[2] J. Angove, op. cit., p. 59. Cape Select Committee on Labour Market,
1879, p. 59, q. 9,639, ev. A. G. Watermeyer.
[3] (Cape) Blue Book on Native Affairs, G. 20, 1881, p. 130.
[4] Ibid., G. 33, 1882, p. 181; G. 2, 1883, Appendix, p. 8; G. 86, 1882, p. 724.
[5] Reports of Inspectors of Diamond Mines: G. 27, 1882; G. 34, 1883; G. 30,
1884; G. 28, 1885; G. 40, 1886; G. 26, 1887; G. 28, 1888; G. 22, 1889; G. 11, 1890.

labourers' wages were considerably lower. The old methods
continued to be used and the diggers remained small independent
entrepreneurs, employing perhaps one or two Natives. In 1886
there were at the river diggings some 1,150 diggers (1,000 'white',
150 'native'), employing 2,250 labourers (250 'white', 2,000
'native'). The wages of Native labourers were from seven shillings
to eight and sixpence, with food in addition, or from twelve and
sixpence to fifteen shillings, without food. On occasion it was
reported that it was difficult to obtain labour at these rates; at
other times, despite the lower rates on these diggings, labour was
obtained without much difficulty.[1]

European wages on the mines at this time were from £4 to £8
a week. Overseers usually received £4 or £5 with a percentage
of the value of the diamonds discovered; mechanics and engine-
drivers from £6 to £8. These rates were necessary to attract
sufficiently skilled labour to the mines; for, at that time, most of
the skilled labour had to be induced to come to South Africa.
The local supply of trained artisans was very small. In 1888, of
the European employees at the Kimberley mine, 55 per cent
were of British extraction, 43 per cent of colonial, and 2 per cent
from other countries; at De Beers mine 65 per cent were of
British, 30 per cent of colonial, and 5 per cent of European and
American extraction.[2]

Thus were established in South Africa the wage-rates which
have there come to be so widely accepted as the proper reward
of the European artisan and even of the European labourer.

The conditions under which Natives worked at the mines were
modified during the 'eighties. In the 'seventies, diggers and
companies had provided accommodation for their Native labourers
usually in the neighbourhood of their 'floors', or had hired labour
from contractors who paid all the expenses, and provided Native
labourers at a price, according to Anthony Trollope, of £1 a
week each. During the 'eighties the 'closed compound system
of housing Native labourers was adopted and by 1888, it had
'entirely superseded the former method of lodging Kafirs in
unenclosed quarters' at the Kimberley and De Beers mines.[3]

Closed compounds were introduced to prevent the theft of
diamonds and also to prevent drunkenness, both of which occasioned great loss to the employers in the 'seventies and early
'eighties.[4] Unscrupulous diamond dealers encouraged Natives to

---

[1] *Report of Inspector of Claims*, Barkly West, G. 26, 1887, p. 12. (Cape)
Blue Book on Native Affairs, G. 20, 1881, p. 128 (Report of Civil Commissioner,
Barkly West.)
[2] *Report of Inspectors of Diamond Mines*, G. 22, 1889, pp. 6, 10.
[3] Ibid., G. 28, 1888, p. 14.
[4] F. Gardner Williams, op. cit., p. 258.

secrete stones and, as the companies grew in size, it became more difficult for employers to detect theft. Special legislation gave claim-holders and companies the right to search their servants, and in some cases the searching of Natives was undertaken by the mining boards.[1] These measures were costly and were not an effective preventative. Drink also, according to the Civil Commissioner of Kimberley, was 'an unmixed evil to the natives themselves and to all employers of their labour'.[2] Before the introduction of the closed compound system it was reported that, at the beginning of each week, 'due to the drunken excesses of the week-end', from half to two-thirds of the mine labourers were absent.[3] Drunkenness led to crime. The eight thousand cases brought before the Magistrate of Kimberley in 1882 were regarded as 'fully up to the average', but not as an exceptional number. This in a district with an estimated population of some twenty to thirty thousand inhabitants.

The Government made some attempt to improve conditions and appointed two official 'Registrars and Protectors of Natives', one at Kimberley and one at Dutoitspan. This measure was barely effective. The Civil Commissioner of Kimberley reported that 'while a good deal of registering, with its consequent taxation, is done, the protectors' duties are not, I fear, quite so well attended to'.[4] A fee of one shilling, which was charged to employers on the registration of their servants, was designed after 1874 to pay for the maintenance of the Native hospital which had been established, and also for a depot where Natives in search of employment might obtain lodging, food, and clothing.[5] In 1883 no such depot existed, the previous one having been closed down, and the fees levied 'to cover the expenses of this system', amounting to £6,470, were paid into the general revenue.[6] Meanwhile, according to the Acting Registrar of Natives, destitute and discharged Natives seeking employment were 'forced to wander about the streets in

[1] In 1887 searching at Kimberley and De Beers mines was undertaken by the companies. G.28, 1888, op. cit., p. 14. At Dutoitspan and Bultfontein it remained in charge of the Mining Boards. Ibid. and G. 41, 1890, p. 26.
[2] (Cape) *Blue Book on Native Affairs*, G. 3, 1884, p. 27.
[3] *Reports of Inspectors of Diamond Mines*, G. 40, 1886, p. 14; G. 11, 1890, p. 21.
[4] (Cape) *Blue Book on Native Affairs*, G. 2, 1883, Appendix, p. 4.
[5] Ordinances Nos. 2 and 28 of 1874. The latter ordinance was permissive and was not put into force immediately. In addition to permitting the establishment of depots, it required that Natives lodging at the depots should be supplied with suitable clothing. The cost of the clothing was to be repaid by the employer engaging a Native. The expense of financing the depots apparently prevented the immediate enforcement of this ordinance. See *Parl. Papers* [C. 2220] 1879, op. cit., pp. 63–71. Report of the Commission upon the Griqualand West Labour Question (1876).
[6] (Cape) *Blue Book on Native Affairs*, G. 2, 1883, Appendix, p. 4.

a starving condition until they found a master, or . . . a night's lodging in gaol'.[1]

The employers claimed, and their statements were corroborated by the Inspectors of Mines, that the 'closed compound system' mitigated these evils. According to the latter, employers could now begin the week with a full complement of Native labourers, and searching for stolen diamonds could be made more effective, as it was only necessary to search Natives when they left the compounds on the completion of their term of service. The noisy drinking-shops were suppressed and the town freed from brawling Natives. Finally, the Natives 'after experience of the compound system, liked it, and, being enabled to save money instead of spending it to the benefit of low canteen-keepers, soon improved in physique and morale'.[2] According to the employers, the health of the labourers was 'out of all comparison better than before compounds were in vogue'.[3]

'In the closed compounds', the Inspector of Mines reported in 1888, 'the Kafir labourers are lodged in comfortable, clean, and well-aired dormitories; food and clothing and smaller necessaries are supplied at a regular tariff within the compound to any employee who chooses to purchase at these stores.'[4]

Certainly the Natives appear to have shown no universal dislike of the system, for they continued to offer their services at the diamond-mines. Indeed, even after the discovery and development of gold-mining on the Witwatersrand provided a rival market for their services, conditions at Kimberley were such that the labour supply could normally be maintained without resort to organized recruiting through labour agents. The sources of Native labour began to change and some attempts were made to attract Natives from the Cape Colony, but, on the whole, until the end of the century, sufficient numbers presented themselves at the Company's compounds to meet the demand.

(iii) Supply and Sources of Native Labour

In the 'eighties, the sources from which Native labour was drawn continued to be very varied. The following table[5] which shows the tribes of 'new hands' registered in 1884 at the Kimberley and De Beers mines, gives an indication of the diversity and relative importance of the sources:

[1] Ibid., Appendix, p. 5.
[2] *Reports of Inspectors of Diamond Mines*, G. 11, 1890, p. 21.
[3] Ibid., G. 22, 1889, p. 6.
[4] Ibid., G. 28, 1888, p. 14.
[5] (Cape) *Blue Book on Native Affairs*, G. 2, 1885, p. 210. The tribal names are reproduced as listed in the report.

Shangaans	.	.	.	681
British Basutos	.	.	.	195
Sekukuni Basutos	.	.	.	2,215
Zulus	.	.	.	815
Portuguese Zulus	.	.	.	446
Bakhatlas	.	.	.	56
Matabele	.	.	.	120
Colonials	.	.	.	375
Bakwenas	.	.	.	33
Batlapings	.	.	.	277
Swazis	.	.	.	11
Bamangwatos	.	.	.	56
Barolongs	.	.	.	115
Korannas	.	.	.	6
Griquas	.	.	.	3
Batlaros	.	.	.	21
Transvaal Basutos	.	.	.	47
West Coast	.	.	.	2
Damara	.	.	.	1
Mozambique	.	.	.	1

                                                        ————
                                                        5,476

The number of labourers, both European and Native, employed
at the diamond diggings, fluctuated considerably during this decade. The general trend was decidedly in the downward direction,
the downward trend being due to the change in technique, the
growth of companies and, finally, the amalgamation of companies
into a single controlling unit.[1] After De Beers obtained control
of output in 1889, the Bultfontein and Dutoitspan diggings were
left practically unworked until after the end of the century.[2]

The following table, compiled by the Inspector of Mines from
the official reports, shows the number of employees on the four
diggings from 1881 to 1889.

The period for which individual Natives would remain working
at the mines appears gradually to have lengthened. In the early
years it was universally reported to be a matter of three, four, or
five months. It is true that, in 1886, the Acting Registrar of
Natives estimated that the average duration of contracts was two
months,[3] but Natives might re-engage for further periods. In
1889 Natives were engaged on a three-months' contract, but the
majority, sometimes after a holiday outside the compound, would
re-engage for further periods, remaining at work up to nine, or
even, in some cases, up to eighteen months.[4]

[1] Ibid., G. 4, 1890, p. 57.
[2] G. 4, 1891, p. 16, De Beers Consolidated Mines, Ltd., *Annual Report*
(1896, p. 7; 1898, p. 8).
[3] (Cape) *Blue Book on Native Affairs*, G. 5, 1886, p. 5.
[4] Ibid., G. 22, 1889, p. 6.

AVERAGE NUMBER OF EMPLOYEES (EXCLUSIVE OF MANAGERS AND SECRETARIES), EUROPEAN AND NON-EUROPEAN, EMPLOYED ON DIAMOND MINES, 1881–1889[1]

		1881	1882	1883	1884	1885	1886	1887	1888	1889
Kimberley Mine	European	800	700	400	300	450	430	740	560	337
	Non-European	3,000	4,000	2,000	1,500	1,500	2,000	2,500	2,000	2,300
	Total	3,800	4,700	2,400	1,800	1,950	2,430	3,240	2,560	2,637
De Beers Mine	European	300	300	200	250	320	200	500	480	550
	Non-European	2,000	2,000	1,260	1,700	1,700	2,400	3,000	2,500	2,160
	Total	2,300	2,300	1,460	1,950	2,020	2,600	3,500	2,980	2,710
Du Toit's Pan Mine	European	1,000	—	320	400	770	590	420	380	297
	Non-European	8,000	—	2,800	3,300	4,500	4,030	3,200	2,500	1,852
	Total	9,000	—	3,120	3,700	5,270	4,620	3,620	2,880	2,149
Bultfontein Mine	European	1,000	—	220	260	360	290	260	260	88
	Non-European	4,000	—	2,300	2,500	3,600	2,530	2,600	2,600	518
	Total	5,000	—	2,520	2,760	3,960	2,820	2,886	2,860	606
GRAND TOTAL	European	3,100		1,140	1,210	1,900	1,510	1,920	1,680	1,272
	Non-European	17,000		8,360	9,000	11,300	10,960	11,300	9,600	6,830

[1] G. 11 1890, p. 38.

CHAPTER VI
OTHER EMPLOYMENT, 1870–1885

A. NATIVE LABOUR FOR THE DEVELOPMENT OF TRANSPORT

THE mining population of the Kimberley district did not exist in complete isolation. To meet its needs ancillary industries were organized not only in Kimberley, but elsewhere in Africa and even beyond. Within ten years, when the first influx of prospectors was over and the number of diggers had become somewhat more stable, Kimberley and the adjacent mining townships had a population, including Europeans, Natives, and other non-Europeans, of at least eighteen thousand, and was second only to Capetown.[1] In addition, a considerable number of diggers and labourers continued to work the river diggings.

Kimberley in the 'seventies was described as

> A city in the desert—dropped, as it were, from the clouds, so detached does it seem from all the ordinary surroundings of civilized communities. A city built of tent-cloth and corrugated iron and wood, and here and there substantial brick.[2]

Situated in the midst of a barren plain, far from the existing centres of consumption, it had to be provided with food and all the other requirements of a mining centre with a population drawn from all corners of the world.

Transport services had at once to be improvised and developed. In the western part of the Cape Colony road-passes had already been constructed traversing the first mountain ranges which separate the narrow coastal belt from the hinterland. Once the escarpment of the inland plateau, the Karroo, had been climbed distance was the only geographical barrier isolating Kimberley. The country was comparatively flat, with vast plains sparsely covered with drought-resisting shrubs stretching for hundreds of miles. Rainfall was scanty, averaging from five to ten inches a year, and falling in summer in a few heavy thunderstorms. Such storms would make the country temporarily impassable, as they do to this day, but, except for occasional delays from this cause, lack of water and pasturage were the main obstacles to wagon

---

[1] Population of Capetown and suburbs, 1875, 44,000; population of Kimberley and adjacent townships, 1877, 18,000 (European 8,000, non-European 10,000); population of Port Elizabeth, 1875, 13,000; population of Borough of Durban, 1881, 14,200 (European 7,500, Indian 3,200, Native 3,500). Statistics from *Cape Census of* 1875, G. 42, 1876; *Return of Population of Griqualand West*, A. 14, 1876; W. Peace, *Our Colony of Natal* (1883), p. 156.

[2] Morton, op. cit., p. 13.

transport. The lack of pasturage was a serious matter, for it was not practicable to carry or buy food for draught-oxen, and they had simply to be turned loose to graze when halts were made. Consequently halts had to be long and ox-wagon transport was very slow, the journey from Port Elizabeth to the diamond-fields taking a month or even six weeks.[1] The route to the diamond-fields from Port Elizabeth was shorter than that from Capetown. It had the added advantage of passing through the more easterly and less arid parts of the Karroo. Therefore, before the construction of railways, it became the most used route for transporting goods to the diggings.[2] Normally the route taken was that via Graaff Reinet, but in times of drought a more easterly and longer route, passing through Grahamstown, or even Kingwilliamstown, and Queenstown would be used on account of the better pasturage along the way.

In Natal, also, the demand for transport was stimulated. The traders and transport riders of Natal had always had a keen interest in the trade with the interior, but Durban was not so favourably situated for becoming a transport depot for the diamond-fields of Griqualand West. Moreover, other geographical conditions made difficult the supply of transport services. The coastal belt was hilly, and inland the southern escarpment of the Drakensberg was far more formidable than the coastal ranges of the Cape mountains. Rainfall was heavy and the summer storms regularly washed away such roads and bridges as there were. Nevertheless, efforts were made to maintain the rough tracks which served as roads.[3]

In both the Cape Colony and Natal the development of transport led to an added demand for Native labour. Natives were employed by European transport riders as leaders and drivers,[4] and they also engaged in transporting goods as independent contractors.[5] Soon, however, the increase in trade introduced a new demand for their services, for it led to the construction of railways and the improvement of harbours. Before the discovery of diamonds the Governments of the Cape Colony and Natal had both toyed with railway projects, but the depression of the 'sixties and the failure of the existing lines to pay their way had prevented further construction. As soon as it was clear that the new transport demand was likely to be permanent, they bought out the private companies which had built and operated the first lines.

In the Cape Colony rivalry between the ports resulted in the

[1] C. A. Payton, op. cit., p. 84.
[2] J. Noble, op. cit., p. 211; Payton, op. cit., pp. 77–84.
[3] *Parl. Papers*, 1872, XLIII [C. 618], p. 7.
[4] J. Noble, op. cit., p. 293.
[5] See below, pp. 105–6.

Government constructing no less than three lines to connect Capetown, Port Elizabeth, and East London with the diamond-fields. Between 1874 and 1886, 1,730 miles of railway were constructed.[1] The work was carried out by contractors who made their plans on the assumption that unskilled Native labour would be available. The first railway estimates apparently assumed that sufficient Native labour for all unskilled work would be forth-coming at wages of eighteenpence a day.[2] It was soon found that these rates were not sufficiently attractive to induce Natives to travel the long distance—five hundred miles or more—from their homes to the 'Western' line which was being constructed to con-nect Capetown and Kimberley. On the northern part of this line, in the neighbourhood of Hope Town, where the country was sparsely populated and labour had to be drawn from a considerable distance, the supply was reported to have been 'inadequate' throughout the course of the work.[3]

The ease with which Native labour was obtained on the different railway and harbour works varied according to their distance from areas with a Native population. On the Midland (Port Elizabeth-Rosmead) line, too, the supply was small at first, and fell far short of expectations.[4] By 1876, however, it was reported that there had been 'encouraging progress' in the number of men coming forward, both for the Midland line and the north-eastern extension of the line from East London.[5] In 1883 it was reported that the number of men on the railway works had increased and there were no longer complaints of lack of labour.[6] Farther east, where Natives lived close at hand, they offered their services more readily and little difficulty was experienced in obtaining labour for the construction of the Eastern Railway, which ran inland from East London, or for the harbour works at East London.[7]

Another reason why the supply of Native labour persisted in falling short of expectations on some of the lines was that many of the railway works were not popular with the Natives on account of the tommy-shop system which was widespread. The labourers complained that although the money wages, according to prevail-ing standards, were high, as much as three shillings a day being

[1] *Official Year Book*, No. 6, 1910–22, p. 792.
[2] I. Murray, *Early Railway Development in the Cape Colony* (unpublished thesis, University of Capetown), p. 33.
[3] *Report on Construction of Railways*, G. 61, 1883, p. 6.
[4] In 1874, for example, labour contractors arranged to supply six thousand Natives for the Midland line but only twenty-seven arrived. *Memorandum on Immigration and Labour Supply*, by J. X. Merriman, G. 8, 1876, p. 2.
[5] Ibid., p. 2.
[6] G. 61, 1883, op. cit., p. 6.
[7] (Cape) *Blue Book on Native Affairs*, G. 21, 1875, p. 42.

offered, the effective wage was far lower. The prices charged and deducted for provisions were so exorbitant that they received only a few shillings at the end of the month from the contractors, who, in many cases, were also the storekeepers.[1]

Where the Natives who had been out to work reported favourably on the treatment and wages they had received, as they did of the East London works, there was no difficulty in obtaining labour.[2] On the other hand, on one occasion the Natives of Keiskammahoek refused to go to the railway works until they were promised that their money would be paid to them direct, at the end of each week, by an officer especially appointed for the purpose. On these terms, however, the railway contractor was unwilling to engage them.[3] In 1885 nominal wages of three shillings a day failed also to attract Natives from Middledrift, although the district was suffering from drought, and although ten years earlier its inhabitants had been eager to work on railway construction.[4]

The colonial authorities believed that another reason for the small supply of labour was the opposition of the missionaries, and the parents of young Natives, who were thought to be averse to their charges and children going out to the public works, where drink was freely sold to Natives. Whether on balance this did in fact deter is uncertain. It is reported that many Natives preferred the public works for the very reason that drink was easily obtainable there. There is no doubt that there was a lot of drunkenness. The European navvies, who were imported for a time because of the failure of the Natives to come forward in sufficient numbers,[5] were many of them heavy drinkers, and their example, combined with the encouragement of the canteen-keepers, soon introduced the Natives to the habit of drinking strong colonial wine and spirit.[6]

The Government took action to promote the supply of labour to the public works. The influence of magistrates and other officials was enlisted. In 1873, for example, the magistrates in

[1] The profits that were made by storekeepers on the railway construction works were so great that it was possible for Pauling, a railway contractor, to raise the capital he required by selling the monopoly of the catering rights on the works. G. Pauling, *Chronicles of a Contractor*, p. 27. J. Rose-Innes, Civil Commissioner, Kingwilliamstown Division, reported that wages of 1s. 3d. per day with rations would be preferable to the high rates paid without rations; (Cape) *Blue Book on Native Affairs*, G. 12, 1877, pp. 112–13. See also idem, G. 5, 1886, p. 38; Robertson, '150 *Years of Economic Contact*', op. cit., pp. 12, 13.
[2] (Cape) *Blue Book on Native Affairs*, G. 21, 1875, p. 32.
[3] Ibid., G. 5, 1886, p. 38.
[4] Ibid., G. 2, 1885, p. 33.
[5] In February 1874 an application had been made for 200 artisans, and 300 navvies, later further indents for 150 European navvies and then for 1,000 were made. G. 35, 1875, p. 2; cf. G. 8, 1876, op. cit., p. 2.
[6] (Cape) *Blue Book on Native Affairs*, G. 21, 1875, p. 59.

Basutoland (which was administered by the Cape Colony between 1871 and 1884), 'agents' with the tribes beyond the eastern frontier, and the Civil Commissioners of colonial divisions with large Native populations, were officially informed that 'moral supervisors' accompanying parties of fifty or more labourers would be paid five shillings per day[1] in order to encourage young men from the mission stations, and to overcome the objections of parents to the conditions which their children encountered on the railway and other public works.

The following year an official request was made for parties of Natives to be sent from Basutoland to the Western Province, and both there and in the districts beyond the eastern frontier of the Cape Colony parties of Natives were organized and dispatched to the colonial public works by magistrates and official 'agents'.[2] The Government offered to pay the cost of transporting Natives by sea from Port Elizabeth to Capetown, if parties from the eastern frontier districts could be induced to go to the western districts.[3] Further, it established a permanent Native labour agency at Kingwilliamstown and entered into arrangements for obtaining labour from beyond the northern boundary of the Colony. It was not its intention to monopolize the labour so obtained. Native labourers were available for private employers who were prepared to accept its terms, namely, payment of a deposit of £6 for each male adult, and wages of £1 a month and rations.[4]

The Government also made arrangements for obtaining labour from the east coast of Africa and Natives from Portuguese East Africa were brought down by boat to Port Elizabeth and Cape-town, where they were employed both on the public works and by the farmers.[5]

These measures appear to have been fairly successful, for in 1878 the Government was able to discontinue the importation of European navvies. European artisans continued to be imported, after a short interruption in 1878, until 1884.[6] The contractors found the imported European navvies unsatisfactory, and they preferred Native labourers when they could be obtained.[7]

We may summarize the situation by saying that the sources

[1] Circular No. 5 of 1873; (Cape) *Blue Book on Native Affairs*, G. 27, 1874, p. 153.
[2] G. 21, 1875, pp. 32, 111; G. 16, 1876, p. 51; G. 64, 1882, p. 1.
[3] G. 27, 1874, p. 154.
[4] G. 21, 1875, op. cit., p. 59.
[5] G. 64, 1882, p. 1.
[6] H. M. Robertson, 'The Cape of Good Hope and Systematic Coloniza-tion,' *South African Journal of Economics*, Vol. V, No. 4, December 1937, p. 409.
[7] G. 8, 1876, op. cit., pp. 2–3; G. 3, 1884, op. cit., p. 10.

from which Native labour for the railway and other public works in the Cape Colony was obtained were principally the Native locations within the Colony, such as the Peddie locations; the tribes beyond the frontier, particularly the Fingo who had been settled beyond the Kei in 1858, 1864, and subsequently; and Basutoland. Some Natives were also obtained from north of the Vaal River and from Portuguese East Africa.[1]

It is impossible to give statistics of the number of Natives employed on railway construction, for the work was carried out by contractors and no returns are available. Employment was not continuous, the Natives being engaged and paid off as new construction was undertaken and completed.

The number of Native labourers employed on the public works during any period must clearly have depended both on the amount of construction and on the speed at which the work was done. Between 1874 and 1886 a yearly average of 144 miles of railway was laid. In the later years at least, Native labour was largely used on the Midland line, and it was used throughout on the Eastern line. As early as 1874 there were reported to be three hundred and ten 'kafirs' and three hundred and sixty Fingo employed on the railway and harbour works at East London.[2] In the division of Middelburg, through which the Midland line passed, at one time as many as two thousand Natives were employed on railway construction.[3] Where pass regulations apply, pass statistics give some indication of the number of labourers going out to work, although allowance must be made for understatement on account of evasion. From Fingoland the Government 'agent', Mr. Matthew Blyth, who was one of the most distinguished of the Cape Native administrators, and who had taken great care that a complete pass system should be instituted, reported that in 1875 one thousand Fingo were employed on Government works within the Colony[4] and, the following year, that at least that number were constantly so employed.[5]

The period for which individual Natives would go to the public works was usually from three to six months,[6] and the shortness of the period made it uneconomical to obtain labour from far afield if transport costs had to be paid.[7]

In Natal the influence of the growth of the diamond diggings

[1] G. 21, 1875, op. cit., pp. 32, 111; G. 35, 1875, p. 8; G. 12, 1877, op. cit., p. 4 (R.M. Cornet Spruit); p. 8 (R.M. Thaba Bosigo); G. 64, 1882, p. 1.
[2] (Cape) Blue Book on Native Affairs, G. 21, 1875, p. 42.
[3] Ibid., G. 3, 1884, p. 42.
[4] Ibid., G. 21, 1875, p. 32.
[5] Ibid., G. 16, 1876, p. 51.
[6] Ibid., G. 12, 1877, p. 113; G. 16, 1876, p. 59 (J. Rose-Innes, Civil Commissioner, Kingwilliamstown).
[7] G. 35, 1875, p. 8.

on the transport system was in some respects different. On the one hand, Natal was not so favourably situated for becoming a forwarding centre for goods sent from Europe to the diamond-fields. On the other hand, Natal produced certain goods, notably sugar and coffee, which were in demand at the diggings, and which were not grown elsewhere in South Africa. Throughout South Africa the rise in the demand for transport led to a rise in the cost of transport oxen. This had particularly serious consequences in Natal, for it threatened both to make unprofitable the carrying trade with the Orange Free State and the South African Republic and to hinder the development of agriculture within Natal. The mortality of the oxen engaged in transport was very heavy; in 1871 it was estimated that during the previous dry season four thousand head had died 'from over-work and want of sustenance'. The increased cost of oxen made such losses particularly serious. The authorities therefore decided to extend the railway system in the hope that, in addition to carrying local products to Kimberley, the railway would tap the wool trade, and assist in the development of trade in grain between Natal and the northern and eastern Orange Free State and the South African Republic.[1]

Lines were constructed both north and south along the coast, to serve the sugar and coffee plantations; and also inland, where the main line was intended to cross the Drakensberg escarpment and the Orange Free State, to connect Durban and Kimberley. In practice railway construction proceeded slowly, on account of the hilly coastal belt. The main line had reached a point only fifty miles from Durban by 1880, when industrial depression reduced the revenue of the country. For two years little progress was made with the railway.[2] In 1886, by which time the Witwatersrand had become the magnet attracting all the South African railways, the Natal line had reached Ladysmith.

As in the Cape Colony, railway construction led to a rise in the demand for Native labour. In Natal forced labour had previously been used for public work, principally the construction and maintenance of the roads.[3] It continued to be used for such work. The Natives performing this compulsory labour were paid, but the rates were below those that could be earned in the towns.[4] In 1883, indeed, the Colonial Engineer estimated that if the

---

[1] *Parl. Papers*, 1872, XLIII [C. 618]. Correspondence *re* Construction of Railways in Natal, p. 7. Report of Select Committee for the Consideration of Railway Projects, 1871.

[2] J. van der Poel, *Railway and Customs Policies in South Africa*, p. 10.

[3] For a description of the Natal roads, see *Parl. Papers*, 1872, XLIII [C. 618], op. cit., p. 7.

[4] *Natal Blue Book*, 1880, JJ., p. 46.

Government had obtained its labour in the open market it would have had to spend half as much again on the roads.[1] This forced labour was obtained through the Native chiefs who ordered out their tribesmen on the requisition of the magistrates. The period for which individual Natives had to work was six months. Compulsory service for the Government was very unpopular with the Natives on account of the low wages paid,[2] and also because there was nothing to prevent the Native chiefs ordering out the same men again and again.[3] The number of Natives supplied to the Colonial Engineer for compulsory service on road construction and maintenance was considerable. It rose from 1,330 in 1880 to 2,340 in 1884.[4]

Under this system the Government did not directly bid up wage-rates as did the Cape Government. Nevertheless, in Natal, the colonists complained that the compulsory service exacted reduced their labour supply. It interfered with private agreements between Europeans and Natives for labour to be given 'at the busy season'.[5] These complaints apparently resulted in changes in the administration of the system, for in 1875 the Secretary for Native Affairs reported that Natives were leaving the reserves for private land, the payment of rent being preferred to compulsory service at low wages.[6] In 1882 the Natal Native Commission recommended that Natives living on private farms should not be compelled to serve on the roads without the consent of their landlords, and that those in service, or under registered agreement of service, should also be exempt.[7] Thereafter, compulsory service was exacted only in the Native reserves of Natal and, later, in those of Zululand.

The construction of the Natal railway-lines was carried out by private contractors who bid up the price of labour. In 1883, on the railway construction works in the Weenen district, where rates had previously been from ten to fifteen shillings per month, contractors paid thirty shillings a month and in addition supplied rations.[8] Conditions on the Natal railway works appear to have been better than on many of the Cape lines. Rations were supplied to labourers by some, if not all, of the contractors. There do not appear to have been serious complaints from contractors about difficulty in securing labour In later years, indeed, the Government resorted to them to obtain labour for railway maintenance

[1] Ibid., 1883, FF, p. 76.   [2] Ibid., 1880, JJ, p. 46.
[3] *Natal Native Affairs Commission*, 1906–7, para. 118.
[4] *Natal Blue Book*, 1880, JJ, p. 86; 1884, HH, p. 1.
[5] *Natal Government Gazette*, 1871, p. 46.
[6] Secretary for Native Affairs, No. 369 5/8/1875, quoted Axelson, op. cit., p. 45.
[7] *Natal Native Affairs Commission*, 1881–2, para. 34.
[8] *Natal Blue Book*, 1883, GG, p. 53.

work.[1] But while the contractors were apparently satisfied with the supply of labour, the colonists complained about the competition of the railway construction works and the consequent rise in wage-rates.[2]

B. NATIVE LABOUR FOR URBAN DEVELOPMENT

The new market in the interior led to the growth of towns and villages to supply it with goods and services. Towns which were suitable forwarding centres, such as the ports, junctions, and convenient halting-places on the routes to the interior, grew rapidly. People congregate in towns and villages partly in order to take advantage of the opportunities which concentration affords for securing the economies of specialization and division of labour. Those centres which had already come into existence for this reason found in the development of the Kimberley market some degree of new stimulus to further growth; and some new and, at first, small centres came into existence for the same reason.

Statistics relating to the growth of towns are unsatisfactory for this period, since no census was taken between 1875 and 1891, but the figures for those dates, compared with those for the 1865 census, do give some indication of the rate of expansion which must have taken place in the 'seventies and early 'eighties.

Table showing the population of the three principal ports and three of the larger inland towns in the Cape Colony in 1865, 1875, and 1891.[3]

	1865	1875	1891
Cape Town (and suburbs) .	37,800	45,200	51,200
Port Elizabeth . .	10,800	13,000	23,300
East London . .	—	2,100	6,900
Paarl . . .	4,900	5,800	7,700
Graaff Reinet . .	3,900	4,600	5,900
Queenstown . .	1,200	2,300	4,100

In all the towns, and particularly at the ports, where the increase in foreign trade led to great activity, the demand for labour rose and the use of Native labour became more general for both unskilled and semi-skilled work. In 1884 it was reported from Port Elizabeth that Native men were employed 'in stores, shops, as grooms and general indoor servants'. Their wives and daughters

[1] 'The dearth of labour which has been referred to in my two previous reports has continued during the year. The expensive system of obtaining Kafirs through contractors has therefore had to be continued, and by this means all requirements have been fairly well met.' Report of the General Manager of Railways, *Natal Blue Book*, 1890–91, C., p. 93; and cf. 1893–4, C., p. 3.
[2] *Natal Blue Book*, 1876, JJ, p. 9; 1882, GG, p. 48; 1883, GG, p. 68; 1886, B, p. 69; 1887, B, pp. 68, 73.
[3] G. 42, 1876, Part I, p. 9; G. 6, 1892, p. 16.

were employed as 'washerwomen, cooks, and housekeepers'.[1]
According to the Civil Commissioner of the division, it was

> A remarkable fact that natives may now be seen everywhere in
> responsible situations at Stores, Railway, Beach, and as Overseers
> to labour parties, with watch and chain to keep their time correctly.
> In hard manual labour they quite supersede the white, in trenching,
> digging, and carrying at three shillings a day.[2]

And a year later he reported that

> Whenever hard work is required, the natives are taken on in
> preference to white men, in the streets and on the farms. Even as
> experts and foremen they are gradually advancing in estimation.[3]

Even in Capetown, far as it was from the Native territories,
private employers began to introduce and use Native labour for
stevedoring. A few Native labourers had previously been employed, principally in building operations and by market gardeners.
In 1884, owing to the difficulty experienced in obtaining labour
locally, the largest firm of landing and delivery contractors erected
a location within the Docks area where it housed and fed approximately five hundred Natives, most of whom were obtained in
the Transkei.

Contemporary reports of the period state, however, that in the
Cape Colony, in spite of the efforts at the industrial schools to
instruct Natives in skilled crafts, such as carpentry, smithing,
and shoemaking, they did not make a success as independent
craftsmen or as highly skilled employees,[4] and that they even
failed to practise the crafts for which they were trained.[5]

Against this evidence may be set the statistics furnished in an
official return of 1886, showing the occupations of Natives who
had been pupils of industrial schools.[6] Among ex-pupils of these
institutions there were then:

Ministers	59
Evangelists, etc.	114
Journalists	5
Law agents	10
Clerks and interpreters . . .	95
Telegraph messengers and letter carriers .	23
Teachers	580
Sewing teachers	59

---

[1] (Cape) *Blue Book on Native Affairs*, G. 3, 1884, p. 55.
[2] Ibid., p. 54.   [3] Ibid., G. 2, 1885, p. 51.
[4] G. 3, 1881, op. cit., p. 55 (I. W. Wauchope, Civil Commissioner, Port
Elizabeth).
[5] *Select Committee on the Supply of the Labour Market*, 1879, p. 66 (ev.
Rev. G. Brown, M.L.A., Alice).
[6] G. 1, 1887.

Farmers and petty cultivators	326
Carpenters	211
Wagonmakers	36
Blacksmiths	36
Tinsmiths	28
Thatchers	4
Masons	30
Millers	6
Sawyers	3
Furniture makers	15
Printers	30
Bookbinders	22
Tailors	36
Shoemakers	39
Shopkeepers	8
Shopmen and storemen	134
Policemen	63
Transport riders and wagon drivers	103
Married women	281
Domestic servants (female)	239
Do. (male)	95
Labourers	94
Miscellaneous	162

In the towns and villages throughout South Africa Natives were employed in domestic and manual work. Anthony Trollope, who has vividly described his travels in South Africa during 1878, remarked that throughout the country Natives and Coloured people appeared to do all the manual work. Describing his observations in a small town in the Orange Free State, he wrote:

In regard to the question of work, I found that in the Free State, as in all the other provinces and districts of the country, so much of its work as is done for wages is invariably done by coloured people. . . .
I had little else to do and watched the while that I was there—but I did not see a single white man at work. I heard their voices—some Dutch, though chiefly English; but the voices were the voices of masters and not men. Then I walked round the place with the object of seeing, and nowhere could I find a white man working as a labourer, and yet the Orange Free State is supposed to be the one South African territory from which the black man has been expelled. The independent black man who owned land has been expelled—but the working black man has taken his place, allured by wages and diet.[1]

At this time wages in the towns, particularly the ports, were much higher than those which had previously been paid on farms. In Port Elizabeth the usual rate for Natives doing hard manual

[1] A. Trollope, op. cit., Vol. II, pp. 239, 240.

work was three shillings a day. Between 1867 and 1884 the ruling rate at the Capetown docks, for Coloured labourers and such Natives as were employed, was also three shillings a day. Thereafter, between 1884 and 1896, three rates, of thirty, forty, and fifty shillings a month were paid, with free quarters and rations,[1] the rate presumably depending upon the nature of the work.

In Capetown one firm which used Native labour obtained it through a chief in the Transkei, who sent his own sons to accompany the labourers dispatched. In towns nearer the Native territories it would appear that Natives found employment without the intervention of agents. Many Natives preferred to seek work in the towns where cash wages were higher, hours of work shorter, and life freer than on the farms.[2]

In Natal the increasing tendency of the Natives to go to the towns to seek daily work, which could be obtained at much higher rates than those customary for monthly or yearly engagements,[3] led to the institution of a system of registering daily labourers, or 'togt' men, as they were called. A proclamation issued in 1874 provided that no Native was to remain within the Boroughs of Pietermaritzburg or of Durban for more than five days unless he was the proprietor or renter of a house or land or in the employ of such a proprietor or renter, or unless he was a duly registered 'togt' man, or day labourer. Such a labourer had to pay a fee of two shillings and sixpence a month in advance, for the 'privilege' of wearing a 'togt' badge. He was required, if unemployed, to work at the current rate of pay for any householder who might demand his services. Magistrates were required to state the minimum wages for different types of work 'upon the offer of which the labourer shall be bound to work'.[4] This proclamation remained in force until 1902, when it was superseded by an Act empowering boroughs to make by-laws regulating the conditions under which 'togt' labourers might live in towns.

The period for which Natives would work in towns varied considerably. Some would take service for a few months, but in many towns some of the Native workers were already becoming permanent residents.

C. NATIVE LABOUR FOR FARMING

The rise of Kimberley stimulated farming over a very large

[1] *South African Native Affairs Commission*, 1903–5, Vol. V, pp. 10, 11. Report of N. Adams Lowe, Superintendent of the Native Location, Table Bay Harbour Board.
[2] G. 3, 1884, op. cit., p. 54.
[3] *Natal Government Gazette*, 1874, p. 152. Extract from memorandum by the Secretary for Native Affairs.
[4] Ibid., p. 15. Proclamation, 27 March, 1874.

area of South Africa, at a time when wool production and ostrich-breeding were also proving themselves to be profitable farming operations. Before the discovery of diamonds, farming had provided the only important field of employment for Native labour. Wherever European farmers had settled in regions with a Native population they had sought to employ some of the Natives on their farms and in their houses. But, except in the western districts of the Cape Colony and in the coastal belt of Natal, the demand for labour had been diffuse. Each European farmer had required simply the continuous services of a very limited number of labourers to tend the sheep and cattle and for domestic work. For the rest the demand for labour was seasonal. Field-workers were required for ploughing and harvesting and sometimes for cleaning the growing crops, but the amount of cultivation on most European farms was very small, agricultural produce usually being grown only for domestic purposes. On the sugar and coffee and tea plantations of Natal, on the grain farms, and in the vineyards of the western districts of the Cape, the more intensive farming involved more labour, both continuously and at the busy seasons.

Throughout most of the country the workers on pastoral farms were hired by the year and paid in stock. In the Transvaal and Orange Free State seasonal labour had previously been obtained through the labour tax, which appears to have developed into the system now known as labour tenancy. Under this system Natives living on land owned by Europeans give unpaid service instead of paying rent. A similar system was also common in Natal, where it was the usual means of obtaining labour in the midland and upper districts.[1] There, however, the period of service was usually longer than in the Republics, six months being the common period, and low cash wages were often paid to the labour tenant while he was working. In the Cape Colony the system of labour tenancy appears to have been less general, one reason no doubt being that relatively fewer Natives lived on European farms. The eastern districts of the Cape Colony drew both seasonal and more permanent labourers from the locations within the Colony and even from Basutoland. When continuous field labour was required it was not generally supplied by Natives. In the western districts the Cape Coloured population supplied the bulk of the farm labour, both seasonal and continuous. In Natal the demand for field-workers for the plantations was met by importing indentured Indian labourers to supplement Native labour. To obtain Native labour for such work as clearing bush, colonists sometimes

[1] *Natal Blue Book*, 1876, JJ., p. 12; 1883, GG., p. 19; 1884, B., pp. 17, 29; 1886, B., p. 17.

had resort to recruiting through the chiefs, who were paid from ten to twenty shillings for each man supplied.[1]

Within a few years of the rise of Kimberley the price of trek-oxen suitable for transport-riding rose from five or six pounds to sixteen, and as a result cattle-breeding became very profitable.[2] The price of sheep, both for slaughter and breeding also rose, fat 'hamels' (wethers) and well-bred stock ewes selling in 1875 for seventeen shillings each, whereas three or four years previously they had been worth only eight shillings and sixpence. Nevertheless, meat was relatively cheap on the diamond diggings; beef and mutton sold at fourpence or fivepence a pound.

Vegetables, on the other hand, fetched fabulous prices on the Kimberley and Dutoitspan markets. In 1870 cabbages sometimes sold at as much as ten shillings each, and in 1871 they sold readily for two shillings and sixpence each. Potatoes were sixpence a pound or more, rice and sugar ninepence a pound. Other vegetables were almost as expensive.[3] Maize was also much in demand at the diggings, for it was the staple diet of the Native labourers, while wheat was wanted by the European diggers. Grain was supplied by the European farmers of the Orange Free State, and, to a limited extent, by those of the Western Transvaal, by the Natives of Basutoland, by farmers from the Cape Colony, and by importation from abroad.

The demand for transport also induced many farmers to engage in the carrying trade, and transport-riding became a sideline or the main occupation of many of them.[4]

At the same time that the demand for farm produce was rising as a result of the new markets dependent upon the production of diamonds, other causes were leading to a revival in demand after the depression of the 'sixties. In Natal in 1869, after an interval of four or five years, but before there can have been much reaction from the diamond discoveries, sugar planters and farmers were sufficiently confident of the future to renew their petitions for Native and Indian labour.

The rise in the price of farm produce led to a rise in costs. The supply of labour presented the greatest problem to the European farmers who wanted to increase production. Many of the developments which were causing the prices of farm produce to rise were also resulting in a demand for labour in other

---

[1] Ibid., 1881, GG., p. 58; 1883, GG., p. 46.   [2] J. Noble, op. cit., p. 273.
[3] C. A. Payton, op. cit., pp. 152, 197.
[4] In 1875 Noble wrote: 'Many or nearly all of the farmers in the Zuurberg district are not only cattle breeders but "kurveyors" (transport riders), and have always some wagons on the road. A span consists of 16 oxen, so that a few wagons take a hundred head, counting supernumeraries. Some men we know have thus employed 500 oxen.'—op. cit., pp. 272-3.

occupations. New opportunities were available to the Natives, both as labourers under European supervision and as independent suppliers of produce and such services as transport. At the diamond diggings, in the towns, and on the public works higher wages were being offered than those customary on farms. At the same time, other conditions were often more attractive. For pastoral work farmers required continuous service and, as we have seen, in many areas such workers had been hired by the year. After 1870, in a few months at the diggings, in the towns, or on some of the public works, Natives could earn as much as they had previously been paid for a year's service. Moreover, in the 'seventies the desire to acquire guns was an important incentive, causing Natives to go out to work for Europeans, and guns could be acquired more easily by service there than on farms, where wages were often paid in stock. The taste for European liquor was also spreading among the Natives of the eastern Cape Colony, and is reported to have led some Natives to prefer service in the towns and on the public works, where drink was more easily obtained and less supervision exercised. Hours of work, too, were usually longer on the farms, where labourers were required to work from sunrise to sunset. All these factors led many Natives to prefer the alternatives which were now available to continuous work on the farms.

Where farmers required seasonal labour for shearing and reaping they did not experience so much difficulty in obtaining it,[1] at least in the Cape, where the rate of pay rose. In the midland and upper districts of Natal, where labour tenants had usually provided the farm labour, young Natives began to find life in the towns and at the diamond-fields more attractive than working for their fathers' landlords. Complaints about the lack of parental discipline and the failure of young Natives to fulfil their labour obligations began to be heard.[2]

In the 'seventies the complaints about the scarcity of Native labour which were common throughout South Africa were particularly clamorous in the Cape Colony and Natal.[3] In the coastal

[1] (Cape) *Blue Book on Native Affairs*, G. 21, 1875, p. 41.
[2] *Natal Blue Book*, 1883, GG., p. 19.; 1886, B., p. 17.
[3] In 1875 a writer in the *Cape Monthly Magazine* declared that 'the only platform upon which all stand agreed is this, that the prosperity of the country is retarded for want of a sufficient supply of labour, and that something ought to be done to remedy the evil.' ('Native Labour and Labour Policy,' p. 1).
In 1878 farmers in the South African Republic complained to Anthony Trollope of the scarcity of labour which, they said, combined with the lack of transport to make unprofitable the production of agricultural products for sale. Trollope, op. cit., Vol. II, p. 109.
In 1875 Noble wrote, 'There are localities in the colony where anything will grow, if it gets plenty of *water*; and with water we may grow anything if we have *labour*. These are the great requirements of the country.'—op. cit., p. 292.

colonies the competition of employers in the towns and on the public works led to a rise in the price of labour. But there were wide regional disparities in the change in wages. The rise in wages was greatest in the neighbourhood of those towns and public works in which the new demand was greatest and which were farthest from the supply. Wages for daily-paid and seasonal work appear to have risen more than those for more permanent workers. Thus, in the western districts of the Cape Colony, 'permanent agricultural labourers of the Coloured class' received from fifteen to twenty shillings a month, with food and quarters, and garden lots to cultivate; occasional labourers, during the harvest and vintage season, were sometimes paid as much as three shillings and sixpence a day, with an allowance of wine in addition.[1]

In the neighbourhood of Port Elizabeth, also, the wage-rates on farms appear to have risen. In 1885 the Civil Commissioner of the division reported that Natives made good reapers, woodcutters, and wagon-drivers and received wages of from two to three shillings a day, or one pound a month, with rations and the right of grazing a few cattle.[2] In the neighbouring district of Alexandria, however, the Inspector of Locations reported that many farmers paid their Native labourers simply by ploughing and sowing the land allotted to them. Where money wages were paid they averaged from ten to fifteen shillings a month.[3] At this time the wages of one pound a month and rations, which the Government proposed should be the rate for labourers obtained through the official agency at Kingwilliamstown, were considered very liberal. At harvest-time, however, reapers paid by the day received from one to two shillings with rations in addition.[4]

In the north-western districts of the Cape Colony, wages do not appear to have risen. In 1881, for example, the Special Magistrate at Kenhardt reported that shepherds received ten shillings a month or a goat ewe, cast-off clothing, a 'not illiberal ration of meat', and a little bread and coffee. Their wives and children were generally required to work at the farmer's homestead.[5] The servants attracted by these terms were unsatisfactory, but, according to the Magistrate, the farmers were 'quite unable or unwilling to pay such wages as would induce good men to serve them well'.[6]

In fact, the complaints of the scarcity of labour arose largely

---

[1] J. Noble, op. cit., p. 293; Select Committee on the Supply of the Labour Market, 1879, p. 21.
[2] G. 22, 1882, p. 51.
[3] (Cape) Blue Book on Native Affairs, G. 5, 1886, p. 7.
[4] J. Noble, op. cit., p. 293; (Cape) Blue Book on Native Affairs, G. 3, 1884, ɔ. 7 (Inspector of Locations, Alexandria).
[5] G. 20, 1881, p. 8.   [6] Ibid.

from the general unwillingness of the farmers to raise the wage-rates to which they were accustomed when faced with competition in the labour market. When they were forced to raise them they complained bitterly. The higher wages which in some cases they had to pay in order to obtain labour had their compensations. In 1875 Mr. Rose-Innes reported from Kingwilliamstown that

> 'while the agricultural interests are directly being inconvenienced by this derangement in the labour market, caused by the increased scale of remuneration, fixed by the Government (for the public works), the decrease in crime, and perceptably in stock stealing, may be looked upon, in some measure, as compensating for that inconvenience.'[1]

In Natal, as in the Cape, complaints of the scarcity of labour were widespread, and in many districts wage-rates rose. In 1876 the Resident Magistrate of the district of Unsinga reported that wages had increased

> 'to the furthest limit that the planters can afford, and complaints are made that farm servants receiving their 15s. a month and rations, do much less work than formerly when 7s. was considered a fair wage.'[2]

The rise in wages was fairly general; wages of ten, fifteen, and even thirty shillings a month being reported to be common.[3] In the upper districts complaints were not so much concerned with the tendency of wages to rise as with the failure of labour tenants to provide the labour expected of them. In some cases money rentals were substituted for labour tenancy. As early as 1876 the Resident Magistrate of the Upper Unkomanzi district reported:

> Large rents are now paid by some Natives in this Division, in some instances as much as £5 per hut; but owing to high prices for produce, and high wages, they do not seem to object to this high rent in favourite localities, provided they are not called upon to furnish labour to the landowners.[4]

and in 1880 we hear from Ixopo that:

> Labour has been, and still is, scarce, many of the Native tenants preferring to pay high rents rather than compel their sons to work. Now that a District Surgeon has been appointed, a number of the farmers intend importing Coolie labour. The annual average rent charged to Natives on private property is about 30s. to 40s. per hut though I have heard of one or two farmers charging £5.[5]

---

[1] G. 21, 1875, p. 41 (J. Rose-Innes, Civil Commissioner, Kingwilliamstown Division).

[2] *Natal Blue Book*, 1876, JJ., p. 11.

[3] Secretary for Native Affairs, 26, No. 125, quoted Axelson, op. cit., p. 107

[4] *Natal Blue Book*, 1876, JJ., p. 13.

[5] Ibid., 1880, JJ., p. 117 (R.M. Ixopo), cf. ibid., p. 109 (R.M. Unvoti) p. 112 (R.M. Weenen).

In Natal the Zulu war of 1878–9 further upset the labour market. Both Europeans and Natives were required to render service.[1] The high rates the Natives were paid, together with the money they obtained from hiring out their wagons and selling their cattle to the military authorities, made them unwilling to work for the farmers and planters while the money lasted.[2]

D. WILLINGNESS TO WORK

The development of diamond production led to a rise in the demand for the produce of Native as well as European farmers, which was augmented by the independent revival in the demand for export products such as wool which Natives also produced. In addition, new opportunities arose for Natives to become independent entrepreneurs, particularly transport-riders. By themselves, such new opportunities would have tended to reduce the supply of Native labour offering for work under European supervision. But at the same time opportunities for employment under European supervision became more varied and attractive. For both reasons direct incentive to Natives to increase their productivity was now much greater than hitherto.

The effect on the supply of labour depended on the relative attraction of the new opportunities and also on the ability and willingness of individual Natives to seek additional income. Changes in wage-rates may affect both ability and willingness to work. A rise in wage-rates may increase or decrease ability according to the extent to which it affects the habits of particular people. In South Africa, where higher wages took the form of better rations and better living conditions, they probably increased ability to work. On the other hand, where drink was easily obtainable and freely taken the new opportunities may have reduced it.

The effect of an increase in the wage-rate on willingness to work is more complex. The response depends on whether under the new conditions the individual wishes simply to maintain his former standard of life or to increase his income. In the former case the amount of labour he is prepared to supply will certainly decrease, for at the higher wage-rate the same income can be obtained for less labour. If he seeks to increase his income, the effect on the supply of labour will depend on the extent to which he seeks to do this, that is, on whether he is prepared to work more under the new conditions or not. The total supply might increase, remain constant, or even decrease.

[1] Between Dec. 1878 and Oct. 1879, 2,500 Natives were called out and supplied to the military authorities for transport service. *Parl. Papers*, 1880, LI C. 2676] p. 18. Further correspondence *re* Affairs of S.A.
[2] *Natal Blue Book*, 1879, JJ., pp. 5, 7, 9, 12.

In the period following the discovery of diamonds, wage-rates in South Africa increased and the prices of Native produce rose, that is, the terms on which Natives could sell their produce and services improved. At the same time new incentives arose and increased pressure was applied to Natives to sell their produce and their labour. In the first place, they were acquiring new wants which could be satisfied only through exchange. Secondly, new obligations were being enforced upon them by the governing authorities. The smallness of individual land-holdings, lack of capital, and failure generally to adopt more productive techniques continued to restrict their efforts as independent producers and to force them out to work under European supervision.

On balance the net effect of the interaction of these different forces was to cause an increase in the supply of Native labour. During the 'seventies, there were undoubtedly in South Africa more Natives working under European supervision than in any previous decade. There may have been some transfer of Natives from work on farms to other occupations, but, since there was also an increase in the supply of Native labourers, it is very doubtful whether, in spite of complaints of 'labour shortage', farmers employed fewer Native workers in the 'seventies than before. In some cases, it is true, they had to pay higher wages.

(i) The Response to New Opportunities as Independent Producers

There is fairly convincing evidence that the trade in Native produce increased in response to the more favourable terms on which they could dispose of their produce. In the Cape Colony, Kingwilliamstown and Queenstown were the centres for trading with Natives within and beyond the frontier. These towns were also, it is true, on the most easterly route to the diamond-fields. Their rapid growth cannot, however, be attributed to the latter cause alone, for the produce was not all of a kind wanted by the diggers. By 1875 Kingwilliamstown was the fourth town in the Colony in size and had a population of five thousand. Between 1865 and 1875 the population of Queenstown nearly doubled.[1]

The purchasing power of the Natives served by these centres was estimated to be not less than £400 thousand a year.[2] They produced wool, angora hair, hides, horns, goat and sheepskins, tobacco, and cattle, valued at three-quarters of a million,[3] and exchanged what they did not consume. Wool was the staple commercial product of the Fingo, Thembu, and Xhosa; and,

---

[1] Population of Kingwilliamstown, 1875, 5,169 (1865, no return—Kingwilliamstown was not then within the Colony); population of Queenstown, 1865, 1,225; 1875, 2,320. Census of 1875, G. 42, 1876, p. 9.
[2] J. Noble, op. cit., p. 231.   [3] Ibid., p. 231.

in some parts, cattle were beginning to give place to sheep.[1]   In
the Herschel district 'a great deal of grain' was raised and sold,
while it was estimated that in 1874 the Basuto supplied three
hundred thousand bushels of grain to the Orange Free State and
Diamond Fields.   The Gcaleka and Pondo produced and exchanged 'considerable quantities' of leaf tobacco, while the Pondo
near the St. John's River carried on 'a large trade in cattle', taking
blankets and other articles in exchange.[2]

In Natal, too, the Natives sold what produce they could, but
their ability to increase their incomes in this way was largely
dependent upon their proximity to towns.   In 1880 the Magistrate
of the division in which Pietermaritzburg was situated reported
that the supply of labour from Native sources 'has year by year
become more inadequate, as the Natives become richer, and yearly
cultivate a larger acreage with the plough, besides engaging in
transport-riding on their own account'.[3]

Native women would travel long distances on foot to offer fowls,
eggs, and milk to the European colonists.   Yet the amount of
Native produce sold or bartered in Natal cannot have been great.
In the Cape the staple article produced for exchange was wool.
In Natal, in 1884, it was estimated that the number of wool-
bearing sheep owned by Natives was only six hundred.[4]   Moreover, in the upper districts, the only products of even the European
farms which were marketable, on account of the cost of transport,
were wool and crude butter.[5]   Many of the Natal Natives lived
in reserves and on farms in remote and inaccessible areas where
they could not have increased their incomes to any extent by the
sale of produce.

The occupations and numbers in which Natives succeeded as
independent entrepreneurs were very limited.   They appear to
have been most successful as independent transport-riders.   Those
who became traders were so successful as to evoke comment.[6]   In
1880, in the Cape Colony, it was reported that Native transport-

---

[1] (Cape) *Blue Book on Native Affairs*, G. 21, 1875, pp. 36, 60–3.

[2] J. Noble, op. cit., pp. 230, 231.   In 1874 the Fingo 'agent' reported that there
were 45 trading stations in Fingoland (the area to which Fingo had migrated
from the Colony in 1858 and 1864) and he estimated that the value of the
import and export trade was at least £150,000.   Ibid., G. 21, 1875, p. 33.

[3] *Natal Blue Book*, 1880, JJ., p. 89 (R.M. Umgeni Division); cf. idem., 1881,
GG., p. 37.

[4] W. Peace, *Our Colony of Natal*, 1883, p. 58.

[5] 'On remote farms butter and wool . . . have remained almost the only
produce that is capable of transport in the conditions of the colony.   It still
continues to be a pressing and interesting problem, how best some additional
remunerative industries may be found for up-country settlers who are far away
from the advantages of ready markets.'   H. Brooks, *Natal*, etc. (1876), p. 289.

[6] Thus the census report of 1875 calls attention to the fact that one Fingo
described himself as a merchant, while several shopkeepers and traders were
returned as belonging to the 'aboriginal races'.   Census 1875, G. 42, 1876, p. 20.

riders had in their hands the bulk of the carrying trade of the Transkei.[1] In the neighbourhood of Aliwal North, Natives also acted as transport-riders, and some owned wagons and spans of ten or twelve oxen.[2] Natives from Tembuland, in the intervals between farming operations, engaged in transport-riding and even, it is reported, bought timber which they took to the upper (north-eastern) districts of the Cape Colony and the Orange Free State, where they sold it at a profit.[3] In Basutoland all the mail con-tractors were Natives. In Natal it was 'the daily custom of merchants and farmers alike to entrust to them waggons and oxen laden with loads of merchandise of all kinds, including both food and drinks', and theft or misappropriation of goods was rare.[4]

(ii) The Effect of the Emergence of New Wants

The increase in trade involved new opportunities to buy European goods as well as to sell Native produce, and the oppor-tunities were taken. To what extent this was due to the fact that such goods could be obtained on more favourable terms or to an increased willingness to work originating in the emergence of new wants cannot be determined.

We have seen how Natives went to Kimberley first to acquire articles such as knives and brass-wire, and, later, guns. The desire to acquire guns played its part in inducing Natives to go to the Cape public works, but there were also many other important incentives. During this period, in the Cape Colony and the Native territories east of the Kei River, the use of European clothes, ploughs, wagons, saddles, and household utensils spread rapidly.[5] Coffee, sugar, salt, and candles were in use in most kraals. Even those least influenced by European customs discarded karosses in favour of blankets and acquired such articles as beads, brass-wire, chains, red ochre, arm-rings, and ear-rings.[6] In the early 'seven-ties Noble estimated that sixty thousand blankets were disposed of in the course of a year at Kingwilliamstown.[7] By 1876 the sale of blankets there was diminishing and giving place to the sale of European clothing.[8] The increase in the consumption of European liquor and the

---

[1] (Cape) Blue Book on Native Affairs, G. 13, 1880, p. 153.
[2] Ibid., G. 21, 1875, p. 50.   [3] Ibid., G. 13, 1880, p. 134.
[4] W. Peace, op. cit., p. 49.
[5] E. Glanville, 'The Industrial Progress of the Natives of South Africa.' Society of Arts, 1876, pp. 448–56; (Cape) Blue Book on Native Affairs, G. 27, 1874, pp. 31, 35, 42, 44; G. 21, 1875, pp. 33, 36, 37, 38, 41; G. 12, 1877, p. 114; G. 33, 1879, p. 59; G. 13, 1880, p. 136.
[6] J. Noble, op. cit., p. 230; (Cape) Blue Book on Native Affairs, G. 33, 1879, p. 119 (British Resident, Pondoland).
[7] J. Noble, op. cit., p. 230.
[8] (Cape) Blue Book on Native Affairs, G. 12, 1877, p. 114.

drunkenness which resulted were matters of concern to Native administrators. In the 'seventies and early 'eighties many officials in the eastern districts of the Colony and in the territories east of the Kei River reported that drunkenness among Natives was increasing, and that a growing number 'squandered' their money on drink and became demoralized.[1]

The new wants were not limited to European commodities. Officials remarked upon an increasing desire to obtain European education for their children and a new readiness to pay for it.[2] As early as 1871 the Fingo, who were living east of the Kei River, themselves subscribed nearly fifteen hundred pounds to establish in Fingoland a school and industrial institution similar to Lovedale.

Methods of cultivation changed rapidly, the plough supplanting the Native hoe. In 1874 the Civil Commissioner of the Kingwilliamstown Division reported that there the Native hoe had been 'entirely superseded by the plough'.[3] By 1878 the same report was made as far to the east as the Umzimkulu district of Griqualand East.[4] Native ploughing was, however, 'very rude'.[5]

The use of the plough made the cultivation of larger areas more practicable. Partly, perhaps, on this account, but no doubt also because of the new opportunities for the disposal of produce, there were reports of Natives beginning to buy and lease land.[6] Their need to go out to work was clearly reduced by that development.

In Natal the introduction of European goods was slower. In 1881 the Magistrate of the Klip River Division, the most northerly in the Colony, reported of the Natives:

> 'Civilization among them is advancing, a large portion having taken to dress, and when mounted, which is becoming the mode of travelling, delight in appearing in gay-coloured clothing. The use of farming implements (especially the plough, which is taking the place of the primitive "pick") is coming into favour; several now possess wagons and valuable teams of oxen, which are used for "transport" purposes.'[7]

[1] Ibid., G. 27, 1874, p. 16; G. 21, 1875, p. 40 (Civil Commissioner, East London), p. 55 (Acting Civil Commissioner, Fort Beaufort); G. 3, 1884, p. 31 (Special Magistrate, Kingwilliamstown); p. 40 (Civil Commissioner and Resident Magistrate, Komgha); p. 120 (Resident Magistrate, Cala, Tembuland).
[2] Ibid., G. 33, 1879, p. 38.   [3] Ibid., G. 27, 1874, p. 13.
[4] Ibid., G. 33, 1879, p. 38 (Resident Magistrate, Umzimkulu, Griqualand East).
[5] Ibid., G. 13, 1884, p. 30 (Civil Commissioner, Kingwilliamstown).
[6] Ibid., G. 21, 1875, p. 41; G. 33, 1879, pp. 38, 95.
[7] *Natal Blue Book*, 1881, GG., p. 37. At this time the Natal Native Affairs Commission, 1881–2, reported: 'We are satisfied that the Natives have made some progress towards civilization during the last thirty-five years. This is shown in the success or influence of missionary settlements, in the acquirement of property, both immovable and movable, in the greatly increased wearing of clothing, in the use of ploughs and wagons, in the diminution of forced marriages of girls, and in the more extensive purchase of manufactured goods. Among

In Basutoland also the Natives were acquiring and using European goods, such as guns, clothing, sugar, and tea, while in Bechuanaland cattle, grain, ostrich feathers, and karosses were traded for European goods.[1]

The Natives to the north and east of the South African Republic were less touched by European influences, but even there many of them had visited the diamond-fields, and guns, at least, were a common possession.[2]

To obtain European goods the Natives had to sell either their produce or their labour. The extent to which they could satisfy their wants by the sale of produce was limited by the scarcity of land, the system of land tenure, and their lack of capital equipment and of knowledge of more productive agricultural technique. Transport facilities, too, were few and uncertain. The new railways did not pass through the Native territories and the roads in these areas, almost to this day, have been rough tracks crossed by dongas and washed away in summer by frequent rain-storms.

The increased crowding of the Natives was commented on by many administrative officials.[3] In some cases it was caused by European occupation of land previously occupied by Natives. Thus, in 1883, the Civil Commissioner of Queenstown reported that during the previous five years Crown land in the division had been cleared of 'rebels' and sold, with the result that 'the Natives are much more closely packed than I remember ever before to have seen them in a twenty-five years experience',[4] and he added:

'It is all very well to say that they should go out and work for the Colonists; so they should, but they do not see it in this light, and love their homes as much and as dearly as Europeans.'[5]

the last, no doubt we have to regret the increased consumption of ardent spirits.'
   In 1884 the Native population of Natal was estimated to number 375,000, and they were said to possess: ploughs, 6,103; harrows, 153; wagons, 723; carts, 213; Peace, op. cit., p. 58.
   [1] In 1880 it was estimated that the annual value of wagons and soft goods coming from the Colony was £50,000 (exports, valued at £100,000, were cattle, cereals, ostrich feathers, and karosses). The total population was about 67,500 and the Natives owned some four hundred wagons. Memorandum by Captain Harrell, 27 April, 1880. *Parl. Papers*, 1883, LXIX, p. 180 et seq., quoted J. A. I. Agar-Hamilton, *The Road to the North*, p. 159.
   [2] A. Aylward, op. cit., p. 142; Morton, op. cit., p. 15.
   [3] For example, in 1873 it was reported from Victoria East that in 1867 there had been a large migration to the Transkei, but that the population was already nearly as large as before the exodus. (Cape) *Blue Book on Native Affairs*, G. 27, 1874, p. 3; G. 21, 1875, pp. 35, 59. ('Agent' with Kreli.)
   [4] Ibid., G. 2, 1883, p. 13.
   [5] Ibid., p. 15. A writer in the *Cape Monthly Magazine* (1875) said that this attitude of the Europeans restricted the supply of Native labour, for the 'Natives realize many whites think they ought to be compelled to work, and this prevents their coming forward readily.' ('Native Labour and Labour Policy,' p. 5.)

During this period the Cape Colony annexed Fingoland and Griqualand East (1879), Port St. Johns, Gcalekaland, Tembuland, and Bomvanaland (1884–6). These annexations were undertaken largely for administrative reasons and only in a few instances resulted in European occupation. After the insurrection of 1880 Europeans were allotted certain land in the districts of Xalanga, Tsolo, Maclear, and Matatiele. European villages have also been established throughout these territories at the centres of the magistracies, and European traders have been allowed to occupy trading sites and lease a limited quantity of land. With these exceptions the Natives have continued to occupy the Transkeian Territories.

Some of the complaints of the increasing scarcity of land were no doubt due to the fact that new opportunities had arisen for using it to advantage. There are no statistics available to show whether there was an actual increase in the Bantu population of South Africa or even in the numbers of the south-eastern group of the Bantu, those who lived within and on the borders of the Cape Colony and Natal. The first census within the Transkeian Territories was not taken until 1891, and, even then, Pondoland was not included, for it was not annexed until 1894.

Natives both bought and leased land within the Cape Colony, and, in spite of official prohibition, migrated to the less crowded territories. In many cases the Natives who bought and leased land set up as farmers and were quite successful. But where they moved off eastwards (many went from Basutoland, the Herschel Reserve, and Fingoland to Griqualand East) they moved away from the colonial and Kimberley markets. The only marketable products of the more distant parts of the Native territories were cattle, wool, hides, and skins. To supplement their incomes and obtain money, these Natives had to a large extent to go out to work. Moreover, the less crowded areas filled up rapidly.[1]

[1] In 1886 the Chief Magistrate of Griqualand East, which had hitherto been the Mecca of the landless, wrote: 'East Griqualand during the past year has suffered least of the three territories from drought and consequent scarcity of food. It is also not so thickly populated as the Transkei and Tembuland, and there is thus more grazing ground available and the quantity of stock owned by each individual is relatively larger. But notwithstanding the restrictions placed upon natives from the Colony and other territories there has been a continual stream pouring in throughout the year, Fingoes being the most numerous immigrants, and in spite of every effort being or to be made a few years more will probably find East Griqualand in the same state as Fingoland, parts of Tembuland, and the locations in the Colony, and have a superabundant population without further room for it to spread into.
'Hitherto the conditions have been favourable to rapid increase in the native tribes. There has always been land available for them to colonize and enable them to continue their natural semi-pastoral life. These conditions are now fast changing. The last of the vacant land is taken up, and the real struggle for

The Natives in Natal were probably less crowded than in the Cape, but, on the other hand, opportunities for selling produce were fewer. According to the Lieutenant-Governor, the Natives were land-holders and producers and their production was gradually increasing, but not

> to such an extent as to prevent their supplying from among them to the colonists a very large body of labourers for wages.

Moreover, he reported that the location lands within the Colony were

> here and there already becoming crowded. Pressure to work for wages is from this and other causes falling ever more and more upon the natives in the colony.[1]

E. OFFICIAL MEASURES TENDING TO INCREASE THE SUPPLY OF LABOUR

To supplement these forces, which were in any case tending on balance to increase the supply of Native labour, the Governments of the Cape Colony, Natal, and the Republics adopted various other measures. Some were deliberately designed, in part or in whole, to increase the supply of labour, in other cases the effect may have been incidental. Three types of measure call for special notice: the imposition of taxation, the subdivision and issue of individual title deeds to land, and the promotion of immigration.

(i) Taxation

Between 1870 and 1886 there were important and significant changes in both the amount and the nature of the taxes levied upon the Natives of South Africa. Taxes were imposed and collected as European control was extended to new areas, notably to the Transkeian Territories, and as administration became more effective in the Orange Free State and the South African Republic. In the latter States, the increase in the circulation of goods and money made it possible for the Governments to levy taxes in money in place of the labour tax, where previously it would have been impracticable. Natives living on privately owned land (nearly all the land in the Republics was by this time owned by

existence between the different tribes themselves, and again between the natives as a whole and the Europeans may be said to have commenced.
'The native can no longer pack up his few household goods and start off to "fresh fields and pastures new" when he finds himself too closely surrounded by neighbours, and he must either accommodate himself to his changed surroundings and become more of an agriculturist and acquire handicrafts, or he must disappear. . . .' (Cape) *Blue Book on Native Affairs*, G. 5, 1886, p. 90.
[1] *Natal Government Gazette*, 24 June, 1871. Lieutenant-Governor Keate to Lord Kimberley (No. 88).

the Europeans) were, however, still required to work for their landlords during a part of the year in return for their right to occupy the land.

Taxes were levied for different reasons. Some were imposed in order to pay the costs of administration in Native reserves and locations; some because it was felt that the Natives ought to contribute directly to the general revenue; and some with the definite object of forcing the Natives to work for Europeans. For whatever purpose it was levied, the extension and increase in taxation had the effect of increasing the number of Natives working for Europeans.

Some of the changes in Native taxation did not discriminate between Natives in different occupations. Thus, in Natal, in 1870, the registration of Native marriages was made compulsory and a registration fee of five pounds imposed. Five years later this tax was repealed, but the hut tax was raised from seven shillings to fourteen shillings, and it was made applicable to all Native huts. Only 'houses of European construction inhabited by Natives having only one wife and otherwise conforming to civilized usages' were exempt from the tax.[1] This meant that Natives living on the farms on which they were employed were no longer exempt from the hut tax.

In the Orange Free State all 'coloured' persons (a term which there was used to include Natives) working on public diamond diggings or employed in digging for gold, or other precious metals, were required to register and pay a fee of one shilling a month.[2] Outside public diggings a poll tax of ten shillings a year was levied on every 'coloured' adult male between the ages of eighteen and seventy.[3]

Such other direct taxation of Natives as there was in Natal and the Orange Free State, and most of the taxation in the Cape Colony and the South African Republic was closely connected with the occupation of land. To understand the systems of taxation adopted and to appreciate their effects, it is necessary to realize the differences in status of Natives occupying land in the various parts of South Africa. Then, as now, many Natives lived in Native reserves, or, as they were then more generally called, Native locations, which had been set aside for their especial use. In such reserves the land was usually occupied in some more or less modified form of tribal tenure.

---

[1] Law No. 13, 1875.
[2] Where hospitals had been established for their benefit 'coloured' persons employed in mining were required to contribute one shilling a month towards the upkeep; if working in other capacities 6d. a month. Oranje Vrystaat Wetboek, 1854–91. Chap. LXX.
[3] Ibid., Chap. LXXI.

A few Natives lived on land which they had purchased either individually or in common with others. They also lived, in large numbers, on unalienated Crown land, and on farms owned by Europeans, while the number living in or on the outskirts of towns and villages was increasing.

In the Native reserves in the Cape Colony and Natal a hut tax of ten and seven shillings respectively had usually been imposed at the time when each reserve was established. In Basutoland, too, a hut tax of ten shillings had been levied soon after its annexation. These taxes had been originally levied to pay the costs of administration, but, as we have seen, in Natal taxation soon came to be looked upon as a lever which might be used to force the Natives out to work for the European colonists. In the Orange Free State, a hut tax of ten shillings was levied in the most important of the three small reserves within the Republic. In the South African Republic no reserves were set aside for Natives before 1880;[1] thereafter some reserves were set aside, but this did not noticeably affect the taxation system.

Natives living on land which they had purchased were not subject to special taxation.

Natives living on unalienated Crown land were mostly to be found in Natal and the Cape Colony, for in the Republics the European burghers had acquired practically all the land. During this period the fact that Natives had been allowed to remain or to settle on Crown land was much criticized, particularly in Natal, on the ground that it reduced the supply of labour and the number of tenants seeking to hire privately owned land; and, further, that the insecurity of tenure on Crown land was a danger, since evictions might lead to unrest.[2] In many cases 'squatters',[3] as these Natives were called, had no legal right to occupy the land on which they lived, although often they had been in occupation before it had been appropriated.

In 1873, in Natal, a Select Committee appointed to consider 'by what means the supply of labour from within the Colony might be increased' had recommended that Natives squatting on Crown land should be charged a rent.[4] The Natal Native

[1] *Natives Land Commission* (Beaumont Minute), U.G., 25, 1916, para. 12.

[2] *Natal Native Affairs Commission*, 1881-2, para. 30: 'We greatly regret that squatting on Crown lands without rent being demanded was ever allowed by the Government. The mischiefs are manifold, such as lessening the supply of labour for farms, unfairness towards private owners wishing to procure native tenants, and danger to be feared in consequence of eviction. We do not, however, see why these evils should not at once be corrected by rents being now imposed. . . . We think that the rent to be charged should be the average rent of the neighbourhood under similar circumstances.'

[3] The term 'squatter' was generally applied to Natives living on Crown land, to Natives renting European-owned land, and often also to labour tenants.

[4] *Natal Legislative Council, Sessional Papers*, 1873, No. 21.

Commission of 1881-2 repeated this recommendation, and in 1884 it was adopted, a charge of one pound per hut in addition to the ordinary hut tax being levied on all Natives living on Crown land.[1] It is reported that it applied to about six thousand huts.[2]

In the Cape Colony it was considered desirable to exercise more control over groups of Natives living on both Crown and privately owned land. For this purpose a series of Acts, known as the Location Acts, were passed. The chief object of the earlier Acts appears to have been the prevention of the theft of stock by Natives, but later amendments were designed to discourage, through taxation, the renting of land to Natives. In 1869 a tax of ten shillings a hut had been levied on huts on Crown land occupied by Natives. In 1876 provision was made for the appointment of officials to supervise Native 'locations'[3] of more than one hundred huts on Crown land. To defray part of the expenses in connexion with the control of livestock which was attempted, a graduated tax not exceeding ten shillings per hut was levied in locations for which inspectors were appointed. The Act proved too complicated to function successfully, and in 1884 it was repealed and a uniform tax of ten shillings a hut levied on Natives occupying huts on Crown lands reserved for them.[4]

It was in the case of Natives living on land owned by Europeans that the attempt to influence the distribution of the population by taxation was most marked. At this time, in the South African Republic and the Orange Free State, almost the whole of the Native population lived on such land; in Natal almost half the Native population;[5] in the Cape Colony a much smaller proportion of the Native population lived in this way, but, nevertheless, the

[1] Law 41 of 1884.
[2] *Natal Parliamentary Papers*, 46, No. 57 of 1883.
[3] This Act, No. 6 of 1876, defined a 'native location' as 'any number of huts or dwellings exceeding five within an area of one square mile occupied by any of the native races such as Kafirs, Fingoes, Basutos, Hottentots, Bushmen, and the like, such occupants not being in the *bona fide* employment of the owner of the land upon which such huts or dwellings are situated if the said land is private property, and such huts not being situated within the limits of any municipality.'
[4] Act 37 of 1884. This Act repealed Acts 2 of 1869, and 6 of 1876. It distinguished between a 'Native Location on Private Property' and a 'Native Location on Crown Land'. The latter was defined as follows: 'By Native location on Crown land is meant any number of huts or dwellings occupied by any of the Native races as Kafirs, Fingoes, Basutos, Hottentots, Bushmen, and the like, on certain Crown lands reserved for the purpose of Native Tribes within the Colony, commonly known as Native locations.'
[5] In 1881 it was estimated that the Native population of Natal was 375,000 and was located as follows:

On Locations and other Native Trust Lands	169,800
On Private Lands as Tenants	162,600
On Crown Lands as Squatters	42,600

Natal Native Affairs Commission, 1881-2, p. 35. Appendix G.

numbers were considerable. Natives occupying such land would pay for their right to use it either by working for their landlord for part of each year, or in rent paid either in cash or in kind. Such Natives were often called 'squatters'. Confusion as to the exact meaning of the term,[1] combined with the reluctance of farmers to admit that they permitted 'squatting' on their farms, makes it impossible even to estimate the total or the relative number of Natives living in these different ways.[2] In 1875 the census report stated that of the 'considerable class of byowners' (persons occupying land on the share-farming system) only 77 persons had been returned as such, while 1,314, of whom 50 were Europeans, had been described as squatters.[3]

During this period the systems of labour tenancy, share-farming, and the renting of land to Natives for cash were all severely criticized on the ground that they reduced the supply of labour by keeping Natives, or allowing them to remain, on land where their labour was not used. In some cases, indeed, farmers deliberately kept a reserve of Native labour on their land.

In the Cape Colony the Location Acts were in part designed to prevent this. Thus, the Act of 1876, which imposed a tax on both the landowners and the Natives living in locations on private land, exempted Natives 'in the *bona fide* employment of the owner of the land'. The amended Act of 1884 exempted only Natives in the '*bona fide* and continuous employment of the owner'. A uniform tax of ten shillings a hut was to be paid by the owner of the land. There was, of course, nothing to prevent attempts to pass on the tax. These amendments, in some districts at least, had the effect of reducing the number of Native tenants. It was reported from the Division of East London, for example, that the Location Act of 1884 had been 'strictly enforced', that the tax

[1] For example, the Inspector of Native Locations in the Division of Bathurst distinguished between Natives, 'the majority', who were farmers hiring land at 5s. an acre or farming 'on halves', the share-farming system, and 'squatters' who paid a nominal rent for the waste parts of farms. (Cape) *Blue Book on Native Affairs*, G. 2, 1885, p. 11.

[2] In the Cape Colony in 1865 a Native Affairs Commission had made specific inquiries into the number of squatters on European farms, but few of the farmers who replied to the questionnaire admitted that there were squatters on their land, although they quite frequently reported that there were squatters on their neighbours' farms. Similarly field-cornets reported that there were no squatters in their wards, although they, too, sometimes said that there were squatters in neighbouring field-cornetcies. *Native Affairs Commission*, 1865, Appendix 2.

[3] Census of 1875, op. cit., p. 20.
In 1886 the Civil Commission of Bathurst reported: 'The natives living in this Division are principally located on private property, portions of which are let to them on the halves, or at a fixed annual rent by the proprietors, who are generally speaking, non-residents or absentee landlords.' G. 5, 1886, op. cit., p. 9.

had in most cases been paid by the proprietors, and that very many of them had cleared off their tenants.[1]

In the South African Republic attempts were also made to impose differential taxes, Natives in the employment of the European farmers being exempted or taxed more lightly than the others.[2] At the same time taxes were imposed on Natives passing through the country, with the object of forcing them to take service with the farmers. It was, however, impossible for the Republican authorities to collect these taxes.[3] In 1880 the British administration repealed them and imposed a uniform hut tax of ten shillings which remained in force until 1895.

It is not possible to measure quantitatively the extent to which these various measures diverted Native labour to farm work or increased the total supply. In the Cape Colony the exemption from tax of the huts of Natives in the employment of the owners of the land must have rendered farm work more attractive than it would otherwise have been. It would tend to divert labour to farm work. One reason suggests itself for this exemption. On farms, wages were often paid in stock, by ploughing and sowing for the labourer, or simply by allowing him to cultivate a piece of ground and graze a few animals. Where cash wages were paid they were usually very small and were only a part of the total real wages. Under these circumstances taxation would have caused farm-labourers to leave the farms to earn money to pay their taxes, in the same way that to-day labour tenants have for the most part to leave the farms on which they live to earn what money they require. It has been pointed out above that the imposition of this differential taxation in 1884 led farmers to turn off tenants,[4] whereas previously the number of tenants had been on the increase.[5] In Natal, where in 1875 such differential taxation was abolished, there was a tendency for cash tenancy to be substituted for labour tenancy.

The general effect of taxation was undoubtedly to increase the

[1] G. 12, 1887, op. cit., p. 13.

[2] Parl. Papers, 1877, LX [C. 1748], Transvaal Native Affairs, 1875–6, p. 3. R. Southey, Lieutenant-Governor, Griqualand West, to Sir Henry Barkly.
Parl. Papers, 1880, LI [C. 2584], pp. 101–2. Further correspondence re affairs of South Africa.

[3] Ibid. [C. 2584], pp. 101–2.
Ibid., 1882, XXVIII [C. 3219], p. 23. Royal Commission on Settlement of the Transvaal, ev. Kruger re the enforcement of the tax law No. 3 of 1876. 'Circumstances were not such that the law could clearly be put into operation'. Ibid. [C. 3114], p. 31. It was not until 1879 that the British administration was able to collect taxes from 'the large and hardly manageable native population of the northern districts', and it was unsuccessful in collecting taxes from Mapoch and his subjects. Parl. Papers, 1883, XLIX [C. 3486], Correspondence re Transvaal, 1882–3, p. 4.

[4] G. 12, 1887, op. cit., p. 13.

[5] Select Committee on the Native Location Acts, A. 26, 1883, p. 23.

supply of labour, although in some instances Natives were able to meet taxation from the sale of produce. For example, in Basutoland, provision was made whereby Natives could pay their taxes in produce, which was sent into the Cape Colony and sold, and at the first collection the greater part of the tax was paid in grain, cattle, and goats, and only a small part in money.[1] In other districts where markets were close at hand, as in the district of Glen Grey, in the Ciskei, and in the neighbourhood of Pieter-maritzburg, it was possible for Natives to obtain money to pay taxes by the sale of grain and other agricultural produce.[2] In the more remote districts, however, the export of grain was impossible, because of the lack of transport facilities. Consequently traders would pay in money only for cattle, wool, and hides.[3] The Natives were reluctant to sell their cattle, their traditional and principal store of wealth, and therefore, as opportunities for employment within the Native reserves were few, they went out to work for Europeans to secure money for the payment of taxes. Just after its annexation the magistrate of the Xalanga district in Tembuland reported that:

> In order that money might be obtained to pay hut tax hundreds of young men have been sent into the Colony by their relatives to work in the towns and among the farmers. The frequent recurring necessity of having to find money for their friends will gradually force the young men out of the groove in which they have been living and moving from day to day, and from year to year.[4]

In Natal, too, taxation was met by the sale of both produce and labour, but, as we have seen, opportunities for selling produce were few, while the amount of tax collected was considerable.[5] It must have been met largely through the sale of labour.

[1] G. M. Theal, *History of South Africa since 1795*, Vol. V, 3rd ed., p. 63.

[2] For example in 1888 it was reported from Middledrift in the Ciskei that 'in consequence of this superabundance of grain, and the great scarcity of money, the people cannot obtain cash for their surplus stock, and are obliged to barter it away to the traders for goods. This presses heavily upon the people, who depend principally upon their grain to obtain money to pay their taxes'. G. 6, 1888, op. cit., p. 17.

[3] Ibid., G. 12, 1887, p. 68; G. 4, 1891, p. 37; G. 7, 1892, op. cit., p. 31.

[4] G. 13, 1880, op. cit., p. 135; cf. (Cape) *Blue Book on Native Affairs*, G. 33, 1879, pp. 58–9. Magistrate with Makaula, Mount Frere 'Hut tax': This was not paid as promptly as the first collection owing partly to an order issued by me during the disturbed state of the country, namely: no person was to leave the district for any lengthened period, therefore they were unable to proceed to places where employment was to be had.'

[5] Direct taxes collected from Natives in Natal, 1870 to 1880: 1870, Hut tax, 7s. plus Marriage Fee, £28,000; 1871, ditto, £33,000; 1872, ditto, £38,000; 1873, ditto, £40,000; 1874, ditto, £41,000; 1875, ditto (for six months), £34,000; 1876, Hut tax, 14s., £57,000; 1877, ditto, £59,000; 1878, ditto, £60,000; 1879, ditto, £61,000; 1880, ditto, £63,000. C. Axelson, op. cit., p. 108. Discussing the ability of the Natives to bear the increase in taxation in 1875, the Secretary for Native Affairs stated that he considered the increased taxation

(ii) Individual Tenure

During this period the grant of individual title deeds to Native land-holders came to be looked upon by some people in the Cape Colony as a possible means of increasing the number of Native labourers. Thus, in 1876, Mr. J. X. Merriman, then Commissioner of Crown Lands and Public Works, expressed the hope that the introduction of the system of individual tenure would force lazy Natives to earn their keep and stimulate others to obtain the means to buy land.[1] The way in which the introduction of individual title was expected to bring about an increase in the supply of labourers was clearly expressed by the Civil Commissioner of Peddie.

> He wrote, 'The cry for more land is prevalent . . . no reason exists why the children and grandchildren should be provided with land and so on in perpetuity . . . this general fancy that all future generations are to be furnished with land by the Government, would be in a great measure obviated if the locations were surveyed for villages and garden lots, and individual titles issued to such as are now considered entitled to them. This would prevent all over-crowding and much grumbling, as those coming after would clearly see that if they could not inherit the gardens of their parents or relatives they would have to go out in the world and labour for themselves.'[2]

It was not, however, only for this reason that the issue of individual title deeds was advocated. Missionaries and educationalists had great hopes that it would hasten the spread of European civilization. Many experienced Native administrators continued to advocate the grant of individual titles, in spite of the comparative failure of nearly all the early attempts to institute it. They considered, however, that individual title deeds should be granted only where improvements had already been made.[3]

Within the Cape Colony proper, that is, excluding the Transkeian Territories, the survey of Native locations was continued for the purpose of issuing individual title deeds to garden and village allotments. In 1869 the survey of locations in the Ciskei had been begun. After 1877 some of the locations in the division

did not 'exceed the powers of the Native people to pay without inconvenience' owing to the increase in their wealth and the fact that when the 7s. tax was introduced wages were usually 5s. a month and rarely exceeded 10s., and their poultry fetched 3d. and 4d. a head, while in 1876 wages were from 10s. to 15s. a month and even 30s., according to ability, and the price of poultry was from 1s. 6d. to 2s. per head. S.N.A. 26, No. 117, quoted C. Axelson, op. cit., p. 107.

[1] Memorandum on Immigration and Labour Supply, G. 8, 1876, p. 1.
[2] G. 33, 1882, p. 140.
[3] A. 52, 1882, p. 8; G. 33, 1882, op. cit., p. 6; G. 2, 1885, op. cit., p. 23; G. 12, 1887, op. cit., p. 54.

of Queenstown were also surveyed. In all these cases, under the
title deeds granted, the allotments could not be transferred without
the consent of the Government. As in the case of the earlier
surveys, many of the title deeds were not taken up. Where they
were taken up the legal formalities of transfer were not subsequently observed. Moreover, the village allotments were not
occupied, the Natives with garden allotments continuing to live
beside them, often squatting on the commonage. Others who
had not taken up their title deeds or who were not regarded as
entitled to garden allotments also squatted on the commonage.[1]
The result was that the survey of these locations had little effect
in stimulating agriculture, in preventing overcrowding, or in
forcing landless Natives out to work.

(iii) Organization of Immigration

In the Cape Colony and Natal official attempts were also made
to increase the number of labourers by promoting immigration
both from abroad and from other parts of Africa.

In 1873 and 1874 the scarcity of labour in the Cape Colony
was much discussed in the newly created Legislative Assembly.[2]
No less than three motions were passed on the necessity for
obtaining labourers from Europe,[3] from the 'Border Tribes',[4] and
from India and China.[5] Artisans and navvies were imported from
Europe for the early railway construction. The navvies, who for
the most part came from Britain and Belgium, were found to
be expensive and unsatisfactory, and the Government looked
elsewhere for cheaper labour.

By the 'seventies, except when skilled workers were required
for particular undertakings, such as the construction of railways,
immigration had come to be regarded simply as a means of
supplying the demand for cheap labour. Thus, in 1876, Mr. J. X.
Merriman wrote:

> 'In the Cape the Government is called on to "survey mankind from
> China to Peru" in the hope of creating and maintaining a class of
> cheap labourers who will thankfully accept the position of helots
> and not be troubled with the inconvenient ambition of bettering
> their conditions.'[6]

The European farmers in particular, in spite of their complaints
of the scarcity of labour, were not generally in favour of the
importation of European farm-labourers. Their experience of the

---

[1] *Report on Native Location Surveys*, U.G. 42, 1922, pp. 2–4.
[2] The Cape Colony was granted responsible government in 1872.
[3] Cape of Good Hope, Votes and Proceedings of Parliament, 6 May, 1873.
[4] Idem, 15 May, 1873.   [5] Idem, 30 July, 1874.
[6] G. 8, 1876, op. cit., p. 1.

German peasant immigrants whom Sir George Grey had introduced led them to fear that imported labourers would rise to the
level of independent farmers and increase the competition for
labour.[1]

The Government considered various schemes for importing
Indian, Italian, and Chinese labourers. It had actually contracted
to introduce four hundred Chinese labourers when the Imperial
authorities vetoed the plan. None of the other schemes came to
anything, and in 1879 a Select Committee appointed to inquire
into the supply of the labour market advised the colonists to make
use of the State-aided immigration scheme to introduce English
and German families and young European farm-labourers. At
the same time it recommended that the Government should
introduce, in groups of not less than a hundred, Native African
labourers from Delagoa Bay, on the east coast, and Damaraland,
on the west coast.[2]

As early as 1874 the Cape Government had attempted to take
advantage of the Langalibalele incident in Natal to obtain additional labour. At that time the followers of this insubordinate
Hlubi chief were given the choice of returning to Natal, taking
service on the public works, or entering the service of colonists
for periods of not less than one year.[3] In 1878, also, after the
Gcaleka 'war', friendly and hostile Natives who were in distress
were brought to the western districts, where they were engaged
under contract by farmers. Some three thousand men, women,
and children were introduced. Although the number was comparatively small and most of the workers left when, or before,
their period of service was completed, the terms under which
these Natives were engaged are interesting. The period of contract was three years. During the first six months no cash wages
were to be paid, thereafter cash wages were to be five shillings a
month until the end of the first year, seven shillings and sixpence
during the second, and ten shillings during the third. Food,
lodging, and 'rough clothing' were to be provided and, on account
of the inquiries from masters and complaints from the Natives,
the official supervising the engagement of these Natives suggested
a scale of rations.[4]

In 1881 and 1882 effect was given to the recommendation of the
Select Committee that Native labourers should be introduced from
Delagoa Bay and Damaraland. The importation of these labourers
was not continued after 1882. An outbreak of smallpox at Delagoa
Bay and the withdrawal of the steamship service interrupted

[1] e.g. Select Committee on the Supply of the Labour Market, 1879, p. 11.
[2] Ibid., pp. iii–iv.   [3] G. 27, 1874, op. cit., p. 154.
[4] Parl. Papers, 1880, L. [C. 2482], S.A. War, Corresp., 1879–80, p. 354.

supplies from that source; there were disturbances in Damaraland, and the growing commercial depression at the same time reduced the demand for labour. The number of immigrants introduced was a little over a thousand, nearly all of whom came through Delagoa Bay. They came under long-term contracts and were employed both as railway labourers by the Government and on farms.[1] In the western districts where they were employed, they were, on the whole, popular with the farmers, and there were many applicants for their services.[2]

Natal was more successful than the Cape in its attempt to obtain labourers from abroad. The Government did not attempt to introduce labourers from Europe, but the subsidized importation of Indian indentured labourers was continued. They had already been imported primarily for the plantations of the coastal belt, where the system of labour tenancy was not practicable, but the importation had been discontinued in 1866, when industrial depression reduced the demand. By 1872 all the Indians in Natal had completed their indentures. It was estimated that there were then some five thousand seven hundred within the colony, about half of whom had remained at work, as free labourers, on the sugar and coffee plantations and in other employment in the coastal districts. The rest were distributed through the colony as servants, traders, storekeepers, gardeners, and fishermen. Some Indians had left Natal and made their way to the diamond-fields.

The usual rate of wages paid to the Indian labourers who had completed their indentures was fifteen shillings a month; specially skilled workmen were paid from thirty shillings to two pounds, with rations in addition to cash wages. On the Durban railway able-bodied Indian labourers were paid from twenty to thirty shillings a week and rations.[3]

In 1869 applications for indentured labourers began again. Importation was not resumed, however, until 1874. The delay was largely due to the refusal of the Indian authorities to sanction the immigration until certain improvements had been made in the conditions under which the Indians were introduced.[4] Thereafter large numbers were imported and, as few of the indentured labourers elected to return to India when their indentures were

---

[1] G. 64, 1882, p. 1.   [2] G. 79, 1883, p. 2; G. 58, 1884, p. 6.
[3] *Natal Legislative Council, Sessional Papers*, 1872, No. 1. Report of Coolie Commission.
[4] Under the new arrangements, as before, the Indians were imported under contract and the initial period of service was for five years. After five years they were free. If they re-engaged they received a bonus of two pounds a year. If they remained in Natal for five years after their indentures had expired, ten years altogether, they were entitled to free return passages to India. Indian indentured labourers had to be provided with quarters, food, and medical attention in addition to cash wages. Ibid., 1876, No. 6, p. 7.

completed and the Indian Government refused to sanction contracts which made their return compulsory, the Indian population
of Natal increased rapidly. The number of Indians rose from
five thousand in 1872 to nearly thirty thousand in 1886, and to
sixty thousand in 1899. Less than a third were indentured at the
latter dates.[1] Employers of indentured Indians paid them cash
wages, which rose from ten shillings per month in the first year
of service to fourteen shillings in the fifth. Food and lodging
were also provided.[2] In addition, employers paid two-thirds of
the cost of importation, superintendence, and return passages,[3]
which totalled approximately thirty pounds per adult male.[4]

Most of the indentured Indians were employed on the sugar
plantations and in the sugar mills, later they were also to be
employed in coal-mining. A few up-country farmers employed
indentured Indians, but language difficulties and the necessity for
providing medical services, which were required by the regulations, prevented the widespread use of such labour on inland
farms. For some years Indian labour was chiefly confined to the
coastal districts[5] because it was found more suitable for working

[1] Indian population of Natal:

1886:	Men	Women	Children	Total
Free Indians	10,680	4,817	6,431	21,928
Indentured Indians	4,805	1,857	999	7,661
			Total	29,589
1899:				
Free Indians	15,946	8,295	17,431	41,672
Indentured Indians	11,858	4,752	2,474	19,084
			Total	60,756

Natal Blue Book, 1881, A, p. 11; 1899, A, p. 11.

[2] *Natal Legislative Council, Sessional Papers*, 1876, No. 6. Report of the
Protector of Immigrants, p. 5.

[3] Law No. 20, 1874. In 1894 the contribution from the general revenue to
the cost of Indian immigration was withdrawn. Act No. 37, 1894.

[4] *Natal Legislative Council, Sessional Papers*, 1875, No. 29. Receipts and
Payments by the Indian Immigration Trust Board, p. 3.

[5] *Population of Natal*, 1881 :

	Whites	Indians	Natives
Borough of Pietermaritzburg	6,085	754	3,305
County of Pietermaritzburg	3,859	965	85,485
Borough of Durban	7,494	3,224	3,480
County of Durban	2,209	3,227	17,884
„ Klip River	2,875	98	31,386
„ Victoria	1,815	9,919	56,890
„ Umvoti	1,555	155	32,478
„ Weenen	1,391	43	26,937
Alexandra County	530	1,811	21,990
Alfred County	286	—	22,900
Umsinga Division	364	—	26,518
Totals	28,463	20,196	329,253

W. Peace, op. cit., p. 156.

under supervision in large gangs than for general farming operations.[1]

In the early 'seventies attempts were also made to increase the supply of Native labour from beyond the north-eastern frontier of Natal. According to the Lieutenant-Governor the reason why the colonists wanted additional labour was that the Natives of Natal, being land-holders and producers, were not wholly dependent upon wages.

'The majority of them', he wrote, 'are apt in consequence to offer their labour on terms and conditions more suitable to themselves than to the colonists who employ them. The latter want to secure long terms of service at small wages, the former prefer short periods of service terminable almost at their own discretion, with wages on a more liberal scale, though still remarkably small as compared with the rate of wages in most other countries. . . .'[2]

The Natives from beyond the frontier were prepared to work continuously for longer periods.[3]

To stimulate the local supply of labour, and also to increase the number of labourers coming from beyond the frontier, Law No. 15 of 1871 was passed. It provided that employers wanting labourers might apply to the magistrates, paying a fee of ten shillings for each labourer for whom they applied. Magistrates were to inform the Natives in their districts that they could obtain employment by applying at the magistrate's office. If the applications from employers exceeded those from the labourers the deficiency was to be met by the introduction of Natives from beyond the frontier.[4]

The number of labourers from the north-east actually employed in Natal was considerable.[5]

[1] *Natal Blue Book*, 1880, JJ., p. 117; 1882, GG., p. 39. W. Peace, op. cit., pp. 53, 54.

[2] *Natal Government Gazette*, 24 Jan. 1871 (No. 88). Lieutenant-Governor Keate to Earl of Kimberley.

[3] Ibid.

[4] Law No. 15 of 1871, *Natal Government Gazette*, 1871, p. 532.

[5] Returns showing the number of Natives entering Natal in search of work and the number returning to their homes:

	Zulu		Amathonga	
	Entering	Leaving	Entering	Leaving
1880	1,965	603	2,895	191
1881	7,130	8,550	2,227	5,183
1882	3,104	2,397	2,114	1,918

Natal Blue Books 1880–83, JJ., p. 87, FF., p. 115; FF., p. 48. Cf. the following report from Durban: 'The complaints of scarcity of native labour have not been so great as in former years; the wants of the European inhabitants on this respect being met by the large numbers of Amatonga labourers who come to seek employment here and by the Indian immigrants, Zanzibar liberated slaves, and other foreign importations. It is, however, from this class of men in a much greater degree than from our own natives that most of the crime in the Borough has arisen.' *Natal Blue Book*, 1880, JJ., p. 93.

F. OFFICIAL MEASURES TENDING TO RESTRICT THE SUPPLY OF LABOUR FROM THE NATIVE AREAS.

While all these efforts were being made to increase the supply of labour, restrictions on movement were at the same time tending to make the search for employment a hazardous undertaking which might end in imprisonment for the would-be labourer.

In the Cape Colony a severe vagrancy law was passed in 1879, making it an offence for any person to be without 'legal and sufficient means'. The harbouring of such 'idle and disorderly' persons was also prohibited. This Act did not differentiate between races, but there is no doubt that it was designed to supplement the location laws and prevent the congregation of groups of Natives, and other non-Europeans, who were not in regular employment. In practice it is reported to have had conflicting effects upon the supply of labour. On the one hand, within the Colony it is said to have increased the number seeking work. Thus, in 1883 the Civil Commissioner of Komgha in the Ciskei said that the enforcement of the law had resulted in numbers of Natives seeking employment, both with the farmers and in the towns.[1] On the other hand, it was reported to have acted as a deterrent to Natives desirous of entering the Colony to look for work. The Chief Magistrate of Tembuland wrote:

'Desire for clothing and to use other necessaries of life is rapidly increasing, and the men are quite willing to work in order to procure them if paid labour could be had within the territories; but they have a dread of pass, trespass, and other laws in force in the Colony, and many would almost rather starve than come under them.'[2]

Within the Cape Colony, the pass law (Act 22 of 1867), which required Natives to obtain written permits before moving about, ceased to be applicable to Natives from the Transkeian Territories, as these territories were annexed, for it applied only to Natives whose principal chief lived beyond the colonial frontier. Nevertheless, in practice all Natives within the eastern districts were required to carry passes or certificates of citizenship.[3] Native administrators criticized the pass system on the ground that it wasted the time of Natives desiring to seek work within the Colony, that it was an irritation, and therefore a 'drag on the

[1] G. 2, 1883, op. cit., p. 6.
[2] (Cape) *Blue Book on Native Affairs*, G. 12, 1887, p. 69.
[3] 'Your Committee . . . find that although an almost universal practice has prevailed in the Eastern Province, of requiring all natives to carry passes, the present law is defective, and almost impracticable, owing principally to the difficulty in determining what natives really come under its operation.' Select Committee on the Pass Laws, A. 11, 1886, *Report*, p. iii.

supply of labour'.[1] The Commission of 1883 on Native Laws and Customs recommended the abolition of the system.

> 'We have', it said, 'come to the conclusion that in the now altered circumstances of the Colony, this Pass Law should be repealed and the natives encouraged to seek employment in the colony without the irritation and inconvenience and loss of time entailed by what is known as the Pass System.'[2]

During the next few years the pass system, already *ultra vires* in its application to a large number of Natives, fell into general disuse.

In Natal the pass system seems to have been less hampering to the movements of Natives: at least this aspect of it gave rise to little comment. A law of 1884 required Natives entering or leaving the Colony to obtain passes, but this requirement, which was not very effectively enforced, did not prevent a very considerable exodus of Natives after the opening of the Witwatersrand gold-fields in 1886. In the towns of Durban and Pietermaritzburg the registration of daily labourers, the 'togt' system, was designed to control the movements of Natives, but there is little evidence that it affected the supply of labour.

In the Republics, Natives moving about were required to carry written passes signed by the local field-cornets, or, in some cases, by other officials. According to instructions issued in 1858 to field-cornets of the South African Republic, passes were not to be granted permitting Natives to leave this territory.[3] Later, in the 'seventies, attempts were made to collect heavy fees for the issue of passes to Natives who were not resident with'n the Republic nor in employment there.[4] There were complaints that these measures prevented Natives making their way to Kimberley, and, although large numbers undoubtedly evaded the pass laws, these impositions must have made the journey more hazardous and thereby reduced the attractiveness of employment, while some labourers were probably diverted to the farmers of the Republic.

The general effect of the pass law and vagrancy laws in this, as in later periods, was to make travel and work for Europeans more onerous and thus to reduce the aggregate supply of labour, although these restrictions on the movements of labourers may have increased the supply in certain localities.

[1] Select Committee on Pass Laws, 1883, p. 1, ev. John Hemming.
[2] Commission on Native Laws and Customs, 1883, *Report*, p. 50. For similar opinions see (Cape) *Blue Book on Native Affairs*, 1882, p. 3 (Matthew Blyth, Chief Magistrate, Transkei); p. 128 (Chalmers, Civil Commissioner, Kingwilliamstown); 1884, p. 38; 1885, pp. 35, 122.
[3] Instructions to Field-cornets. G. W. Eybers, *Select Constitutional Documents*, pp. 414–16.
[4] See above, p. 115.

CHAPTER VII

GOLD MINING, 1886–1899

A. THE GOLD-FIELDS OF THE SOUTH AFRICAN REPUBLIC BEFORE 1886

THE demand for Native labour coming from the early attempts at exploiting the gold resources of South Africa was sporadic and localized in character. Such was the case in the 'seventies at Tati, to the west of the South African Republic, and within the Republic at Marabastad and Eersteling in the neighbourhood of Pietersburg, at Letaba, and in the Murchison Hills in the north-east.[1] The alluvial diggings in the district of Lydenburg were more productive and significant, but even there the demand for labour was small compared with that at the diamond diggings in Griqualand West, although the kind of work was similar. European prospectors and diggers would each employ a few Natives to help in the work of digging out and washing the gold-bearing soil. Committees were elected to regulate the working of the gold-fields and, as on the diamond diggings, they made regulations determining the size of claims and, in some cases, limited the number which might be held by individuals or companies.[2] Even where shafts were sunk to mine gold ore, as at Tati and in the Murchison Hills, concerns were small and scattered.

Native labour was obtained in various ways. Some of the prospectors and diggers brought their Native servants with them. Other Natives were attracted by the opportunity of earning money, goats, beads, and other articles. Guns, too, were much in demand, although it was against the law of the South African Republic to provide Natives with guns.[3] To supplement such labour, gangs of Natives were brought from Delagoa Bay to the diggings in the east of the Republic.[4]

At Barberton, where in 1885 the rich Sheba reef was discovered, conditions were different. It was soon realized that shafts would have to be sunk and that considerable capital expenditure would be required to extract the gold. There European miners and artisans did the skilled work while Natives were employed on the less skilled. By 1886 there were already fifteen hundred Natives so employed.[5]

---

[1] T. Baines, *The Gold Regions of South Eastern Africa* (1877), pp. 3–6, 75–88.
[2] Ibid., p. 86.   [3] Ibid., p. 99.   [4] Ibid., p. 137.
[5] 'The public have been warned over and over again that these are no "poor man's diggings" (p. 486). The great question is, what is to be the future of these fields? I must say that, after careful investigation, I am not sanguine as to the Kaap Valley being able to carry any large population for a long time to

B. THE WITWATERSRAND GOLD MINES: TECHNIQUE AND THE DEMAND FOR LABOUR

The Barberton finds were soon overshadowed by the discovery and development of the gold-bearing beds of the Witwatersrand. Previously, in South Africa, gold had been found in rich nuggets, alluvial deposits, or patchy, contorted reefs. On the Witwatersrand it is present in uniform, continuous, and extensive beds of a hard conglomerate, known as 'banket'. The first gold was obtained by crushing and washing the 'outcrop' of these beds, but as they dipped steeply to the south, shafts had soon to be sunk to extract the gold-bearing rock. The gold was in fine particles, and to obtain it the ore had to be extracted, crushed, and chemically treated.

Considerable capital expenditure was necessary to acquire the right to mine, to buy, and erect the plant necessary to crush and treat the ore, to sink shafts, to equip them with haulage gear, drive tunnels and do the preparatory work necessary to ensure a continuous supply of ore. Capital was readily available, for the Kimberley diamond magnates soon became interested in the gold discoveries. They used their resources to float gold-mining companies and also to assist in mobilizing overseas capital.

In the South African Republic the laws controlling gold prospecting and production had been consolidated by the Gold Law of 1885. Proved gold-fields might be declared open to the public. The landowner and prospector of such fields were then entitled to a certain number of claims, the remainder being available, subject to the payment of licence fees, to any European who could acquire them. Large-scale enterprise was no longer hampered by restrictions on the right to amalgamate claims.

Within a few months of the discovery of the main reef in 1885 the Kimberley magnates bought up, at prices ranging from seven thousand to seventy thousand pounds, the bare pastoral farms along the Witwatersrand. Numerous mining companies were floated, both in South Africa and overseas. By the end of 1887 there were two hundred and seventy gold-mining companies in

come, and even then the population will be a purely working one, men toiling for regular wages, miners, engineers, and skilled artisans employed by companies. The average English labourer will be driven out of the fields by native labour, 1,500 natives being at present employed, and there will be no such thing as a poor man jumping into a fortune except by some extraordinary stroke of luck. I cannot too strongly impress on those without capital, that Barberton is no place for them, that is unless they are prepared to be contented with wages no better, proportionately, than they can earn in any other part of the world. The skilled artisan or experienced miner may be fortunate enough to obtain a succession of highly profitable engagements, but this is very far from being a certainty. . . . Were this an alluvial gold-field my advice would no doubt be different.' J. W. Matthews, op. cit., pp. 486, 491–2.

the Transvaal;[1] by 1889 there were forty-five companies producing gold and a population of twenty-five thousand Europeans and fifteen thousand Natives on the Witwatersrand.

The cost of supplies, such as machinery and most stores, was high, because they had to be imported and transported, first by rail, and then by ox-wagon from the railheads at Kimberley, in the Cape Colony, and Ladysmith, in Natal. European skilled labour was also expensive, for high wages had to be paid to attract experienced miners and artisans to the Rand. There were no large prizes for the man without capital. Moreover, the Rand was far from large mining and industrial centres, the cost of most provisions was extremely high, and conditions were primitive. On the other hand, coal and Native labour were available.[2]

Between 1890 and 1895 bore-holes were sunk to test whether the gold-bearing conglomerate continued to the south. At the same time the development of the cyanide process of chemical treatment increased the percentage of gold which could be extracted from between fifty and sixty to over ninety-five. This improvement in technique promised to make mining the ore profitable at depths of two, three, and even four thousand feet. By 1895 mines were being developed along the 'Main Reef' from Modderfontein, about twenty miles east of Johannesburg, to Randfontein, about the same distance to the west. To the south, shafts were being sunk to mine at deeper levels.[3]

The demand for labour which resulted was much greater than that which had followed the discovery of diamonds. Nevertheless, it was in many respects similar. Moreover, the first development of the Rand was largely undertaken by men who had had experience at Kimberley. Consequently, and for the same reasons, the organization of the labour force was adopted which had been developed at Kimberley, on the basis of European engineers, miners, and overseers, supervising Native labourers. Skilled engineers and miners were required underground to direct shaft-sinking, 'development', and the mining of ore. On the surface they were required to superintend the erection and maintenance of plant, and the crushing and treatment of the ore. The cost of European labour was high. During 1894 the average wages of European employees on the gold-mines were £23 1s. per month.[4]

Native labourers could be obtained at much lower rates. In 1889 the average cash wage of some six thousand Native labourers employed was fifteen shillings a week. Food was also supplied.[5] Consequently Native labour tended to be employed wherever

[1] G.T. Amphlett, op. cit., p. 109.
[2] C. S. Goldmann, *South African Mining and Finance* (1895–6), p. xvii.
[3] Ibid., p. vi.   [4] Ibid., p. xvii. Working hours were 9·6 per day.
[5] *Chamber of Mines, First Annual Report*, 1889, p. 10.

possible. As on the diamond-mines, Natives helped to sink the shafts, to break down and load the rock underground, to sort out the 'waste' rock, and to perform various other tasks according to the nature of the plant used for crushing and treating the ore. The proportion of European to Native employees in 1894 and 1895 was approximately one to seven.[1]

C. TERMS AND CONDITIONS OF WORK AND RECRUITMENT OF NATIVE LABOUR

From the beginning the cost of labour has been a high proportion of the cost of gold-mining. In 1894, out of a total of four and a half million pounds sterling spent by sixty of the principal companies, wages and salaries accounted for £3 million. The cost of the salaries and wages of miners, millmen, and other managing officials was one and a half million; that of Native labour, including the cost of food, another one and a half million; fuel consumed, principally coal, half a million; explosives, fuel, etc., half a million; other stores, such as mining timber, candles, drill-steel, etc., half a million.[2]

Since the money wages of skilled European labourers were of necessity high, the terms on which Native labour could be obtained were a matter of vital concern. The problem of attracting a continuous supply of Native labour occupied both individual mine managers and the leaders of the mining industry. The matter was complicated. Some believed that an increase in the wage-rate, the normal method of attracting additional supplies, would result in the long run in a decrease in the supply of labour to the industry; they considered that the Natives who came to the mines wished to earn a fixed amount to satisfy certain definite wants, and therefore, that if wages were raised the Natives would work for a shorter period. Thus, Mr. Hennen Jennings, Consulting Engineer to Messrs. H. Eckstein and Company, told the Industrial Commission of Inquiry of 1897 that: 'They come, in fact, only in order to make enough money to return to their kraals with sufficient means to enable them to marry and live in indolence.'[3]

Competition for Native labour between the different mines tended to raise Native wages and also on occasion to lead to corrupt practices. The first report of the Witwatersrand Chamber of Mines makes this clear:

'So long', it says, 'as the total supply is deficient, it is to be feared that eager competition between managers to secure labourers will

---

[1] In 1894 5,500 Europeans and 42,500 Natives were employed on the average. At the end of 1895 7,000 Europeans and 51,000 Natives were employed. C. S. Goldman, op. cit., p. xvii.
[2] Ibid., p. v.   [3] Industrial Commission of Enquiry, 1897, p. 219.

be inevitable. This competition has in some cases taken the regret-table form of overt attempts to bribe and seduce the employees of neighbouring companies to desert their employers. Even without resort to actual attempts to bribe, a manager finding himself short of labour which is urgently required, has standing alone scarcely any other remedy than to raise his rates of pay. The result has necessarily been a steady rise of rates all round, which is adding a very heavy additional expense to the working of the mines.'[1]

On the assumption that higher wage-rates would lead to a decrease in the supply of labour to the industry as a whole,[2] attempts were made to reduce wages and to establish a fixed scale of wages on all the mines. Co-operation between the different managements was relatively simple, partly because the individual units were large and also because many of the financiers controlling the mines were interested in several properties. The beginnings of the present 'group' system of management, under which large financial houses control the working of numerous mines, was present even in the 'nineties. As early as 1887 an unsuccessful attempt had been made to establish a central co-ordinating body; in 1889, under a new constitution, the Witwatersrand Chamber of Mines was established.[3] It immediately directed its attention to the cost and supply of Native labour.

There were two aspects to the question of the cost of Native labour. On the one hand, there was the cost of money-wages, food, and quarters. In addition, there was the cost of recruiting, for the sudden demand for labour led enterprising individuals, acting independently or in the employ of contractors and mining companies, to scatter all over South Africa and engage Natives for work on the mines. Native labourers were engaged in their home districts, in other centres of employment, on the road to the gold-mines, and on the Rand itself.[4] Recruiting agents charged a fee for their services which might be as much as £4 for each Native labourer supplied.[5] Even where mines employed their own recruiters the cost of obtaining Native labourers and bringing them to the Rand was heavy. Such preliminary expenses were the more serious since there was no guarantee that the employers

[1] *Chamber of Mines, Annual Report*, 1889, p. 9.

[2] 'In support of a general reduction of wages, if possible by a fixed tariff, it is forcibly argued that the high wages now paid are themselves a principal reason of the short supply . . . it is found that the average period of service among our Kafirs is much shorter than in districts in which a lower rate of wages is paid.' Ibid., 1889, p. 10.

[3] C. S. Goldman, op. cit., p. xxix. In 1897 the name of this association was changed to the Chamber of Mines of the South African Republic, in 1900 it became the Transvaal Chamber of Mines.

[4] *Chamber of Mines, Annual Report*, 1895, p. 18.

[5] [Cd. 1897], 1904, p. 20, pp. 387–9, ev. Mr. Maxwell, a general mining contractor.

who paid them would be able to retain the services of the Natives supplied.

The Chamber of Mines directed its attention to reducing the money-wages paid to Natives, to establishing a fixed scale of wages on all the mines, and to reducing the cost of recruiting. During the 'nineties it was only partially successful in these attempts. Agreements to reduce wages were made on several occasions, and resulted in temporary reductions, but when the supply of labour forthcoming at the agreed wage-rate fell short, competition between employers forced the wage-rates up above that level.

Thus, in 1889, the average weekly wages of some six thousand Natives had been fifteen shillings a week with food in addition.[1] The next year an agreement to reduce wages was signed by sixty-six companies. In December of that year Natives were paid according to the rate agreed upon, which effected a reduction of 25 per cent and a saving of £15,000 a month. The reduced rate did not last long, for, according to the report of the Chamber of Mines for 1891, some managers soon raised their rates to maintain their supply of labour:

> As the winter advanced, however, and through the increased demand for labour, caused by railway construction and the requirements of the mines, the supply of Kafirs fell off, and some managers, who were unable to maintain their supply by other means, gradually raised their rate of wages. This, of course, brought about a general rise, and in July and August the scale suggested by the Chamber was being generally exceeded. In no case, however, did the rates rise so high as they had been before the Chamber began to move in the matter. . . .[2]

The agreement was not renewed, although the Chamber of Mines continued to advocate combination with the object of reducing the cost of Native labour.[3] In 1895 no two mines paid alike, the Native labourers being paid 'according to the varying value of their work'. According to the Chamber's Native Labour Commissioner the usual wage-rates were from £2 to £3 a month, but skilful drillers might earn up to £3 10s.[4]

In 1896 another agreement to reduce wages was arranged, and at the same time it was agreed to standardize conditions as regards

[1] Average weekly wages, as shown by the returns of 53 companies: 3,059 Natives working underground, 14s. 11d.; 1,748 Natives working above ground, 14s. 2d.; 1,171 Natives working for contractors, 17s.; average 5,978 Natives 15s. a week. Chamber of Mines, Annual Report, 1889, p. 10.

[2] Ibid., 1891.

[3] 'Your Committee strongly recommend the companies to render all the assistance in their power towards helping the managers to combine for the purpose of controlling and cheapening native labour.' Ibid., 1894, p. 64.

[4] Letter from the Chamber of Mines' Native Labour Commissioner to Mr. Tainton, Cape Government Labour Agent in the Transkei. Quoted, ibid., 1893, p. 52.

hours of work and rations. In order to prevent competition between mine managers taking the form of offering better food and shorter hours of work, minimum hours of work and maximum rations were agreed upon, in addition to maximum and minimum rates of pay.[1]

In the following year the schedule of Native wages was revised and rates were again reduced, the highest rate being fixed at two shillings and sixpence and the lowest at a shilling. In order to allow managers to reward specially skilled Natives, $7\frac{1}{2}$ per cent of the Natives employed might be paid at special rates. (At this time the system of reckoning a month as thirty working days was introduced.) Inspectors were appointed to see that the agreement was kept. In spite of this measure the agreed schedule of wage-rates was in some cases exceeded. Nevertheless, the Chamber of Mines expressed the opinion that individual companies endeavoured to keep to it and that the agreement and the system of inspection had reduced wage-rates.[2]

At the same time that the Chamber of Mines tried to reduce wages it attempted to increase the supply of labour and reduce the cost of recruiting. There was much complaint against the system of recruiting by competing labour agents. It was argued that it increased the cost of labour in various ways. In the first place, it was said, recruiters engaged and charged fees for supplying Natives who would have found their own way to the mines;[3] secondly, competing recruiters molested and 'jumped' Natives who had been engaged by others, or who were going to the Rand independently, and so increased the hazards of the journey and made Natives unwilling to undertake it;[4] further, the misrepresentations of recruiters concerning conditions and wages on the Rand led to Natives being disappointed on arrival there, and as a result work on the gold-mines became unpopular.

[1] Ibid., 1896, p. 157.

[2] 'In some cases the Schedule had been exceeded, in a few considerably, but this was made known to the companies and instructions were given by Boards to conform to the rates fixed. The moral effect of the inspections has been found to be good, as the engagement having been voluntarily entered into for the general benefit no company likes to appear as the one taking advantage of the others by paying higher wages than those allowed. It cannot be said that the Schedule is rigidly maintained, but there is a distinct endeavour to abide as closely as possible by it, and the net result is that the rates of wages are far lower than they would have been if, in the first instance, the companies had not combined and adopted uniform rates, and in the second, if the tendency to compete had not been checked by the inspection system.' Ibid., 1898, p. 56.

[3] 'Generally, "touts" infest the main roads and induce natives to go with them under various promises, the result being that those promises are not fulfilled, and the "boys" are discontented, and, on the other hand, companies are compelled to pay premiums for labour which, if not interfered with, would have come voluntarily to them.' Ibid., 1894, p. 5.

[4] Ibid., 1893, p. 5; 1898, p. 86; Transvaal Labour Commission, Evidence. [Cd. 1897], 1904, p. 28, q. 641.

Some thought that a centralized system of recruiting would reduce the cost of obtaining labour, both by eliminating unnecessary capitation fees and by bringing to an end many of the abuses which had arisen from uncontrolled recruiting. It was not, however, considered feasible to organize a centralized system of recruiting until contracts of service with Natives could be enforced, for any such system would involve considerable outlay and, unless contracts of service could be enforced, the companies paying the cost of recruiting would not necessarily benefit from the labour brought to the Rand.[1]

To make recruiting profitable it was necessary to ensure that the services of the recruit repaid this cost in addition to his wages. In practice, in the early days the amount of premium paid was actually deducted from the nominal cash wages of recruited labourers.

In the 'nineties employers on the Rand frequently paid large sums to agents who supplied Natives engaged under long period contracts.[2] Such Natives, however, frequently left their service before they had fulfilled their contracts. The reasons for this were numerous. The misrepresentations of recruiters concerning wages and other conditions were, no doubt, partly responsible, but even without deliberate misrepresentation many Natives must have failed to understand the nature of the contracts which they undertook to carry out. Before arriving on the Rand few could have had any conception of the nature of mining work, particularly work underground. Some, indeed, refused to go underground. Some found that they had agreed to work for wages lower than those generally prevailing and either insisted on being paid the current rates or deserted their employers and went to others who were prepared to pay the usual rate.[3] Others, too, sought work

---

[1] 'Besides these direct measures for improving the native labour supply with a view to ultimately lowering wages, the Committee considered proposals from Messrs. Remingfield, Wilhelm, and Best and Williams, to bring Natives from the East Coast. Owing, however, to each of these, though in varying degree, involving a considerable outlay, which the companies would have to make good, in addition to paying a bonus, in the present state of insecurity with regard to the retention of native labourers none could be adopted. Upon proclamation of the Pass Regulations, it will, however, be possible to organize a supply from the East Coast, either through independent agents or by the direct action of the Chamber's Native Labour Department.' Ibid., 1894, p. 3, cf. 1898, p. 12.

[2] Mr. Maxwell, a general mining contractor, told the Transvaal Labour Commission, 1904, that the highest bonus paid by him before the war had been £4 per head. [Cd. 1897], 1904, p. 20, q. 387-9. In 1895 the Wolhuter Gold Mines, employing 1,105 Natives, paid £2,520 in premiums, £234 of this was refunded by deductions from the wages of recruits. In 1896, when 1,641 Natives were employed, £6,570 was paid out and £453 refunded. *Industrial Commission of Enquiry*, 1897, p. 112, ev. C. S. Goldmann.

[3] 'Apart from the fact that Colonial natives are disinclined to work underground, the great difficulty which attended this endeavour to supply the labour demand of the Rand at a reduced rate of wages by importing natives from the

in occupations which appeared more attractive than mining. In some cases Natives were induced to desert by recruiting agents who would take them to another employer and from him receive a capitation fee.[1]

The practice of deducting capitation fees from the wages of recruited labourers was a great inducement for Natives to desert and seek work independently, for then no premiums would be paid to agents, and consequently no such deductions made.

Other Natives again, according to their own accounts, were 'sold' to recruiters by their chiefs.[2] Consequently, they came to the mines unwillingly and deserted at the first opportunity.

To prevent Natives from breaking their contracts with impunity the Chamber of Mines endeavoured to persuade the Government of the South African Republic to enact a pass law which would give greater control of the labour force in districts where large numbers were congregated.[3] At length, in 1895, the Volksraad passed such a law,[4] drafted by the leaders of the mining industry, and designed to give employers greater control of the movements of Native labourers.[5] Giving evidence before the Industrial Commission of Inquiry of 1897, Mr. C. S. Goldmann said:

'I may mention that the whole intention of the law is to have a hold on the native whom we have brought down, be it from the East Coast, South, or from the North, at considerable outlay to ourselves. . . .'[6]

The law provided that on entering a gold-field which had been proclaimed a labour district a Native had to provide himself with a District Pass, authorizing him to seek employment for three days, with provision for extension of the period on payment of a

Colony was, that the experiment was made on too small a scale. The "boys" who came here, and many thousands more who were willing to come, would have been quite satisfied to work on the surface at 40s. per month, but they were not disposed to take lower wages than other natives working around them; for the mere fact of their having agreed to do so before leaving their districts was regarded by them as being of no importance whatever. In addition to this, labour was scarce, and by deserting they were able at once to get employment at full current rates. The experiment, therefore, failed, and there was no desire to repeat it.' *Chamber of Mines, Annual Report*, 1893, p. 30.

[1] Idem, 1896, p. 153, *Transvaal Labour Commission*, Evidence [Cd. 1897], 1904, p. 204, ev. Sir Herbert Sloley, Resident Commissioner of Basutoland.

[2] Reasons advanced by the Native Council of Basutoland why the Basuto did not go to Johannesburg more freely included misrepresentation by Labour agents and complaints that they were 'sold' by their chiefs, and that this made service outside the country unpopular. [Cd. 1897], 1904, p. 204, ev. Sir Herbert Sloley.

[3] *Chamber of Mines, Annual Report*, 1893, p. 4; 1894, p. 4; 1895, p. 13.

[4] Law No. 23 of 1895.

[5] '. . . in order to get a workable pass law at all the Chamber had to prepare it in every detail'; *Industrial Commission of Enquiry*, 1897, p. 106, ev. C. S. Goldmann; cf. J. P. Fitzpatrick, *The Transvaal from Within*, p. 61.

[6] *Industrial Commission of Enquiry*, 1897, p. 110.

fee. When a Native found work, the employer took possession of the District Pass and retained it until the Native was discharged, the Native employee being provided with an Employers' Pass. Natives found without a pass were liable to be arrested. Penalties were imposed for contravening the pass regulations which, moreover, made it an offence for employers to engage Natives not furnished with District Passes in proper order. In practice, however, according to the Executive Committee of the Chamber of Mines, the administration of the law was ineffective and consequently the pass law failed to achieve its purpose.[1]

After its enactment the Chamber of Mines went ahead with its own recruiting organization. In 1896 the Native Labour Supply Association was formed for 'the purpose of introducing native labour to the Witwatersrand'.[2] It was intended that this central organization should recruit for all collaborating mines instead of each employing independent and competing agents.

Hitherto the Chamber of Mines had attempted to increase the supply of labour by spreading information about conditions and wages on the Rand among Native chiefs, Government officials, and others likely to be able to promote the supply. It had also attempted to improve conditions both on the routes to the mines and on the mines themselves. In 1893 a Native Labour Commissioner had been appointed for this purpose.[3] It also made frequent representations to the Government of the South African Republic, asking it to protect Natives who were travelling to and from the gold-mines against molestation and robbery.[4] According

---

[1] *Chamber of Mines, Annual Report*, 1895, p. 7.   [2] Ibid., 1896, p. 157.
[3] The Native Labour Commissioner was appointed '(1) to organize and regulate the native labour supply; (2) to act as the medium of communications between the mining companies and the Government officials, Native chiefs or others who may arrange for the supply of native labour; and (3) to watch, in a measure, over the welfare of the natives during their period of engagement.' Chamber of Mines to Honourable Superintendent of Natives, Pretoria. Quoted, ibid., 1893, p. 33.
According to the report of 1894, active steps were taken by these means to increase the supply of labour. It said: 'During the year the Committee through the Chamber's Native Labour Commissioner, has kept up a constant communication with the native chiefs within and beyond the boundaries of the Republic, disseminating information with regard to local labour requirements, and encouraging natives to come here to seek employment. In particular, measures have been adopted for deriving greater benefit from the existence of a teeming native population in the northern districts of this country. The Native Labour Commissioner personally visited a large number of chiefs in the Zoutpansberg district.' Ibid., 1894, p. 3.
Depots were also established on the northern route where Natives might obtain food and shelter and proper travelling passes. It also arranged for responsible 'indunas' to accompany gangs to protect them from molestation. Ibid., cf. 1895, p. 12.
[4] In 1893 the Chamber of Mines presented memorials to the Volksraad on the following subjects: (1) Supply of Native labour; (2) Pass Law; (3) Liquor Law; (4) Molestation of Natives. Ibid., 1893, p. 4.

to contemporary accounts, in addition to the frequent violent
robbery of Natives returning from the Rand with the money and
goods they had earned, those proceeding there were sometimes
detained by officials of the Republic under the pretext of vaccina-
tion and pass regulations and money extorted from them.[1] It
was also alleged that officials in the north required and were paid
ten shillings or £1 a head for the Native labourers they sent to
the mines.[2]

After 1895 the Chamber tried, on the whole unsuccessfully, to
centralize recruiting for the mines and also to obtain a monopoly
of recruiting in South Africa. The centralization of recruiting
was most successful in Portuguese East Africa, where, according
to the report of the Rand Native Labour Association, the services
of 'every Labour Agent in Portuguese Territory whose opposition
was of any moment' were secured at a cost which did not 'materially
affect the price of natives landed on these fields'.[3] Within the
Republic it was less successful. There, even companies which
were members of the central association competed with its agents
to obtain labour. The result, according to the Native Labour
Commissioner, was that the cost of obtaining Native labourers
from the north was raised.[4]

The attempt of the Association to obtain from the Governments
of the South African colonies and protectorates a monopoly of
recruiting was likewise unsuccessful, except in the case of Portuguese East Africa.[5] Some authorities opposed the grant of such
a monopoly on the ground that there were other employers of
labour who used recruiters.[6] They did not, however, oppose the
migration of Native labourers to the Rand. Indeed, in many
instances, they encouraged it. This was done sometimes by
supporting the representations of recruiting agents,[7] sometimes

[1] Ibid., 1893, p. 5; 1894, pp. 5, 67; 1895, pp. 15, 69; 1898, p. 86.
[2] *Industrial Commission of Enquiry*, 1897, pp. 14, 23, ev. Mr. G. Albu.
[3] Report of Rand Native Labour Association, *Chamber of Mines, Annual Report*, 1898, p. 446.
[4] 'From the northern districts of the Transvaal we have succeeded in getting 12,233 natives. Here the opposition was of a far more serious nature than on the East Coast. Companies, some of which are members of the Association, instead of allowing me to collect boys for them at prices obtained during the latter months of the year 1897, sent their own representatives to compete against mine. These circumstances account for the price of Northern boys being raised to £3 10s. 0d. per head.' Ibid.
[5] In September 1899 the Portuguese Government issued a decree against competitive recruiting, but this did not come into force owing to the outbreak of the South African War.
[6] *Chamber of Mines, Annual Report*, 1898, pp. 68, 75.
[7] Letter from Resident Commissioner, Bechuanaland Protectorate. Quoted *Chamber of Mines, Annual Report*, 1898, p. 66: 'Some months since I used a certain amount of influence with the Chief Khama to get his consent to allow Mr. Poultney, a labour agent, to engage some of his followers to proceed to the mines in Johannesburg. . . . Khama has lately been informed by Mr.

by attempts to control recruiting so as to eliminate misrepresentation and other abuses which tended to make employment on
the Rand unpopular. To this end the Government of Natal, in
1896, and of the Cape Colony, in 1899, passed Acts making it
compulsory for recruiting agents to take out licences, imposing penalties for wilful misrepresentation of conditions and for
inducing Natives to break contracts of service.[1]

To encourage Natives in the Transkeian Territories to go to
the Rand the Cape Government used the influence of officials
and Native chiefs. It also established depots from which labourers
were dispatched to the Rand.[2] Both the Natal and Cape Governments appointed official agents in Johannesburg to assist colonial
Natives working there and to make remittances for them to
relatives in the colonies.[3]

D. THE SUPPLY AND SOURCES OF NATIVE LABOUR

Between 1890 and 1899 the total number of Natives employed
on the gold-mines rose from approximately fourteen thousand[4] to
ninety-seven thousand.[5] Native labourers went to the gold-mines
from all over Southern Africa. The most important source was
Portuguese East Africa. In 1897 it was estimated that half of the
labour employed came from there, a fifth from 'the North', and
the remainder from Bechuanaland, Basutoland, Swaziland, Natal,
the Transkeian Territories, and the Cape Colony 'proper', i.e.
excluding the Transkeian Territories.[6] The Natives of the South
African Republic itself, it is reported, did not go to Johannesburg
in large numbers. In July 1896 it was said that of nearly forty-
three thousand Natives employed within a three-mile radius of

Poultney that a number of the boys engaged are suffering from sickness, and
that a number are already dead. . . . I am very anxious to assist as far as
possible the employment of Protectorate natives by high-class mines at the
Rand, and the furnishing of the information as is now asked for by Khama will
assist materially in gaining their confidence and getting them to go to work and
so feed their families instead of letting them starve, which they are doing at
present.'

[1] Act No. 36, 1896 (Natal); Act No. 6, 1899 (Cape Colony).

[2] 'I should like to point out to you what the Cape Government has done in
the supply of natives. They have given notice through their kaffir chiefs to
collect native labour, and the Government have brought it to Imvani Station,
where we have taken delivery during the months of January and February last
of between 400 and 500 natives, and 2,797 during the eight months of 1896.
The Cape Government have depots at Umtata. I can further show you letters
we have received from the Commissioners of Natives in the Cape Colony,
telling us that their depots are full, and urging upon us to take the natives.'
Industrial Commission of Enquiry, 1897, p. 118, ev. C. S. Goldmann.

[3] *Parl. Papers*, 1896. [C. 7944-ZI], No. 169, Zululand, Annual Report for
1895, p. 10; (Cape) *Blue Book on Native Affairs*, G. 50, 1900, p. 67.

[4] *Chamber of Mines, Annual Report*, 1898, p. 55.

[5] [Cd. 1897], 1904. Exhibit No. 1.

[6] *Industrial Commission of Enquiry*, 1897, p. 116, ev. C. S. Goldmann.

the centre of Johannesburg less than a thousand were from the Republic.[1]

Although the total number of Native labourers employed on the gold-mines increased rapidly, the numbers going to the Rand from some territories fell during the second half of the decade. The reason was said to be the conditions which prevailed both on the routes to the Rand and on the Rand itself. Thus it was reported from the Transkei that the number going to the South African Republic had fallen owing to the hardships which the Natives encountered on the way.[2] According to pass statistics the number of Natives going from Natal to the South African Republic also fell.[3]

The Natives were not insensitive to changes in wages and other conditions. After the concerted reduction in wages which took place in 1890, it was reported in 1892 that 'difficulties were before very long experienced in obtaining a sufficient supply of labour', the agreement had been evaded while it lasted and was not renewed.[4] Similarly, in 1897, when wages were reduced by agreement the supply of labour fell off and the Secretary of the Chamber of Mines reported that 'consequent on this action, a rather greater number of Natives than usual are leaving the Rand'.[5]

In the same year the Report on Trade, Commerce, and Industry of the South African Republic suggested that such changes in conditions might account for the scarcity of labour complained of. It said:

'The dearth of native labour is one of the most serious questions, and is a most difficult problem to solve. . . . The inadequate supply of labour may be ascribed to various causes. The Chairman of the Chamber of Mines in his last annual address, said that owing to the rapid development of the industry the demand for natives had increased during the last few years from 30,000 to 40,000 to 80,000 to 100,000. This, no doubt, is one of the causes, but the wages now offered are not so attractive as formerly, and the hardships

---

[1] It was stated that the actual number employed was 42,553, of which less than 754 were Transvaal Natives. At this time the male adult Native population was estimated to be 150,000. *Report on Trade, Commerce and Gold Mining Industry of the South African Republic* for 1897. *Parl. Papers*, 1899, LXIV [G. 9093], p. 10.

[2] 'Owing to the very frequent robberies and other ill-treatment, few natives now go from these territories into the Transvaal in comparison to the numbers that did so formerly.' Chief Magistrate, Transkei. (Cape) *Blue Book on Native Affairs*, G. 31, 1899, p. 71. The number of passes issued in the Transkeian territories to natives for the purpose of seeking employment in the South African Republic was: 1896, 15,491 (G. 19, 1897, p. 126); 1897, 22,120 (G. 42, 1898, p. 146); 1898, 18,302 (G. 3, 1899, p. 126); 1899, 7,105 (G. 50, 1900, p. 71). Cf. J. P. Fitzpatrick, op. cit., p. 102.

[3] 1896, 26,487; 1897, 20,092; 1898, 16,386. [Cd. 1897], 1904, p. 544.

[4] *Chamber of Mines, Annual Report*, 1892, p. 10.

[5] Ibid., 1897, p. 116.

natives were subjected to in years gone by, and indeed at the present time to some extent, in travelling to and fro, have probably been communicated to the various tribes and have possibly had the effect of making the natives chary of seeking work in the Transvaal."[1]

In spite of the rapid increase in the demand for Native labour, the repeated complaints of its scarcity were intermittent, for at times the supply caught up with or was even in excess of the immediate demand. Thus, in March 1896, and again in March 1897, the supply was said to be in excess of the demand.[2] Employers in the gold-mining industry were already beginning to experience an inconvenience arising from the use of migratory labourers who relied on farming for a part of their income and who liked to be at home during the ploughing season and, moreover, tended to remain at home when crops were good.

[1] *Report on Trade, Commerce and Gold Mining Industry of the South African Republic* for 1897, op. cit., p. 10.
[2] *Chamber of Mines, Annual Report*: 1895, p. 41; 1897, p. 111.

CHAPTER VIII

OTHER EMPLOYMENT, 1886–1899

A. NATIVE LABOUR FOR TRANSPORT DEVELOPMENT

THE effects on the South African economy of the development of gold-mining on the Witwatersrand were similar to those which followed the growth of diamond production in Griqualand West. Johannesburg soon surpassed Kimberley as a consuming centre of unprecedented size in South Africa. By 1889 it had a population of twenty-five thousand Europeans and fifteen thousand Natives. To supply the mines with machinery and other stores and to meet the varied wants of the community which established itself on the Rand, ancillary industries were organized in the neighbourhood of the mines, as well as elsewhere in South Africa, and beyond.

Before the development of gold production the population of the South African Republic had consisted almost exclusively of farmers. Moreover, among both Europeans and Natives subsistence farming had predominated. Many of the farmers owned large herds of cattle and sheep. They were not accustomed to selling their produce. To obtain commodities such as sugar, coffee, rice, gunpowder, textiles, and iron goods, they had been accustomed to barter their wool or cattle. Hunters would barter ivory, skins, and ostrich feathers. Beyond this there had been little trade. Cultivation had for the most part been carried on only for domestic purposes.

The response of the farmers of the South African Republic to the new market for their produce was slow. Consequently, even such foodstuffs as maize, the staple ration of the Natives employed at Kimberley and on the Rand, had to be imported either from other parts of South Africa or from abroad,[1] the local supplies being very small. All machinery and most manufactured goods had also to be imported from abroad.[2] Consequently, as in the case of the development of diamond production, the first reaction of the growth of the new mining centre was upon the transport services. At first transport-riders conveyed goods to the Rand from the colonial railheads at Kimberley, in the Cape Colony, and

---

[1] D. M. Wilson, *Behind the Scenes in the Transvaal*, p. 254.

[2] Imports of machinery through Cape ports rose from £283,000 in value in 1887 to over £2,000,000 in the later 'nineties. The greater part of this machinery was imported for the mines and railways, although imports of industrial and agricultural machinery trebled in value. D. W. Gilbert, 'The Economic Effects of the Gold Discoveries upon South Africa,' *Quarterly Journal of Economics*, August 1933, p. 564.

Ladysmith, in Natal. Transport by rail, however, soon began to supersede the ox-wagon, for the colonial railways were rapidly extended towards Johannesburg, and the construction of a line from the Portuguese port of Lourenço Marques was begun. On the Rand the 'Boksburg Tramway', in reality a light railway, was constructed to connect the gold-mines with the coal deposits of the eastern Rand. The Cape railway was extended through the Orange Free State and reached Johannesburg in 1892; the line from Lourenço Marques reached Johannesburg in 1894; and that from Natal in 1895. All the lines to Johannesburg passed through the territory of more than one political unit. Political considerations influenced to some extent their construction and were to have important reactions on railway policy. Further, in the future, the supply of Native labour from Portuguese East Africa was to be intimately connected with railway policy.

The immediate effect of the renewal of railway construction was to increase the demand for Native labour, for Natives did most of the unskilled work. Between 1888 and 1890 2,014 miles of railway were constructed in South Africa, 889 in the South African Republic, 442 in the Orange Free State, 390 in the Cape Colony, and 293 in Natal. In addition, some 50 or 60 miles were laid in Portuguese East Africa.

As in the case of earlier construction, statistics of the number of Natives employed are unobtainable. According to contemporary reports, however, the employment of Native labour for this purpose had important repercussions on the supply of Native labour in other industries. Thus, in 1889 the Chamber of Mines reported that the competition of other mining districts and railway construction works in Natal, the Cape Colony, and on the Rand itself (where fifteen hundred to two thousand Natives were employed, at 'very high rates of pay') weakened its power to pay lower wage-rates without thereby adversely affecting the supply of labour.[1] In Natal the alleged scarcity of labour for work on the roads and on farms was attributed in part to the high wages paid on the railway works.[2] From East London in the Cape Colony, it was reported in 1890 that a great many Natives had left the division for work on the railways.[3]

---

[1] 'In support of a general reduction of wages, if possible by a fixed tariff, it is forcibly argued that the high wages now paid are themselves a principal reason of the short supply. . . . But it is to be remembered that the local mining industry is subject to outside competition in the native labour market. Other mining districts offer wages almost as high as the Rand, the railways being constructed in Natal and the Cape Colony draw away a large number of Kaffirs and the Boksburg Tramway is employing 1,500 to 2,000 Kaffirs at very high rates of pay.' *Chamber of Mines, Annual Report*, 1889.

[2] *Natal Blue Book*: 1888, C, p. 39; B, p. 4; 1889, B, p. 78; 1890–91, B, p. 120.

[3] (Cape) *Blue Book on Native Affairs*, 1890, G. 4, p. 9.

In Natal the demand for labour for work on the roads increased with the increase in traffic. Compulsory labour continued to be used for this purpose, but the Natives were reluctant to go out for road work and considerable difficulty was experienced in obtaining the labour required.[1]

In 1889 wages on the roads were fixed at twelve shillings and sixpence per month, rations also being provided and, as the reward of good service, blankets. The number of labourers supplied to the colonial engineer for road work rose from 1,854 in 1886 (it had been somewhat higher between 1881 and 1884) to 3,799 in 1893–4.[2]

At the colonial ports the increase in imports resulting largely from the development in mining led to more labour being required for stevedoring, and for this work Natives were largely employed at all the ports. At Capetown private firms continued to supplement the local supplies of 'coloured' labour by the introduction of Natives from the eastern parts of the Colony.[3]

B. NATIVE LABOUR FOR COAL PRODUCTION

The development of the coal-mining industry, resulting largely from the discovery of the Witwatersrand gold deposits, created a new demand for Native labour. Previously it had been known that there were coal deposits in Natal, in the South African Republic, and in the north-eastern districts of the Cape Colony. Farmers living in the vicinity of coal deposits had mined coal for their own use, but the absence of markets close at hand and of transport facilities had hindered development.[4] In 1879 coal had been discovered at Vereeniging on the Vaal River, in the extreme south of the South African Republic. Lewis and Marks, of Kimberley, had bought the coal-field and coal was mined to supply fuel to Kimberley. It had, however, to be transported three hundred miles by ox-wagon, and this prevented large-scale production. The development of gold-mining on the Rand provided a market much closer to hand. It also led to the opening of collieries at Witbank in the Middelburg district, sixty miles north-east by east of Johannesburg, and at Brakpan and Springs on the

---

[1] 'The supply of Native labour for the maintenance during the year of the augmented strength of the Road Parties throughout the Colony was a matter of peculiar difficulty. The great drain upon the labour market, caused by the demand for natives at the Gold Fields, and for our railways, made itself distinctly felt.' Report of Colonial Engineer, *Natal Blue Book*, 1888, C, p. 39.

[2] *Natal Blue Book*, 1881 FF, p. 114; 1882 FF, p. 47; 1883 FF, p. 76; 1884 FF, p. 1; 1886 H, p. 1; 1887 H, p. 36; 1888 H, p. 8; 1889 H, p. 8; 1893–4 H, pp. 3, 799.

[3] *South African Native Affairs Commission*, 1903–5, Vol. V, pp. 10, 11. Report of N. Adams Lowe, Superintendent Native Location, Table Bay Harbour Board.

[4] *Parl. Papers*, 1890 [C. 5897], p. 3, No. 104, Natal. Report on Bluebook for 1889; J. McPhee: 'Coal in the Transvaal,' *Proceedings of the Empire Mining and Metallurgical Congress*, 1930.

eastern Rand.[1] The coal output of the South African Republic increased rapidly. In the years 1893 and 1894 it averaged 670,000 tons, and in the years 1895 to 1899, 1,563,000.[2]

A large part of the coal produced was consumed by the mines. In the Transvaal from the beginning of gold-mining the production of gold and coal have been closely associated, for the financiers who bought up the gold deposits also bought up many of the coal-fields.

In Natal, although coal-mining was developed independently of gold production, large-scale production was an indirect result of the exploitation of the Witwatersrand gold-fields, for the railway line from Durban to Johannesburg passed through some of the Natal coal-fields and it was the extension of this line beyond Ladysmith that made production profitable for any but local purposes.[3] After 1889, when the railway was extended through the coal-fields, the industry expanded rapidly. In 1889, 29,000 tons of coal were produced, between 1890 and 1894 production averaged 130,000 tons annually, and between 1895 and 1899, 299,000. The number of labourers employed was small in relation to those employed in diamond and gold production. In 1889 the producing collieries employed 50 Europeans, 42 Indians, 359 Natives; by 1898 the numbers had risen to 118 Europeans, 854 Indians, and 1,753 Natives.[4] Rates of pay on the Natal coal-fields were high by local standards, but not so high as those in Johannesburg.[5]

In the Cape Colony coal-mining was also carried on in the district of Indwe in the north-east. Production was relatively small, but it rose from an average of 23,000 tons between 1885 and 1889, to 46,000 (1890–4) and 144,000 (1895–9). The number of Natives employed was consequently not large, and they were obtained from tribes in the vicinity.

C. NATIVE LABOUR FOR URBAN DEVELOPMENT

The increased trade due to developments on the Rand led to urban expansion throughout South Africa, and particularly at the ports. The demand for labour for all types of work kept pace with the growth in the size of the towns. In the Republics, in Natal, and in the eastern part of the Cape Colony, Native labourers did nearly all the manual work. It was only in the towns and

[1] Graham and Lategan, *The Coals of the Witbank District*, p. vii.
[2] *Official Year Book*, No. 9, 1926–7, p. 527.
[3] *Parl. Papers*, 1890 [C. 5897], p. 3, No. 104, Natal. Report on Bluebook for 1889.
[4] *Transvaal Labour Commission*, Evidence. [Cd. 1897], 1904, 11. 12,565, 12,582.
[5] *Natal Blue Book*, 1897, B, p. 74 (Report of Resident Magistrate for Newcastle.)

villages of the western districts of the Cape that Native labourers were the exception.

In the towns and villages in South Africa, and particularly at the ports and in Johannesburg, the cash wages paid to Native labourers continued to be much higher than on farms. At Port Elizabeth, for example, in 1893, the Associated Boating Companies employed three hundred Native labourers at wages of from 3s. to 4s. 6d. per day, hours of work being from 5 a.m. to 6 p.m.; the Harbour Board employed over a hundred Natives at 3s. per day for new hands and 3s. 6d. for old hands, hours of work being, summer months, 6 a.m. to 5 p.m., winter months, 6.30 a.m. to 5 p.m.[1] Native labourers in the building trade received from 2s. to 3s. a day.[2] From the small inland town of Steynsburg it was reported that coloured labourers received 2s. 6d. to 3s. a day, without food; or 1s. 6d. to 2s. a day, with food; while Native labourers employed on farms were usually paid in stock; but if paid in money they received 10s. a month and rations.[3]

Natives who came to work in urban areas usually lived either on their employers' premises or in mere hovels on the outskirts of the towns or villages. Usually some areas would be set aside, either by custom or by law, for Natives and other non-Europeans. The terms on which Natives were permitted to reside in towns varied somewhat in the different colonies and republics. In the South African Republic only Natives in the employ of Europeans were permitted, apparently, to live in towns, for the 'Town Regulations' provided that 'every male coloured person above the age of 12 years, residing in any town or village, shall be provided with a printed Town pass, setting out the name of his master and term of service'.[4] They further provided that 'coloured persons' (including Natives) might not reside in any place abutting on a public street, but that every householder, or owner of an 'erf' (plot) might keep 'in his backyard' whatever servants he required for domestic service. In the Orange Free State, under Act No. 8 of 1895, municipalities and village management boards were empowered to appoint locations for coloured people and to make regulations controlling residence in them, the grazing of cattle and other matters. Stringent pass regulations were subsequently enforced by many urban local authorities. In Natal, as we have

---

[1] (Cape) *Labour Commission, Report*, G. 3, 1894, p. xxviii. Vol. I of the evidence given before this Commission was published in G. 39, 1893 and Vols. II–IV were published together with the report in G 3, 1894.

[2] Ibid., p. xliv.   [3] Ibid., p. xlviii.

[4] Regulations for towns in the South African Republic, being a modification and amendment of the Regulations drafted in 1858 . . . accepted by First Volksraad, Article I, 256, dated 18 September 1899, section 37.

seen, 'togt' regulations which had been promulgated in 1874 controlled those Natives in Durban and Pietermaritzburg who were neither in monthly or yearly employment, nor the owners or renters of fixed property. In the Cape Colony there were no general provisions regarding the residence of Natives in urban areas, but certain municipalities were empowered to make regulations setting aside locations and controlling the residence of Natives within their boundaries.

The effect of such provisions on the labour market depended on whether they made work in urban areas more or less attractive than it would otherwise have been. In some cases, where pass laws and curfew restrictions were stringent, it almost certainly rendered work less attractive to Natives. Even so, there was usually more freedom for Native employees in urban areas than on farms occupied by Europeans. In some cases urban employment provided freedom from irksome tribal or parental control.

D. FARMING

The development of gold-mining augmented the stimulus to farming which had resulted from diamond production. For some years the Witwatersrand was dependent upon ox-wagon transport for nearly all its supplies, and the coming of the railways did not by any means completely displace it. Consequently transport-riding and cattle-breeding continued to be most profitable occupations. Agriculture also was stimulated, for prices on the Rand were extremely high. The prices of goods in demand at Johannesburg rose throughout South Africa.[1] European farmers in many parts of the country sought to increase their production and required more labour. But, as in the 'seventies, the forces which induced an increase in the demand for labour for farm work also provided many Natives with new opportunities for the sale of both their produce[2] and their labour.

[1] According to an index number of prices in the Cape Colony compiled by Mr. D. W. Gilbert from statistics in the Cape Statistical Register, the prices of domestic foods fell sharply from 1883 to 1886 and more slowly till 1888, then they rose rapidly from an index of 90 in 1888 to 105 in 1889; after a slight fall they continued to rise and in 1898 the index stood at 115. D. W. Gilbert,'The Economic Effects of the Gold Discoveries upon South Africa,' *Quarterly Journal of Economics*, August 1933, pp. 571–2.

[2] In 1890 the Civil Commissioner of the district of Herschel reported that: 'Prices of stock, especially trek oxen, and grain, have advanced at least one hundred per cent. during the past year, in consequence of the demand for transport to the gold-fields and the drought. A considerable number of trek oxen have been purchased at these advanced rates, as also larger quantities of grain, and this together with the substantial rise in the price of wool has been the means of circulating a large amount of money in the district. I have been informed by traders of standing in the district that there is more cash in circulation at the present time in this division than there has been since the Basuto War.' (Cape) *Blue Book on Native Affairs*, G. 4, 1890, p. 12.

Employment in the mines, in the towns, on the railways, and on the other public works was now available at wages higher than those hitherto prevailing on the farms. The farmers in the eastern part of the Cape Colony felt the competition of the diamond-fields. Previously most of the labour on the diamond-mines had come from the north and east. The development of the Rand diminished the supply from these sources[1] and employers on the diamond-fields now tried to attract labour from the south. Thus in 1889 the Civil Commissioner for the division of Peddie reported:

> The demand for labour from this district for the diamond-fields must materially affect all the divisions from this to George, Sneeuberg, and Middleburg, as hitherto large numbers of shearers and reapers have been accustomed to visit the farms within the area described, but as from 13s. to 15s. a week with rations and lodgings, and transport by rail is freely offered for labour for the diamond fields, the supply for other purposes will be reduced unless the farmers can afford to compete against such wages.[2]

Natives from the Transkeian Territories and Basutoland preferred work on the diamond- and gold-fields and railways, unless work offering on the farms was both close at hand and also for short periods. Natives from these areas would do seasonal work on farms in the Orange Free State and north-eastern Cape, but they were reluctant to go farther afield for farm work.[3] In Natal large numbers of labour tenants and their dependents sought work on the Rand.[4]

The increase in the competition for the services of Natives led to many complaints from the farmers. In Natal farmers and landlords complained, and magistrates reported, that labour-tenants evaded their obligations by going to the Rand where wages were 'exorbitant'. The report for 1897 of the Magistrate of Weenen gives a typical description of the exodus to Johannesburg. He wrote:

> The sole cause of the trouble continues to be the constant exodus of Natives to Johannesburg, where, attracted by the high wages paid them there, they persist in going, despite damages sued for by their landlords under their contracts and prosecution and punishment under the Masters and Servants (Native) Act, on their return.[5]

---

[1] cf. the report of the Resident Magistrate for the district of Upper Umkomanzi, Natal, that : 'Very few natives now obtain passes for Kimberley.' *Natal Blue Book*, 1893–4, BB, p. 36.

[2] (Cape) *Blue Book on Native Affairs*, G. 3, 1889, p. 21. The period for which natives going to the diamond-mines were required to contract was three months.

[3] *Cape Labour Commission Report*, G. 3, 1894, p. xii; Annexure.

[4] *Natal Blue Book*, 1894, pp. 3, 53.

[5] Ibid., 1897, B., p. 69; cf., 1888, B, pp. 75, 81.

In the Cape Colony complaints were directed principally
against the necessity for paying seasonal workers higher wages
and against the 'squatting' system, which, it was said, reduced
the supply of labour by enabling Natives to live without working
for Europeans,[1] and also led to the theft of stock. Often the
system was resorted to in order to secure a reserve supply of
labour.[2] Nevertheless, it was much criticized by those farmers
who wanted to get more labour without raising wages. In the
Cape Colony complaints about the scarcity of farm-labour led in
1890 to the appointment of a Select Committee, and, in 1893, of
a Commission to inquire into the labour problem. Neither the
Select Committee nor the Commission found that the scarcity of
labour was universal throughout the Cape Colony. The Select
Committee reported that in the western districts the competition
of public works had detrimentally affected the corn and wine
farmers, but its recommendation that Native labour be imported
for the public works from the eastern districts, Mozambique,
Delagoa Bay, and Damaraland shows that it considered the
shortage to be a local one.[3]

The Commission of 1893–4 was also of the opinion that the
scarcity of farm-labour was regional, and that it was greatest in
the western and north-western districts. Further, the Commissioners found that throughout the Colony some employers were
well supplied with labour while their neighbours complained that
they were short of labour.[4] They considered that there was a
considerable potential supply of labour and that the problem was
to induce labourers to go to those parts where they were most

[1] (Cape) *Labour Commission Report*, G. 3, 1894, ev. Vol. II, qq. 10,458;
11,088; 11,309; 13,320; 13,970; 15,571; 16,529; 18,461; 18,705–8. Vol. III,
q. 25,244.
   [2] ev. Vol. II, ibid., qq. 12,039; 13,132; 16,532; 21,773.
   [3] 'Your Committee having examined a number of witnesses and considered
the petitions and such papers as were laid before them, are of opinion that the
evidence later superabundantly establishes the fact that, in the Western Districts, the employment to any large extent of the so-called Cape Boys on railways, harbours, and other public works, or the conditions of pay and other
privileges offered to such labourers by those in charge of such works, does
materially and seriously affect the labour market to the detriment of both corn
and wine farmers, especially at certain seasons of the year, such as pruning,
wine-making, ploughing, and reaping.' (Cape) *Select Committee on Labour*,
1890, A. 12, p. iii.
   Farmers from the Caledon district who gave evidence before this committee
complained that since public works had been under construction in the neighbourhood they had had to pay wages 'as high as 2s.' a day, or even 2s. 6d., and
3s. in the ploughing and reaping seasons, whereas previously wages had been
1s. 6d. Similarly at Paarl, wages in the reaping seasons were said now to be
2s. 6d. and 3s. a day, with food in addition, whereas previously they had been
1s. 6d. and 2s. On the government public works wages were from 3s. 6d. to 4s.
a day, and hours were regular and shorter than on farms. Ibid. Minutes of
ev. p. 2, *et passim*.
   [4] (Cape) *Labour Commission, Report*, G. 3, 1894, para. 7.

urgently required. Farmers, moreover, had failed to avail themselves of the opportunity for attracting labour from a distance.[1]

They pointed out that, although competition had raised the
wages of daily labourers, the wages of monthly servants on farms
had remained stationary for a long time. According to their
report such wages did not vary greatly throughout the Cape
Colony, Natal, and the Orange Free State, nor did they compare
unfavourably with the wages paid in towns when facilities for
grazing stock and other privileges enjoyed by farm servants were
taken into account. They said:

> 'Although as a rule it might be said that their wages are from ten
> shillings a month and upwards in cash, yet when all is calculated
> which is provided for the servants besides the money wage or its
> equivalent in stock, which is commonly preferred, the total often
> comes up to considerably above three pounds a month; and besides
> this such servants, on pastoral farms especially, have certain
> privileges; for instance, their stock running free with that of their
> employer's and benefiting by his entire animals, salt, dipping,
> etc., so that the monthly farm servant can often lay by much more
> than the town or day labourer.'[2]

Farm-labour was not, however, attractive to the migratory
labourer anxious to obtain money for the payment of taxes and
the purchase of goods.

E. OFFICIAL ATTEMPTS TO PROMOTE THE SUPPLY OF NATIVE LABOUR

In these circumstances many employers throughout South
Africa looked to Government action to promote the supply of
Native labour. Others were less optimistic, if not sceptical. The
Cape Labour Commission of 1893–4 considered that official action
might be desirable,[3] but it rather doubted the efficacy of measures
designed to that end. It concluded its report by emphasizing

---

[1] 'There exists material in considerable quantity for a labour supply in parts
where the European population contains many of the poorest class, and in parts
where the native population abounds, but the difficulty is to induce members
of these populations to work or move towards where they are wanted to work.
Government and other great employers of labour occasionally employ agencies
to obtain the labourers they want, and they have succeeded in inducing a supply
to come from some parts, and the supply is slowly increasing; but farmers have
no workable organization among themselves and make only isolated and ill-
directed and generally ineffective attempts to attain this end.' Ibid., para. 14.

[2] Ibid., para. 9.

[3] 'It may be the case that they (farmers) look too much to Government; but
it is found wise elsewhere for Government to undertake the promotion of
labour supply, and by doing so here, it would benefit itself as a great employer
of labour, do good to farmer and labourer alike, and promote the well-being
and productiveness of the Colony.' Ibid., p. xvi, para. 14.

that employers by improving their relations with their labourers could do more to increase the quantity and quality of labour than 'anything the Commission could recommend or Government carry out'.[1]

In the Cape Colony the attempt to increase the supply of Native labour by imposing taxes on Natives renting European-owned land was redoubled. In 1892 the location law was amended.[2] The amended law required the owner of every private location[3] to take out a licence, for which £1 was charged, for every male adult Native resident on his land who was not required for the 'due working' of any private property. The purpose of this measure was said to have been 'to place an impost, a tax of £1, upon the lazy native and not upon the industrious native or the employer of such a native'.[4]

The Act is reported to have caused considerable dispersion of the Native population within the Cape Colony, partly because landowners turned Native tenants off their land rather than pay the increased tax (presumably they were unable to pass on the tax), and partly because many Natives migrated, being disturbed by the measure, which they did not fully understand. According to the Civil Commissioner for Alexandria three thousand Natives for these reasons left that division.[5]

An attempt was also made by the imposition of a 'labour tax' to force Natives living within Native reserves to go out to work. Under the so-called 'Glen Grey' Act of 1894 a tax of ten shillings per annum was imposed, in the districts to which the Act was applied, on 'every male native residing in the district, exclusive of natives in possession of lands under ordinary quitrent titles, or in freehold, who in the judgment of the Resident Magistrate is fit for and capable of labour'. Natives who had been employed beyond the borders of their district for not less than three months during the preceding year, or for a total period of three years, and those who had been employed for 'adequate remuneration' within the district, were exempt from the tax.

The labour tax was alleged to be a *quid pro quo* for the reservation of land for the use of Natives.[6] Supporters of this provision of the Glen Grey Act appear to have expected it to have important repercussions on the supply of Native labour. The Prime Minister,

[1] Ibid., para. 48.   [2] Act No. 33 of 1892.
[3] Under this Act, No. 33 of 1892, the number of male adult natives whose occupation of huts or dwellings on any one farm constituted a Native location was to be determined in each division by the Divisional Council, subject to the provision that it was to be not less than three or more than seven.
[4] *Cape Hansard*, 1899, p. 77. W. P. Schreiner.
[5] (Cape) *Labour Commission, Report*, G. 3, 1894, para. 28.
[6] *Select Committee on the Glen Grey Act*, A. 33, 1898, p. 49, ev. Cecil J. Rhodes.

Cecil Rhodes, when introducing the Bill, paid great attention to
this aspect of it. He spoke of the effect the 'gentle stimulant of
the labour tax' would have on the Natives:

> 'You will', he told the Legislative Assembly, 'remove them from
> that life of sloth and laziness, you will teach them the dignity of
> labour and make them contribute to the prosperity of the State,
> and make them give some return for our wise and good government.'[1]

Further, he promised that if the Bill were passed, 'in order to
assist the western farmer', he would propose

> 'that the Commissioner of Crown Lands should deal with the
> question of putting native labour from the East on the railways.
> He anticipated, as a result of the taxes, they would have considerable
> pressure of labour.'[2]

The Bill was passed, but in practice the labour tax broke down
almost at once. It was unpopular, both with the Natives and
with their magistrates who had to administer it and who regarded
it as both irritating and unnecessary.[3] This provision of the Act
soon became a dead letter and was repealed in 1905.[4] Meanwhile
it was partly responsible for delaying the extension of the Act
within the Transkeian districts, as it made the Natives suspicious
of the whole measure.[5]

Other provisions of the Glen Grey Act dealing with the grant
of individual tenure and the imposition of local taxation also
seemed likely to affect the supply of Native labour. The Act
made provision for the survey of the district of Glen Grey (the
old Tambookie location) in the neighbourhood of Queenstown
and the issue of title deeds for arable allotments to individual
Native land-holders. The rights of the title-holders were restricted in various ways. Allotments had to be beneficially
occupied. They could only be transferred subject to official
approval. On the death of the title-holder the allotment passed
to his heir according to the official interpretation and regularization
of Native custom. At the same time the legal formalities of
transfer were simplified and the cost reduced, for where individual

---

[1] *Cape Hansard*, 1894, pp. 362–9.   [2] Ibid.
[3] *Select Committee on the Glen Grey Act*, A. 33, 1898, pp. 8, 9, 12, 14, 40;
(Cape) *Blue Book on Native Affairs*, 1901, p. 80; *South African Native Affairs
Commission*, 1903–5. Vol. V, p. 21, Annexure 10; *Transvaal Labour Commission,
Report* [Cd. 1896], 1904, para. 7.
[4] Act No. 14 of 1905.
[5] H. G. Elliot, Chief Magistrate of Tembuland, Transkei, and Pondoland,
giving evidence before the Select Committee of 1898, said: 'I think the labour
tax extremely objectionable and irritating; and it has been without any benefit
whatever. . . . Had it not been for that labour tax I am satisfied a lot of other
districts would have applied to come under the Act.' *Select Committee on the
Glen Grey Act*, A. 33, 1898, p. 24.

tenure had previously been introduced the legal formalities of transferring land had seldom been observed by the Natives.

We have seen that Native administrators had long advocated the introduction of individual tenure as an essential condition for the progress of agriculture and that some people had advocated it as a means of increasing the supply of Native labour. During the 'eighties and early 'nineties support for the measure increased on the latter ground. In 1894 the Cape Labour Commission reported that suggestions were made in many different quarters that 'a royal road' to increase the supply of labour was

> by furnishing all the natives in the Eastern and Transkeian terri-
> tories with individual titles, and preventing all who had no title from
> occupying land.[1]

The Commissioners, however, considered that neither the Natives nor the country were prepared to pay for the necessary surveys and that the Natives generally did not appreciate, understand nor ask for individual title, although they were of the opinion that some form of fixity of tenure should be granted both as regards arable holdings and commonages.

Some supporters of the grant of individual title to land appar- ently desired the right of transfer to be unrestricted, their opinion being that Natives to whom such grants were made would sell their land. The Commissioners of 1894 reported that they did not think that such a step would have the effect of creating a large class of landless Natives who would be forced to earn their living by working for Europeans. They said: 'the natives where they have received titles, have not, so far as the Kaffir race is concerned, shown so much disposition to part with them as some expected would be the case; there have hardly been any instances as yet while many of the Fingoes and others have, on the other hand, bought land largely.'[2]

In contrast to a large section of local opinion they considered that in any case the introduction of individual tenure could only have a very gradual effect on the supply of labour. Experience was to justify their expectations. The survey of Native reserves and the issue of title deeds to garden allotments did not have any very marked effect on the occupation of the land, for the Natives who did not receive allotments under the new system continued to live in the reserves and to cultivate fields and graze their cattle on the commonages. Further, the system introduced did not in itself bring about any considerable changes in farming methods and so did not result to any great extent in increasing agricultural

---

[1] (Cape) *Labour Commission Report*, G. 3, 1894, para. 35, cf. Appendix U.
[2] Ibid.

production. Nevertheless, modifications in Native land tenure were necessary for the adaptation of the old methods of subsistence farming to the changing conditions.[1]

Although, therefore, the 'Glen Grey' tenure did not have much effect on agricultural technique it increased the pressure on Natives to enlarge their cash incomes, for title-holders had to meet part of the expenses of the survey and the quitrent which was charged for allotments (fifteen shillings for allotments up to five morgen[2] and three shillings for every additional morgen) was greater than the hut tax of ten shillings which had previously in practice entitled Natives to cultivate fields of varying sizes[3] and to the use of the commonages.

In addition, the Glen Grey Act instituted a system of district councils which were to levy rates for local purposes. In practice the rate levied was ten shillings, payable by registered holders of 'Glen Grey' titles and by all other male adult Natives 'fit and capable of labour' with the exception of those holding land under ordinary quitrent or freehold title. Thus, apart from the labour tax the new system increased the cash requirements of Native land-holders. The system was first applied in the Glen Grey

[1] In 1884 R. J. Dick, Special Magistrate in the Kingwilliamstown Division had reported: 'The system under which natives obtained land from their Chiefs or Headmen in times gone by answered fairly well, and gave rise to no dissatisfaction, simply because there was more land than the people required. But it is a very different matter now. The locations are all becoming densely populated, and in addition are very heavily stocked. The consequence is that unless the commonage and grazing ground is brought into use as garden land, the newcomers and freshly married men are not able to cultivate. The land, although held in common by the tribe, is very unequally apportioned, each man or family having claimed or cultivated as much as he or they pleased when land was plentiful, so that some have about 40 acres of garden land while later comers cannot find a garden plot.' (Cape) *Blue Book on Native Affairs*, G. 3, 1884, p. 31.

[2] One morgen = 2·12 British acres.

[3] The following extract from the report of the Departmental Committee, Native Tax (Consolidated) Bill, gives a review of Native taxation in the Cape Proper and in the Transkeian territories before Act. No. 41 of 1925: 'In the Province of the Cape of Good Hope Proper a fixed annual amount of 10s. as hut tax is payable by the occupiers of each hut situate on Crown land, in reserves known as Native locations. This tax was at one time uniform throughout reserves in the Cape Proper, but, at different times and under varying conditions, certain areas were surveyed for individual tenure, and payment of quitrent by title holders was substituted for the payment of hut tax. . . .

'As successive portions of the Transkeian territories came under the Cape Government the payment of a hut tax was made one of the conditions under which they were taken over.

'Land administration was from the first a very important function of the Magistrate, and in course of time the hut tax developed into a land tax of 10s. per allotment. The Districts of Butterworth, Nqamakwe, Txome, Idutywa, Umtata, Xalanga, and Engcobo have been surveyed and in these districts quitrent is payable by title-holders, and hut tax by occupiers of huts on the Commonage as in the Glen Grey Districts.'

On the size of allotments in the Ciskei, see above, footnote 1.

district, but it was designed for extension to the Transkeian Territories, and was immediately, in 1894, applied to four Transkeian districts.[1] Later it was applied to other districts in the Transkeian Territories.

In the South African Republic during this period, as in the Cape of Good Hope, the Government attempted to increase the supply of labour. In 1895 it revised the taxation of Natives in order to take advantage of the new sources of revenue and to increase the pressure forcing Natives to work. Under Law No. 24 of 1895, a so-called 'Hut Tax' of ten shillings was levied. Each male Native above twenty-one years of age who was unmarried or had only one wife was assessed as one hut, and each additional wife as an additional hut. Consequently the tax was in reality a poll and wife tax.[2] A poll tax of two pounds was also levied on male Natives over twenty-one years old. Exemption from this tax was granted to Natives who by reason of age or chronic disease were prevented from working and were at the same time in needy circumstances, and also to Natives who resided among white people as servants, and to those Natives employed by Commissioners and Sub-commissioners of Natives in the country districts who drew no Government wage. According to a memorandum prepared by the Department of Native Affairs:

> The second tax, the Poll Tax, was primarily raised for the sake of revenue, but it was also a strong endeavour to force the Natives to work as it was quite impossible for those residing away from European centres to raise the necessary money to pay the above-mentioned taxes, and many were thus forced to come and work in the towns and on the mines.[3]

In 1898 it was further decreed that these taxes were to be collected from Natives and coloured persons on the gold-fields and in the towns.[4]

In the same year that the taxation of Natives was increased, a 'squatters' law'[5] was passed limiting to five families the number of Natives allowed in respect of every farm or divided portion of a farm, except where special permission for an increased number was obtained from the Government. This law could not be enforced. Whole tribes were living on land which had come into the occupation or possession of private owners. On many farms throughout the Transvaal and especially in the Zoutpansberg,

---

[1] Proclamation No. 352 of 1894.

[2] In addition a road tax of 2s. 6d. a year was levied from 1894 on all male natives above the age of twenty-one who were not in service.

[3] Memorandum on Native Taxation, Transvaal. Submitted in evidence to the Native Economic Commission, U.G. 22, 1932.

[4] First Volksraad Resolution of 14 July, 1898.

[5] Law No. 21 of 1895.

Lydenberg, Waterberg, and Middelberg districts large unauthorized locations continued on private farms, the Natives paying rent either in labour or in money.

In the Orange Free State, too, as in the Transvaal, attempts were made to bring about a redistribution of the potential Native labour force. In 1893 a 'squatters' law' was passed limiting to five families the number of Natives who might normally reside on farms occupied by Europeans. Landdrosts were given authority to allow up to fifteen families to reside on one farm, but a tax of five pounds per annum was to be levied for each family in excess of ten. Only two Native families might reside on land not occupied by Europeans.[1] This law, like the 'squatters' laws' in other parts of South Africa' could not be effectively enforced.

Although the specific attempts to increase the supply of labour by measures such as the Cape labour tax and the 'squatters' laws' of Natal and the Republics failed because they were not effectively enforced, nevertheless the supply of Native labour was on the whole increasing. Within a generation new opportunities and new wants on the one hand and taxation on the other were causing Natives to go out in unprecedented numbers to work for Europeans. Pass statistics give some indication of the number of Natives leaving the Transkeian Territories and Natal for work in other centres. The number leaving the Transkeian Territories rose from 38,400 in 1896 to 61,000 in 1898,[2] while the number going to the South African Republic from Natal averaged over 20,000 a year between 1896 and 1898. Large numbers also went out to work from the British Protectorates of Basutoland and Bechuanaland, and from Swaziland. By the end of the century only in the more remote districts of the Northern and Eastern Transvaal and Zululand were the Natives of South Africa relatively independent of working for wages under European supervision.

[1] *South African Native Affairs Commission, 1903–5*, para. 115.
[2] Return showing number of Passes issued in 1898 in the Transkeian territories to Natives to proceed to various centres in search of employment:

	Natal	Orange Free State	South African Republic	Other Centres	Total
Tembuland	42	334	5,940	11,358	17,674
Transkei	40	3,469	5,990	17,138	26,637
Pondoland Port St. Johns }	1,941	102	1,322	762	4,127
East Griqualand	2,211	242	5,049	5,093	12,595
Total	4,234	4,147	18,301	34,351	61,033

(Cape) *Blue Book on Native Affairs*, G. 31, 1899, p. 126.

PART III

THE PROBLEM OF THE TWENTIETH CENTURY COMPETITION BETWEEN EUROPEAN AND NATIVE

CHAPTER IX
INTRODUCTORY

IT has been argued in the preceding sections that during the earlier part of the nineteenth century the first preoccupation of the majority of Europeans in South Africa in the problems arising from contact with Bantu tribes had been with defence and personal security, and that, subject to the need for defence, they were concerned to obtain labourers. In the latter part of the century, as the need for defence grew less, their attempts to induce and compel the Natives to work for them became more systematic. The predominant European attitude was that of an employer class concerned to increase the supply of labour without raising its cost.

During the twentieth century some new forces came into being and the situation became more complex. During the nineteenth century the development of mining had introduced skilled European employees whose interest had coincided with the desire of employers to increase the supply of Native labour. At that time European and Native labour were co-operant factors of production and an increase in the supply of one class of employee tended to increase the productivity and wages of the other.

In the twentieth century a cleavage of interest appeared between the European employee, on the one hand, and, on the other, the European employer and Native labourer. There were two aspects of this cleavage of interest. Some of the Native labourers began to acquire skill and to compete for work with European-skilled artisans, and particularly with the European miners. At the same time it became apparent that some of the Europeans who had no land were losing such means of support as were hitherto available to them. They had consequently to compete with Natives and other non-Europeans for unskilled work. In both cases Natives and Europeans became competing factors of production, and it was in the sectional interest of groups of Europeans to exclude Native competitors. The attempt of such groups to maintain or create a privileged position for themselves has been one of the dominating forces in the labour market in South Africa.

In the mining industries it has led to the creation of a statutory colour bar, to the restriction of Natives to kinds of work generally designated as unskilled or semi-skilled, and to the maintenance of the organization of the labour force on the basis of a relatively large number of low-paid migratory Native labourers and a small proportion of highly paid European miners and supervisors. Accepting the bar to the advancement of Natives, employers in the gold-mining industry contend that Native labourers work to obtain a more or less predetermined sum of money, to meet such obligations as taxes and debts already incurred, and that consequently it pays them to combine to keep down the level of Native wages. Higher wages, they consider, would result in their Native labourers working for a shorter period and consequently the supply of labour would be reduced.

The gold- and coal-mines of the Transvaal have succeeded in establishing a combination of employers for the purpose of buying Native labour and there is ground for believing that its importance in the market is sufficient to enable it to depress the level of Native wages throughout South Africa below that which would result from competitive bidding.

Successive governments have sanctioned this policy. They have considered that it increases the profitability of mining and consequently its capacity to employ Europeans.

At the same time mining, and particularly gold-mining, has been taxed directly and indirectly to foster farming and manufacturing industries. Before the South African War (1899–1902), in the days of the South African Republic, the gold-mines had been officially regarded primarily as a source of revenue for the State. The majority of the men engaged in gold production were 'uitlanders', who were useful as long as they contributed wealth to the burghers of the Republic. Under the British administration this attitude was modified, but not fundamentally changed. The mines were wasting assets to be exploited rapidly so that they might provide revenue for reconstructing the late Republics and for establishing a strong British element, rural as well as urban, throughout the conquered territories. Subsequently, after the Transvaal secured responsible government in 1906, and more particularly after the formation of the Union of South Africa in 1910, the same policy of taxing the mines was continued, and the proceeds have been used to promote other industries.

Varied and widespread attempts have been made to assist European farmers, to protect European-skilled artisans from Native competitors, and to create employment in manufacturing industry for those Europeans not engaged in professional work, farming, or the skilled trades. To this end attempts are being made to restrict the freedom of the Native population to migrate to industrial centres for employment other than mining.

Simultaneously with these new developments official measures to increase the supply of Native labourers have continued, but there has been a growing tendency to attempt to confine them chiefly to domestic service, 'unskilled' work in mining, and work on farms. The policy has gained ground of regarding the Native population as hewers of wood and drawers of water only, and of restricting them to the less skilled types of manual work.

It has thus come about that one of the most striking characteristics of the South African economy is the authoritarian attempt to regulate the distribution of resources between different industries and different racial groups. An outstanding example is the development of the racial policy known as 'segregation'. The former policy of protecting the Natives within the Cape Colony and Natal from some of the effects of sudden contact with European ideas and legal systems, by reserving land for their use, has developed into an official Union policy of demarcating European and Native areas within each of which the supposed interests of the different racial groups are to be dominant.

The effect of these measures on the labour market is to divert resources from one industry to another. What the general situation would have been had there been no such diversion can only be conjectured. The forces operating are far too numerous and conflicting to permit of confident judgment. As to the effects of particular measures, analysis can be more fruitful; and in the chapters which follow the attempt is made to ascertain their economic significance in the market for Native labour.

CHAPTER X

THE SUPPLY OF UNSKILLED LABOUR FOR GOLD MINING, 1901–1907

A. THE IMMEDIATE POST-WAR PROBLEM

THE South African War of 1899–1902 for a time disrupted the growing economic interdependence of the different parts of South Africa. Resources were diverted to wartime purposes. Mining came to a standstill. On the Rand the European mining population either enlisted or sought sanctuary at the coast. In the Transvaal and Orange Free State, and also in parts of Natal and the Cape Colony, farming was suspended, for war ranged over the countryside. Before the end of the war most of those of the rural population of the Republics who were not in the field were swept into the towns, which had been captured by the British forces, or into concentration camps.[1] Their sheep and cattle were commandeered by one side or the other, and many of their homesteads destroyed.

At the ports, through which military supplies came, activity was feverish. The boom caused by military expenditure was unprecedented even at the Cape, where 'prosperity' and war had been linked since the re-victualling station had been established.

Britain annexed the two Republics long before the fighting came to an end, and when peace was signed, in May 1902, the work of reconstruction had already begun. From the start Milner based his policy upon the prosperity and rapid development of gold-mining.[2] He regarded the rapid exploitation of gold as essential; the faster it could be got out of the ground the greater would be the 'over-spill', the excess over the profits required to remunerate the capital invested, and 'it is that over-spill which benefits the local community and fills the coffers of the State, and can be used for the general advantage of the country'.[3] A prosperous mining industry was to be the basis for building up other resources and for establishing British settlers on the land to strengthen the British element throughout the conquered territory.[4]

The mines were permitted to reopen as soon as it became

[1] At the end of the war there were 200,000 persons, including 80,000 Natives, in the different concentration camps. Walker, *History*, op. cit., p. 499.

[2] *Parl. Papers*, 1903, XLV [Cd. 1552], p. 3. Milner to Chamberlain. Dispatch on the Finances of the Transvaal and Orange River Colony.

[3] *Milner Papers*, ed. C. Headlam, Vol. II, p. 491. Milner speaking at the March session of the Inter-Colonial Council, 1904.

[4] [Cd. 1552], 1903, op. cit. *passim*; cf. E. A. Walker, op. cit., pp. 501, 507; H. A. Wyndham, 'The Formation of the Union, 1901–1910', *Cambridge History of the British Empire*, p. 613.

possible to spare transport from the requirements of the army and the concentration camps. Before the end of the war 2,000 stamps had been restarted; the number in operation before the war had been 6,340.

Before the war Portuguese East Africa had been the most important source of Native labour employed on the Rand gold-mines, and towards the close of 1901, before the end of the war, Milner arranged the *modus vivendi* to ensure a continuation of the supply of labour from Portuguese East Africa. By this agreement the Transvaal Government promised that the pre-war railway tariffs and classification of goods would be maintained, and that if modifications were made on the colonial lines the rates on the Lourenço-Marques–Johannesburg line would be modified in proportion in order that the port of Lourenço Marques should get the same share of the railway traffic as before the war. In return recruiting in Portuguese Africa was to continue to be permitted.

The British Administration also considered the wishes of employers of Native labour when framing the Pass Laws, and other legislation concerning Natives, in the newly acquired Colony. Much of the legislation of the Republican Government was taken over and proclaimed, the aim of the British authorities being to preserve the laws and regulations of the late Republic where they were not in conflict with British policy.[1]

The pass system was regarded as necessary for all Natives, 'as much for the security and protection of themselves as for the white people', but it was hoped that impartial administration would remedy such abuses as the capricious refusal of masters and officials to issue passes and the exaction of personal service or other payment in return for the issue of a pass.[2] Passes were not, however, to be issued to Natives under contract of service except with the consent, in writing, of the employer.[3]

The pass system was in fact a means of enforcing contracts. In labour districts, special regulations were designed to record 'the whole of a man's service, his movements and character, and so to control his career as to check the vicious habit of desertion formerly prevailing'.[4] Unscrupulous labour agents were considered

---

[1] Memorandum by Sir Godfrey Lagden upon Proclamations relating to: (1) General Pass Regulations; (2) Special Regulations for Labour Districts; (3) Regulations for controlling, procuring, and engaging of Native labourers and their management at mines; (4) Coloured Person's Exemption; (5) Prohibition of supply of Intoxicating Liquor to Coloured Persons (Amendment of Law 19 of 1898). *Parl. Papers*, 1902, LXIX [Cd. 904], p. 19.

[2] Ibid., p. 20.

[3] Native Passes Proclamation, No. 37 of 1901, Schedule, General Pass Regulations, Sec. 18.

[4] Memorandum by Sir Godfrey Lagden, op. cit. [Cd. 904], 1902, p. 20.

to have been largely responsible for the extent of desertion, as they both misrepresented conditions of service and encouraged Native labourers to break their contracts. To mitigate such abuses it was made obligatory for recruiting agents and compound managers to secure licences from the Government. These licences could be cancelled if the holders abused their position. In addition, severe penalties were imposed for misconduct.[1]

Inspectors were appointed in mining areas whose functions were to guard the interests of Natives working on the mines, supervise contracts, prevent ill-treatment, and, at the same time, 'insist upon the natives performing their contracts and take measures for the detection and adequate punishment of deserters'.[2]

Thus, while an attempt was made to check the abuses to which recruiting and the system of capitation fees had given rise, the mining industry was assured of the continuance of a criminal sanction to contracts of service, and more effective administration promised an increase in actual control as compared to the Republican days.

The end of the war saw an extravagant gold boom. Two hundred and ninety-nine new gold-mining companies were floated[3] and they and the older companies all clamoured for labour. The war, however, had disturbed the supply of Native labour, for the mines had been closed down;[4] the Natives returned to their homes, and once there they were averse to going far afield for long periods while conditions were unsettled. In addition, the military authorities had employed a large number of Natives, offering high money wages and plenty of food, often combined with very little work.[5] Activity at the ports was great during the war and immediate post-war period. The result was that as the diamond- and gold-mines reopened they felt keenly the effects both of the disturbance to the supply of labour and of the competing demands.[6]

The De Beers Diamond Mines, which had previously been able to maintain their supply from labour offering itself at the compounds, had to have recourse to recruiting, and for a short time after they reopened they experienced great difficulty in obtaining or retaining men with sufficient skill and experience for

---

[1] Labour Agents and Compound Overseers Proclamation, No. 38 of 1901.
[2] [Cd. 904] 1902, op. cit., p. 20.
[3] *Transvaal Labour Commission, Report* [Cd. 1896], 1904, p. 74.
[4] A few mines were allowed by the Republican authorities to continue working, their output being taken over by the State. On the British occupation of Johannesburg milling operations were prohibited. *Transvaal Chamber of Mines, Report for 1900 and 1901*, p. 124.
[5] *De Beers Consolidated Mines, Ltd., Annual Report*, 1902, p. 5.
[6] Ibid., 1901, pp. 4, 28; (Cape) *Blue Book on Native Affairs*, 1902, G. 25, pp. 3, 4, 21, 25, 29, 33, 38, 70; 1903, G. 29, pp. 5, 7.

drilling.[1] By the middle of 1903, however, the situation had eased and they had plenty of labour and no fears concerning their future supply.[2]

On the gold-mines the supply of Native labour fell far below expectations and threatened to bring the boom to an abrupt end. The mines had been organized on the basis of a large number of cheap Native labourers and a small number of European miners and supervisors. As we have seen, high wages had to be paid to attract skilled miners to the Transvaal, and it was largely the plentiful supply of cheap Native labour which had made possible the proving and working of the relatively low grade ore of the Witwatersrand.

B. THE NATIVE LABOUR POLICY OF THE TRANSVAAL CHAMBER OF MINES

From the beginning, combination for the reduction of Native wages had been one of the chief aims of the Chamber of Mines. During the war the system of engaging Native labourers and the rates of pay had been reorganized on paper in a further attempt to prevent competition between the mines bidding up wages and the costs of recruiting.

On the ground that competitive recruiting increased the cost of labour without increasing the supply, and, also, that the abuses of misrepresentation and fraud were due to competitive recruiting and might even reduce the supply of labour through giving the gold-fields a bad name, the engaging of all Native labour was centralized.[3]

The Witwatersrand Native Labour Association was constituted in 1900 to replace the Native Labour Supply Association. Its regulations provided that:

> No Company, whilst a member of the Witwatersrand Native Labour Association, will be allowed under any circumstances to engage any but white labour, except through the agency of the Association. This will apply: (1) to all natives who, from having previously worked on your mine, or who from any cause may come forward and seek such work voluntarily; (2) to those who have been recruited within or without the Transvaal—in fact to all natives or coloured men employed either above or below ground on your property.'[4]

---

[1] (Cape) *Blue Book on Native Affairs*, 1902, p. 3; *De Beers Consolidated Mines, Ltd., Annual Report*, 1901, p. 4.

[2] *De Beers Consolidated Mines, Ltd., Annual Report*, 1903, p. 9.

[3] *Transvaal Labour Commission*, Evidence [Cd. 1897], 1904, p. 31, q. 746; ev. Mr. F. Perry, Chairman and Managing Director, Witwatersrand Native Labour Association.

[4] *Transvaal Chamber of Mines, Report for 1900 and 1901*, p. 112.

It was not a profit-making concern, but an association of the various mines for the purpose of engaging and distributing Native labour among themselves. Describing the Association in 1903, the Chairman said:

'It is often referred to as a monopoly, and it is stated that it has secured special privileges from the Transvaal Government. This is not the case. In fact, the Association is merely a co-operative society, all the members of which are shareholders. All the members agree to deal with the society only. The only penalty for breach of this agreement is exclusion from the Society. Any individual member is perfectly at liberty to secede from the Society and deal elsewhere if he thinks it be in his interest to do so.'[1]

Thus, it was admittedly a voluntary monopoly and, in addition, it had obtained an official monopoly of recruiting within Portuguese East Africa from the Government of that colony.[2]

In addition to controlling the engagement and distribution of the Native labour force the Association decided to reduce the rate of pay to a maximum of thirty-five shillings and a minimum of thirty shillings per month of thirty working days, subject to certain exceptions.[3]

Most of the Transvaal collieries were under the control of the same financial groups as the gold-mines, and were members of the newly organized Witwatersrand Native Labour Association. It was thought that such a powerful combination of employers would be in a position to dictate wage-rates. Moreover, the new rates had the appearance of a rise, because, early in the war, the Republican Government had, by proclamation, reduced to 20s. a month the wages of those Natives who were allowed to remain on the Rand. Before the war, however, rates had been higher. In 1899 the average rate had been 49s. 9d. per month, rising to 53s. 9d. in August. In 1895 rates had been from £2 to £3 a month.

Apart from their natural desire to reduce wage costs many of the leaders of the mining industry believed that most of the Natives who went out to work desired a fixed sum of money to

[1] *Transvaal Labour Commission*, Evidence, op. cit., p. 31, q. 746, ev. Mr. F. Perry.

[2] Notice No. 323, Boletin Official, 7 July, 1900, quoted in *Transvaal Chamber of Mines, Report for 1900 and 1901*, p. 104; 1906, pp. 40–44.

[3] *Transvaal Chamber of Mines Report for 1900 and 1901*, p. 12. The exceptions were: 'B. That the rate of wage to be paid to natives known as piccaninnies shall be 15s. per month of 30 days, or 6d. per diem; C. That a maximum of 7½ per cent. of the total number of natives employed on any mine may receive special wages; D. That the maximum rate of wage to be paid for shaft sinking on non-milling mines shall be at the rate of 50s. per month of 30 days, or 1s. 8d. per diem; but for producing companies the maximum shall be 40s. per month of 30 days, or 1s. 4d. per diem, except in cases of companies sinking an independent shaft, when the maximum wage may be paid.'

satisfy specific wants and obligations, and that, therefore, if wages were higher their periods of work on the mines would be shorter and more intermittent, and that consequently in the long run the supply of Native labour would be reduced.

In discussion of the supply of Native labour in South Africa, there has been much confusion between the possibly divergent effects of an increase in wage-rates upon the supply to individual employers and upon the total supply. Under competitive conditions individual employers can only increase their supply by offering better terms, but the effect of higher rates in general may be to lessen the supply of labour available for all. There is room for difference of opinion on the latter point, and evidence upon it is not conclusive. The South African Native Affairs Commission (1903–5) made specific inquiries into the effect of wage-rates on the supply of labour. It was not able to do more than collect opinions,[1] but it came to the conclusion that there was

> A measure of truth in the suggestion that while increased wages might have the effect of tempting a larger number of labourers into the market; on the other hand, such increased gains would enable them to remain for a longer period at their own homes.'[2]

The mining industry reduced wages and centralized the system of recruiting and engaging Native labour in the belief that the same or a larger supply would be obtained at a lower average cost.[3]

Its plans were frustrated; for after the wartime dislocation of the labour market and under the new conditions as regards pay and engagement the Natives were not prepared to work on the mines even in pre-war numbers. The number employed was reduced from 88,627 in 1898 and 96,704 in 1899 to 42,587 in 1902 and 64,454 in 1903.[4]

Some mine managers considered that the most effective means of increasing the supply of Native labour to the mining industry was to raise wage-rates, and the central labour association modified its schedule of wage-rates. In 1902 a recommendation was made that the average earnings of the Natives on any mine should not exceed fifty shillings per head for a month of thirty shifts, either for piece or for day work. Mine managers were to be free to fix their rates of pay subject to this maximum average of fifty shillings, and the extension of piece-work was recommended.[5]

· The system of fixing a maximum average wage rather than a

[1] *South African Native Affairs Commission*, 1903–1905, Vol. V, Appendix D, pp. 1–431, written replies to circular of questions.
[2] Ibid, *Report*, para. 378.
[3] *Transvaal Chamber of Mines, Annual Report*, 1902, p. 7.
[4] *Transvaal Labour Commission*, Evidence [Cd. 1897], 1904, Exhibit No. 1.
[5] *Transvaal Chamber of Mines, Annual Report*, 1902, p. 56.

simple maximum rate was designed to achieve a double purpose. As before, it was intended to prevent competition between mine managements bidding up the average rate of wages on the gold-mines, and at the same time it was designed to allow the different managements some latitude in organizing their labour forces and adjusting wage-rates to individual capacity and effort, which were recognized to be subject to considerable variations. This system does not appear to have lasted for long, if indeed it came into force at all, for in January 1903 the Association decided to revert to the pre-war schedule of pay, and in April a further rise in wages was sanctioned, the simple maximum pay for surface and skilled underground labourers being fixed at fifty shillings and sixty shillings respectively per month of thirty days.[1]

The rise in wages did not have an immediate effect on the labour supply. Native confidence had been badly upset, and it could only slowly be restored. Moreover, the Natives disliked the centralized system of engagement,[2] and this was continued, although it was modified early in 1903 when District Managers of the Witwatersrand Native Labour Association were given authority to engage Natives for any particular mine to which they wanted to go. Unless a Native expressed such a wish when he was engaged, he signed on for the mines in general. A Native who had previously worked on a mine was given a further chance of returning to that mine on his arrival on the Rand. Other Natives, as far as possible in the gangs in which they arrived, were distributed among the various mining groups in such a way that each group under the same financial control should have approximately the same percentage of its total 'complement' of labour. 'Complements' were determined by the Consulting Engineers' Committee and were revised from time to time.[3] The groups themselves were free to decide to what mine or mines within the group the labour was sent.

Before the claims of the various gold-mining groups were considered the collieries were supplied with labour 'on the basis of their output'.[4]

Complaints continued that Natives were sent to mines to which they did not want to go; they were indeed inevitable under any

[1] *Witwatersrand Native Labour Association, Ltd., Annual Report*, 1903, p. 5.
[2] *Transvaal Labour Commission*, Evidence, [Cd. 1897], 1904, pp. 332–9. Evidence of Mr. Wm. Grant, who had been the Chamber of Mines' Labour Commissioner from 1893–7. Cf. ibid, p. 97, q. 2036.   Evidence of Mr. Mello Breyner, Diplomatic Agent for Witwatersrand Native Labour Association in Lourenço Marques; ibid., p. 160, q. 3544; ibid, p. 164, q. 3650.
[3] *Witwatersrand Native Labour Association, Annual Report*, 1903, p. 5.
[4] Ibid., p. 5. No specific details are available as to how output was determined.

system designed to distribute the labour force without discrimination between popular and unpopular mines.

While organization on the mines was being altered so radically and centralization was taking the place of direct personal contact, the demand for Native labour in other occupations had increased greatly owing to the post-war boom and the work of reconstruction in the ex-Republics. There was plenty of alternative employment available for any Natives who might have been dissatisfied with the new conditions.[1] The ports, railways, and other construction works competed with the mines for the supply of labour, and the Natives apparently were not slow in seeking employment where wages and conditions were most attractive.[2] Mr. Fred Hellman, General Manager of the East Rand Proprietary Mines, when urging the Chamber of Mines to agree to a rise in wages in 1902, said:

'It is a fact that, of all the competitors for native labour, the Mining Industry, which in importance ranks first, offers the smallest inducement to natives to enter its employ. The native to-day is in possession of probably more money than he has ever had before and his position is further strengthened by the excellent crops of the past season, so that he requires greater inducement to leave his kraal and come and work in the mines than ever before. He is master of the situation and is able to dictate terms to the industry and to other would-be employers, and, if the industry is to go on, his terms must be accepted until the conditions change or an extraneous source of supply shall be available. It is frequently stated that the rate of pay is a matter of indifference to the native, and that a higher rate would not induce him to come forward in increased numbers. I do not believe this to be the case. I find that natives are constantly leaving the service of the mines to engage elsewhere for higher rates than the mines are paying, and I beg to point out that the Chamber itself has recently admitted, in a letter addressed to the Director of Railways, that the rates paid by the railway constitute a serious obstacle to the recruiting of natives for the mines, and has asked the railway to reduce its rate to that paid by the mines. . . .'[3]

C. 'LABOUR SHORTAGE'

The failure of the labour supply to come up to expectations was a serious blow to all who had plans for the rapid development

[1] *South African Native Affairs Commission*, 1903–1905, Vol. V, p. 55.
[2] (Cape) *Blue Book on Native Affairs*, G. 25, 1902, p. 11; *Transvaal Labour Commission*, Evidence, op. cit., p. 20, qq. 387, 389.
[3] *Transvaal Labour Commission*, Evidence [Cd. 1897], 1904, p. 426. Letter from Mr. Fred Hellman to the Secretary, Transvaal Chamber of Mines. Mr. Hellman was not contending that a rise in wage-rates would necessarily increase the total supply of labour but, he considered, it was the only way in which the mining industry could secure a larger share.

of South Africa. A severe drought had hindered and increased the expense of repatriation and settlement in the rural areas. Agricultural and commercial depression resulting from the drought had already begun to bring to an end the post-war boom. When the expected supply of Native labour to the mines failed to materialize, this threatened to super-impose a reduction in activity in the mining industry. Anxiety about the supply of labour became widespread, and when the South African Customs Conference met in March 1903, it discussed the question and came to the conclusion that the Native population of Africa south of the Zambesi did not 'comprise a sufficient number of adult males capable of work to satisfy the normal requirements of the several Colonies, and at the same time furnish an adequate amount of labour for the large industrial and mining centres'.[1] It therefore recommended the opening of new sources of supply. It failed, however, to establish any criterion of what constituted a 'sufficient' or 'adequate' supply of labour. Estimates of labour 'requirements', particularly in regard to Native labour, have frequently been made in South Africa, but they have tended to overlook the fact that any such calculation is simply based on an estimate of the number it would pay to employ at a particular rate of wages.

Before the war employers in the gold-mining industry had begun to explore the possibility of importing unskilled labourers from abroad. Some of the leading mine-owners now began a campaign in favour of the importation of Chinese labourers. The High Commissioner, Lord Milner, was also considering the possibility of importing indentured Asiatic labourers for unskilled work.[2] In July 1903 the Transvaal Labour Commission was appointed

> To enquire what amount of labour is necessary for the requirements of the Agricultural, Mining, and other Industries of the Transvaal, and to ascertain how far it is possible to obtain an adequate supply of labour to meet such requirements from Central and South Africa.'

[1] [Cd. 1640] 1903, p. 13.
[2] On the 1st April 1903, he wrote to a friend: 'I believe that when everything is done that can be, we shall still be short and very short, of unskilled labour for the enormous industrial development (far greater than anyone who has not seen this country recently can picture) which is within the reach of the Transvaal and of all South Africa, if only workmen can be found . . .' *Milner Papers*, Vol. II, p. 460.
A week later he wrote: 'I am coming to the conclusion that in all probability we must have some Asiatics—not necessarily Chinese—here for our industrial development. I am dead against the Asiatic settler and trader, but I do not believe that the indentured Asiatic would prove uncontrollable. And, without the impetus he would give, I do not see how we are to have that great influx of British population—for the superior skilled work, trades, professions, and agriculture—which is the ultimate salvation. . . .' ibid, p. 461.

The Majority Report, signed by eleven of the thirteen members of the Commission, came to the conclusion that the demand for Native labour in the Transvaal for agriculture, mining, and other industries was 'in excess of the present supply', that the disparity was likely to increase, and that there was 'no adequate supply of labour in Central and Southern Africa' to meet the labour requirements of the Transvaal.[1] An attempt was made to estimate these 'requirements', and the following table[2] was drawn up to demonstrate the 'shortage' of labour:

	Estimated number required	At work	Shortage
Agriculture . .	80,000	27,715	52,285
Mining . .	197,644	68,280	129,364
Other Industries .	69,684	69,684	No data obtainable
C.S.A. Railways:			
Open Lines . .	16,000	12,402	3,598
New Construction .	40,000	3,848	36,152
	403,328	181,929	221,399

A minority of two[3] considered that the demand for labour for both mining and agriculture had been exaggerated; that the evidence of the Chamber of Mines as to the labour requirements of the industry had been accepted without question, and that the existing scarcity of labour was partly due to temporary causes arising from the wartime dislocation and partly to the action of the Chamber in reducing wages. They considered that the evidence of Mr. William Grant, who had been Native Labour Commissioner for the Chamber of Mines from 1893 to 1897, had been dismissed too lightly.[4] He was of the opinion that:

The actions and blunders of the past year, instead of attracting, have distinctly alienated natives, and no proof whatever has been afforded that the number of men required cannot be made available provided conditions of service are satisfactory, not to the employer only, but also the employee. . . . It is beyond question that the abortive attempt to reduce wages is responsible for the deficient supply of natives. . . .[5]

[1] *Transvaal Labour Commission*, Majority Report [Cd. 1896] 1904, para. 101.
[2] Ibid., para. 39.
[3] Messrs. J. W. Quinn and P. Whiteside.
[4] *Transvaal Labour Commission*, Minority Report [Cd. 1896] 1904, paras. 9, 12, 28–57, 62.
[5] Idem, Evidence, pp. 333–4.

On the other hand, the South African Native Affairs Commission (1903–5)[1] confirmed the opinion that there was an 'absolute shortage' of labourers to fill the requirements of South Africa, and estimated the 'shortfall' at 307,528 labourers.

The central association of the mine-owners, the Transvaal Chamber of Mines, wanted to obtain additional supplies of labour, and, despite the evidence of many witnesses before the Transvaal Labour Commission emphasizing the important influence of conditions of work on the supply of labour, it was not inclined to rely upon the possibility of gradually increasing the supply by offering improved conditions.

The Chamber of Mines was just as little prepared to adopt the plan proposed by Mr. F. H. P. Creswell,[2] that European labour be employed in the 'unskilled' grades in which Natives had previously been employed. It argued that such a policy would raise costs and result in a great curtailment in the grade of ore which it would pay to mine; that forty-eight of the seventy-nine producing mines would be ruined and the profits of the remainder seriously diminished.[3]

It was said by some supporters of the 'white labour policy' that the financial interests which controlled the mines feared that the growth of a large European labour force would lead to labour disputes, and so were not favourably disposed to experiments with European labour.[4]

Three engineers, reporting on Mr. Creswell's experiments with white labour on the Village Main Reef Mine, of which he was manager, considered that it might be possible to increase the scope of European employment to some extent. They thought that, as a result of such a policy and of the use of mechanical labour-saving devices, the amount of Native labour required might be reduced without raising costs above the level of 1899.[5] These opinions were, however, subject to the assumption that the Native labour procurable fell 'far short' of estimated requirements; for these engineers considered that, notwithstanding its inefficiency and other disadvantages, 'at anything near the present rate of wages' it was much the cheapest and most profitable tool for working the gold-mines.[6]

[1] Para. 368.
[2] Mr. (later Colonel) Creswell became the first Minister of Labour when the Department of Labour was created under the Nationalist-Labour Government in 1924.
[3] *Transvaal Labour Commission*, Evidence, op. cit., p. 403. (This calculation was based on the assumption that the unskilled white labourer would be paid 12s. per day and would do twice as much work as the Native labourer.)
[4] Idem, Minority Report, op. cit., paras. 9–11. Idem, Evidence, paras, 9, 13, 958.
[5] Idem, Evidence, p. 574, q. 13083. Report of Messrs. Price, Skinner, and Spencer, 4 Nov., 1902.   [6] Ibid., p. 574, q. 13083.

The advocates of white labour were only a small group, and their policy did not provide an immediate or easy solution to the difficulties of the mining industry. The reaction from the activity of the first few months of peace was serious.[1] Emigration from the Transvaal began and threatened Milner's plan of founding there a strong British community. An intense campaign of propaganda in favour of the importation of Chinese labour for the mines was carried on by the Chamber of Mines, and many who had at first opposed the introduction of Chinese labour began to turn to it as the only solution. For example, the European miners' trade union, the Transvaal Miners' Association, which had been established in 1902, at first vigorously opposed the introduction of Chinese labourers, but later agreed to it. Early in 1904 the Transvaal Legislative Council[2] passed an Ordinance authorizing the importation of Chinese indentured labourers. The Ordinance was duly sanctioned by the Imperial authorities and importation began immediately.

The Chinese were introduced under conditions laid down in the Transvaal Labour Importation Ordinance, which were designed to prevent them from competing with European labour for the more highly paid work. They were to be employed on 'unskilled labour' only, which was defined as

> such labour as is usually performed in mines in the Witwatersrand district by persons belonging to the aboriginal races or tribes of Africa south of the Equator,[3]

and were specifically debarred from all skilled trades and occupations, which were enumerated in a schedule.[4]

Under the mining law[5] of the South African Republic no coloured person had been permitted to hold an engine-driver's certificate of competency, and in practice, blasting certificates were not granted to non-Europeans. In this matter the law and

[1] *Times History of the War in South Africa*, Vol. VI., p. 101.
[2] The Transvaal Legislative Council was a nominated assembly of official and unofficial members, with official members in the majority.
[3] Ordinance No. 17 of 1904.
[4] Schedule 1 to Transvaal Labour Importation Ordinance, Ordinance No. 17 of 1904: 'Amalgamator, assayer, blacksmith, boiler-maker, brass-finisher, brassmoulder, brickmaker, overseer, bricklayer, banksman, carpenter, coppersmith, clerk, cyanide shiftsman, drill sharpener, driver of air or steam winch, driver of mechanical or electrical machinery, engineer, electrician, engine-driver, fitter, fireman-overseer, ganger, ironmoulder, joiner, mine storeman, mechanic, machinist, millwright, machine sawyer, mason wine overseer, machine rockdriller, mine carpenter, miller, overseer in any capacity other than the management and control of labourers, onsetter, patternmaker, plumber, painter, plasterer, pipeman, pumpman, plate-layer, quarryman overseer, rigger, stone-cutter, signaller, skipman, sampler, turner, tinsmith, timberman, time-keeper, wiresplicer, woodworking machinist.'
[5] Law No. 12 of 1898.

practice of the Republic were taken over by the British administration. The legal restrictions on the field of employment of the Chinese went far beyond the previous legislation, and are important because the occupations designated in the schedule have continued to be claimed as belonging exclusively to Europeans.[1]

The Chinese experiment did not last for long. Humanitarian opposition in Britain to the employment of Chinese indentured labourers on the Rand led to the prohibition of the issue of further licences for recruitment at the end of 1906,[2] and in 1907 the legislature of the now self-governing Transvaal repealed the Labour Importation Ordinance and decided that the Chinese coolies should go home as their contracts expired.[3]

The average cost of Chinese labour was about fifty shillings a month of thirty shifts; in addition to free food and quarters.[4] The number of labourers imported was 63,453, the maximum number employed at any one time being 57,828 in January 1907.[5] The introduction of the Chinese enabled the organization of the mining industry to continue on the basis of a large number of low-paid non-Europeans at a time when it was seriously threatened. The price paid was an extension of racial discrimination.

In a memorandum written at the beginning of 1906 on the effects that would follow a prohibition of importation of Chinese labour the Chamber of Mines stated that the number of stamps then in operation which would be hung up would be 3,135, and that 6,405 skilled European labourers would have to be dismissed. Furthermore, it considered that

> there is no justification for expecting the normal supply of Kaffir labour can be kept at a higher figure than at present, viz. 87,673 or, excluding those employed on collieries, 79,484.[6]

Events were to belie its expectations; for as the post-war boom collapsed throughout South Africa the demand for Native labour in other occupations fell, and Natives went to the Transvaal gold-mines in increased numbers.

[1] *Native Economic Commission*, 1930–32, U.G. 22, 1932, para. 842.
[2] Spender, *Campbell Bannerman*, Vol. II, p. 228.
[3] *Parl. Papers*, 1907, LVII [Cd. 3528], p. 159.
[4] Persia Campbell, *Coolie Emigration to Countries within the British Empire*, p. 183.
[5] *Transvaal Chamber of Mines, Annual Report*, 1909, p. xlii.
[6] Ibid., 1906, p. 77.

CHAPTER XI

THE 'POOR WHITE' PROBLEM AND THE COLOUR BAR IN THE MINING INDUSTRY

A. THE NATURE AND GROWTH OF THE 'POOR WHITE' PROBLEM

THE severe and prolonged depression (1904–9) which South Africa experienced after the feverish war and post-war activity brought into prominence what is known as the 'Poor White Problem'. Poverty was not a new phenomenon in South Africa, nor has South Africa been alone in having to face the problem of poverty. The differential racial composition of the population has, however, introduced factors not present in countries with a more homogeneous population. Further, in South Africa the rapid development of mining brought about a quick transition from a predominantly subsistence-farming economy to a more complex economic system with very different standards of living. Readjustment to the changed situation was in many cases slow. Moreover, partly as a result of the presence of a large Native population, many Europeans failed to find a footing in the new economy. Even without the discovery of minerals the old system could not have endured unchanged, because of the necessity for supporting an increasing population on a limited amount of land. The development of the diamond- and gold-fields had postponed the emergence of the evil day by providing immediate employment for many of the poorer Europeans, particularly as transport-riders and overseers. The construction of railways had brought to an end the palmy days of the transport-rider, and the development of underground mining required more skilled supervision of the Native labourers. Thus the rapid development of the diamond- and gold-fields provided temporary employment only for many of the landless Europeans.

Many of the European farmers in the interior responded very slowly to the increased demand for agricultural produce and consequently failed to benefit from the new markets. Further, in 1896, the Rinderpest, a severe cattle disease, had swept through the country and impoverished the pastoral farmers. Thus, before the war, poverty had been increasing among the less adaptable of the European farmers. It was already noticeable that the landless Europeans were tending to congregate about the towns and villages where they were largely dependent on private or public assistance. The South African War intensified the distress of the rural population. The war both impoverished landowners, whose stock disappeared and whose buildings were generally demolished, and swept into the towns, in a destitute condition, a very large number who owned no land and who had been sinking into poverty.[1] The burgher settlements, founded after the war as a measure of rehabilitation, failed; and in 1906 the Transvaal Indigency Commission was appointed to inquire into the circumstances of the European poor.

European poverty was not, however, confined to the northern provinces. It had already appeared as a serious problem in many of the older districts of the Cape. The Cape Labour Commission of 1893–4 had called attention to the poverty of many Europeans, and before the end of the century the Dutch Reformed Church had founded the Kakamas Settlements to try and settle indigent Europeans on the land as small farmers.

The problem of adjustment to these changed conditions was particularly difficult in South Africa, where the tradition of slavery and the presence of a large non-European population had led to a customary division of labour between Europeans and non-Europeans, and a reluctance on the part of the European to seek employment as a manual labourer. The Transvaal Indigency Commission reported in 1908:

> We have been impressed with the frequency with which it has been stated in evidence that unskilled labour was 'Kaffir's work' and as such not the kind of work which a white man should perform. This opinion is due not to anything which is inherently unpleasant or degrading in the work, but to the fact that such labour is ordinarily performed in South Africa by the natives.
> This attitude of the white man has greatly affected his efficiency as a labourer. He has never regarded unskilled labour as an ordinary field of employment. When he has had to do unskilled work he has done it grudgingly as being Kaffir's work, and therefore inefficiently. . . . The white man's prejudice against 'Kaffir 'work, his inefficiency as an unskilled labourer and the higher wage he requires, have had the natural result that coloured labour, inefficient though it is, is cheaper to the employer for unskilled work than white labour. The demand, therefore, for unskilled white labour has been extremely small, and it has been difficult for the white man to get employment at such work. . . . It is essential to realize the importance of the practical monopoly of the unskilled labour market possessed by the native.[2]

This stratification of the labour market into European and Native preserves was most marked in the northern colonies. In

[1] *Transvaal Indigency Commission*, 1906–8, T.G. 13, 1908, paras. 13–38.
[2] Ibid., paras. 46–50.

the Cape Colony the 'Cape Coloured' were employed on all grades
of skilled and semi-skilled work, the sole class of work in which
they had no share being that of control and management.[1] In
Natal time-expired indentured Indians and their children sought
employment in increasing numbers in skilled and semi-skilled
work.[2]

In the Transvaal the official decision to repatriate the Chinese
labourers as their contracts expired and the prohibition on further
importation left the mining industry once more faced with the
question of the organization of its labour force. The alternatives
before it were either to extend the employment of Native labourers
on the more skilled and responsible work or to expand the unskilled labour force by employing European unskilled labourers.
The first alternative received support from mine managers and
technical experts. Natives were already being employed on some
types of skilled work and many had proved to be highly efficient,
as mine managers testified;[3] for example, Mr. Peterson, General
Manager of the Geldenhuis Estate Gold Mining Company, giving
evidence before the Mining Industry Commission, said:

'We have some of the Kaffirs who are better machine-men than
some of the white men. I have boys who have been working on the
mine from twelve to fifteen years, and they are better than many on
the Rand nowadays.
'Q. "Can they place holes?"
'A. "Yes, they can place the holes, fix up the machine and do
everything that a white man can do, but, of course, we are not
allowed to let them blast."
'Q. "If the law was not what it is, do you think they could blast
with safety?"
'A. "I do not think; I feel sure about it. I have had experience
with natives since 1879, and I know what a native can do." '[4]

Many mine managers and engineers considered that an unnecessary number of Europeans were employed on the mines,
and that economies could be effected by employing less European
labour.[5] According to the evidence of Mr. Way:

The trouble with the mines is that underground the white labour
so-called is not labour at all; it is merely supervision.
One of the greatest economies to be made in my opinion is at
present we have far too many whites employed on the mines. In my
opinion two men are employed underground doing work one man

[1] *Economic Commission, Report*, U.G. 12, 1914, para. 62.
[2] Ibid., para. 58.
[3] *Transvaal Mining Industry Commission*, 1907–1908, Majority Report,
para. 270.
[4] Ibid., Evidence, p. 909, qq. 13372; 13373.
[5] Ibid., Majority Report, paras. 235–8. Evidence Messrs. George Albu,
Drummond Chaplin, Hellman, and Hoffman.

could do easily. The white man underground is not a working man at all; he has not to work as in other countries where there is no large supply of unskilled coloured labour.[1]

By this time, however, the European miners were becoming alarmed at the prospect of Native competition.[2] They were, moreover, backed up by a growing body of political opinion, which was perturbed by European poverty and unemployment and was increasingly able to influence policy after 1906, when the Transvaal secured responsible government. Thus there were serious obstacles to the reorganization of the labour force of the gold-mining industry.

B. THE 'WHITE LABOUR POLICY' AND THE TRANS-VAAL GOLD MINES

A wide gap between the rates paid for skilled and supervisory work and those paid for unskilled work accompanied the division of the labour market into European and non-European spheres. High wages came to be looked upon as the privilege of the European, to be defended at all costs. The higher the wage-rates demanded by Europeans the more limited the number which could find employment, and political support grew for a policy of protecting Europeans from the competition of Natives.

The terms of reference, composition, and report of the Mining Industry Commission appointed in 1907 are significant of the development of this policy. It was appointed to investigate:

1. In what direction, and in how far, the use of mechanical appliances can be extended on the mines, and the effect of such extended use upon
   (a) the employment of white labour;
   (b) the cost of production;
   (c) the demands of the mining industry for native labour;
   (d) the mining industry generally.

2. The means best calculated:
   (a) to increase the employment of white labour on the mines;
   (b) to secure the more efficient use of native labour; and
   (c) generally to secure greater economy and efficiency in mining operations.

The Commission consisted of five members: Andries Stockenstrom, Peter Whiteside, Frederick Hugh Page Creswell, Max Francke, and Charles Hugh Spencer. Of these, Max Francke resigned and appended a memorandum of his conclusions, and C. H. Spencer signed a minority report.

[1] Ibid., para. 269, p. 149, qq. 1219 and 1252, cf. ibid., para. 237; evidence, p. 1,346.
[2] Ibid. paras., 273–81.

The remaining three commissioners, in the majority report, interpreted these terms of reference to assume the desirability of an increased employment of white men on the mines and considered that it was 'only putting into words the general policy and conviction of this community' when it stated that the chief and only real and permanent value of the mining industry was the means it afforded of building up and maintaining a large and prosperous white population.[1] Their report shows very clearly the political opposition to the full utilization of the Native labour force. It emphatically rejected what was termed 'the Coloured labour policy' of the Chamber of Mines, and considered that a large European population was the ultimate goal; that this could best be achieved by the extension of the employment of Europeans on the mines and need not entail a rise in costs.[2]

The minority report by C. H. Spencer alleged that nearly all the evidence quoted in order to show that the costs of working with white labour would be no greater, or less, than those of working with coloured labour was obtained by picking certain parts of the evidence of practical men, mine managers, and engineers, who had themselves come on their whole experience to exactly the opposite conclusion.[3]

The majority considered that the pass laws made the employment of Natives more attractive than the employment of Europeans because under the pass laws breach of contract was a criminal offence, and so it was possible to enforce continuous employment for Natives.[4] There was considerable justification for this opinion. When European labourers had been employed one of the chief disadvantages had been their irregular attendance.[5] The Rand Unemployment Committee, which in 1908 had arranged for certain mines to put unemployed European men on to unskilled work, reported:

> Results obtained by these men have been in many cases unsatisfactory owing to want of persistence on the part of the men. Where men have stayed at their work for some considerable time, they have shown, as a rule, marked improvement in efficiency, but unfortunately in many cases they have thrown up their employment for no adequate reason or have been dismissed for unsatisfactory conduct. This has happened in some cases where the men have been earning high rates of wages.[6]

[1] Ibid., Majority Report, para. 189.   [2] Ibid., paras. 228–879.
[3] Ibid., Minority Report, p. 104.
[4] Ibid., Majority Report, para. 862.
[5] *Transvaal Labour Commission, Evidence* [Cd. 1897], 1904, op. cit., p. 525, q. 11940.
[6] Report of Rand Unemployment Committee reprinted in *Annual Report of the Transvaal Chamber of Mines for* 1908, p. 27.

The Manager of the Nourse Mines said:

'The first batch of men had to be taken off the tramming and shovelling work owing to their irregular attendance at work after pay day, when they were responsible for considerable extra cost and anxiety lest their absence should cause the mill to be hung up. . . . They were an exceptionally fine lot of men physically, most of them having done similar work before having come to this country.'[1]

There can be little doubt of the superior attractions of Native labourers who were engaged on long-term contracts and subject to penal prosecution for desertion.

To assert, however, as the Majority Report of the Mining Industry Commission did, that the conditions which made coloured labour more attractive than white were 'almost entirely conditions created by legislation and administration'[2] was going too far. The control of the labour force by legislative sanction was of great assistance to the mining industry, but the benefit was not all on one side; as a set-off against this were statutory conditions regarding recruiting, the registration of contracts, and the management of compounds.

Although the Majority Report of the Mining Industry Commission explicitly stated that it did not recommend that special occupations be reserved for white men by legal enactment,[3] it proposed that to extend the scope of white employment it should be made obligatory for a miner holding a blasting certificate to be attached to each machine-drill. It considered that the effect of this regulation would be the employment of Europeans to operate these drills; and that it would tend to offset the measures which promoted the competition of non-Europeans.[4] The Report of the Commission is more interesting for the light it throws on the political development of the 'white labour policy' than for any importance that it might be thought to possess as an impartial review of conditions in the mining industry.

The desirability and expediency of protecting Europeans from the competition of Natives was not unquestioned at this time. The Transvaal Indigency Commission, for example, was convinced that the restriction of the Native to unskilled work could not be permanent,[5] and opposed such restriction on the grounds that, in the first place, it was unfair to the Native who had been encouraged to leave his tribal lands and come and work for the European on whom he was now dependent; and, in the second

---

[1] Ibid.
[2] *Transvaal Mining Industry Commission*, Majority Report, para. 897.
[3] Ibid., para. 302.   [4] Ibid., para. 919.
[5] *Transvaal Indigency Commission*, 1906–1908, para. 52.

place, because such action would ensure higher wages for Europeans, dependent entirely upon their privileged position, and

'To protect the white man from native competition at this stage is simply to bolster up the aristocratic tradition for a few years longer, without doing anything to qualify the white man for the ultimate struggle for economic superiority over the native. The cost of production with white labour in South Africa should not be artificially maintained above that which obtained in other new countries. South Africa cannot really progress until her standards are assimilated to those of the leading peoples of the world.'[1]

The reports of these commissions show that legislation to protect the European worker from Native competition was under consideration in the Transvaal before the formation in 1910 of the Union of South Africa.

C. LEGISLATIVE ACTION: THE MINES AND WORKS ACT AND THE NATIVE LABOUR REGULATION ACT

Immediately political union was achieved the new South African Parliament turned its attention to the revision and consolidation of legislation, and in 1911 two Acts (Nos. 12 and 15) which have had important and lasting effects on the market for Native labour were passed. They were the Mines and Works Act and the Native Labour Regulation Act.

The Mines and Works Act is important because regulations framed under it attempted to impose and extend a legal bar to the employment of coloured workers on many kinds of work on the mines. Under mining regulations framed under this Act certificates of competency are required by individuals performing many kinds of work. Such certificates were not to be granted to 'coloured persons' in the Transvaal or Free State,[2] and certificates granted to 'coloured persons' in Natal and the Cape were not valid in the northern provinces. In addition, it was laid down that many types of work were only to be carried out by 'white' men. In 1920 the employment of white men was prescribed by the regulations in thirty-two occupations on the mines in which 7,057 persons were employed, and Trade Union influence had extended it to nineteen others in which 4,020 persons were employed.[3]

The Native Labour Regulation Act consolidated the laws in regard to the recruitment and employment of Native labour along the lines of those already in force in the Transvaal. The Act covers a wide range of topics and is designed to protect the

[1] Ibid., para. 84.   [2] Regulation No. 285.
[3] *Low Grade Mines Commission*, Final Report, U.G. 34, 1920, para. 164.

Native by enforcing standards of accommodation, etc., to diminish the abuses to which recruiting is liable to give rise; and to assist the employer by continuing the provision that breach of contract on the part of a Native labourer[1] is a criminal offence. It provides for the proclamation of 'labour districts' within which special regulations apply, both in regard to the pass system and the registration of contracts, and to the provision of housing, food, and hospital accommodation.

As we have seen, there is something to be said for the view that the action of the State in backing up the sanctity of contract has made the employment of Native labour more attractive; for instance, it is a criminal offence for Natives under contract to strike. This penal sanction appears to have been very effective, for strikes of Native workers on the mines have been few and very short-lived, whereas employers have learnt how costly strikes of European workers can be. Against the criminal sanction for breach of contract must be set the provisions which control the employer of Native labourers. These include the licensing of recruiting agents and employers and the employment and licensing of compound managers; the requirement of a written contract, explained to the Native in the presence of a magistrate; the power of the Director of Native Labour to cancel contracts; and the regulations concerning the keeping of books and the payment of cash wages, the housing, feeding, medical attention, and repatriation of Native labourers.

The Mines and Works Act, as amended in 1926, and the Native Labour Regulation Act provide the legal framework within which employers in mining industries have to organize their labour force.

After 1911, despite a temporary relaxation in some directions during the Great War of 1914–18, the colour bar became more rigid. This was a result in part of the extension of the statutory colour bar and in part of the increase in the power and co-ordination of trade unions, composed of European-skilled workers, both on the mines and in other industries.

In South Africa, during the first decade of the twentieth century, trade unions had little power and their growth was slow. In 1910, as far as can be ascertained (statistics are incomplete, for the rendering of statistical returns was not compulsory until 1919), the total membership of trade unions and other associations of employees was only nine thousand.[2] In 1911 the Transvaal Federation of Trades was established, and nearly all the trade unions in the Transvaal became affiliated to it. Two years later, in 1913, when a strike on one of the gold-mines spread and

---

[1] Defined in the Act as one employed on mines and works.
[2] *Official Year Book*, No. 9, 1926–7, pp. 212–14.

involved all the gold-mines and many other trades on the Witwatersrand, this Federation was recognized by the Government
and negotiated a settlement with members of the Cabinet. In
1915, for the first time, the Transvaal Chamber of Mines officially
recognized the trade-union movement and a conference was held
to discuss certain demands which were put forward by the South
African Industrial Federation on behalf of its affiliated unions.[1]
In the Transvaal the trade unions were exclusively European,
both on the mines and in other trades. On the mines the unions
were concerned to improve the pay and working conditions of
the European miners. They attempted to do this by insisting on
the maintenance of the colour bar.[2]

During the Great War a large number of white miners enlisted
and, by consent, some latitude was then permitted to enable
non-Europeans to do semi-skilled work, such as drill-sharpening,
underground.[3] There was, however, constant friction concerning
the spheres of work of Europeans and non-Europeans, for costs
on the mines rose rapidly, and this, combined with the scarcity
of European labour, inevitably led to the employers attempting
to use non-European labour more extensively.

In July 1918 the Chamber of Mines and the South African
Industrial Federation came to an agreement, known as the Status
Quo Agreement, whereby it was agreed that the then existing
position with regard to the relative scope of employment of European and coloured employees should be maintained. Although
the colour bar prevented the full utilization of the non-European
labour force, the employers in the mining industry were not
prepared to force the issue and face a strike. In evidence presented
to the Commissioner appointed in 1918 to inquire into Native
unrest on the Witwatersrand, the Chamber of Mines stated:

'It is impossible to deny that the colour bar as laid down in the
Government Mining Regulations imposes an artificial restriction
on the advancement of the coloured and native population. But
much more important than the Government Mining Regulations is
the force of custom. Public opinion is not prepared to see the substitution of coloured or native workers for white skilled and semi-
skilled workers, and any attempt to employ the non-white workman
on mining work at present occupied by white men would cause a
strike of white employees on the mines, who would be supported
by the great bulk of the white population of the Rand.'[4]

Events were to prove this prophecy correct.

[1] Ibid.
[2] *Dominions Royal Commission*, South Africa, Evidence, Part II, qq. 2040–
2113, F. S. Malan (Minister of Mines and Industries, 1912–24), 'The Union of
South Africa', *Cambridge History of the British Empire*, p. 653.
[3] F. S. Malan, op. cit., p. 660.
[4] *Transvaal Chamber of Mines, Annual Report*, 1918, p. 92.

In practice the Status Quo Agreement applied to certain work classed as semi-skilled, such as drill-sharpening, waste-packing, pipe-laying, rough timbering, whitewashing, and similar work which had for some time been carried out by Europeans on some mines and by Natives on others. As the Natives received about three shillings a day for such work and the Europeans twenty shillings, the inducement for mine managers to substitute Native for European workmen is obvious.[1]

It was the desire to amend this agreement and generally so to reorganize the underground labour force as to make a better use of Native labour to counteract the rising costs, that led to the strike of 1922, the most serious industrial dispute that has yet occurred in the Union. The strike started at the Transvaal collieries and spread to the gold-mines. It involved twenty-two thousand European gold-miners and was supported by a general strike on the Rand, lasting eleven days, the strike on the collieries lasting seventy-six days, and that on the gold-mines sixty-seven days.[2] Martial law was declared, troops were rushed to the Rand, and for some days a minor civil war was waged.

The gold-miners went back to work unsuccessful in their resistance to all changes in organization. The immediate result of reorganization was the temporary elimination of a number of Europeans and a substantial reduction in wages, leading to a reduction in costs, an increase in the scale of operations, and in the mining of low-grade ore.[3] Although the strikers failed to prevent these developments, the influence of the Rand 'revolution' has been very great. Alarmed by previous strikes in 1913 and 1914, the Government had begun before the war to embark on social legislation. The 1922 strike showed the lengths to which European labour was prepared to go in the endeavour to protect its position, and there is no doubt that memories of the strike have been behind subsequent industrial legislation, much of which has been designed to protect Europeans from Native competitors.[4]

[1] *Report of Mining Industry Board*, 1922, para. 12.
[2] *Official Year Book*, No. 6, 1910–22, p. 332.
[3] *Low Grade Ore Commission*, 1932, U.G., 13, 1932, para. 9.
In 1923 the average proportion of non-European (mostly Native) to European employees on the Witwatersrand gold-mines was 10·1 to 1. Between 1911 and 1921 it had averaged 8·1 to 1, the highest number of non-Europeans per European being 9·1 (in 1916) and the lowest 7·4 (in 1919). After 1923 the proportion of non-Europeans declined. Between 1924 and 1933 it averaged 9·2 to 1, the highest number per European being 9·7 (in 1924) and the lowest 8·9 (in 1929). Since 1933 the rapid expansion of gold-mining and the difficulty experienced in securing an equivalent expansion in the number of Native labourers has led to a continuous fall, from 9·1 to 1 in 1933 to 7·5 to 1 in 1939, in the proportion of non-Europeans employed, although their absolute number has risen from some 227,000 in 1933 to 303,000 in 1939. *Annual Reports of the Government Mining Engineer*, 1911–39.
[4] cf. F. S. Malan, op. cit., p. 655.

In 1923, the year after the strike, the regulations comprising the legal colour bar were declared *ultra vires*. Employers in the mining industry did not, however, alter their labour policy, which had been influenced at least as much by custom, public opinion, and fear of the trade unions as by the legality of the colour bar, which indeed had long been considered doubtful.[1] Three years later the bar was reimposed, this time against Natives and Asiatics only, under an amended Mines and Works Act.[2] A Mining Regulations Commission had reported in 1925 on the encroachment of Native upon European labour, the result of which it considered was bound to be the elimination of the European worker 'from the entire range of mining operations'.[3] The reimposition of the colour bar was recommended

> to secure to mineworkers generally an adequate measure of protection against accident and disease in the exercise of their highly dangerous and unhealthy calling, and to rescue the European miner from the economic fetters which at present render him the easy victim of advancing native competition.[4]

It being the opinion of the Commission that

> What we have called 'colour-bar' regulations will, we venture to think, go some way towards effecting both of the purposes mentioned in paragraph (125), in the direction, that is, not only of safety and health generally but also of counteracting the force of the economic advantages at present enjoyed by the native.'[5]

The Mining Regulations Commission was remarkably frank about the dual purpose of the regulations. It is sometimes contended that they are necessary in the interests of safety and health because the Native, though possibly competent technically

---

[1] *Low Grade Mines Commission*, 1919–20, Final Report, para. 163. *Native Economic Commission*, 1930–32, U.G. 22, 1932, *Typescript of Evidence*, p. 9133, evidence of Chamber of Mines Representatives.

[2] The Mines and Works Amendment Act, No. 25 of 1926, provides that certificates of competency (which, by statutory regulation, must be held by mine managers, mine overseers, mine surveyors, mechanical engineers, engine-drivers, miners entitled to blast, and such other persons as may be determined by the Governor-General) 'in such provinces, areas or places as may be specified in the regulations . . . shall be granted only to the following classes of persons, namely, (*a*) Europeans; (*b*) persons born in the Union and ordinarily resident in the Province of the Cape of Good Hope who are members of the class or race known as 'Cape Coloured' or of the class or race known as 'Cape Malays'; (*c*) persons born in the Union and ordinarily resident in the Union elsewhere than in the Province of the Cape of Good Hope who would if resident in that Province, be regarded as members of either of the classes or races known as 'Cape Coloured' or 'Cape Malays', and (*d*) the people known as Mauritius Creoles or St. Helena persons, or their descendants in the Union.'
Thus Natives and Asiatics may be, and have been, prevented by statutory regulation from acquiring certificates of competency.

[3] *Mining Regulations Commission*, U.G. 36, 1925, para. 119.

[4] Ibid., para. 125.   [5] Ibid., para. 219.

is unable to enforce his authority, it being alleged that accidents have actually arisen through Natives being overruled by Europeans. The Department of Mines stated that an occupation such as that of engine-driver is closed on these grounds to Natives. The regulations, however, go far beyond such occupations. One provides that when amalgam or other precious materials are unlocked or handled it must be done in the presence of two white persons. According to the Department of Mines:

> The reason for this is that in the case of whites we are dealing with persons whose position in society and whose personal history and character are ascertainable and offer a fair guarantee of their honesty, whereas in the case of natives their antecedents and character are unknown and they cannot be placed on the same footing as the white man for this purpose.[1]

Presumably it is considered necessary to prevent mine managers from being too trusting in the allocation of duties among their staff.

The decision to reimpose the legal bar by passing the Mines and Works Amendment Act was taken in spite of the fact that the Economic Commission (1914), the Native Grievances Inquiry (1913-14), the Low Grade Mines Commission (1920), and the Mining Industry Board (1922) had all condemned the restriction of the sphere of the Native by legislation. The mining regulations have been amended so as to exclude Natives from nearly all ostensibly responsible positions.

Under the Mines and Works Act, as amended, regulations may be applied to industrial as well as mining occupations, but as yet no such regulations have been applied outside the mining industry.

The manner in which labour policy on the gold-mines has been governed by colour-bar regulations has been indicated by representatives of the Chamber of Mines. Giving evidence before the Native Economic Commission (1930-32), they said:

> 'If we had a free hand to reorganize our work, with all due regard to safety and health, there is not the slightest doubt that we could do with a materially smaller number of Europeans; and that in consequence of the reorganization we would have to employ a larger number of leading hands and natives of the boss-boy type. We would have to increase their numbers; and to that extent there would be an enlarged scope for the employment of natives at a higher rate of pay.'[2]

The Government Mining Engineer was also of the opinion that a reduction in the number of Europeans employed underground

[1] Evidence of Government Mining Engineer to Native Economic Commission, 1930-32.
[2] *Native Economic Commission*, 1930-32, Typescript of Evidence, p. 9139.

would reduce mining costs and increase the opportunities available for Natives.[1]

A general issue arises here. If a government wishes to finance and implement programmes of social relief and reform, is there not a general presumption that it will be able to do so upon a larger scale if it avoids all expedients which raise the costs and reduce the scale of the industry expected to yield the revenue to finance the schemes? In the particular case of the South African gold-mine, the question may be posed thus: Would it not be more expedient to allow the mines to maximize their taxable output, by adopting freely every cost-reducing innovation, and thus to maximize the contribution from taxes which the industry can make to the national exchequer, from which all social services should be financed—instead of so arranging the burden that it inflates the costs and reduces the scale of operations (and the aggregate gross turnover) of the mining industry?

[1] Summary of evidence submitted to Low Grade Ore Commission (1932) by D. H. Pirow, Government Mining Engineer.

CHAPTER XII

WAGE POLICY AND RECRUITING IN THE MINING INDUSTRY

A. CONDITIONS OF LIFE FOR NATIVE LABOURERS: THE COMPOUND SYSTEM

THE attempts to protect sections of the European population from the competition of Native employees have had important results in the conditions of work on the mines. There is no doubt that both the living conditions and the organization and payment of the Native labour force have been influenced by the social policy characterized by the colour bar. As a result of the restrictions on the employment of Native labour on the mines, only to a very limited extent has it paid employers to offer conditions which will attract a permanent Native labour force. For the most part employers have continued, for fifty years, to rely on migratory labourers who work on the average for periods of ten to twelve months (subject to wide variations from the average in comparatively few cases), returning home to their peasant life in rural areas between spells of work on the mines. To accommodate such a labour force the system of housing Native employees in barracks, known as compounds, which had been adopted on the Kimberley diamond-mines, has been taken over and adapted to the needs of the gold- and coal-mines.

In South Africa residence in compounds is compulsory for the vast majority of the Native labourers employed in mining. On the gold-mines a compound generally accommodates from three to six thousand Natives,[1] on the coal-mines fewer Natives are employed and the compounds are smaller. On the Kimberley diamond-mines the system of housing Natives in enclosed barracks was adopted in part in order to minimize the theft of diamonds, and Native employees are not allowed to leave the mine premises during their period of service. On the gold- and coal-mines the Native employees are not confined to the compounds, but may leave them when not at work; subject, of course, to pass-law regulations.

Some of the gold- and many of the coal-mines have married quarters for part of their labour force. On the gold-mines such accommodation is very limited. In 1930, on the Rand gold-mines, 1,474 out of a total of nearly 200,000 Native labourers were

---

[1] Dr. A. J. Orenstein (Chief Medical Officer, Rand Mines), 'Diet of Natives on the Witwatersrand Gold Mines'. *Race Relations*, Vol. VI, No. 1, 1939, p. 16.

accommodated in married quarters. The number has not since increased appreciably. The Natives living in married quarters are workers whom the mines do not want to lose, such as Native clerks and other specially trained and skilled men. They form a small permanent labour force, their families grow up at the mines, and in some cases have begun work on them.

The administration and control of married quarters has been a matter of some difficulty. In 1914 the Native Grievances Commissioner reported that most of the mine managements wished to abolish their 'mixed locations' because of the prevalence in them of the illegal sale of liquor and prostitution. He considered that on the whole these charges were justified and advocated the provision of better housing, at a substantial distance from the compounds, for those married Natives for whom it was considered desirable to provide permanent homes. The married quarters of the Dynamite Factory at Modderfontein were cited as an example of this type of accommodation.[1]

At this time, as now, the system of allowing Native workers to live on the mine premises with their wives and families was found chiefly on the coal-mines in both the Transvaal and Natal. The Economic Commission of 1914 reported that its 'steadying effect' on the supply of labour was clear. It quoted the Government Mining Engineer, Mr. (now Sir) R. N. Kotze. Referring to the Transvaal, he said that whereas the Native labourers on the gold-mines remained for about eight or nine months their average stay on the coal-mines was much longer. The coal-mines were usually situated on privately owned farms, where there was plenty of land. The companies permitted some of their labourers to erect huts outside the compounds, and they became permanent residents on the mine, living with their families and cultivating small patches of ground around their huts.[2]

In connexion with the gold-mines, Mr. Taberer of the Native Recruiting Corporation, at this time considered that the desire of the Natives to bring their people to the mines was increasing. He said:

'It is not only a strongly expressed wish, it is a growing wish, especially now. You will understand that in most parts of the country they have lost their cattle through diseases . . . and they say, "Having lost my cattle there is no tie to keep me here. My home is my work, and I should like to have my wife and children with me at my work." '[3]

The Commissioners called attention to the advantages to be derived from a permanent Native labour force, but added that

[1] *Native Grievances Inquiry*, U.G. 37, 1914, paras. 134, 135.
[2] *Economic Commission*, U.G. 12, 1914, para. 52.   [3] Ibid.

there were also disadvantages which were particularly likely to arise if 'married compounds' were situated in close proximity to large towns, and that in view of the 'grave issues involved' they were not prepared to make any recommendation on this matter.[1]

In 1930 representatives of the Chamber of Mines, giving evidence before the Native Economic Commission, testified to the difficulty which had been experienced in checking prostitution and the selling of illicit liquor where mine labourers had been allowed to live in villages on mine property. Such difficulties, however, they considered had been overcome in small villages, or locations, of specially selected and privileged Natives. The extension of the married quarters was not regarded as practicable, for they considered it only paid to accommodate 'special boys' in this way, and there was already sufficient provision for them.[2]

It is interesting to note that at some of the Natal collieries employers have found it profitable to provide extensive married quarters, some collieries accommodating as much as 50 per cent of their labour force in this way.[3] This provision is believed to induce many of the Native labourers to stay at the mines for years on end, although in many other respects conditions of work and pay on the collieries are inferior to those on the gold-mines. In some cases the married quarters on the collieries consist of single *rondavels*. Such accommodation is not suitable for permanent family life, for, according to Native custom, adolescent children sleep in separate huts. Where no provision is made for them, the older children are usually sent away to live with relatives in the rural kraals. In such cases the provision of married quarters does not lead to the growth of a large permanent industrial population at the collieries. But it does lead to a more permanent labour force than is usual where accommodation is almost entirely confined to barracks.

Government authorities have opposed the extension of married quarters on the mines. They are able to make their opposition effective because, in terms of the Native Labour Regulation Act, plans for the erection of compounds have to be approved by the Department of Native Affairs. By refusing to approve plans for married quarters, this Government Department can prevent, and in some cases is alleged to have prevented, the extension of such accommodation. Originally it appears that this opposition was

---

[1] Ibid.
[2] *Native Economic Commission*, 1930–32. Typescript of evidence, pp. 9123–9130. Evidence given on behalf of the Transvaal Chamber of Mines, and Native Recruiting Corporation, by Messrs. F. G. A. Roberts, F. L. Butlin, Harold Mayer, A. J. Limebeer, and J. B. Gedye.
[3] Letter from the Secretary of the Natal Coal Owners' Society, 22 September 1938. Interview with Chief Compound Manager, Dannhauser, July 1938.

due to the difficulty which had been encountered in controlling the locations which had grown up. Latterly, official policy has tended more and more to oppose the creation of a class of permanent industrial workers among the Native population. This is probably due both to the policy of protecting groups of Europeans from the competition of Natives and to the ostensibly humanitarian policy of preventing the Native population from becoming wholly dependent upon the industrial system introduced by Europeans.

In 1925 Messrs. Mills, Clay, and Martin, who signed the Chairman's Report of the Economic and Wage Commission, considered that the assimilation of the Native population into the economic system of Western civilization was inevitable. They thought the system of housing mine labourers in compounds was desirable as a temporary expedient, because it provided sheltered conditions which eased the inevitable difficulties of transition from primitive to civilized economic conditions.[1]

Many Europeans in South Africa do not believe that the complete incorporation of part of the Native population into the Western industrial system is desirable or inevitable, although, admittedly, industry, particularly mining and farming, are dependent upon Native labour. The system of migratory labour, of which the compound system is a corollary, is not regarded as a temporary expedient, but as a permanent feature of the organization of Native labour on the mines, in spite of the fact that migratory labourers are inevitably relatively inefficient, both as mine labourers and as peasant farmers. For the mine labourers lose some of the efficiency they have acquired during their prolonged absences, and they also tend to lose interest in the life and work of the kraal, regarding their spells at home as long holidays. Both mining and farming suffer from the lack of specialization consequent upon the system of migratory labour. Moreover, the compound system separates mine labourers from their wives, it breaks up family life, and leads to immorality both in the compounds and in the kraals.

If, in spite of these drawbacks, one accepts migratory labour as the foundation of industry the compound system has certain advantages. In the mine compounds in South Africa the Native labourers are provided with a scientifically calculated diet; their quarters are ventilated and cleaned; medical and other services

---

[1] 'The insulation,' they wrote, 'of the natives employed in large industrial and mining centres from the demoralizing influences of an urban community alien to his ways of life, which the system of compounds effects, seems to us to be the best compromise possible in the difficulties of this transitional stage in the native's economic development.' *Economic and Wage Commission*, op. cit., p. 157, paras. 284, 285, 286.

are provided, including a certain amount of entertainment, all at a cost below the price at which they could be bought if purchased individually. The Native labourer has, however, to accept the planned service as a part of his wage, even although he might prefer to provide for himself.

The provision of these services may incidentally have an important educative effect on the development of Natives, both as suppliers of labour and as consumers.

Such advantages as may arise from the mass provision of food and accommodation are not, however, altogether incompatible with conditions designed to attract a permanent labour force. It is interesting to note the contrast between the conditions on the gold- and coal-mines of the Transvaal and those on the copper-mines of Northern Rhodesia and the Belgian Congo. In the latter countries there is no colour bar and employers consider that it pays them to attempt to attract a permanent labour force by making provision for family life on the mines.

It is frequently argued that the system of stimulating the growth of a population wholly dependent upon mining has disadvantages as serious as those of migratory labour and the compound system. For, it is said, should the demand for the product of the mines fall, such a population is subject to unemployment, whereas migratory labourers retain a link with the land and have something to fall back upon. Further, it is argued that mining is essentially a temporary industry doomed to extinction as ore reserves are used up, and that it is therefore socially undesirable to allow a section of a primitive population to specialize in this line of production. The argument is not usually extended to the case of European miners.

In the case of gold-mining on the Witwatersrand, it is also argued that migratory labourers are less subject than permanent workers to industrial diseases such as 'miners' phthisis'.

The social problem which arises from the first of these disadvantages, that of the specialization of a section of the population in an industry subject to fluctuations in demand, is whether there is a resultant loss of flexibility which increases the cost of readjustment to a fall in demand to such an extent as to outweigh the economies of specialization.

Secondly, it is true that the gold-mines are inevitably wasting assets. But the system of migratory labour may simply mask a condition of dependence upon them which is in any case the actual fact.[1] In South Africa the whole economy is based upon the

[1] cf. the opinion of the Chief Native Commissioner of the Transkeian territories: 'It is scarcely an exaggeration to say that the mines proved the salvation of the Natives during 1936. All available labour was absorbed and

exploitation of the country's gold resources. The standard of life of the Native, as of the European population, is dependent upon the production of gold. The maintenance of a relatively inefficient labour force shortens the life of the industry. It reduces both the product of the mines and that of peasant farming below that which might be obtained were specialization encouraged.

With regard to the argument that the incidence of 'miners' phthisis' is reduced by the system of migratory labour, there is some evidence that the incidence is lower among Natives who have worked intermittently than among Europeans with equal length of total service, whereas it appears to be about the same among Natives and Europeans who have worked continuously.[1] There is, however, little knowledge concerning the medical history and causes of death of ex-mine-workers who return to their homes. This may serve to conceal the prevalence of the disease.[2]

While silicosis may be reduced by the system of migratory labour, the incidence of general tuberculosis appears to be increased. There is some evidence that Natives are particularly susceptible to the latter disease during their first year of service of the mines, whether on first engagement or on re-engagement, their liability to contract it being greatest on first engagement.[3] The spreading of employment thus increases the risk of illness and death from this cause.

B. THE ORGANIZATION OF RECRUITING

The social policy which has resulted in the continued use of migratory labour and the compound system has had further consequences in influencing the organization of Native labour on the mines. Employers in the mining industries are prevented from making full use of the capacities of Natives. Consequently they employ Native labour as a relatively undifferentiated mass,

recruits went forward in great numbers to earn money for the relief of their people at home. There was, of course, the usual drop in numbers of recruits coinciding with the ploughing season towards the end of the year.' *Report of the Department of Native Affairs for the years* 1935–6. U.G. 41, 1937, p. 73.

[1] 'Tuberculosis in South African Natives with special reference to the disease amongst the mine labourers on the Witwatersrand.' *Publications of the South African Institute for Medical Research*, No. XXX, Vol. V, March 1932, p. 174.

[2] 'The Magistrate, Flagstaff, reports that in interviewing applicants for relief, he made the discovery that many of the male applicants were ex-miners who were suffering from phthisis and silicosis, but who were not in receipt of compensation. The question of compensation was taken up with the Director of Native Labour, and by the end of 1936 thirty-two families had benefited to the extent of £1,650. The assistance thus obtained under the Miners' Phthisis Act was of great economic value to the district.' *Report of Department of Native Affairs*, U.G. 41, 1937, p. 72.

[3] 'Tuberculosis in South African Natives. . . .' op. cit., pp. 141–3, 350.

and on the Transvaal gold- and coal-mines they have turned their attention rather to preventing competition from driving up the rates of pay and the cost of recruiting than to devising widespread incentives to Natives to increase their efficiency.

(i) The Centralized Control of Recruiting and of Wage-rates

Bowing before the colour bar and fortified by the fact that the Union Government had sanctioned the system of recruiting and long-term contracts by passing the Native Labour Regulation Act, the leaders of the industry, in 1912, once more set about reorganizing the methods of recruiting and paying the Native labour force.

It will be illuminating before describing the system adopted to trace the fortunes of the organization for the collective buying of Native labour. The Witwatersrand Native Labour Association had been reorganized in 1900. It had been intended that it should be the sole buyer of Native labour for its members, but its monopoly had soon broken down outside Portuguese territory.

The costs of recruiting were higher than anticipated and recruiting fees were raised repeatedly. Between 1903 and 1904 fees rose as follows:

> Natives on 12 months' contract, from £3 5s. 0d. to £5; Natives on 6 months' contract, from £1 12s. 6d. to £2 10s. 0d; local Natives engaged for 3 months or less, from £1 to 1 5s. 0d., with a further liability of £1 5s. 0d. on renewal of contract after three months' service.[1] Later fees on local voluntary boys were as high as £2.[2]

In 1906 the Robinson Group obtained permission through the British Government to recruit independently in Portuguese East Africa,[3] and resigned from the Witwatersrand Native Labour Association. It soon rejoined the Association, but the centralized recruiting system had broken down. The constitution of the Association was altered, and, while members were still bound to recruit only through the Association in Portuguese East Africa, they were now left free to recruit independently elsewhere.[4]

Independent recruiting does not appear to have been less costly, for, in 1911, the Executive Committee of the Chamber of Mines reported that the most serious aspect of the labour supply was the ever-increasing cost of recruiting and an increase in the wages

---

[1] *Witwatersrand Native Labour Association, Annual Report*, 1903, pp. 4, 5. *Transvaal Chamber of Mines, Annual Report*, 1904, p. 414.

[2] *Transvaal Chamber of Mines, Annual Report*, 1906, p. 576.

[3] Ibid., pp. 40–44.

[4] Before the defection of the Robinson Group, the fees charged on local and voluntary boys had been reduced to 2s. 6d., and those on boys coming direct from 'open' districts, were abolished in 1907. Ibid., 1907, p. 483.

of Natives,[1] and in the following year the Native Recruiting Corporation was formed to take over recruiting for the gold-mines in British South Africa. The Robinson Group, however, did not join the Corporation until 1919,[2] when Sir J. B. Robinson sold his controlling interest in the Group. The Native Recruiting Corporation then secured the monopoly of recruiting for the Witwatersrand gold-mines in the Union and the Protectorates.

In order to prevent the different mines from competing for labour by offering higher wage-rates, the Native Recruiting Corporation, in addition to laying down the rates for different classes of Natives on time-work, insisted that earnings from piece-work should be limited. Its schedule of wage-rates provided that the average daily wage for certain classes of Natives employed on piece-work was not to exceed two shillings and threepence per shift on any mine.[3] This system is known as the *maximum average*. The maximum average wage, which may not be exceeded under penalty of a fine to the mine concerned, has been modified from time to time.[4] But the principle of restricting the earnings of Natives employed on piece-work has been maintained, although the dissatisfaction to which such limitation of wages gives rise has been recognized by employers:

> To expect that the natives will be for ever content with their present position and limitations is absurd. . . . It behoves us to endeavour to remove, before they become acute, but with due regard to the position of the white workmen, the real grievances from which the natives are suffering—the chief of which, so far as the mines are concerned, is this impossibility of advancing in earnings beyond a very limited point.[5]

The wage-rates laid down by the Native Recruiting Corporation apply to all Natives employed on the Witwatersrand gold-mines and not only to those engaged through the Corporation.

(ii) The Recruiting System

Labour for the Witwatersrand gold-mines is obtained through the two central recruiting organizations, the Witwatersrand Native

---

[1] Ibid., 1911, p. xliv.

[2] W. A. Mostert, an independent contractor, supplied Native labour to the Robinson Group until 1919.

[3] *Native Grievances Inquiry*, op. cit., para. 263.

[4] In February 1914 a sliding scale was introduced whereby when not more than 25 per cent of all Natives employed on lashing and tramming were employed on contract (piece-work) the maximum average was raised to 2s. 6d., descending to 2s. 3d. where 100 per cent were on contract. ('Lashing' is the name given to the process of shovelling broken rock; 'tramming', that given to the work of pushing trucks.)

[5] *Transvaal Chamber of Mines, Annual Report*, 1918, p. 70.

Labour Association and the Native Recruiting Corporation, and also from Natives who present themselves independently at the mines seeking employment. At current wage-rates and under conditions of work and life on the gold-mines, recruiting and the long period contract have been necessary in order to keep up the supply of labour.[1]

The proportion of recruited to non-recruited labour from the Union and the British Protectorates in South Africa has diminished, yet these areas now supply a larger proportion of the labour force. During the five years 1910–14 these areas supplied to the mines an annual average of 148,000 Natives, of whom 61 per cent were ·recruited. During the period 1935–9, when the average number from these sources had risen to 236,000, the proportion of recruits had fallen to 41 per cent.[2] On the other hand, all Portuguese Native labourers now come under contract, and Natives are being obtained under long-period contracts from Nyasaland.

In South Africa in the early days much prominence was given to abuses such as misrepresentation of terms of service and other kinds of fraud which are frequently associated with uncontrolled recruiting among primitive people. In the different colonies legislative attempts were made to check abuses and these were consolidated in the Native Labour Regulation Act of 1911. One practice which had arisen from competitive recruiting was that of making large advances to Natives. At one time sums of £20 to £30, and even up to £60, or their equivalent in cattle, were advanced to a single man, and a Native often received payment for his whole contract in the form of cattle handed him at his kraal.[3]

In 1910 the amount of advances was limited to £5. Limitation of advances was continued under the Native Labour Regulation Act, the amount of advances and the conditions under which they might be given being modified, and in 1921 the system of limiting advances was extended[4] to agents and employers not falling under the earlier Act. On mines, works, and plantations, advances in consideration of a Native accepting employment were limited to £2, or £3 where the period of employment was to be for nine

---

[1] *Native Grievances Inquiry*, op. cit., para. 426; *Low Grade Mines Commission, Final Report*, U.G. 34, 1920, para. 227.

[2] *Witwatersrand Native Labour Association, Annual Reports*, 1919, Table B. & E; 1939, Tables B & D. During 1933 when there was an exceptionally large supply of Native labour offering in the Union and British Protectorates, it might have been profitable temporarily to cease recruiting but for the desirability of maintaining contracts to accept a minimum monthly quota from recruiting agents. *Transvaal Chamber of Mines, Annual Report*, 1934, Presidential Address for 1933; *Witwatersrand Native Labour Association, Annual Report*, 1935, Chairman's Speech.

[3] *Native Grievances Inquiry*, op. cit., para. 505.

[4] *Natives Advances Regulation Act*, No. 18 of 1921.

months or longer.[1] The principle of limiting advances was supported by the Chamber of Mines,[2] but was opposed by traders
in the Transkeian Territories, who desired that the Natives should
spend their earnings in the Territories, and not in Johannesburg.[3]
The system of advances encouraged desertion, for wages having
been spent, the temptation to evade the labour promised was
great, and desertion was most common among Natives who had
received large advances.[4]

The system of using labour agents lends itself to abuse, but
nevertheless it has certain advantages, both for the labourer and
the employer. Discussing recruitment, Major Orde Browne,
formerly head of the Labour Department of Tanganyika, says:

'The labour agent is frequently represented as a completely
unscrupulous and wholy undesirable parasite, who makes enormous
profits out of the cunning exploitation of ignorant natives; he is
considered the modern successor of the slaver, wholly indifferent
to the welfare of his chattels, and capable of any sort of roguery or
deceit to cajole his victims into his power.

'In actuality, while labour recruiting undeniably lends itself to
knavery and oppression, there is another side to the question; if
respectable persons are selected for the work, and suitable rules and
restraints govern their activities, most valuable services may be
rendered by them to all concerned. Indeed, it may be said that the
labour agent in some form is indispensable.'[5]

The Economic and Wage Commission regarded the long-period
contract, recruiting and compound systems as necessary corollaries
to a social policy designed to maintain the Native reserves as the
home of the labour force.[6] Given a population residing a long
way from the labour centres, labour agents can perform useful
services in arranging for the transport, wayside accommodation,
and provisioning of recruits. Those services are most useful in
remote areas where there is no regular transport.

Large centralized recruiting organizations, such as those of the
gold-mining industry, have certain advantages and certain disadvantages for both employers and employees, as compared with
the individual agent operating on his own. They are in a better
position to provide rest-camps and organize transport, but, on
the other hand, they tend to favour the unpopular employer, who
cannot obtain labour without resort to recruiting.

The Witwatersrand Native Labour Association engages Natives

[1] Proclamations No. 175 of 1921 and 231 of 1923.
[2] Transvaal Chamber of Mines, Annual Report, 1912, p. 13.
[3] Native Grievances Inquiry, op. cit., para. 596.
[4] Ibid, para. 563.
[5] G. St. J. Orde Browne, The African Labourer, p. 50.
[6] Economic and Wage Commission (1925), U.G. 14, 1926, para. 285.

for work upon the Reef generally and not for any particular mine. Between 1912 and 1933 it recruited Natives in Portuguese territory only. Since 1933 it has also recruited in British territory north of latitude 22 degrees south. A certain number of its recruits, who are known as 'specials', and their 'brothers'[1] are engaged for work on particular mines. These Natives must have worked on that mine before, and they must state, when first taken on, that they wish to go back to that mine, and prove by the production of passports or otherwise that they have actually worked there. The percentage of Natives who might choose their own mine was limited by the Articles of Association of the Witwatersrand Native Labour Association to $32\frac{1}{2}$ per cent, but in practice, in addition to those who originally stipulate that they desire to go back to their old mine, others who can prove they have previously worked on a mine, together with their 'brothers', are allowed to return to it. This extension was the result of the discontent and dissatisfaction which the previous system of allotment had caused. In 1914 about 50 per cent of Witwatersrand Native Labour Association recruits and their 'brothers' returned to mines on which they had previously worked.[2]

Natives recruited by the Native Recruiting Corporation are engaged for service on a particular mine subject to their labour being required by that mine. The reservoir of unappropriated recruited labour is available for filling up the complements of unpopular mines. It is very valuable to them, for it enables them to obtain a share of the labour supply without offering more attractive conditions than other mines.

Employers allege that Native workers are slow to recognize and respond to improved conditions of work, and that once a mine has obtained a bad reputation it retains it for years, although conditions on it may have been improved. The system of allotment would help to counteract a slow reaction to improved conditions.

The recruiting organizations themselves attempt to induce their members to improve conditions, for otherwise they have difficulty in securing recruits. Nevertheless, in so far as the centralized system of recruitment and wage policy prevent employers from competing by offering better terms of work, they keep down real wages.

From the point of view of the labourer, one of the disadvantages of a central organization is that, if such an organization has a monopoly of recruiting, Natives may have to accept the terms offered or stay at home. This would appear to be the situation in Portuguese East Africa, where the Witwatersrand Native

---

[1] Relatives.   [2] *Native Grievances Inquiry*, op. cit., paras. 409, 412

Labour Association has the monopoly of recruiting for employers in the Union. Since 1928 Portuguese Natives not employed on the mines of the Transvaal have been regarded as prohibited immigrants, and they are officially required to obtain special permission to remain within the Union. The immigration of Portuguese Natives to employment other than on the Transvaal mines was prohibited for a time after 1928, and it is now subject to regulation. Neither the Natal collieries nor sugar planters have been able to obtain permission to recruit Native labour in Portuguese territory.[1]

(iii) The Strength of the Natives' Desire for Income

The policy of restricting earnings on the mines is partly explained by the belief that the Natives' demand for money income is inelastic. In spite of the experiences in 1902 and 1903 the labour policy of the gold-mining industry has continued to be influenced by the belief that a rise in wages would lead to a falling off in supply through a reduction both in the period of work and in the efficiency of the worker, who, it is contended, would remain at home for longer intervals and forget what he had learnt.

A witness giving evidence before the South African Native Affairs Commission (1903–5) had said:

'A large increase in wages will defeat its object, as the Native will more rapidly attain his object and therefore work a shorter period.'

This opinion was fairly general, although not universal even in 1904.[3] It has, however, continued to be the official view of the Chamber of Mines and was clearly stated by the Native Recruiting Corporation in 1925:

'The Corporation is convinced that any increase in the level of native wages would be followed, to only a small extent, by an increase in the native standard of living; that the main result would be that the native would work for a shorter period than at present; and that consequently the native labour available to industry in the Union would be reduced.[4]

It is noteworthy that the Native Recruiting Corporation did not state that the probable effect of a rise in wages on the mines

[1] Evidence to *Economic and Wage Commission* (1925) qq. 16562–3; *Report on Native Labour in Zululand, Transkei*, etc., 1935, para. 48. Department of Native Affairs, G.P.S. 5941–1935.
[2] *South African Native Affairs Commission*, 1903–1905, Vol V., p. 9, Mr. Biggs, Butterworth.
[3] *Transvaal Labour Commission*, Evidence [Cd. 1897], 1904, p. 255, qq. 6,102–6,106; *South African Native Affairs Commission*, 1903–1905, Vol. V, Appendix D, pp. 1–431, esp. pp. 12, 15, 25, 27.
[4] *Economic and Wage Commission* (1925), op. cit., para. 58.

would be a reduction in the supply of Native labour to the gold-mines, but that 'the native labour available to industry in the Union would be reduced'. This implies that individual employers, firms, and even industries, might be able to increase their supply of labour by raising wages, but that the results of raising wages all round would be a reduction in the total supply of labour, and that by keeping wage-rates down employers as a whole obtain more Native labour than would be forthcoming at higher wage-rates.

The Low Grade Mines Commission of 1919–20 was of the opinion that an increase in wages would not 'appreciably' increase the number of Natives employed by industries in South Africa. Discussing possible means 'towards securing an adequate supply of native labour' for gold-mining, it said:

> The second suggestion, made particularly by various native witnesses, is to pay higher wages. It is true that the wages paid on the gold-mines have increased only to a slight extent since 1914, but unless a sufficient number of unemployed natives is obtainable from present sources of supply, an increase in wages on the gold-mines would merely divert natives from other industries. These would then increase their rates of pay and, in the long run, although natives' wages had been increased all round, and the distribution of the natives amongst employers perhaps altered, the total number of natives employed by the industries of South Africa would not have increased appreciably, and an industrial crisis might result.'[1]

The argument of the Native Recruiting Corporation is based on the assumption that the supply of Native Labour will contract as wage-rates rise because, it contends, Natives on the whole go out to work to meet definite predetermined and limited wants. If wages were raised, they would work for a shorter period. The Low Grade Mines Commission in its Interim Report assumes that the supply of labour is relatively inelastic, in that a rise in wage-rates would not 'appreciably' increase the number of Natives employed in industry.[2] In the final report, however, it draws attention to the fact that the supply of labour could be increased by offering Natives greater incentive to increase their efficiency.[3]

The factual evidence for determining whether higher wages would reduce the supply of labour is meagre; but the Native Recruiting Corporation is undoubtedly in a very favourable position for collecting evidence on the subject and its considered opinion cannot be lightly dismissed. One circumstance must be taken into account, and that is that under present conditions employment on mines, especially underground, is not a popular occupation with many Natives. The Natives who are employed

[1] *Low Grade Mines Commission*, Interim Report, U.G. 45, 1919, para. 41.
[2] Ibid.   [3] Ibid., Final Report, U.G. 34, 1920, para. 199 et seq.

by the mines are on the whole those least touched by European civilization. Representatives of the Chamber of Mines told the Native Economic Commission that 'the average town Native would not under any conceivable circumstances work on the mines, even if you increase the wage, say by 3*d*. a shift'.[1] The limit of any increase in wages to which, apparently, their imagination could run was not a very high one. Nevertheless, it is probably true that urban Natives are reluctant to seek work on the gold-mines under present conditions, which include compulsory residence in compounds and very small rewards for increased efficiency.

The wants of the rural Native have not expanded so much as those of the more urbanized; their life still centres to a large extent in the economy of the kraal, although its subsistence basis is rapidly breaking down and European goods now find their way to the most remote Native areas, while everywhere the imposition of taxation has led to the necessity for cash.

In many cases Natives appear to be content with a very restricted range of European goods and living at home is often preferred to moving long distances for work. It is therefore commonly assumed that leisure is more attractive to the Native than the European without considering how far this may be due to the restricted opportunities open to the Native. These restrictions apply to opportunities for both earning and spending.

Over long periods, nevertheless, it is certain that as they get opportunities to buy and use new products, such as for instance, bicycles, they do take them increasingly;[2] and will continue to do so.

The elaborate recruiting system organized by the mines makes it easier for a rural Native who is not initiated into the intricacies of pass laws and other legislation to find his way unhindered to the mines than to other employment. This circumstance may have led the recruiting organizations to make generalizations about the reactions of Natives to changes in wage-rates which, while applicable to the majority of labourers employed on the mines, have not the same weight when extended to cover the increasingly differentiated gradations of the Native population of South Africa.

C. THE WAGE POLICY OF THE TRANSVAAL CHAMBER OF MINES

(i) 'Monopsonistic Bargaining'

The opinion of employers concerning the effect of changes in

[1] *Native Economic Commission*, 1930–32, Typescript of Evidence, p. 9127.
[2] cf. *Low Grade Mines Commission*, 1919–20, Final Report, op. cit., para. 173.
I. Schapera, 'Present-day Life in the Native Reserves', *Western Civilization and the Natives of South Africa*, p. 43. M. Hunter, *Reaction to Conquest*, pp. 142, 455.

wage-rates upon the supply of labour is important because it may lead them to combine to keep down wage-rates. The more steeply the cost of attracting additional labour rises, the greater will be the advantages of this policy. The amount of labour forthcoming at the wages offered will, of course, depend on the conditions of supply. If, as the Native Recruiting Corporation contends, an increase in wages will actually cause the total supply of labour to contract,[1] the advantage to an industry of keeping down wage-rates may be very great, as more labour will be forthcoming than at higher rates. Under these conditions the incentive to employers to combine is extremely strong.

It was argued before the Economic and Wage Commission of 1925 that exploitation of Native labour, in the sense of payment of a wage below the equilibrium level of competitive conditions, was a characteristic of the South African labour market, and that it was assisted by provisions subjecting 'Native labourers' to penal prosecution for breach of contract and permitting the recruiting and compound systems, which, it was said,

> prevent the native from receiving as favourable a rate of pay as the normal play of supply and demand would otherwise enable him to secure.[2]

This argument is based on the opinion that employers in the gold-mining industry are in a monopolistic, or rather 'monopsonistic'[3] position, and that, believing the Natives' demand for income to be inelastic, they take advantage of the immobility of many Natives, and use the recruiting system to offer less favourable terms of service. For instance, they can insist upon a long period of service, which can be enforced through criminal sanction once it has been undertaken. They can also fix wage-rates below those that would result from competitive bidding between the individual employers. The Commissioners also reported:

> Everywhere we were informed that there was a shortage of Native labour, yet the ordinary result of such a shortage—a rise in wages sufficient to reduce the demand to equality with the supply—does not take place.'[4]

That condition indicates that competition is not effective. The amount of labour employed will be the amount at which the cost of the last unit employed (in the case of the gold-mines, wages plus recruiting expenses) will just equal the value which it adds

---

[1] i.e. if the supply curve of labour is 'backward-sloping'.
[2] *Economic and Wage Commission* (1925) op. cit., para. 58.
[3] I use the term introduced by Mrs. Joan Robinson in her *Economics of Imperfect Competition*, and now generally adopted to describe a buyers' monopoly in order to distinguish it from a sellers' monopoly.
[4] *Economic and Wage Commission* (1925), op. cit., para. 58.

to the product. Where the supply of labour is inelastic[1] the cost
of obtaining additional labour will rise steeply. Where there is a
monopsonistic buying of labour, some employers may find it
profitable to employ more labour at the existing rate of wages
than is forthcoming, although it may not pay the collective association to raise wage-rates or spend more on recruiting in an endeavour to attract more labour. In such a case some system has
to be adopted of rationing and distributing the limited amount of
labour actually forthcoming.

The gold-mining industry has continually complained that it
suffers from a 'shortage' of Native labour. This simply means
that at the present average cost of wages and recruiting it would
pay mine managements to employ more labour than is forthcoming.
It has frequently been stated that the Native labour force is not
'adequate' to enable the mines to work at 'full capacity', and that
an increase in the supply of labour would lower very considerably
the average cost per ton of mining and crushing ore. Thus, the
Low Grade Ore Commission argued:

> It is of fundamental importance to the gold-mining industry of
> the Witwatersrand, based as it is upon the employment of natives
> for unskilled work, that the supply of this class of labour should be
> sufficient to allow the individual mines to work to the full capacities
> of their reduction plants.
>
> When so working, each mine can operate at a lower cost per ton
> milled than would otherwise be the case, as it is then in a position
> to distribute over the maximum tonnage its overhead and standing
> charges, such as those for hoisting, shaft maintenance, pumping,
> main ventilation, compounds, phthisis compensation, insurance,
> licences, supervision, and head office.
>
> An adequate supply of native labour by lowering the cost per ton,
> thus not only ensures the winning of greater profit per ton, but also
> brings within the range of profitable mining ore that would other-
> wise be left unmined.[2]

The problem arises why, over a period of fifty years, mines should
continually have been equipped with 'surplus capacity'.[3]

Part of the *apparent* 'surplus capacity' is explained by the
seasonal and cyclical fluctuations in the supply of Native labour.
It can be regarded as additional equipment to enable the mines

---

[1] i.e. where the supply of labour expands or contracts less than proportionately to a rise or fall in the rates of wages. Inelasticity of the supply of
labour to an industry as a whole would probably seldom be considerable in the
absence of barriers imposed by organized labour, or by the State on its behalf
or on behalf of other interests, to the movement of labour to other industries.
But it is obviously more likely, the larger the industry; cf. Hutt, *Collective
Bargaining*, pp. 91–2.

[2] *Low Grade Ore Commission*, U.G. 16, 1932, Interim Report, para. 16.

[3] 'Surplus capacity' is not confined to reduction works; cf. below, p. 203,
note 2.

to take advantage of seasonal and cyclical increases in the supply
of labour. But complaints that the supply of labour is inadequate
for the most economical working of the mines, on the basis of
their fixed equipment, have been continual. With the exception
of the brief period between 1933 and 1936, they have characterized
the industry from its beginning, in spite of the fact that in fifty
years the number of Native labourers employed has increased
from fifteen hundred to over three hundred thousand.[1] After
1929, depression in farming and manufacturing industry led to
an increase in the supply of labour to the mines, and for almost
the first time on record the President of the Chamber of Mines
stated that a surplus of Natives suitable for mine-work was
available in the Union and the three British Protectorates.[2] By
1936, however, the leaders of the gold-mining industry were again
anticipating a 'shortage' of Native labour and, in spite of a very
considerable increase in the numbers employed, complaints have
again arisen that the supply of Native labour is insufficient to
meet the 'requirements' of the industry.[3]

On the assumption of chronic 'shortage', the question remains
why the mines should organize on the basis of permanently surplus
equipment. One explanation may be that a large part of the
initial expenditure in deep-level mining is in sinking the shafts
to reach the ore, and that the expense of sinking additional shafts,
or increasing the size of those already sunk, is much greater than
that of sinking a larger shaft at the outset. It may, therefore, be
decided that if the risk of sinking a shaft is justified, it is better
to undertake the risk of sinking one sufficiently large to allow for
possible expansion rather than the alternative risk of having to
enlarge it later on at much additional expense. Other equipment, such as reduction works and underground development,

[1] The Annual Reports of the Transvaal Chamber of Mines, 1905–22, show
that the number of Natives employed at the 31st December was consistently
below the full complement. In 1927 the President of the Chamber of Mines
was still complaining of the scarcity of Native labour: '. . . our requirements
in the way of native labour are constantly increasing. A year ago my predecessor
told you that 195,000 natives were needed to work the mines at a maximum
economy. To-day, we have 200,000 at work, yet need more, and this tendency
must continue as long as operations increase. . . .' *Transvaal Chamber of
Mines, Annual Report*, 1927, p. 58.
[2] Ibid., p. 46.
[3] The gold-mining industry began to expand in 1929 with the fall in working
costs which accompanied he world-wide depression in other industries. The
rise in the price of gold which followed the widespread suspension of the gold
standard (Britain, September 1931, South Africa, December 1932) and the
devaluation of currencies in countries which retained the gold standard, further
stimulated gold mining and accelerated expansion. Consequently the demand
for labour rose continuously during this period; cf. *Transvaal Chamber of Mines,
Annual Reports, passim*, especially the Reports for 1933, pp. 40–42, 46; 1936,
pp. 48, 51, 52; 1937, p. 47; *Witwatersrand Native Labour Association, Annual
Report*, 1935, Chairman's Speech; idem for 1937, Chairman's Speech.

can, for technical reasons, be extended more gradually as mining proceeds.[1]

With a given technical equipment it will, of course, pay to employ labour up to the point at which you have planned to carry on operations, if the desired amount of labour can be obtained at the prearranged price.[2] Where there is centralized control of the payment and distribution of labour, if wages are fixed at a level at which it pays individual employers to engage more labour than is forthcoming, some system of rationing will have to be adopted, and in consequence particular employers may continually report 'shortage' as compared with their planned 'full complement'.

An additional explanation of continued 'surplus capacity' is that in view of the method of distributing the Native labour force, it may pay mine managements deliberately to engineer an appearance of 'surplus capacity', in order to secure a larger quota of labour.[3] Under the centralized system of engaging and distributing Native labour on the Witwatersrand gold-mines a technical Committee of the Chamber of Mines, after investigating the reduction plant and the capacity of the mine to supply it, assesses the number of Natives required to run each individual mine at its 'full capacity'; this number is known as the mine's 'complement'.[4] It is understood that the recruiting organizations distribute labour on a basis dependent on the requirements of the various individual mines, but information as to the precise basis of allocation is not available for publication.

Competition to obtain an increased supply of labour is keen between individual mine managers, but, in so far as the central control is effective, it is not permitted to take the direct form of offering higher wages.[5] Mine managements may therefore resort to devices such as enlarged fixed equipment in order to be allotted

[1] 'Generally speaking, it is deemed to be expedient to minimize the risk by starting operations with a smaller mill, and gradually extending the development.' Ross E. Browne, *Working Costs of the Witwatersrand*, Appendix 3, quoted, W. J. Busschau, *The Theory of Gold Supply*, p. 67.

[2] cf. Busschau, op. cit., p. 36, 'With a given technical equipment, unit working costs will fall up to the point of capacity.'

[3] cf. W. H. Hutt, *Theory of Idle Resources*, Chap. VII.

[4] 'The native labour complement of a mine is the number of natives required to run it at its full capacity, and is assessed by a technical committee of the Chamber of Mines after investigation not only of its reduction plant but also of the capacity of its mines to supply it, after giving due consideration to such factors as sorting of waste rock, support of workings, etc.' *Low Grade Ore Commission*, U.G. 16, 1932, para. 44, cf. *Low Grade Mines Commission*, Final Report, U.G. 34, 1920, paras. 230–33.

[5] In 1914 the Native Grievances Commissioner reported: 'The demand for labour is greater than the supply; and the employers, despite their close organization, are not really loyal to their agreements with each other. For example, all mines comprised in the Native Recruiting Corporation have agreed upon a

larger complements. The effect of an increased assessment is to put the mine in a more advantageous position for securing additional labour and to give it a prior claim should the supply fall off.[1]

The 'shortage' of Native labour is not felt by all mines equally, in spite of the centralized system of distributing labour, for there is not sufficient 'allotable' labour to 'bring up to their complement the unpopular mines'.[2] In 1929, for example, when the average percentage by which complements were short on thirty-two mines was 7·22, the percentage 'deficiency' on individual mines varied between 10·59 and ·95. At that time the richer mines of the Far East Rand, whose working conditions were generally better, were most popular, and it was on the low-grade mines—'the mines with the least resilience and little in the way of cash resources'[3] —that the deficiency was greatest between the number employed and the full 'complement' of the mine.

The effect on the production of gold of the fixation of Native wages below the competitive rate is the same, for those mines which secure labour, as that of any other cost-lowering device. It lowers the grade of ore which it pays to mine, but at the same time

> the tonnage of ore milled is smaller than if the mines were free to attract more labour by raising wages. Thus the amount of ore worth milling is increased, but the number of tons milled a year, and probably also the average grade of ore milled, are reduced. The annual output of gold is therefore lower, but the lives of the mines are more than proportionately lengthened.[4]

Over the whole life of the industry the effect of this fixation of wages, by increasing the total amount of ore which will be worth milling, will be to increase the total employing capacity. More labour will be employed by the industry in these circumstances than would be if the individual mines competed for labour by raising the rate of wages offered, for, *ex hypothesi*, a higher rate of wages would actually reduce the total number of man-hours.

uniform rate of wages; but it is very generally believed (and I have no doubt that the belief is well founded) that there are many evasions of this agreement.' *Native Grievances Inquiry*, op. cit., para. 418.

[1] *Low Grade Mines Commission*, 1919–20, Final Report, op. cit., para. 231.

[2] 'As all the natives from the Union and the three Protectorates choose the mines on which they work, the natives obtained from Portuguese East Africa are used to make good the deficiencies on the less popular mines. But about one-fourth of the Portuguese natives, being time-expired, also have the privilege of choosing the mines on which to work, with the result that the allotable natives remaining may not be sufficient to bring up to their complement the unpopular mines.' *Low Grade Ore Commission*, op. cit., para. 44.

[3] Evidence of Gold Producers' Committee of the Chamber of Mines to *Low Grade Ore Commission*, op. cit., Statement No. 7, para. 21.

[4] F. W. Paish, 'Causes of Changes in Gold Supply,' *Economica*, Vol. V (New Series), No. 20, November 1938, p. 383.

The centralized control of wages and the distribution of labour between the mines determines, in part, the production of individual mines. Under this system it is possible that the richer mines are prevented from mining ore which would be payable under competitive conditions while production on the poorer mines may be maintained under conditions which would not be profitable if the rate of wages were not kept down by the collective action of employers.[1]

In so far as the centralized control of the Native labour force assists the mining of low-grade ore, it is in accord with official Government policy, for successive governments have feared the consequences of any contraction in the gold-mining industry,[2] and have attempted to promote the mining of low-grade ore.

The labour policy of the gold-mining industry clearly affects also the distribution of labour between gold-mining and other industries. The labour market outside the mining industry is considered later.

(ii) Average Wage-rates of Native Labourers

The centralized control of recruiting and of wage-rates has been successful in keeping average wages from rising, despite the continual complaints about the 'shortage' of Native labour.[3] Money wages were lower in 1913 than in 1896, in spite of the greater efficiency of the Native.[4] In 1913 the average monthly wages were 52s.[5] In 1896 they had been 60s. 10d.[6] The average pay for all Natives for thirty shifts had been:

[1] In 1918, when the mining industry was suffering from rising costs and scarcity of Native labour, the Chamber of Mines proposed (the Consolidated Gold Fields of South Africa dissenting) that the situation could be met by temporarily closing down six of the low-grade mines (it proposed that the Government should provide a subsidy to cover the cost of pumping operations and the maintenance of plant). It considered that gold output would not be reduced, for 'the remaining mines would be of higher grade than those closed down.' *Select Committee on Gold Mining Industry*, 1918 [S.C. 3, 1918], p. 5, Statement of Chamber of Mines presented by the President, Mr. E. A. Wallers.
The Government Mining Engineer was also of the opinion that the closing down of a few mines would ease the situation without reducing the gold output. Ibid., p. vii.
[2] cf. the appointment in 1916 of the State Mining Commission in 1918, of the Select Committee on Gold Mining Industry, in 1919 of the Low Grade Mines Commission, and in 1930 of the Low Grade Ore Commission.
[3] cf. *Low Grade Mines Commission*, Final Report, op. cit., paras. 127–37. *Report of Mining Industry Board*, 1922, para. 152. *Economic and Wage Commission*, op. cit., para. 58. *Inter-departmental Committee of the Labour Resources of the Union*, 1930, paras. 25–46. *Annual Reports of the Transvaal Chamber of Mines, passim*, cf. footnote p. 269 below.
[4] *Economic Commission*, 1914, U.G. 12, 1914, para. 51.
[5] *Report of Government Mining Engineer* for 1913.
[6] *Transvaal Labour Commission*, Evidence [Cd. 1897], 1904 Exhibit, No. 1.

		s.	d.	
1902	.	34	8	(or 1 1.9 per shift)[1]
1906	.	56	0	(or 1 10.3 per shift)
1910	.	54	1	(or 1 9.6 per shift)

Since then money wages have remained much the same, the average rate per shift having been:

			s.	d.
1914 .	.	.	1	11.7[2]
1921 .	.	.	2	2.1[3]
1930 .	.	.	2	1.7 (June)[4]
1939 .	.	.	2	3[5]

The wages of the majority of Native employees in the gold-mines deviate little from the average. In April 1931, of the 198,602 Natives employed in the gold-mines, both on the surface and underground, the cash wages per shift of one-quarter were less than 1s. 11d.; half received between 1s. 11d. and 2s. 2d., and one-quarter over 2s. 2d. Eighty-six per cent received less than 2s. 6d. Only 1,000 received over 5s. 4d., 524 over 6s. 3d., 210 over 7s., and 25 between 9s. 3d. and 11s. 6d.[6] Since that date, expansion in the number of Natives employed in gold-mining has been general throughout all wage-groups except the lowest. The absolute number, as well as the percentage, of Natives receiving less than 2s. has fallen. This is because Natives who have previously worked underground for 120 shifts are now paid a minimum cash wage of 2s. per shift on re-engagement, consequently this becomes a minimum for a large number of Natives. In November 1938 the proportion of Natives receiving less than 1s. 11d. was 14 per cent (as compared with one-quarter in 1931); 63 per cent received between 1s. 11d. and 2s. 2d., and less than one-quarter over 2s. 2d. Eighty-six per cent still received less than 2s. 6d. The number receiving over 5s. 4d. had increased from 1,000 in 1931 to 2,676, while 1,200 received over 6s. 3d., 582 over 7s., and 63 between 9s. 3d. and 12s. 8d.[7]

In addition to wages paid in money, food, quarters, and medical

---

[1] *Native Grievances Inquiry*, op. cit., para. 250. Until 1912 there was no uniformity in regard to the payment of railway fares. Some mines deducted fares paid from wages and some did not.

[2] *Report of Mining Industry Board*, 1922, para. 168.

[3] Ibid.

[4] *Native Economic Commission*, 1930–32, op. cit., para. 818.

[5] *Annual Report of the Government Mining Engineer*, 1939, U.G. 22, 1940, p. 22.

[6] *Native Economic Commission*, 1930–32, op. cit., Annexure 21, IV.

[7] The statistics for 1938 were obtained for me by the South African Institute of Race Relations.

and other services are provided for Natives on the gold-mines. While money wages have shown little variation the standard of food and accommodation has improved. In 1899 the provision of fresh vegetables and meat was the exception, and the air-space per boy rarely exceeded 200 cubic feet. In 1902 rations consisted almost exclusively of mealie meal. The introduction of the Chinese labourers led to an improvement in housing conditions, for minimum standards were laid down for the Chinese, and when they left these quarters were used for Natives.

Under the Native Labour Regulation Act of 1911 minimum standards of food and accommodation were laid down, and in 1914 Mr. H. O. Buckle reported:

> Generally speaking, I do not think there is much to complain of in the food supplied to native labourers on the mines. The prescribed scale appears to be generally adhered to, although strict adherence is not insisted upon; if the mine provides food of approximately the quantity and food value laid down, no objection is taken to minor variations in accordance with the view of the compound manager and medical officer concerned. I think this is a wise course: it allows for experiment and improvement.
>
> There were not a great number of complaints as to the food provided.[1]

In 1914 the cost of food to the gold-mines was about 4d. to 6d. per head per day.[2] In 1922 the Mining Industry Board thought that the provision of quarters, food, and services was equal to an additional 1s. a day.[3] In 1932, according to statistics from a number of mines, the cost of food was 3·85 per Native per shift worked. (3·16 per Native per day in service.) The total cost to the mines of food, quarters, medical and other services, excluding interest on compound buildings, was 10·31d. per shift worked. It was estimated that the cost of the food and services supplied to the Native would, if purchased individually, have been about 1s. 4d. or 1s. 5d. per day.[4] In 1939 the estimated cost to the mining companies of food and quarters was 1s. 1d. per shift worked.[5]

The Chamber of Mines considers that the rise in the cost of food and compound services at some periods, particularly towards the end of the Great War and in the years immediately following it, involved an increase in the real wages of Natives although cash wages had remained stationary.[6] The increase was not, however,

---

[1] *Native Grievances Inquiry*, op. cit., paras. 128, 129.
[2] Ibid., para. 126.   [3] *Report of Mining Industry Board*, 1922, para. 165.
[4] *Native Economic Commission*, 1930–32, op. cit., paras. 819, 820.
[5] *Annual Report of the Government Mining Engineer*, 1939, U.G. 22, 1940, p. 22.
[6] *Low Grade Mines Commission*, 1919–20, Final Report, op. cit., paras. 191, 197.

nearly proportionate to the rise in the wages of European miners during the same period.

(iii) Efficiency and Method of Remuneration

The fixation of Native wage-rates has not been achieved without cost. It has hindered the development of piece-work and made it extremely difficult for mine managers to organize a wage policy which provides effective incentives for Natives to increase their efficiency in those types of work which the colour bar permits them to perform.

Discussion of the supply of Native labour in South Africa has tended to overlook the fact that the supply of labour depends on both numbers and efficiency, and that efficiency may increase as a result of greater incentives. There is evidence that the restriction on earnings imposed by the mines has affected the nature of the labour supply. The result of the limitation on earnings enforced under the Native Recruiting Corporation Agreement of 1912 was that some mines had to cut their piece-rates solely to comply with it. At that time there was a system of piece-work on the Nourse Mines under which lashing and tramming boys earned up to 8s. per shift. This had to be altered; the average pay for lashing and tramming boys fell to 1s. 9.2d. per shift and the mines lost that set of highly efficient Native workers, although the manager considered that the earlier arrangement had been more satisfactory to the mine as well as to the Natives. On the Crown Mines piece-work rates had to be cut again and again, and reduced from 1s. to 5d. per truck. As a result they lost 600 boys within a few days and 400 more soon afterwards. Average earnings of this class of Native fell from 4s. to 2s. 1d. per shift.[1]

The Commissioner appointed to inquire into Native Grievances, Mr. H. O. Buckle, commented:

> It is quite evident that when a mine is driven, as in this instance, to cut rates, not because the management think that they are not getting value for their money, but merely to comply with an arbitrary clause of this kind, the work must suffer.
>
> The effect of this clause is that, whenever the general run of natives on this work becomes more efficient, the management is compelled to reduce the rate, thus actually penalizing efficient work. This does not seem to me the way to get the best out of a labourer.
>
> The purpose of the clause is, of course, to prevent the mines out-bidding each other for piece-work labour, just as the prescribed rates prevent them with respect to day's pay labour. It seems to me, for the reasons given above, to be unsound in principle, and it has certainly caused dissatisfaction, which is to nobody's interest.[2]

[1] *Native Grievances Inquiry*, 1914, op. cit., paras. 263–6.
[2] Ibid., paras. 267–9.

The Native Grievances Inquiry Commission, the Dominions Royal Commission, and the Economic Commission of 1914 all recommended the abolition of the maximum average and the extension of piece-work with no limitation on possible earnings. The Economic Commission reported:

> Your Commissioners feel no doubt that the productive powers of the native are being held in check while at the same time a sense of injury is being generated by the device of the maximum average in particular, and in general by a failure on the part of the gold-mines to pay natives more frequently on a system which furnishes an incentive. . . . The native desires to be paid according to his strength; and he complains of the small amount he earns. Your Commissioners understand that the question of an extension of piece-work for natives is closely engaging the attention of the gold-mining industry, and are convinced that much can be done in this direction to increase the efficiency of native labour. They agree with Mr. Taberer, who stated that he preferred piece-work (for natives) in the interest of the mine, of the native, and of the industry.[1]

The Commissioners considered that an alteration in the Native wages system would not affect costs of production adversely, because, in their opinion, Native labour was used extravagantly, and insufficient attention was paid to its organization and to the possibility of increasing its efficiency by providing adequate incentives.[2]

The Low Grade Mines Commission (1919–20) and the Mining Industry Board (1922) also recommended the extension of piece-work.[3] The former considered that improved opportunities for increased earnings would stimulate the energy of Natives and 'assist to make good the shortage of labour'. It drew attention to the fact that a smaller but more efficient labour force might give as good results as a larger complement.[4]

The *maximum average* system is opposed to the principle of piece-work because, if efficiency increases, wage-rates have to be cut. In addition, the technical difficulties of determining piece-work rates are made very much greater by the highly centralized control of the wages of the Native labour force.[5]

Mine managements, it is reported,[6] have repeatedly considered the extension of piece-work; nevertheless, despite its recognized

---

[1] *Economic Commission*, 1914, op. cit., para. 54.
[2] Ibid., para. 55.
[3] *Low Grade Mines Commission*, op. cit., Final Report, para. 200. *Report of Mining Industry Board*, 1922, para. 154.
[4] *Low Grade Mines Commission*, op. cit., paras. 209–10.
[5] cf. H. M. Robertson, '150 Years of Economic Contact. . . .' op. cit., p. 19.
[6] *Transvaal Chamber of Mines, Annual Report*, 1907, p. 112; *Economic Commission*, 1914, op. cit., para. 54; *Low Grade Ore Commission*, 1932, op. cit. para. 14.

advantages in increasing efficiency, the proportion of Native labour employed on this system has not increased. In 1913 the proportion on piece-work on the Reef was 33·7 per cent, the proportion on individual mines varying from 13·8 to 66 per cent. In 1925 about 31 per cent and in 1930 about 33 per cent of the total Native labour force was on piece-work.[1] In 1932 the Low Grade Ore Commission found that in spite of the recommendations of the Low Grade Mines Commission (1919–20) and the Mining Industry Board (1922), the system of piece-work amongst Natives had not been extended, but that, on the contrary, a smaller proportion of the Native labour force was on piece-work than in 1922. The reason stated was that drilling and to a minor degree shovelling and tramming were the only underground operations which lent themselves to piece-work. In drilling there had been a considerable decrease in the number of Natives employed, owing to the more general adoption of the jack-hammer drill, while at the same time there had been an increase in the number and proportion of Natives engaged on support of workings, to which, it was said, piece-work was quite inapplicable.[2]

Actually, a powerful motive preventing the extension of piece-work is fear lest it lead to increased competition for Native labour between mine managements and to a rise in average wages. This is clearly demonstrated in a memorandum submitted by the Chamber of Mines to the Native Economic Commission (1932), which, after detailing various technical difficulties inherent in all systems of piece-work, such as the keeping of accurate tallies and the prevention of scamped work, states that other difficulties are the beliefs, based on experience, that it would lead to 'a certain amount of pirating of natives as between mine and mine' and to 'an increase in the general level of wages without any corresponding advantages'.

(iv) Period of Labour Contract

The long-period contract is said to be necessary to repay the employer for the expenses of recruiting.[3] At the same time it is of great advantage to employers in that it enables them to mitigate to some extent the disadvantages of the seasonal fluctuations in the supply of labour. Where the labourer's home is on the land

---

[1] *Native Grievances Inquiry*, 1914, op. cit., para. 259; *Native Economic Commission*, 1930–32, op. cit., para. 829.

[2] *Low Grade Ore Commission*, 1932, op. cit., para. 14.

[3] In 1930 the cost of recruiting Natives and of the services of the Witwatersrand Native Labour Association, excluding the cost of the Assisted Voluntary System, was approximately £435,784, or 1·78d. per Native per shift worked by all Natives, not merely those recruited, an amount equal to nearly one half of the feeding costs per shift worked. *Native Economic Commission*, op. cit., para. 805.

his industrial life is influenced by the seasons. Bantu peasants like to be at home for the ploughing season and again to enjoy the fruits of the harvest. Thus good harvests reduce the supply of labour to the mines, while there is also a distinct seasonal variation in the supply of labour.[1] The Native Economic Commission considered that the main value of recruiting to the gold-mining industry was that it reduced the seasonal falling-off in the supply of labour which generally began between February and May and was greatest in December.[2] Recruited Natives are contracted for from 270 to 313 shifts. By careful distribution of orders to recruiters it is possible to counteract partially the seasonal fluctuations in supply.

Before the formation of the Native Recruiting Corporation in 1912, British South African Natives were recruited for different periods varying from two to eight months.[3] There were several changes in the contract period while the Witwatersrand Native Labour Association was still attempting to control recruiting in British South Africa. These changes were, generally, in the direction of shortening the period of contract, subject to the Native refunding the cost, or a portion of the cost, of his railway fare.[4] The 'voluntary' Natives who were engaged locally were seldom on more than monthly contracts.[5] Many Natives preferred to make their own way to the labour centres, for they obtained greater choice of employment, and sometimes better terms, especially in the form of shorter contracts of service.[6]

Portuguese Natives under the *modus vivendi* were recruited on a twelve-months (313 shifts) contract, and the Transvaal-Mozambique Convention of 1909 limited their service to a total period of two years, except by special permission of the Curator of Portuguese labour, which appears to have been freely given. By subsequent arrangement from July 1914, all Portuguese Natives were recruited on an eighteen-months contract, the first twelve months being on deferred pay. Thus half the contract wages were payable in Portuguese territory on the return of the labourer.[7] Under the Mozambique Convention of 1928 the maximum period of service of Portuguese Natives was limited to eighteen months, the initial contract being for 313 shifts (twelve months) and any subsequent contract being limited to 156 shifts.

[1] (Cape) *Blue Book on Native Affairs*, G. 25, 1902, pp. 23, 80.. Schapera, 'Labour Migration from a Bechuanaland Reserve,' *Journal of the African Society*, vol. xxxiii; *Report of the Department of Native Affairs*, 1922–6, U.G. 14, 1927, p. 12; *Native Economic Commission*, 1930–32, op. cit., para. 804, Annexure 18; cf. below, p. 218.
[2] *Native Economic Commission*, 1930–32, op. cit., para. 804.
[3] *Report of the Witwatersrand Native Labour Association for* 1903, p. 16.
[4] *Transvaal Chamber of Mines, Annual Report*, 1906, pp. 577, 586.
[5] Idem, 1904, p. 15.   [6] Idem, 1906, p. 573.   [7] Idem, 1912, p. 410.

After the first nine months' service and during any period of re-engagement one-half of the wages earned have to be paid to the Natives in Mozambique on their return.[1]

When the Native Recruiting Corporation was organized in 1912 a minimum contract of ninety shifts (between three and four calendar months) was introduced and contracts varied between this period and a year.[2] 'Voluntary' Natives at this time were engaged for different periods by different mines. In 1914, out of a total of sixty-seven mines:

34 engaged voluntary Natives for a minimum of				30	shifts[3]
7	,,	,,	,,	60	,,
12	,,	,,	,,	90	,,
9	,,	,,	,,	120	,,
1	,,	,,	,,	150	,,
4	,,	,,	,,	180	,,

In 1932 only four mines would engage by the month Natives who came to them voluntarily. Others took them for not less than a three-, four-, or six-months' period.[4]

The minimum period for which British South African Natives were recruited was raised in 1919 to 180 shifts[5] (approximately seven months' service). The Low Grade Mines Commission (1919–20) recommended that the period of contract of recruited Natives be reduced, but this advice was not followed. On the contrary, the period of contract of Natives recruited by the Native Recruiting Corporation was raised in 1924 from 180 to 270 shifts[6] (from approximately 7 months to $10\frac{1}{2}$ calendar months' service) in the case of Natives from the Union and Basutoland. This had the result of retaining in service Natives recruited in January, when the supply was most plentiful, and helped to counteract the falling-off in the supply which became acute during the winter.[7] In 1928, however, the Assisted Voluntary System was organized to cater for those Natives who preferred a shorter period of contract and greater freedom of choice in selecting the mine at which to work. Under this system a Native wishing to go to the Witwatersrand to work on a mine has his railway fare advanced and may receive in addition the loan of £2, which is usually made to a recruited Native. On arrival in Johannesburg the

[1] *Native Economic Commission*, 1930–32, op. cit., paras. 802, 811. *Official Year Book*, No. 17, 1934–5, p. 1014.
[2] *Native Grievances Inquiry*, 1914, op. cit., para. 420.
[3] Ibid., Annexure 19.
[4] *Native Economic Commission*, 1930–32, op. cit., para. 802.
[5] *Low Grade Mines Commission*, 1919–20, Final Report, op. cit., para. 224.
[6] *Transvaal Chamber of Mines, Annual Report*, 1924, p. 52. *Low Grade Ore Commission*, U.G. 16, 1932, para. 6.
[7] *Report of Native Affairs Department*, 1922–6, U.G. 14, 1927, p. 12.

'Assisted Voluntary' Native is in the position of the non-recruited worker in that he can choose his own mine and engage for any period of service for which the mine he selects is prepared to engage labour.

The advantage of this system to a Native is that it saves him interest upon his railway fare and upon any additional money he may require before setting out for the mines. Previously a Native who did not wish to be recruited and who did not have sufficient resources of his own had to borrow from a local trader, and, in the opinion of the Native Economic Commission, traders sometimes charged usurious rates of interest.[1]

The system has proved popular, and in the years 1935–9 it was used by 44 per cent of the Natives coming to the Transvaal mines from the Union and the Protectorates, the areas to which it is applicable.[2]

Statistics of the actual length of stay of Natives at the gold-mines are difficult to obtain. Various isolated investigations have been made and these samples show that, on the average, Portuguese Natives remain at the mines for longer periods than British South African Natives. An investigation which was made in 1923 showed that 19·9 months was the average period of service of the seven thousand East Coast Natives who left or died in the service of the Transvaal gold- and coal-mines during September and October of that year. Individual service varied from twenty years downwards, the most common period being one and a half year (the records were taken to the nearest quarter year). The investigation has not been repeated, but in 1931 the Chamber of Mines considered that there had been no fundamental changes prior to the Mozambique Convention of 1928. The Chamber was then also of the opinion that ten or eleven months was the average period of service of British South African labour.[3] By 1934, however, the average period of service of Union and Protectorate Natives had increased and was slightly over twelve months.[4] The reason for this increase was no doubt the reduced alternative means of obtaining a living resulting from drought and economic depression.

The investigations which have been made do not demonstrate any striking difference in length of service between recruited and non-recruited Natives, except that one relatively small sample

[1] *Native Economic Commission*, 1930–32, op. cit., para. 800.
[2] *Witwatersrand Native Labour Association, Annual Reports*, 1935–9.
[3] Statement prepared by Chamber of Mines for Native Economic Commission on 'The effect of the Convention of 1928 on the service of Portuguese Natives and on the labour force generally,' dated June, 1931.
[4] *Report of the Department of Native Affairs on Native Labour in Zululand, Transkei*, etc., 1935, p. 11.

showed that of 2,043 British South African Natives discharged in November, 1930, the average service of the different classes was:

	Natives	Months
Recruits . . .	785	11.21
Non-Recruits from Territories .	969	10.80
Assisted Voluntary System .	191	7.39
Non-Recruits (Local) . .	98	15.77
Total . . .	2,043	10.88[1]

In 1935 the average period of service of labourers using the Assisted Voluntary System had risen to 11·74 months, and that of recruited labourers to 13·69.[2]

A few Natives remain at work on the mines for years, and many return again and again. In 1918 75 per cent of the East Coast recruits had previous mine experience, and in 1929 over 70 per cent.[3] In 1933, when recruiting in Portuguese East Africa was being conducted on a restricted scale, 95 per cent of the 38,458 Natives engaged had previously worked on the mines.[4] A test check made by the Director of Native Labour, Johannesburg, dated April 1931, showed that of 7,391 arriving for work on the mines 82·10 per cent had been previously employed on the Witwatersrand.[5] It is not shown whether the previous employment was on the mines or not, but on the whole, except in periods of acute industrial depression, the drift of employment is from mine to other work.

In order to encourage Natives to remain at work continuously a bonus of five shillings a month of twopence a shift was paid to Natives who remained at work after the completion of their contracts. Natives who went home, but did not stay away more than four months, in the case of a British South African, and six months in the case of a Portuguese Native, did not forfeit this bonus,[6] but the bonus was discontinued in 1932 because it was considered to have been ineffective in inducing Union Natives to remain on. Seventy-five per cent of the Natives who had drawn it were Portuguese Natives, who, it was considered, would in any case have renewed their contracts.[7]

[1] Evidence of Chamber of Mines to Native Economic Commission, 1930–32
[2] Report . . . on Native Labour in Zululand, etc., op. cit., p. 12.
[3] Transvaal Chamber of Mines, Annual Report, 1919, p. 256; W. Gemmill 'The Organization of Native Labour', Proceedings of the Third (Triennial Empire Mining and Metallurgical Congress, Part II, p. 3.
[4] Witwatersrand Native Labour Association, Annual Report, 1933, p. 2.
[5] Native Economic Commission, 1930–32, op. cit., Annexure 21, III.
[6] Ibid., para. 817.
[7] Report on Native Labour in Zululand, etc., op. cit., para. 92.

In recent years the Government has endeavoured to limit the period of service of British South African Natives on the mines, and in 1935 the Chamber of Mines agreed to limit the period of consecutive service of tramming and shovelling boys (i.e. the less skilled workers) to two years, such Natives not being re-engaged until a period of four months had elapsed. The fact that the mines would not agree to this provision applying to boss boys and special haulage boys indicates that it is probably customary for such boys to remain at the mines for longer periods.

This limitation of the period of work was desired by the Government on the grounds of health and social policy. It feared the ill-effects upon Native family life of unduly long absences on the part of the husband and desired to maintain the Native reserves as reservoirs from which Native labour could be drawn and returned as required.[1] It also desired to spread employment on the mines over a larger number of Natives to alleviate the unemployment which resulted from depression in other industries. The attempt to limit the period of service has, however, been abandoned.[2] Previously the policy of the mines had been to try to extend the period of work so long as this could be done without raising wages.

D. SOURCES OF NATIVE LABOUR

The restrictions on the opportunities for advancement and for earning higher wages have combined with the compound system to make work on the mines unattractive to many of those Natives who have become accustomed to urban conditions. Consequently mine labourers have been drawn very largely from the rural areas, particularly the Native reserves within the Union, the British Protectorates, and Portuguese East Africa. On the whole, in South Africa Natives go to the mines to supplement the incomes which they obtain from the land.

It is interesting to note that the number of Natives transferring directly from other employment on the Witwatersrand to mine work has fallen very considerably since the introduction in 1912 of the stringent restrictions on earnings. In 1911 some 17,000 Natives went from other types of employment to the mines. The average number transferring in the five years 1907–11 was 13,000; in the years 1921–5 it had fallen to 5,000; and in 1932–4 to 2,000; since then it has risen to 4,000.[3] The fall, which took place in 1932–4, at a time when depression in other industries would lead one to expect a rise, is probably accounted for by restrictions

[1] Interview with Mr. A. L. Barrett, Director of Native Labour, 1935.
[2] Interview with Assistant Director of Native Labour, 1938.
[3] *Witwatersrand Native Labour Association, Annual Reports*, 1919, Table E; 1937, Table D.

SOURCES OF NATIVE LABOUR EMPLOYED IN THE TRANSVAAL GOLD- AND COAL-MINING INDUSTRIES, 1904-39[1]

Territorial Analyses of Natives employed by members of the Witwatersrand Native Labour Association, Ltd., and contractors[2] as at 31 December, 1904–39, showing the percentage from each source and the total number employed.

Year	Cape Province	Natal & Zululand	Orange Free State	Transvaal	Basutoland	Bechuanaland	Swaziland	East Coast[3]	Tropical[4]	Other Sources	Total number employed
1904	12·7	3·49	·3	6·96	2·91	·69	·64	66·23	5·91	·17	77,000
1905	6·08	2·60	·17	5·77	1·94	·73	·79	73·19	8·71	·02	81,000
1906	13·71	4·81	·31	3·97	2·62	·40	·72	70·97	2·47	·02	81,000
1907	14·47	4·4	·38	6·09	2·33	·18	1·75	69·37	·99	·02	106,000
1908	24·38	5·13	·47	9·15	3·09	·82	1·01	54·98	·85	·02	149,000
1909	24·31	6·31	·34	7·98	2·48	·65	·90	54·32	2·69	·02	157,000
1910	26·02	6·67	·40	7·49	3·17	·39	1·45	51·96	2·43	·02	179,000
1911	23·19	8·61	·48	8·06	3·82	·49	2·07	51·59	1·66	·03	174,000
1912	26·17	7·34	·37	8·87	5·22	·60	1·94	47·93	1·54	·02	191,000
1913	22·04	6·54	·39	8·77	5·68	1·20	1·87	52·15	1·34	·02	155,000
1914	24·97	5·96	·48	7·76	7·44	1·87	2·89	47·71	·90	·02	156,000
1915	33·00	5·54	·40	8·23	6·24	1·49	2·48	42·09	·52	·01	198,000
1916	30·94	4·11	·34	8·93	7·63	1·68	2·05	43·73	·58	·01	191,000
1917	29·79	4·42	·34	7·47	7·04	1·33	2·10	46·93	·57	·01	176,000
1918	26·14	4·25	·35	6·97	6·55	1·15	2·61	51·46	·51	·01	158,000
1919	32·37	3·53	·30	6·82	6·92	1·03	2·55	46·14	·33	·01	177,000

Year										
1920	26·70	2·14	·22	5·20	7·33	·83	1·62	55·60	·35	·01	173,000
1921	30·82	2·13	·24	5·50	10·56	1·11	2·28	47·08	·27	·01	188,000
1922	34·52	2·12	·24	6·28	7·91	1·47	2·99	44·24	·22	·01	183,000
1923	32·57	1·95	·32	7·42	7·18	1·50	2·52	46·29	·24	·01	196,000
1924	33·05	2·43	·43	7·59	9·15	1·18	2·19	43·88	·18	·01	199,000
1925	30·22	2·36	·40	7·94	7·13	1·16	2·58	47·98	·22	·01	192,000
1926	29·75	2·63	·47	8·37	10·93	1·01	2·12	47·54	·17	·01	203,000
1927	28·86	2·22	·45	7·77	8·03	·69	1·70	50·08	·20	·00	215,000
1928	29·21	2·35	·46	7·30	7·99	·84	1·86	49·78	·21	·00	213,000
1929	29·99	2·73	·56	5·72	10·53	1·14	1·94	47·15	·19	·00	205,000
1930	35·33	2·75	·73	7·20	13·17	1·38	2·15	37·11	·18	·00	222,000
1931	36·31	4·13	·96	8·40	13·62	1·49	2·24	32·71	·14	·00	226,000
1932	42·08	4·50	1·00	8·94	13·61	2·13	2·52	25·10	·12	·00	233,000
1933	42·86	4·66	1·18	1·87	14·34	2·16	2·51	22·34	·08	·00	248,000
1934	41·96	4·62	1·23	8·60	13·03	2·48	2·60	24·67	·80	·01	266,000
1935	40·46	4·86	1·05	8·18	13·01	2·54	2·56	27·07	·27	—	291,000
1936	39·23	4·85	1·10	7·00	14·46	2·25	2·21	27·83	1·07	—	318,000
1937	34·53	5·09	1·21	7·34	12·94	2·77	2·26	30·30	3·56	—	300,000
1938	34·23	4·84	1·38	7·82	14·44	3·04	2·09	27·09	5·07	—	324,000
1939	33·92	4·88	1·49	7·82	14·98	2·72	2·07	26·11	6·01	—	323,000

[1] The figures in this table are from the annual reports of the Witwatersrand Native Labour Association, 1904–39. Nearly all the Transvaal gold- and coal-mines belong to this Association.

[2] Before 1924 Natives employed by contractors were excluded.

[3] East Coast, i.e. Portuguese East Africa, including districts north of latitude 22 deg. south.

[4] Tropical (areas) include Northern and Southern Rhodesia, British Nyasaland Protectorate, that part of British Bechuanaland Protectorate north of latitude 22 deg. south, and South West Africa Protectorate. The percentage of labour from the last source fell from ·87 in 1904 to ·03 in 1914, since when it has been negligible.

imposed by the recruiting associations on the engagement of voluntary labour by individual mines in order that the centralized system of recruitment and distribution should not break down owing to the temporary increase in the supply. The earlier fall may have been due in part to the same cause, but it may also be explained by the development of other more attractive openings at a time when opportunities for individuals to earn high wages on the mines were being restricted by the maximum average system.

The preceding table shows the sources from which Native labourers have come to the Transvaal gold- and coal-mines.

E. THE IMPORTATION OF NATIVE LABOUR

A significance attaches to the policy of importing Native labour from Portuguese East Africa which has not hitherto been sufficiently stressed. The supply from Portuguese East Africa can be adjusted to counteract both seasonal and cyclical fluctuations in the numbers of Natives from the Union and British Protectorates. The Natives from Portuguese territory are, moreover, to a marked degree miners of experience, and they can be drafted by the central authority to one mine or another with greater freedom than those from other South African sources.

The table on the preceding pages shows the extent to which, since 1904, the gold-mines have drawn their labour from Portuguese East Africa. The table slightly exaggerates the average amount of labour coming from this source; for the figures published by the Transvaal Chamber of Mines show the numbers employed on the 31st December of each year, and at this time the proportion of Portuguese Natives employed is somewhat higher than the average, owing to the seasonal decline in the supply of labour from other sources.

The chief seasonal decline takes place because many Native mine labourers, who, it must be remembered, are also peasant farmers, return home for the ploughing season, which is from October to December, according to when the first summer rains fall. Earlier in the year, usually in June and July, there is often a smaller seasonal decline, a decline which is particularly marked in years of good harvest and which is due to the fact that many Natives like to take part in the beer drinks with which they celebrate a good harvest after the maize and millet crops are gathered in.[1]

The supply of Portuguese Native labour does not show the same decline, partly because the Natives from this source contract to work for longer periods than the majority of Union and

[1] Annexure 18 to the *Report of the Native Economic Commission*, 1930–32, shows the seasonal fluctuations in the supply of labour between 1925 and 1931.

Protectorate Natives, and their engagement has been regulated to counteract to some extent the seasonal fluctuations in the supply from the latter sources.

Native labourers from Portuguese East Africa have also been engaged to counteract cyclical fluctuations in the supply of labour from other sources. For it has been found possible by more active recruiting to increase this supply when the number from the Union and the Protectorates has fallen off as a result of a rise in the demand in other industries or of good harvests in the reserves.

Further, Portuguese Natives have been employed in mining since the discovery of diamonds at Kimberley, and many of them have become skilled miners in fact, although opposition to the employment of Natives on skilled work may prevent their being officially termed skilled workers.

Finally, Native labour from Portuguese East Africa can be used to maintain the labour quotas of the less popular mines. For recruits from this source who have not previously worked on the Rand are not generally permitted to choose the mine on which they work. Moreover, a large proportion of the Portuguese Native labourers have always been recruited and to-day they are all engaged through the central recruiting association, the Witwatersrand Native Labour Association. A larger proportion of these labourers is therefore available to be drafted to any mine than in the case of labour from the Union and the British Protectorates, all Natives from these sources being permitted to choose their own mine, subject to its willingness to employ them.

The importance of the supply of labour from Portuguese territory had forced Lord Milner to arrange the *modus vivendi* in 1901. In terms of this agreement employers in the Transvaal mining industry secured the right to recruit Natives in Portuguese territory, and a proportion of the Transvaal railway traffic was guaranteed to Lourenço Marques. In 1909, just before the Union of South Africa was constituted, the Transvaal-Mozambique Convention was negotiated to replace the *modus vivendi*. It provided that Portuguese authorities were to allow the recruiting for the mines to continue, and the Transvaal guaranteed that, by periodical revision of the railway rates, from 50 to 55 per cent of the railway traffic to what is known as the competitive area (the area bounded by lines drawn between the goods traffic depots serving Pretoria, Springs, Vereeniging, Welverdiend, Krugersdorp, and back to Pretoria) should come through Lourenço Marques. Other provisions dealt with customs matter. This Convention became applicable to the Union of South Africa when it was constituted in 1910.

In 1928 a new Convention limited the number of Portuguese recruits who might be employed, the number being fixed at:

31 December 1929	100,000
31 December 1930	95,000
31 December 1931	90,000
31 December 1932	85,000
31 December 1933	80,000
and thereafter	80,000

The length of period of service of East Coast Natives was also reduced. Under the Convention of 1928 no East Coast Native may serve for more than eighteen months without being repatriated, and he may not be re-engaged before at least six months have elapsed.[1]

After 1929 the supply of labour available for the mines from the Union and British Protectorates increased greatly as a result of depression in other industries. Recruiting in Portuguese East Africa was reduced and the number of Portuguese Natives employed on the mines fell to 55,000 in December 1933.[2] In 1934 the terms of the Convention were revised. The maximum of 80,000 Natives was adhered to and a minimum of 65,000 Natives to be employed by the mines was laid down. The maximum and minimum numbers fixed were subject to arrangements between the two Governments if any difficulties arose in regard to Native labour.[3] In 1936 the maximum number to be employed was raised by agreement to 90,000,[4] and the agreement was renewed in 1937.[5] In 1940 the maximum number permissible was raised to 100,000.[6]

It was anticipated that the limitation, by the Convention of 1928, of both the number that might be employed and the period of service would seriously affect the labour supply of the mining industry; although no immediate reaction was felt owing to the gradual reduction of the maximum number that might be employed and to the increased supply of Union and Protectorate labour, the mining industry began to look elsewhere for amenable labour to fill the gap. It turned to Central Africa.

After the South African War the Witwatersrand Native Labour Association had attempted to get permission to recruit Natives in Uganda, British East Africa, Portuguese Angola, and the Congo

---

[1] *Native Economic Commission*, 1930–32, op. cit., paras. 808–11. *Official Year Book*, No. 15, 1932–3, pp. 561–3.
[2] *Witwatersrand Native Labour Association, Annual Report*, 1933. Table C.
[3] *Official Year Book*, No. 18, 1937, p. 472.
[4] *Transvaal Chamber of Mines, Annual Report*, 1936, p. 25.
[5] Idem for 1937, p. 4.
[6] *Cape Times*, 7 May, 1940.

Free State.[1] The Imperial authorities refused to sanction recruitment of labour in the British Protectorates or to ask the Government of the Congo Free State to assist the Witwatersrand Native Labour Association in recruiting Native labour there.[2]

In 1904 the importation of five thousand Natives from the British Central African Protectorate (Nyasaland Protectorate) was sanctioned subject to certain conditions, one being that the labourers were not to be introduced during the Transvaal winter.[3] An arrangement was also made with the Rhodesian Labour Bureau whereby it promised to supply the Witwatersrand Native Labour Association with labour not required in the Southern Rhodesian mines, and between May and December 1904, 2,362 Natives were supplied.[4] In the middle of 1905, however, this supply ceased, for the demand for labour was said to be 'in excess of supply' in Rhodesia and the Rhodesian administration opposed the export of labour.[5] In 1906 the British Government decided that it would not allow any further recruiting from Nyasaland for underground work, although the recruiting of five hundred Natives for work on the Premier Diamond Mine was allowed.[6] In 1909 organized recruiting was stopped altogether. Natives were, however, allowed to make their own way to the Rand.[7]

In Portuguese East Africa recruiting north of latitude 22° south continued until 1913, when the Union Government prohibited[8] the introduction of any Natives from districts north of latitude 22° south in consequence of their high rate of mortality. In 1911 their death-rate, chiefly as a result of deaths from pneumonia, had been 67·6 per 1,000 per annum. In 1912 it fell to 49·34,[9] but this death-rate was still regarded as excessive.

The Chamber of Mines protested vigorously against this prohibition, stating that there were then nearly twenty thousand Natives from north of latitude 22° south employed on the mines, and that this class of labour had been working on the Rand since 1902, and the mining industry had spent large sums developing these areas of supply.[10]

In 1918 Parliament refused to sanction the experimental introduction of a thousand tropical Natives which was asked for owing to the 'shortage' of Native labour from which the mining industry was suffering.[11] Two years later the Low Grade Mines Commission

[1] *Transvaal Chamber of Mines, Annual Report*, 1902, p. 9.
[2] Letter from the Foreign Office dated 22 October, 1902, quoted *Transvaal Chamber of Mines, Annual Report*, 1902, p. 18.
[3] *Transvaal Chamber of Mines, Annual Report*, 1904, p. 423.
[4] Ibid., p. 418.   [5] Idem, for 1906, pp. 580, 641.   [6] Ibid., p. 579.
[7] *Report of the Committee on Emigrant Labour*, Nyasaland Protectorate, 1935, pp. 9, 12.
[8] By the Immigrants Regulation Act., No. 22 of 1913.
[9] *Transvaal Chamber of Mines, Annual Report*, 1918, p. 72.   [10] Ibid.   [11] Ibid.

recommended 'the temporary modification' of the prohibition on the employment of tropical Natives on the ground that it would increase the labour supply and consequently improve the position of the low-grade mines. It considered that the discovery of the Lister anti-pneumococcal vaccine and the improvement in the general hygienic conditions on the mines had decreased the likelihood of the heavy mortality which had been experienced before 1913.[1]

The Mining Industry Board also recommended the abolition of this prohibition, but

> subject to condition that no introduction of foreign labour should be allowed if it interferes unduly with the employment of natives from the Union, who are seeking work on the mines. In the past, we fear that sufficient attention has not been given to this matter. Mine managers, not unnaturally, prefer the Portuguese to the Union natives, inasmuch as the former, as a rule, engage themselves for a year, and the latter only for six months.[2]

A writer in *The Round Table*[3] at this time considered that extending recruitment beyond latitude 22° south would make Union industries rely more and more on expanding by means of increasing their unskilled labour force and would weight the scales against any reorganization involving an increase in the proportion of skilled to unskilled labour on the mines.

Since that date official policy appears to have crystallized and the bar to the use of Natives on skilled work has been re-enacted.

Mining employers have agitated continuously for a relaxation of this restriction on recruiting north of latitude 22° south, and in 1933 permission was given for the introduction of an experimental batch of two thousand 'Tropical' Natives[4] (at a time when recruiting in Portuguese East Africa was being restricted at the request of the Union Government). The recruitment of further experimental batches was permitted, and in 1937 the Immigration Act of 1913 was amended to permit Natives from north of latitude 22° south to enter the Union for employment on the mines, subject to the terms of engagement and repatriation being approved by the Union Government.[5] The number of 'Tropical' Natives employed by the gold-mines at 31st December, 1937, was nearly eleven thousand.[6]

The mining industry desires 'Tropical' labour 'to make good

[1] *Low Grade Mines Commission,* 1919–20, Final Report, op. cit., paras. 104, 112.
[2] *Report of Mining Industry Board,* 1922, para. 161.
[3] March, 1922, Vol. XII, p. 431.
[4] *Witwatersrand Native Labour Association, Annual Report,* 1933, p. 4. 'Tropical' Natives are those from north of latitude 22° south.
[5] Act No. 27 of 1937.
[6] The actual number was 10,686. *Witwatersrand Native Labour Association, Report for* 1937, p. 4.

the loss of Portuguese Natives under the Mozambique Convention and assure to the industry a permanently adequate Native labour supply'.[1]

It has frequently been argued that, because it increases the supply, the importation of Native labour for work on the gold-mines depresses the rate of wages within the Union for unskilled labour, both European and Native. On this ground there has been opposition to the introduction of Native labourers and particularly to those coming from Portuguese East Africa and the 'tropical' territories north of latitude 22° south.[2] Opponents of the importation of labour have not usually opposed importation from the British Native Protectorates of Basutoland, Swaziland, and Bechuanaland.[3]

The employment of foreign Native labour on the gold- and coal-mines has a twofold effect on the market for Native labour within the Union. In the first place, there is the direct effect within the mining industry and, secondly, there is the indirect effect in other industries. Consider first the direct effect within the mining industry of such an increase in the supply of labour. It has been argued in preceding sections that employers in the gold-mining industry have been able to establish and maintain wage-rates below the equilibrium level of competitive conditions. If this is so, an increase in the supply of immigrant labour will not necessarily affect the rate of wages. For it will pay to employ additional labour at the established rates until the marginal productivity of labour has fallen to the same level.

A further factor to be taken into consideration when discussing the effect of an increase in the supply of labour on wage-rates in

[1] Evidence of Gold Producers Committee of the Transvaal Chamber of Mines before *Low Grade Ore Commission*, 1932, op. cit., statement No. 7, para. 24.

[2] The opinion of European miners on this subject appears to have changed, if their trade unions can be accepted as representative. In 1920 the South African Mine Workers' Union opposed the introduction of 'tropical' Natives without advancing any reasons. *Low Grade Mines Commission*, 1919–20, Final Report, para. 112.

The Mining Industry Board of 1922 considered that the introduction of foreign labour should not be allowed if it interfered 'unduly' with the employment of Natives from the Union who were seeking work on the mines and that 'the mines should not be permitted to introduce foreign natives if the result would be to keep Union natives out of employment to a greater extent than is unavoidable.' Para. 161. It did not define either 'unduly' or 'unavoidable'.

The Report of the Economic and Wage Commission signed by Messrs. Andrews, Lucas, and Hood, opposed the introduction of foreign Native labour (pp. 323, 325, 332, 347, 348). Mr. Lucas also opposed it in his addendum to the Native Economic Commission, 1930–32, paras. 249–54.

In 1932 'All the workers' bodies were in favour of it, with the exception of the Transvaal Administrative Executive of the South African Labour Party.' *Low Grade Ore Commission*, op. cit., p. 111, Interim Report, para. 46. The Cresswell section of the South African Labour Party, which wants European unskilled labourers to be employed in the mines, has consistently opposed it.

[3] *Economic and Wage Commission* (1925), Clay-Martin-Mills Report, para. 268.

the gold-mining industry is the reaction of Natives to reductions. Cash wages in this industry have been remarkably constant over a long period and any reduction would be likely to disturb Native confidence and the supply of labour. Consequently, unless the increase in the supply was very great it is unlikely that employers would risk reducing the customary rates.

The chief effect of moderate increases in the supply of immigrant labour would probably lead to more Natives being employed at existing rates. This would increase the tonnage mined.

The indirect effect of such an increase would be to stimulate industries dependent on gold-mining. Their employing capacity would increase and, if competition for Native labour were effective in industries ancillary to gold-mines, the money wages of Natives might rise in these industries. Whether real wages would rise would depend upon the relative movements of money wages and of the prices of goods consumed by labour, in the new conditions of increased output.

If, on the other hand, foreign Native labourers were substituted for those from the Union and the Protectorates, instead of being employed in addition to the latter, the supply of Native labour to other industries would increase and this would tend to depress their wage-rates. With labour costs reduced, their output of product would increase. But the lower cost of Native labour on the mines would also lead to an expansion in mining, and so have a secondary effect on industries ancillary to mining, and their demand for labour, even at existing rates of wages, would rise. The net effect on Native wages would depend upon whether the rise in demand for labour by industries ancillary to mining were sufficient to offset the tendency of wage-rates to be depressed by the release of Union Natives from mining.

The effect of a reduction or cessation of the supply of imported labour also varies according to whether this would cause employers in the mining industry to alter their wage-rates. Whether they raised wage-rates or not, the reduction in the supply of labour would curtail the mining of ore and shorten the life of the mines, so that over the whole life of the industry the demand for supplies would be reduced and with it the demand for labour in ancillary industries. Within the mining industry wage-rates might rise, and if, as appeared to be the view held by the Low Grade Mines Commission in 1919–20 and the Native Recruiting Corporation in 1925, wages in other industries are below the equilibrium level of competitive conditions, this might lead to a rise in wage-rates in other industries also. This is not so likely, however, in view of the fact that the demand for labour in industries ancillary to gold-mining would have fallen.

In this connexion the Economic and Wage Commission (1925) considered that the cost to the community of excluding East Coast Natives would be very heavy, and that it was not certain that Native wages would rise as a result.   They said:

'Whatever its effect on the mining industry it would reduce the resources engaged in production in the Union by approximately 80,000 adult male workers—taking the case of the Mozambique native alone. Some branch of industry would be bound to suffer by this curtailment in labour supplies, and it might well be that the reduction of the amount of production would, in the aggregate, affect wages as adversely as the reduction in the intensity of competition for employment would benefit them.'[1]

The Chamber of Mines argues that the importation of Native labour is essential for the maintenance of the industry on its present scale, and that it would not be practicable to substitute Union and Protectorate Native labour. The present organization of labour on the mines, and, indeed, throughout South Africa, is dependent on the importation of Native labour.

It can only be a matter of conjecture whether the cessation of importation would force the employers to break the customary colour bar and enable a partial reorganization of labour to take place. In any case, while the legal colour bar remains no complete reorganization is possible. Present barriers prevent advancement and the effective reward of skilled work by Natives. In such circumstances, it is doubtful whether the reduction of immigration would benefit as a whole even the Native population; and it would certainly reduce national productivity.

F. THE SITUATION ON THE DIAMOND- AND COAL-MINES

In these chapters on Native labour in the mining industries attention has been paid chiefly to conditions on the gold-mines of the Witwatersrand. From the point of view of the amount of labour employed, the wage bill, and the contribution of the industry to the national income, the gold-mining industry is by far the most important single force in the market for Native labour in South Africa. In considering Native labour in the mining industries other than gold, of which the most important are coal and diamond production, some interesting points arise both of similarity and of contrast.

It must be remembered that colour-bar regulations reinforced and extended by trade-union pressure apply to all types of mining. Before the Mines and Works Amendment Act of 1926 the statutory colour bar applied neither in the Cape Province nor in Natal.

[1] Ibid., para. 268.

Nevertheless, opposition was sufficiently strong to prevent the employment of Natives in many types of work.[1]

As in the gold-mines, so in the diamond-mines of the Cape Province and the coal-mines of Natal, there were few opportunities for Natives to rise into the ranks of labour which were officially classed as skilled.[2] In practice, however, the Natives then did, and have continued to do, nearly all the manual work, the European miners' work being largely confined to supervision and direction. In the coal-mines of both Natal and the Transvaal, Natives, together with a diminishing number of Indians, operate the mechanical coal-cutting machines which are used in all the mines. In the coal-mines the ratio of European miners to Native labourers is approximately one to fifty, a fact which demonstrates the extent to which the Europeans' work must be confined to supervision.

The demand for labour for the production of coal and diamonds has shown some contrasts to that for gold production. Cyclical fluctuations have had opposite effects on the production of coal and diamonds, on the one hand, and gold on the other. For whereas in times of relative industrial depression the demand for the former has fallen, the value of gold has risen in terms of other commodities, and its price has also risen when the gold standard has been suspended. Consequently, in the coal and particularly in the diamond-mining industries the demand for labour has fallen in times of depression, whereas in the gold industry it has tended to rise.

Fluctuations in the demand for labour have been particularly marked in diamond production. Since the 1880's a single organization has controlled the sale of diamonds and has adopted the policy of restricting production to maintain prices. Consequently on several occasions when the demand for diamonds has fallen, diamond-mining has been very much curtailed or has temporarily ceased. The fluctuations in employment in diamond-mining are shown on the graph on page 233.

The wages and other conditions of work of the Native labourers employed in the different types of mining show certain typical differences. The most striking fact which emerges is the close

---

[1] 'Custom, public opinion, and Trade Unions are therefore at least as powerful as doubtfully legal provisions in establishing and maintaining an effective colour bar. This is corroborated by evidence given before us of the position at the De Beers mines, Kimberley. Although no legal restrictions are in force here, the colour bar is as vigorously and effectively maintained as on the Witwatersrand mines, and any infringements upon it would be as strongly opposed by the white workmen.' *Low Grade Mines Commission*, 1919–20, Final Report, op. cit., para. 165.

[2] 'Are there any openings for Natives to rise into the skilled ranks of labour?, No.' Evidence of Natal Coal Owners' Association before Economic and Wage Commission (1925). Typescript of evidence, q. 16523.

relation between wage-rates and other conditions of work, and the extent of reliance upon recruiting.

On the diamond-mines Natives have consistently earned higher average wages than on the gold- or coal-mines.[1] Moreover, there are more opportunities for Natives to earn wages substantially above the average. In 1938 the average earnings on piece-work (23 per cent of the total Native labour force was employed on piece-work) on the Kimberley diamond-mines was 3s. 5.53d. a day, which is well above the *maximum average* permissible on the gold-mines. Further, according to information supplied by the General Manager, 'a good loading boy can earn up to 7s. per day'. Bonuses have also been paid for diamonds handed in by individual finders, and this has been an additional attraction.[2]

On the diamond-mines food is not supplied to Native labourers as part of their wage. They buy their own food from stores in the mine compounds and cook it themselves. They work for a minimum period of four months, at the end of which they may renew their contracts for one or more months at the Company's option. During a period of continuous service they may not leave the Company's compounds. In 1938 the General Manager stated that the average period of continuous service was seven months, but that Natives return to work after a few months' rest.

There has been little systematic recruiting for the diamond-mines since the very early days of the industry. In 1906, of 52,078 Natives admitted to the De Beers compounds, 19,988 were sent by agents. In 1909, when the number employed had fallen very considerably, owing to reduced production which followed the American slump of 1907–8, all the labour required was supplied by Natives presenting themselves at the compounds. The number employed fell from 21,923 on the 30th June, 1906, to 11,119 on the 30th June, 1909.[3]

In the following year £133 6s. 10d. only was spent on recruiting, and since then it has not been the general practice to recruit Native labour. No recruiting organization has been maintained, although in periods of exceptional scarcity, as at the end of May

[1] Wages of Natives employed on gold-, coal- and diamond-mines. Average wages per month of 26 working days:

| | Gold | | Coal | | Diamonds | |
	Witwaters-rand	Transvaal	Natal	Cape of Good Hope	Transvaal
1913	52s. 0d.	41s. 3d.	43s. 9d.	89s. 7d.	78s. 0d.
1921	58s. 7d.	52s. 3d.	57s. 6d.	103s. 7d.	90s. 5d.
1932	57s. 7d.	53s. 7d.	49s. 4d.	72s. 6d.	79s. 1d.
1937	58s. 4d.	51s. 11d.	48s. 1d.	78s. 0d.	69s. 0d.

Annual Reports of the Government Mining Engineer.

[2] *Parl. Papers*, 1914–16, XIII [Cd. 7707] *Dominions Commission*, Minutes of evidence taken in South Africa, 1914, p. 21, q. 587.

[3] *De Beers Consolidated Mines, Limited, Annual Report*, 1909, p. 2.

1937, a few hundred Natives have been obtained through labour agents.[1] Similarly, recruiting has not been extensively used to obtain labour, either for the Premier Diamond Mine in the Transvaal, or for the diamond-mines in the Orange Free State.[2]

Nor has there been systematic recruiting for the alluvial diamond diggings, although wage-rates on them have been much lower than on the diamond-, gold-, or coal-mines. Alluvial diamond diggers continue to work on a small scale, each employing only a few labourers, who appear to share to some extent the fortunes of their employers. In 1931, when the price of diamonds had fallen and the industry was depressed, it was reported that in some instances when diggers were doing badly Natives worked for food alone, hoping to be rewarded later. At that time the ruling weekly rates of wages were reported to be from five to fifteen shillings in the Barkly West district (the latter rate was then comparatively rare and was confined to Natives who had been employed for a long time), from seven and sixpence to twelve and sixpence in the Klerksdorp district, and from seven and six-pence to ten shillings at Lichtenburg. Food and shelter were not provided in addition to these wages.[3] Despite the relatively low wages and the poor living conditions on the diamond diggings, the number of Natives employed rose to forty-four thousand in 1928, and the diggings were said to have attracted Natives from farms and contributed to the alleged scarcity of Native farm-labour in the Western Transvaal.[4] This took place without the intervention of organized recruiting.

On the other hand, on the coal-mines, particularly those of the Transvaal, where wages are lower than on the diamond- and gold-mines, a much larger proportion of the labour force is recruited. On the coal-mines, in addition to average wage-rates per shift being lower, work is frequently held up through a shortage of trucks, for the coal produced is not stored at the pithead, but is loaded immediately into trucks. Partly on this account work on the collieries is less regular than on the gold- or diamond-mines.[5]

In the Transvaal the coal industry is closely associated with

---

[1] Idem, 1910, 1913, 1914, 1917. Letter from the General Manager, 25 November, 1938.

[2] *Dominions Commission*, 1914, op cit., qq. 567–8, 587–9, 990–1, 1019–25, 1032–5, 1085–6, 2480. Robertson: '150 Years of Economic Contact,' op. cit. p. 11.

[3] Evidence of the Mining Commissioners at Barkly West and Lichtenburg supplied to the Native Economic Commission, 1930–32.

[4] *Inter-Departmental Committee on the Labour Resources of the Union*, 1930, p. 7.

[5] *Economic and Wage Commission* (1925), op. cit. Typescript of evidence, pp. 1856, 2858, 2876.

gold production, and the majority of its Native labourers are
obtained through the Witwatersrand Native Labour Association
from Portuguese East Africa. In 1925 between 80 and 90 per cent
of the fifteen thousand Native employees came from this source.
The remainder were Natives from districts near the coal-mines
who presented themselves at the collieries.[1] These proportions
are typical.

On the Natal coal-mines there is no centralized system of
engaging or distributing Native labour. The collieries vary considerably in size, and in the organization and conditions of labour.
Some collieries, as we have seen, have found it expedient to
provide extensive married quarters in order to attract and retain
efficient Native labourers. In other respects conditions appear to
be inferior to those on the gold- or diamond-mines, wages are
lower, work more irregular, and the single men's quarters inferior
to those provided on the gold-mines. The relative attractions of
the coal-mines are also said to have been reduced by a system of
credit which was practised by concession stores on mine properties. Native labourers on many mines have pledged their wages
in advance, receiving in return 'tokens' which could only be used
to purchase goods at these stores. This system was sanctioned
by many of the mine managements, who allowed the storekeeper
or his representative to be present at the pay office to collect the
amount due on the disks supplied on credit immediately each
Native had received his pay. It is alleged that this system was
abused and Natives were induced to become constantly indebted
to the storekeepers.[2] According to the Native Affairs Commission
this system reduced the supply of voluntary, as opposed to
recruited, labour to the mines on which it was practised.[3] In
1939 the Native Administration Act was amended in order that
the system might be prohibited, previous attempts to control it
having failed. Stringent regulations have been imposed limiting
credit facilities to Natives on the Natal coal-mines.[4] It is too early
to judge the reactions of the Natives to the new conditions.

Other types of mining are as yet comparatively unimportant

[1] Ibid., p. 2875.
[2] 'Emphasis is lent to the prevailing impression that the token system keeps
the native perpetually in debt by an examination of the official returns of the
estates of natives who have died on the mines. For the year 1937 three large
collieries where the token system is in full operation submitted 61 death
notices; only five out of the 61 estates showed any assets and they amounted in
all to £6 7s. 3d. On the other hand certain other companies where the token
system was not in full operation submitted 45 death notices showing 21 estates
amounting in all to £21 16s. 3d.' Report of the Native Affairs Commission for the
years 1937–8, U.G. 54, 1939, p. 18.
[3] Ibid., pp. 17–18.
[4] Government Notice 1,368, 1939, Government Gazette, 8 September 1939;
Proclamation 332, 1939, Government Gazette, 12 December 1939.

AVERAGE NUMBER OF NATIVES AND OTHER COLOURED PEOPLE EMPLOYED IN MINING AND ALLIED INDUSTRIES IN THE UNION, 1904-1939[1]

Year	Gold Mining Industry	Diamond Mining Industry	Alluvial Diamond Diggings	Coal Mining Industry	Other Mineral Mining Industry	Power Supply Companies, quarries, etc.	Total	Number of Natives employed by members of the W.N.L.A. on 31 Dec.
1904	77,425	—	—	—	—	—	—	76,611
1905	100,785	—	—	—	—	—	—	80,954
1906	94,305	—	—	—	—	—	—	81,231
1907	115,585	—	—	—	—	—	—	106,296
1908	150,729	—	—	—	—	—	—	148,761
1909	173,026	—	—	—	—	—	—	156,708
1910	195,216	—	—	—	—	—	—	179,083
1911	202,993	38,750	—	18,743	5,656	6,521	272,668	174,123
1912	206,374	39,991	—	18,701	6,250	7,344	278,660	191,281
1913	196,462	40,459	—	21,042	5,939	6,424	270,326	155,150
1914	179,837	25,739	—	22,200	5,680	6,018	239,474	156,240
1915	205,834	1,462	5,082	21,223	6,796	5,494	245,891	198,480
1916	214,467	11,422	9,612	24,695	8,585	6,579	275,360	190,778
1917	193,110	18,861	16,860	26,934	9,250	6,466	271,481	176,164
1918	188,019	19,358	13,975	27,161	7,378	3,519	259,416	157,945
1919	179,530	21,938	14,534	28,121	6,820	1,778	252,731	177,420
1920	184,737	23,887	20,275	29,861	6,780	1,729	267,269	173,034

1921 .	181,117	7,710	12,885	35,177	5,519	1,838	244,246	187,834
1922 .	171,458	3,822	15,834	31,383	4,472	1,876	228,845	183,098
1923 .	189,689	10,603	18,374	31,146	6,592	2,012	258,416	196,131
1924 .	191,355	13,203	23,945	33,156	7,556	2,579	271,794	198,786
1925 .	187,797	13,778	22,856	33,162	9,319	2,963	269,875	191,946
1926 .	194,900	17,521	39,715	35,043	13,953	2,694	303,826	202,637
1927 .	199,612	17,664	43,254	34,079	14,621	3,066	312,296	214,679
1928 .	208,482	17,521	44,051	33,537	14,466	3,031	321,088	213,190
1929 .	204,849	17,910	33,368	32,337	18,176	3,116	309,756	204,866
1930 .	213,221	16,027	37,104	29,990	15,781	2,880	315,003	222,257
1931 .	221,335	10,032	28,325	25,279	9,444	2,984	297,399	225,612
1932 .	228,767	2,147	16,983	21,492	5,751	2,698	277,838	232,793
1933 .	243,749	989	21,029	21,894	7,737	2,788	298,186	247,876
1934 .	269,547	1,135	18,954	23,284	10,115	3,201	326,236	265,503
1935 .	299,007	1,782	18,260	26,608	11,451	3,556	360,664	291,210
1936 .	323,451	2,786	14,690	28,511	13,832	10,184	393,454	317,745
1937 .	328,672	5,059	10,879	29,264	16,136	12,019	402,029	299,738
1938 .	343,380	5,115	8,984	31,113	19,349	12,674	420,615	323,771
1939 .	348,048	4,430	8,192	32,090	18,135	13,386	424,281	322,734

[1] Statistics from *Annual Reports, Transvaal Chamber of Mines*, 1904–11; *Government Mining Engineer*, 1911–38; *Witwatersrand Native Labour Association*, 1904–39. Before 1911 the only statistics available are those for the Transvaal gold-mines which are now classified as large mines. At that time the difference was negligible between the numbers employed in these mines and in the whole gold-mining industry.

Indian employees are not included among 'other Coloured People' in this table, and the number of Coloured, as distinct from Native, employees is negligible. A very few Native women are employed in mining industries other than gold and diamond mining, but their number is also negligible.

factors in the market for Native labour. Copper, tin, chromium, platinum, and asbestos are mined in different parts of the country, but until recently the number of Native and Coloured employees in these scattered concerns has been insignificant in comparison with the numbers in the gold-, coal-, and diamond-mining industries. Between 1911 and 1925 the number of non-European employees averaged 7,000 and never exceeded 10,000, thereafter it rose to 18,000 in 1928, fell to 6,000 in 1932, and then rose to a peak of 19,000 in 1938. The demand for labour for these types of mining may, however, be important in the future should their recent expansion continue.

At the moment the gold-mining industry retains its dominant position in the market for Native labour. The graph opposite and table on pages 231 and 232 illustrate this. They show the average number of Natives employed in mining and similar industries between 1904 and 1939, and demonstrate the importance of employment in gold-mining and also the large proportion of Natives employed by members of the Witwatersrand Native Labour Association, the centralized recruiting association of which most of the Transvaal gold- and coal-mines are members.

The importance of the gold-mining industry and its labour policy is further indicated by a comparison of the number of its employees with the total potential Native labour force. In 1921, when (including immigrant labourers) there were within the Union some 1,239,000 male Natives in the age-group fifteen to fifty,[1] no less than 188,000, that is, 15 per cent of the men of working age, were employed by members of the Witwatersrand Native Labour Association. In 1936, when there were 1,700,000 men in this age-group,[2] 318,000 (18 per cent) were employed by members of this organization.

---

[1] *Third Census of the Population of the Union of South Africa* (1921), Part VIII, U.G. 40, 1924, p. 46, Table 6.
[2] *Sixth Census of the Population of the Union of South Africa* (1936), Ages and Marital Condition of the Bantu Population, U.G. 50, 1938, p. 1, Table I.

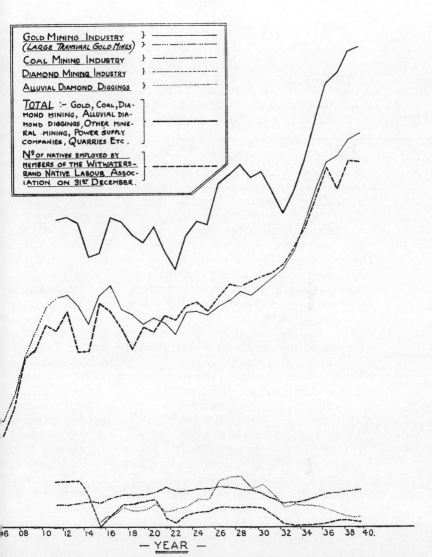

Legend (in figure):

Gold Mining Industry } ————
(Large Transvaal Gold Mines) } — — —

Coal Mining Industry } —·—·—·

Diamond Mining Industry } – – – –

Alluvial Diamond Diggings } ············

TOTAL :– Gold, Coal, Diamond mining, Alluvial diamond diggings, Other mineral mining, Power supply companies, Quarries Etc. } ————

Nº of natives employed by members of the Witwatersrand Native Labour Association on 31st December. } — — —

— YEAR —

'06 08 10 12 14 16 18 20 22 24 26 28 30 32 34 36 38 40.

…RAGE NUMBER OF NATIVES AND OTHER COLOURED PEOPLE EMPLOYED
…MINING AND ALLIED INDUSTRIES IN THE UNION– 1904 ~ 1939.

CHAPTER XIII

OTHER FIELDS FOR NATIVE EMPLOYMENT. (I) URBAN

A. THE INDUSTRIAL SETTING

(i) Urban and Industrial Employment, with Special Reference to the Market for Native Labour, 1900–1914

DURING the twentieth century the population of South Africa has increased more rapidly in urban than in rural areas. The largest growth has taken place amongst the towns of the Witwatersrand, in the neighbourhood of the gold-mines. In Johannesburg itself the population increased threefold between 1904 and 1936, while in the other towns along the Reef it increased well over fivefold. During the same period the population of other inland towns with ten thousand or more inhabitants doubled. The larger coastal towns showed a slightly smaller, but nevertheless considerable, increase, their population nearly doubling.

The increase in urban population has been due to migration from rural areas, and from abroad as well as to natural increase.[1] To a large extent it has resulted from the development of gold-mining. Ancillary industries have continued to grow, both within the towns in the neighbourhood of the mines and at the ports. At the same time, the progress of commercial and specialized farming and the increasing export of farm products have given rise to an additional demand for transport and other commercial and distributive services which has also encouraged urbanization. Within the towns Native labourers have been employed on all types of unskilled and casual work.

During and immediately after the South African War there was great activity at the coastal towns. During the war there was a large trade in military supplies; subsequently the ports received and distributed imports of machinery and other stores for the mines, for railway construction and repair, and for other public works. For all this trade, Native labour was needed. Wage-rates for Natives were high compared with those on the farms and on the mines of the Transvaal, at least while the attempt was being made to reduce wages on the gold-mines below the pre-war levels. At Capetown, Port Elizabeth, and East London, wages, it was reported, were from '2s. 6d. to 5s. per diem, paid in cash every

---

[1] On the growth of urbanization see H. A. Shannon, 'Urbanization, 1904–36,' *The South African Journal of Economics*, Vol. V, No. 2, June, 1937, pp. 164–90.

Saturday'.[1] Consequently many Natives preferred employment
at the ports to work on the farms or on the Transvaal mines. In
addition to the higher wage-rates prevailing, conditions of life
and work were much freer. There were, for instance, no pass
restrictions in the Cape Colony, and in Natal the pass law was
much less severe than in the ex-republics.

A severe and prolonged depression (1903–9), however, followed
the war and post-war boom, and reduced the demand for Native
labour at the ports.[2] This assisted the mines, for from 1904
onwards Natives went to work there in increasing numbers.

Until after 1914 very little manufacturing was carried on in
South Africa. There were some small manufacturing industries,
such as milling, tanning and leather working, carriage-building
and furniture-making, soap-making, and, in Natal, sugar-refining.
The naturally sheltered industries of building and newspaper-
printing were, of course, carried on locally. Most manufactured
goods, however, continued to be imported and exports consisted
almost exclusively of raw materials. Consequently, the chief
demand for Native labour in urban areas was for mining, for
domestic service, for the construction of buildings, railways, and
roads, for transport, and for miscellaneous commercial work.

The principal occupations of the non-European population, the
majority of whom were Natives, are indicated in the census of
1911.[3] There were then 820,000 non-Europeans, 570,000 males
and 249,000 females, in urban areas. Their chief occupations
were:

	Males	Females
Working and dealing in minerals	240,000	
Domestic service	66,000	63,000
Agricultural pursuits	42,000	25,000
Industrial Class:		
Mechanical operations or labour	25,000	
Construction of buildings, railways, roads, and docks	28,000	
Working and dealing in foodstuffs and drink	8,000	1,000
Commercial Class:		
Transport	17,000	
Trade	15,000	

[1] *Transvaal Labour Commission*, Majority Report [Cd. 1896], 1904, para. 51.
[2] According to census statistics at Capetown, which at this time had a very
small permanent Native population, the majority of Natives there being
migratory labourers, the number of Natives rose from 779 in 1891 to 3,341 in
1904; in 1911 it had fallen to 1,388.
[3] Census of 1911. U.G. 324, 1915, p. 664, Table XIV.

Natives were thus employed in a variety of industries, but they were generally employed on unskilled work.[1] At this time a large number of the Natives employed in the towns came from rural areas, to which they returned after spells in European employment. The short period for which most of them were prepared to work made it unprofitable for their employer to go to the trouble and expense of training them for posts demanding a high degree of skill. Nevertheless, the 1914 Economic Commission noted that there were 'a fair number' of Natives doing semi-skilled work, although they did not seriously compete with fully skilled European artisans. On the Witwatersrand, it was reported, the Native labourers who worked with European artisans were beginning to acquire skill and undertake skilled work.[2] Skilled Natives, however, were 'experiencing great difficulty in securing employment, except, perhaps, in remote country districts'.[3] In this respect conditions had not changed since the latter part of the nineteenth century.

In the Cape Province, particularly in the western districts, and in Natal, skilled work was not so usually done by European artisans as on the Witwatersrand. In the Cape Province the Cape Coloured population provided 'a continuous gradation of labour between the white man at the one extreme and the native at the other'.[4] In Natal, Indians, many of them Natal-born, were employed on all types of semi-skilled and most types of skilled work. They were engaged in trading on their own account, and also in building trades, printing, boot-repairing, tailoring, painting, mattress-making, and other miscellaneous callings of the semi-skilled kind, in addition to working on the plantations and in the collieries. Indians able to speak English were employed as cooks, waiters, drivers, vanmen, and as junior clerks and touts in lawyers' offices.[5]

In manufacturing industry and commerce, as in mining, there was usually a wide difference between the wages paid to skilled and unskilled workers. When new industries were established, skilled workers had to be imported from Europe and high wages were necessary to attract and retain them.[6] Consequently, even

[1] 'So far as the skilled trades are concerned your Commissioners find that the position of the native is at present negligible. He confines himself almost exclusively to unskilled work.' *Economic Commission*, 1914, U.G. No. 12, 1914, para. 57.
[2] 'An apprentice from Lovedale, writing from Johannesburg, says that there are many Natives working on the East and West Rand as carpenters who have not been trained in any institution . . . they have been trained by the Europeans who employed them as labourers; the boys are smart enough to pick up sufficient knowledge to enable them to go out as trained carpenters.' Ibid.
[3] Ibid.   [4] Ibid., para. 62.   [5] Ibid., para. 58.
[6] According to the evidence of representatives of the match industry in Natal before the Customs Tariff Enquiry, 1908, in that industry 'the white labour

making allowance for differences in the cost of living, the wages of skilled artisans were higher than those usual in Europe, and were comparable with those in America.[1] Within South Africa the wages of skilled artisans were higher in the Transvaal than in the coastal provinces. According to the Economic Commission of 1914, in the Transvaal the wage in Johannesburg was about twenty shillings a day, equivalent to that for miners paid by the day. In Durban skilled artisans received about fifteen shillings a day, which was much the same as European miners received on the Natal coal-mines.

The wages of unskilled labourers were very much lower. Like the wages of skilled artisans, they varied in different parts of South Africa. The highest rates, according to the Economic Commission of 1914, were found for domestic, commercial, and general service in Johannesburg, and on the diamond-mines; the next highest were those on the Witwatersrand gold-mines (where money wages averaged about two shillings a shift with lodging and food in addition), the coastal towns were next, the wages of Natives now being reported to be lower there than on the gold-mines, in contrast to the situation during the war and immediate post-war period. Wages were lowest on the farms; the Commissioners considered, however, that 'real earnings' on farms were probably higher than they appeared at first sight.[2]

In the western Cape Province, where few Natives were employed, there was not the same gap as in the larger inland towns between the wages of skilled artisans and of unskilled labourers. The wages of the Cape Coloured workers ranged between the two extremes. The wages of skilled workers were somewhat lower and those of unskilled and semi-skilled workers somewhat higher than in other parts of the country.[3] Consequently wage-rates and the organization of industry were more comparable with European conditions.

In Natal the wages of Indians in all types of work were much below those of Europeans in the same industries, but the efficiency of Indians was said to be lower. On the plantations and coal-mines the wages of Indians, both indentured and free, were about the same as those of Natives.[4]

Manufacturing industry and the skilled trades, like mining,

is expensive, all the factory hands being skilled workpeople, imported from Europe, with the result that, in addition to the high scale of wages paid (in the case of mechanics from 12s. to 20s. per diem), additional expenses amounting to approximately 10s. per week on a two years' engagement are incurred in passage money expenses. The coloured labour inside the factories is entirely of Indian extraction—men, women, boys and girls.' *Report of Customs Tariff Enquiry*, March 1908, Part II, Précis of evidence, p. 41.

[1] *Economic Commission*, 1914, op. cit., p. 25, Table XVI.
[2] Ibid, p. 51.   [3] Ibid., para. 62.   [4] Ibid., para. 58.

were organized on the basis of economizing in the use of expensive European labour by employing a smaller number of highly paid skilled men and a larger number of low-paid unskilled or semi-skilled labourers than is probably customary in the same industries in Europe.[1]

One result of this type of organization was that without either an organized apprenticeship system or the opportunity of learning as labourers, European youths failed to become skilled workers. It was the Cape Coloured, Indian, and to a less extent, Native workers who picked up skill from the artisans with whom they worked as labourers.[2] The social system was such that apprenticeship was the only method by which a European could enter the skilled trades without losing 'face'. But regular systems of apprenticeship were not general. Moreover, the prejudice of many Europeans against manual work,[3] and the ambition of parents, who regarded clerical work as superior, combined with fear of competition from non-Europeans and the low wages and poor training facilities given to apprentices to render the skilled trades unattractive to European youths.[4] In the north the dearth of highly skilled artisans remained, and they continued to be imported from Europe. At the same time, Cape Coloured artisans also began to migrate to the Rand[5] in spite of the social and legal disabilities to which they were subject in the Transvaal.

In the general disorganization of European life following the South African War, sections of the European population began to show increasing concern regarding the competition of non-Europeans and the fate of those Europeans who were not finding a foothold in the developing economy. A Cape Select Committee on the Poor Whites (1906),[6] the Transvaal Indigency Commission (1906–8), a Select Committee on European Employment and Labour Conditions (1913),[7] the Economic Commission (1913–14), and the Relief and Grants-in-Aid Commission (1916) testify to the continued preoccupation of the Government with the problem of European poverty. By 1914 many Europeans, particularly in the Cape Colony, even feared that white artisans were suffering from the competition of Cape Coloured workers. The Economic Commission (1913–14) paid particular attention to this aspect of

[1] In the Natal match industry, for example, in 1908 26 Europeans and 405 Indians were employed; a proportion of about fifteen to one. The annual wages bill was said to be £6,150 for Europeans and £6,750 for Indian employees. *Report of Customs Tariff Enquiry*, 1908. Part III, Précis of evidence, p. 41.
[2] *Transvaal Indigency Commission*, 1906–8, para. 308.
[3] In this connexion it is noteworthy that a number of apprentices at the Wolhuter Government Mining School had to be dismissed as they refused to do hand stopping in the course of their training. U.G. 51, 1912, p. 4.
[4] *Economic Commission*, 1914, op. cit., paras. 43–6 and 57.
[5] U.G. 51, 1912, pp. 3, 12.   [6] S.C. 10 of 1906.   [7] S.C. 9 of 1913.

the labour market. It was of the opinion, however, that there was little ground for believing that European labour was being displaced by non-European. On the contrary, the Commissioners considered that during the previous twenty or thirty years a larger proportion of the skilled trades in the Cape had fallen into the hands of Europeans. During the early years of the nineteenth century, as in the eighteenth, most of the skilled work had been done by the Malay slaves and their descendants. During the latter part of the nineteenth century the predominant place was taken by artisans imported from Europe, and the European artisan had fully maintained his position, even if local recruits to the ranks of the partly skilled were more often Coloured than European. Even if European labourers had experienced a relative set-back within the most recent years it did not follow, in view of the expansion of trade, that their actual position was worse than it had been. The wages of Europeans had, in fact, not fallen, but had tended to rise. Reviewing the whole situation with regard to competition between Europeans and non-Europeans in the skilled and semi-skilled callings, the Economic Commission of 1914 reported:

> The competition is greatest with the Cape Coloured, and next in magnitude with the Indians. None of the evidence proved that the sphere of white labour was being absolutely restricted in the Union, and the wages of the whites have not fallen. It is a plausible view that some of the so-called encroachments of the non-whites should properly be regarded as a filling of the gaps left by the attraction of the whites to superior situations, which superior situations could not have existed in the absence of competent people to fill the lower positions. Several witnesses affirmed that there was a dearth of capable white labour, and that a good man soon found a better opening for his talents. The complaints of grinding competition can be understood, since anybody who experiences competition feels it, even if his rivals are losing ground. But here and there white labour may have been displaced, and a constant fear of displacement is prevalent, which is comprehensible, particularly as the non-white workman usually gets a lower wage. The low wage of the non-white, combined with the fact that he readily drops his supply price when demand slackens, is apt to cause a substitution of non-white for white labour when business is depressed.'[1]

(ii) The Development of Manufacturing Industry and the Growth of Employment since 1914

Fear of non-European workmen driving Europeans out of employment had therefore spread beyond the mining industry by 1914. But Government policy took no account of it until the

---

[1] *Economic Commission*, 1914, op. cit., para. 65.

Great War of 1914–18 was over. The war led to the rapid development of manufacturing industry in South Africa and a consequent rise in the demand for labour. The gross value of manufactures[1] rose from £22 million in 1910–11[2] to £71 million in 1918–19, and £98 million in 1920–21.[3] Some of this increase is accounted for by the rise in prices which took place. The official index of the wholesale prices of South African goods rose from 1,000 in 1910 to 2,249 in 1920. Making allowance for the rise in prices, the increase in production was nevertheless very great. The total number of employees rose from 55,000 in 1911 to 180,000 in 1920–21.

After 1920 South Africa experienced the world-wide post-war depression. The demand for South African products fell; competition from goods manufactured abroad increased; and customs tariff protection was granted first to individual industries and after 1924 more widely under a revised tariff providing for maximum and minimum duties. Thereafter the output of manufacturing industry has continued to increase, except for a temporary decline during the depression of 1929 to 1933. The gross value of manufacturing production rose from £98 million in 1920–21 to £150 million in 1935–6; the index of wholesale prices having fallen during this period from 2,249 in 1920 to 1,085 in 1936. The total number of employees rose from 180,000 in 1920–21 to 330,000 in 1936–7.[4]

In the absence of tariff protection this growth of manufacturing industry would have been very much less rapid. But protection was afforded very largely with a view to creating new avenues of employment for the European population. The policy of protection did not, therefore, stand alone. It was merely one manifestation of the attempt to create a privileged position for European workers. To this end a variety of measures were applied. It will be necessary to examine their nature and their incidence before attempting to assess the effects of industrial development upon the market for Native labour.

B. THE PROTECTION OF EUROPEAN WORKERS

(i) *The Protection of Skilled Artisans*

The measures which have been adopted in order to protect European workers from Native competitors have resulted in part

---

[1] On the basis that a factory consists of any premises in which three or more persons are employed, or any form of mechanical power is used, for gain.

[2] C. W. Pearsall: 'Some Aspects of the Development of Secondary Industry in South Africa,' *The South African Journal of Economics*, December 1937, p. 413.

[3] *Official Year Book*, No. 6, 1910–22, p. 347.

[4] *Census of Industrial Establishments*, 1936–7, U.G. No. 39, 1939, p. XVI.

from the growth of trade unions. Except in the Cape Province trade unions have been largely confined to European workers, non-Europeans not being admitted to membership. In the Cape Province trade unions have admitted non-Europeans, and many of the unions have large numbers of non-European members, principally Cape Coloured. Since 1919 attempts have been made to organize separate trade unions among non-European workers in other parts of South Africa, but until very recently they have given little indication of achieving any permanent success. The European unions have attempted to create and maintain a privi-leged position for their members by exclusive devices, such as insistence upon rigid scales of minimum wages and the limitation of entry into trades through apprenticeship regulations. In some cases, such as mining, they have deliberately attempted to prevent the employment of Natives upon skilled work. In other industries the result of the general policy of European trade unions has been to prevent the advancement of Natives.

The first trade unions in South Africa were craft unions, organized during the last quarter of the nineteenth century by skilled artisans who had come from overseas. On the whole the unions were small and had little power. At the end of the century the Typographical Union was the only union organized on a national basis.

After 1900 several new unions were organized, notably the Transvaal Miners' Association. It had endeavoured to protect what its organizers believed to be the interests of European miners, first by opposing the introduction of Chinese labourers, and later by attempting to prevent the employment of Natives on work classed as skilled. The latter attempt was successful. In 1911, as we have seen, statutory regulations were drafted under the Mines and Works Act to prevent the employment of Natives in many types of skilled work.

Similar regulations may be applied to other industries, but so far this has not been done. The exclusion of Natives from most skilled work has been achieved within the framework of legislation ostensibly designed to improve training facilities and prevent industrial strife.

After the founding of the Transvaal Miners' Association, trade unions were organized in other trades on the Witwatersrand, and in other parts of South Africa. The unions which had been previously founded also extended their activities. According to the statistics which are available[1] the membership of trade unions

[1] 'Not until the provisions of the Statistics Act were applied in the year 1919, was it possible to obtain anything approaching complete statistics of employees' associations in the Union.' *Official Year Book*, No. 6, 1910–22, p. 330.

rose from 3,836 in 1900 to 11,941 in 1914, and 135,140 in 1920.[1] Of these 135,140 trade union members, 22,516 belonged to the seven mining unions which had developed. After the strike of 1922 the membership of trade unions declined temporarily, but by 1938 it had risen to 216,000.[2] The existence of these industrial unions at the end of the Great War provided at once the stimulus and the machinery for industrial legislation founded upon the basis of collective agreements.

One of the first expedients suggested to safeguard the position of European employees had been the imposition of statutory minimum wages. It was, however, rejected by successive official inquiries on the ground that any minimum acceptable to white labourers would dislocate and curtail industry. The protection of Europeans by preventing the advancement of non-Europeans was likewise opposed when suggested.[3] European miners in the Transvaal had struck in 1907 in order to coerce the employers to limit the employment of Natives and to increase the employment of Europeans. In 1911 a serious national strike in the printing industry, and during 1913 and 1914 a series of strikes on the Rand, on the Natal coal-mines, and on the railways, induced the government to begin a programme of industrial legislation to placate miners and other workers. The first of a series of Acts was passed in 1911 making provision for the grant of compensation to sufferers from the industrial disease known as miner's phthisis. In 1914 this was followed by the Workmen's Compensation Act and the Workmen's Wages Protection Act. The Great War interrupted industrial legislation. On its conclusion the government continued to implement the programme of industrial legislation and Acts were passed making provision for the regulation of apprenticeship, and the regulation of wages and other conditions of employment, either through industrial councils composed of representatives of employers and employees, or through an official Wage Board.

These measures have resulted in the protection of groups of skilled artisans from competitors, both European and non-European, and in the maintenance of the disparity between the wages of skilled and unskilled workers.

To protect those Europeans who find themselves excluded from the highest ranks, a policy has been adopted of extending their employment in less skilled work. The Government has acted

[1] Ibid.

[2] *Report of the Department of Labour* for 1938, U.G. 51, 1939, p. 35.

[3] *Transvaal Indigency Commission*, 1906–1908, paras. 81–2, 84. *Economic Commission*, U.G. 12, 1914, paras. 57, 66–71. *Select Committee on European Employment and Labour Conditions*, S.C. 9, 1915, para. 37. *Relief and Grants-in-aid Commission*, 1916, para. 73.

in a variety of ways: employing 'civilized' labour in government undertakings, subsidizing other employers of such labour, bringing pressure to bear on employers through the customs tariff, and imposing and enforcing statutory scales of minimum wages for work classed as 'semi-skilled'.[1]

(a) Apprenticeship

We have seen that the low wages paid to apprentices and the poor training given were believed to hinder European youths from entering the skilled trades. To overcome this, in 1918 an Act was passed which provided for the establishment of wage-boards to regulate the wages of women and persons under eighteen, and the employment of apprentices and improvers in certain specified trades and occupations. This was followed, in 1922, by the Apprenticeship Act.[2] Under this Act conditions of apprenticeship (including rates of wages and minimum commencing qualifications) can be determined and given the force of law.

This Act has had the effect of ensuring that Natives should not become qualified to perform skilled work. In the first place under nearly all the apprenticeship regulations the minimum educational qualification is Standard VI, i.e. the highest grade in the primary schools, and few Native children, for whom education is neither free nor compulsory, have the opportunity of attaining this standard.

The Native Economic Commission considered that at an outside estimate schooling facilities were available for some 20 per cent of the Native population between 6 and 16.[3] There is a very large unsatisfied demand for education, which cannot be met for lack of facilities, and of the schools 'many are hopelessly overcrowded and understaffed.'[4] Of the Native children who do attend school few attain Standard VI. In 1935 the percentage of Native children at state and state-aided schools in or above Standard VI was 2·96; the percentage of European children, for whom education is free and compulsory, was 23·60; the number of Native children in Standard VI was 8,400, the number of European, 37,600.[5] Nevertheless competent observers consider

[1] On this, see *Cape Coloured Commission*, U.G. 54, 1937, para. 190. *Report of Department of Labour*, 1933, U.G. 43, 1934, pp. 10–13. Idem, 1935, U.G. 4, 1937, pp. 9, 16. Ivan L. Walker: 'The Civilized Labour Policy and the Displacement of Non-European Labour,' *Race Relations*, Vol. II, No. 5, November 1935. J. D. Rheinallt Jones, 'Economic Maladjustments and the Civilized Labour Policy,' *Race Relations*, Vol. II, No. 2, February 1935.

[2] Act No. 26 of 1922, as amended by Act No. 22 of 1930.

[3] *Native Economic Commission*, 1930–32, op. cit., para. 619.

[4] *Inter-Departmental Committee on Native Education*, 1935–6, U.G. 29, 1936, para. 300.

[5] Ibid., p. 142, Appendix F., Table V; *Official Year Book*, No. 18, 1937, p. 376.

that there are numerous Native children with the statutory educational qualifications who would apply for apprenticeship were it open to them.

Attendance at industrial classes is required of apprentices, and only at Capetown are these classes, which are held at the technical colleges, available to non-Europeans. Thus it is only at Capetown that Natives are able to comply with this requirement, which constitutes an additional obstacle to Natives.[1]

The educational qualifications for apprenticeship are considered to be unnecessarily high in many cases. The Industrial Legislation Commission reported that 'there was reason to believe that in several trades apprenticeship is quite unjustified under existing methods, while in other cases the period of apprenticeship would seem to be unnecessarily long.'[2] Apprenticeship regulations act as an effective barrier preventing Natives from becoming qualified journeymen in many trades.

Entrance to the following trades is controlled by statutory regulation either throughout the Union or in the more important industrial centres: printing, government (building and engineering), railway (building, engineering, and carriage building), mines (building and engineering), building, engineering, food (baking, confectionery, butchery), bootmaking, and leather-working, carriage building, hairdressing, dental mechanician, furniture.

The power given to apprenticeship committees to determine not only the qualifications but the number of apprentices creates an artificial scarcity of qualified artisans who can charge higher prices for their services than would otherwise obtain. Thus wages in these trades are kept high with the incidental effect of tending to depress wages in other parts of the labour market, where the policy of restriction cannot be followed. The representation of employers, in equal numbers with employees, on the apprenticeship committees is no guarantee that this will not happen. If monopoly profits can be obtained by limiting the amount of the product, it will pay employees and employers to combine and divide them. The apprenticeship regulations prevent high wages from having their normal effect of attracting more entrants to the industries in which the value of labour is greatest.

In the Cape Peninsula and surrounding districts, where Coloured artisans were once the rule, the apprenticeship regulations have had the same effect of restricting opportunities for acquiring skill.[3]

[1] *Industrial Legislation Commission*, U.G. 37, 1935, para. 20.
[2] Ibid., para. 20.
[3] R. Leslie, 'Coloured Labour and Trade Unionism in Capetown,' *Journal of the Economic Society of South Africa*, old series, Vol. III, part II. *Cape Coloured Commission*, op. cit., para 273.

(In the three years 1 August 1932 to 31 July 1935, out of 641 apprentices entering into contracts in the Capetown area 36 only were Cape Coloured.)[1] Those able to surmount the statutory obstacles to apprenticeship have difficulty in finding employers willing and entitled to accept their indentures.[2]

The limitation of entry into industries has maintained the scarcity of trained artisans, with the result that in times of rapid expansion such as during the years 1934 and 1935 skilled workers have had once more to be imported.[3]

(b) Statutory Wage Regulation: The Industrial Council System

The employment of Natives is also affected by statutory wage regulation. We have seen how industrial unrest, culminating in the Rand strike of 1922, alarmed the Government. In 1924 the Industrial Conciliation Act[4] was passed to promote industrial peace on the basis of collective bargaining.[5] The Act, which was amended in 1930 and redrafted in 1937,[6] makes provision for the appointment of industrial councils, conciliation boards, and arbitrators, to regulate wages and conditions of work in any industry except agriculture, domestic service in private households, and most branches of government employment. Of these industrial councils have been most important. They consist of representatives of employers and registered trade unions. On registration, industrial councils have wide powers to determine wages, conditions of employment, the grading of employees, the ratio between different 'classes'[7] of employees, and 'any matters whatsoever of mutual interest to employers and employees.'

An agreement which has been approved by the Minister has the force of law, and is binding on all employers and employees in the industry or industries concerned. Agreements may be extended to apply to areas other than the areas for which they were drawn up. The system has been officially described as one of self-government within industry. In practice it gives legal sanction to the exercise of very considerable powers of exclusion, for wage-rates can be established which limit employment to those

---

[1] *Cape Coloured Commission*, op. cit., para. 276.   [2] Ibid., para. 272.
[3] *Report of the Department of Labour for* 1935, U.G. 4, 1937, p. 74.
[4] Act No. 11 of 1924.
[5] *Economic and Wage Commission* (1925), op. cit., para. 82.
[6] Act No. 36 of 1937.
[7] A 'class' of employees is defined as including: 'Such group or section or type of employees as may be specified or defined in the agreement, and in the making of any such specification or definition, any method of differentiation or discrimination based on age, sex, experience, length of employment or type of work or type or class of premises on or in which work is performed, or any other method which is deemed to be advisable may be applied: Provided that no differentiation or discrimination on the basis of race or colour shall be made.' Industrial Conciliation Act, No. 36 of 1937, sec. 24 (2).

whose value to employers is equal to, or greater than, the statutory wage. Under the original Act, Natives subject to certain laws, in practice the great majority of Natives in the Transvaal, the Orange Free State, and Natal, were excluded from the scope of such agreements.[1] The result was that attempts to force up the wages of European employees led employers to substitute Natives who were not subject to the agreements. The Department of Labour in a memorandum to the Native Economic Commission stated that

> the exclusion of pass-carrying Natives . . . meant that there was no wage regulation for a large number of unskilled and semi-skilled workers and some employers soon began to take advantage of this defect in the law by employing persons of the class whose wages were unregulated wherever possible. In some industries, e.g. engineering, which permit of various processes being simplified very considerably by a high degree of specialization and division of labour, it is possible to conduct the work almost entirely with unskilled and semi-skilled workers, and in this way also the incidence of agreements under the Act was evaded by the employment of uncivilized labour at low wages.[2]

The Act was amended in 1930 and industrial councils were then authorized to recommend minimum wages and maximum hours of work for persons (i.e. Natives) who fell outside the scope of the ordinary agreements whenever it appeared that the object of the agreement might be defeated by their employment at rates of wages or for hours of work other than those specified. Such wages became binding for all employers in the industry or industries and areas concerned after approval by the Minister and publication in the official Government Gazette.

In 1937, when the Industrial Conciliation Act was re-drafted, this provision was altered. Under the new Act *any* of the provisions of industrial council agreements may be extended to persons excluded by the statutory definition of 'employee'. At the same time the range of excluded persons was widened to include, among

[1] Industrial council agreements apply only to employers and 'employees', and in terms of the Industrial Conciliation Act of 1924, ' "employee" meant any person engaged by an employer to perform, for hire or reward, manual, clerical, or supervision work in any undertaking, industry, trade, or occupation to which this Act applies, but shall not include a person whose contract of service or labour is regulated by any Native Pass Laws and Regulations, or by Act No. 15 of 1911, Native Labour Regulation Act or any amendment thereof or any regulations made thereunder, or by Law No. 25 of 1891 of Natal or any amendment thereof, or any regulations made thereunder, or by Act No. 40 of 1894 of Natal, or any amendment thereof.' This definition was amended under the Industrial Conciliation Act of 1937.

[2] Memorandum of Department of Labour to Native Economic Commission, dated 6 July, 1931.

others, those whose contracts of employment are subject to the Natives (Urban Areas) Act.[1] Consequently industrial council agreements now apply to Natives in urban areas of the Cape Province only when specifically applied to them. In this respect these Natives are now on the same footing as those in the other provinces.

Statutory recognition of industrial councils, and of the wage-rates and other conditions of employment agreed upon by them, was first given in 1924. Since then the range of industries subject to their control has increased. The number of 'employees' whose wage-rates are directly regulated by them rose from approximately 43,000 in 1928 to 97,000 in 1939. Statistics of the number of Natives in these industries are available for 1938 only. In that year of 154,000 'persons' employed 59,000 were Natives.[2]

Since 1930, when it became possible for industrial councils to recommend minimum wage-rates and maximum hours of work for pass-carrying Natives, many agreements have been extended to regulate these matters. By 1933 such minimum wages and maximum hours of work had been prescribed for the baking and confectionery, canvas and rope-working, and motor industries in Johannesburg and Pretoria, and the tea-room and restaurant trade in Johannesburg. Of thirty-six agreements published in 1937, fourteen were extended to include Natives, of thirty published in 1938 twelve were thus extended. The number of Natives whose wages were directly regulated by industrial council agreements appears to have been about ten thousand in 1938.[3]

As most Natives do not fall within the legal definition of 'employee', and as they are excluded from most of the trade unions officially registered under the Industrial Conciliation Act, they are not represented on the industrial councils by the trade union representatives. The 1937 Act empowered the Minister of Labour to appoint an 'inspector' to represent their interests. The

[1] For purposes of the Industrial Conciliation Act, 1937, by definition 'employee' means 'any person employed by, or working for any employer, and receiving, or being entitled to receive any remuneration, and any other person whatsoever who in any manner assists in the carrying on or conducting of the business of an employer but does not include a person whose contract of service or labour is regulated by Act No. 40 of 1894 of Natal, or, in terms of section *two* of the Masters and Servants Law (Transvaal and Natal) Amendment Act, 1926 (Act No. 26 of 1926), is regarded for the purpose of Act No. 40 of 1894 of Natal as a contract between master and servant, or is regulated by the Native Labour Regulation Act, 1911 (Act No. 15 of 1911), or by the Natives (Urban Areas) Act, 1923 (Act No. 21 of 1923), or by any amendment of, or any regulation made under, any of those laws; and "employed" and "employment" have corresponding meanings.'
[2] *Report of the Department of Labour for* 1933, U.G. 43, 1934, p. 40; idem for 1938, U.G. 51, 1939, pp. 51–5; idem for 1939, U.G. 36, 1940, p. 37.
[3] Idem for 1937, U.G. 30, 1938, p. 46; idem for 1938, U.G. 51, 1939, pp. 38,

'inspector' has no vote, but the Minister's choice is not limited in any way, and it is said that one Minister of Labour expressed his willingness to appoint a nominee of a Native trade union.[1] Such meagre representation is not likely to prevent the wages and conditions of work of Natives from being used as a pawn in the game of collective bargaining conducted in the supposed interests of Europeans.

(ii) The Protection of European Semi-skilled and Unskilled Workers: the 'Civilized Labour Policy'

In spite of the fact that this system of industrial councils was designed to encourage self-government in industry, the Government Department of Labour has attempted to use it to promote the substitution of European for Native workers in certain semi-skilled grades of work. In reporting upon its work for the year, the Department estimated that, during 1935, approximately 3,100 additional European workers were absorbed into industry

as a result of special provision having been made for them in Industrial Council Agreements.[2]

In the Transvaal the Industrial Council for the Motor Industry created a special grade of employee, called a 'service attendant', at a wage of £2 per week; at the same time the wages of labourers were reduced from 24s.[3] to 18s. per week.[4] The Department of Labour was prepared to sanction a reduction in labourers' wages in order to secure employment at higher wage-rates for Europeans, for whom the posts of 'service attendant' were designed, and in which, by the end of the year, 742 Europeans were employed.[5] Similarly, in the building industry agreement for the Witwatersrand and Pretoria it was laid down that a certain proportion of labourers should receive a minimum wage of 1s. per hour in contrast to the wage of from 3s. 4d. to 3s. 6d. per hour for skilled men and 4½d. for unskilled labourers.[6] Such agreements do not specifically exclude Natives from the higher rate, but few Natives are likely to secure such employment, more particularly as employers know they are expected to employ Europeans and they cannot afford to antagonize Government Departments.

[1] Max Gordon, Secretary of the African Laundry Workers' Union, in a memorandum to the Trustees of the Bantu Welfare Trust Fund, 1937. Quoted, R. E. Phillips: The Bantu in the City, p. 6.
[2] Report of the Department of Labour for 1935, U.G. 4, 1937, p. 16.
[3] Govt. Notice 135, Gazette 2 Feb. 1934.
[4] Ibid., 182, 8 Feb., 1935. They were subsequently raised to £1.
[5] Report of the Department of Labour, 1935, op. cit., p. 16.
[6] Govt. Notice 1747, 2 Dec. 1935.

At the same time, in some industries the substitution of machines operated by Natives for the much higher paid European has led the latter to demand an increase in wages of unskilled employees 'to a level at which the European employee can maintain his standard of living'.[1]

Action taken under the machinery of the Industrial Conciliation Act is merely a recent manifestation of the increasing Government interest throughout the present century in the problem of assisting Europeans who have no special training or natural aptitude for skilled or supervisory work. In 1924, when a Nationalist-Labour Coalition Government came into power, it adopted a discriminatory policy which was officially termed the 'civilized labour policy'. This policy involved the employment of European unskilled labourers at wage-rates above those generally prevailing for unskilled work.

It was not an absolutely new expedient. After the South African War a small group led by Colonel Cresswell, who in 1924 became Minister of Labour, had advocated the employment of European unskilled labourers in the gold-mines. His proposals were rejected by the mining companies, although a few European labourers had been employed on unskilled work immediately after the South African War and again when unemployment on the Rand was acute in 1908.[2] At about the same time the Central South African Railways decided to replace Native with European labour as a temporary measure to relieve distress among Europeans,[3] and at the end of 1907 some three hundred European labourers were employed.[4] In 1909, to relieve distress, the Government of the Cape Colony also adopted this expedient. After 1910 the Union Government continued the scheme and by 1912 the number of European unskilled labourers employed had risen to between four and five thousand.

The policy of employing a limited number of European labourers had by then been accepted by the South African railways. The number employed did not vary appreciably until 1924, when the Nationalist-Labour Coalition came into power. The employment of European labourers by the South African railways and Harbours Administration then became a part of the official 'civilized labour policy'.[5]

[1] *Report of the Department of Labour*, 1934, U.G. 11, 1936, p. 80.
[2] 'Report of Rand Unemployment Committee, 1908', reprinted, *Annual Report of the Transvaal Chamber of Mines*, 1908, p. 23.
[3] *Select Committee on European Employment and Labour Conditions*, S.C. 9, 1913, pp. vii and xxv, Appendices C and E.
[4] Report of General Manager, Central South African Railways, quoted 'European Labour on the South African Railways and Harbours,' *Special Bulletin*, No. 135, 1929.
[5] Ibid.

'Civilized labour' was defined in an official circular announcing the adoption of this measure as

> the labour rendered by persons whose standard of living conforms to the standard of living generally recognized as tolerable from the usual European standpoint. Uncivilized labour is to be regarded as the labour rendered by persons whose aim is restricted to the bare requirements of the necessities of life as understood among barbarous and undeveloped peoples.' (*Circular* No. 5, 31 October 1924.)[1]

The equivocal character of this definition needs no emphasis. In practice it has been interpreted to exclude Natives from the ranks of the 'civilized'. The Department of Labour, one of whose functions is to advance the policy,[2] has stated that Natives whose standards of living conform to 'civilized' standards would be regarded as 'civilized' although generally Natives would not come within the definition.[3]

Inspectors of the Department have, however, stated that under no circumstances would Natives be regarded as 'civilized labourers'[4] and many employers believe that the policy is in fact one of fostering the employment of Europeans and excludes Cape Coloured and Asiatics as well as Natives.[5]

The policy is one of employing European labour on unskilled and semi-skilled work at wages higher than those prevailing for that type of work. It is often denied that this is uneconomical for the employer, or at least that the additional cost is small. The Industrial Legislation Commission considered that, although there was some evidence that non-European labour was more efficient than European, the consensus of opinion was that 'given a fair chance' European labour was definitely superior. They reported, however, that

> a fair chance is imperative, especially since most unskilled European labour is not experienced industrial labour, and, therefore, wants the necessary experience and familiarity with the industrial and commercial atmosphere before its efficacy in relation to that of the Native can be judged.[6]

Lack of experience and familiarity with the industrial atmosphere applies also to the Native labourer, and it would appear that to give the European 'a fair chance' is to give him training, and employ him under conditions which are not considered

[1] *Official Year Book*, No. 9, 1926–7, p. 203.
[2] *Report of the Department of Labour*, 1935, op. cit., p. 5.
[3] Secretary for Labour, 20 September 1934, quoted *Race Relations*, Vol. II, No. 5, November 1935, p. 57.   [4] Ibid.
[5] *Cape Coloured Commission*, op. cit., paras. 182, 187.
[6] *Industrial Legislation Commission*, U.G. 37, 1935, para. 150.

necessary in the case of the Native labourer. Even given the better training and additional incentives which are regarded as essential if European labour is to be profitably employed, the Commissioners report that 'even in the case of the most favourable estimates, an equivalent margin above prevailing Native wages would be insufficient to make up for the generally accepted difference in standards of living between the two races'.[1] Thus employment of 'civilized' labour at 'civilized' wages involves additional cost.

(a) Employment in Government Undertakings

In Government employment, where cost is not the deciding factor, and the substitution of European for Native labourers has consequently taken place to a considerable extent, the 'civilized labour policy' has had the result of restricting the demand for Native labour. Direct action has led to the substitution, at higher wage-rates, of European for Native labourers in many official undertakings, and particularly on the South African railways and harbours. Between 1924 and 1933 the proportion of European labourers employed by the Railways and Harbours administration rose from 9·5 to 39·3 per cent and that of Natives fell from 75 to 48·9 per cent. The number of European labourers employed rose from 4,760 to 17,783 and the number of Natives employed fell from 37,564 to 22,008. The total of labourers of all races—European, Natives, Indians, and other Coloured employed—fell from 50,065 to 45,036.[2] Since 1933 the total number of labourers employed has risen, and with it the proportion of Natives. This may have been due to the fact that opportunities for employment in general have been less restricted, so that the rise in proportion of Native workers was less likely to have political repercussions. In August 1936, 38,412 Natives were employed, comprising 59 per cent of the total.[3]

Other Government Departments have followed the same policy. In 1937 they employed some ten thousand Europeans on types of work previously done by Natives, while employment was found on subsidized works for approximately the same number.[4]

The Department of Public Works follows the policy of employing European unskilled labour exclusively in the Orange Free State, Natal, and the Transvaal, as far as work of the Central Government is concerned. In the Cape Province it employs 'civilized' unskilled labour irrespective of race. In Native territories, such as the Transkei, no stipulation is made as to the

---

[1] Industrial Legislation Commission, U.G. 37, 1935, para. 151.
[2] Cape Coloured Commission, U.G. 54, 1937, para. 217.   [3] Ibid., para. 217.
[4] Report of Department of Labour, 1937, U.G. No. 30, 1938, pp. 15, 16.

race of unskilled labour. For services undertaken for the Orange Free State Provincial Administration, it calls for alternative tenders on the basis of European and unrestricted labour, and the latter is generally chosen by the Free State administration. In Natal provincial services no restrictions are placed on unskilled labour.

In spite of the anxiety of the Central Government to promote the employment of European unskilled labour, it has not attempted to depend solely or even largely upon European labour for large undertakings such as the construction of the National roads or the extension of the docks at Capetown.

(b) The Application of the 'Civilized Labour Policy' in Private Industry

Private employers, for whom cost is the fundamental consideration, have not shown the same readiness to follow the civilized labour policy, and various official expedients have been adopted to induce and compel them to follow the lead set by the Government. These include the regulation of wages in industries to which the industrial council system is inapplicable, the manipulation of the customs tariff, discrimination by the Government in accepting tenders, and direct subsidies to employers using 'civilized' labour.

In 1925 the Wage Act was passed to supplement the Industrial Conciliation Act. It made provision for the regulation of wages and of conditions of work in industries in which employers and employees were not organized into trade associations. Agriculture and domestic service, the occupations in which such organization is most difficult, were, however, specifically excluded from the scope of the Act. The Wage Act[1] functions through a Wage Board of three members appointed by the Governor-General. Additional members may be appointed to represent employers and employees in particular investigations. The Board makes recommendations to the Minister, who may make Wage Determinations in accordance with recommendations of the Board. Under the original Act the Board had wide power. It could recommend and determine minimum rates of wages, ascending scales of wages for juveniles, the number of juveniles who might be employed, and 'any other matter whatsoever affecting the remuneration or conditions of employment of any employees'. These powers have been amplified under the 1937 Act.

Unlike the Industrial Conciliation Act, neither the original nor the new Wage Act excludes pass-bearing Natives from the scope

---

[1] The Wage Act of 1925 was amended in 1930 and completely revised in 1937.

of Wage-Board determinations. However the Act of 1925 provided that if the Board found that it could not recommend in respect of the employees in any trade or section of a trade a wage or rate upon which such employees might be able to support themselves 'in accordance with civilized habits of life', it should make no recommendation in regard to such wages or rates, but should report to the Minister on the conditions in the trade and the reasons for its decision. The Minister, on consideration of such report, might direct the Board to make such recommendation as it deemed fit.[1]

At the inaugural meeting of the first Wage Board the Chairman, Mr. F. A. W. Lucas, made a public statement concerning the status and intentions of the Board. He said:

> 'A careful examination of the provisions of the Act will show that there are two underlying aims. The first is to safeguard civilized standards of living for all classes of workers irrespective of race or colour; the second is that the productive energy of the community is not to be hampered, so that full scope can be given to that productive energy subject to the securing of the first aim. The aim of the Board is to establish in the country as soon as it is reasonably possible "a just and balanced system of wage regulation" avoiding as far as possible the irritating contrasts in wages which lead to trouble and the securing of wage levels which will, as far as possible, give satisfaction. The need for action has been clearly pointed out, and the Board will not shrink from taking the responsibility when necessary. The Board's aim is to create a system of justice under which industry will be stimulated and its products justly distributed.'[2]

The Clay-Martin-Mills Report of the Economic and Wage Commission, which reported after the Wage Act had been passed (1925), but before it had come into operation, drew attention to the particular opportunities and dangers confronting wage legislation in South Africa. It pointed out that wages were ultimately determined by the national income, and that legislation could only raise *average* wages by reacting on the efficiency either of individuals or of the organization of labour.[3] Therefore these Commissioners recommended that legislative wage regulations should be made district by district; that it should take existing rates as its starting-point and basis, and it should deal first with the lowest paid classes of labour irrespective of colour; where they considered there was plenty of scope for improvement, both in the physical efficiency of labourers and in the organization of labour.[4]

[1] Act 27 of 1925, sec. 3, sub-sec. (3).
[2] *Report of the Wage Board for the Three Years ended 28th February*, 1929, p. 3.
[3] *Economic and Wage Commission*, op. cit., paras. 108–51.
[4] Ibid., para. 154.

The Wage Board soon found that in all industries in which its reference covered unskilled workers it could not recommend a 'civilized' wage, taking into consideration, as was required, the ability of employers to carry on if they were required to pay higher wages.[1]

In one case only between the years 1926 and 1932 was the Wage Board directed to make a recommendation which was applicable exclusively to unskilled workers.[2] In five cases up to 1935, in which the Board reported that it could not recommend wages for all employees 'at rates on which they could support themselves in accordance with civilized habits of life', it was not directed by the Minister to make any recommendations.[3] Under the first regulations made under the Wage Act it was possible for the Wage Board to consider an application for an investigation from any unorganized body of Natives who could show that they were authorized to make that application. In 1929 the regulations were amended and all persons supporting an application were required to sign it themselves, a provision making it impossible for any large body of Natives, the least organized workers, to make a successful application[4] because of the obvious difficulty in formalizing such procedure where workers in a backward state of cultural development are involved.

The provision requiring special direction from the Minister before wages below 'civilized standards' could be recommended by the Board was dropped from the 1937 Act and a provision was included stating that the Board has no power to 'differentiate or discriminate on the basis of race or colour'. But, in connexion with every investigation the Board, or divisions thereof, is called upon to report specifically

> upon the class or classes of employees to whom . . . it would be equitable . . . that remuneration should be paid at such rates as will enable them to support themselves in accordance with civilized standards of life.[5]

The determination of the amount of wage-rates adequate for a 'civilized standard of life' is a matter involving arbitrary definition and serious conflict of opinion. In 1925 the Economic and Wage Commission commented that

> 'The term "civilized" would appear to be a variant of "living" or "reasonable" as applied to a European in South Africa. So far as

---

[1] *Native Economic Commission*, 1930–32, Addendum by Mr. Lucas (Chairman of the first Wage Board), paras. 317–18.

[2] Ibid., para. 319.

[3] *Industrial Legislation Commission*, U.G. 37, 1935, para. 506.

[4] *Native Economic Commission*, op. cit. Addendum by Mr. Lucas, para. 320.

[5] Wage Act (No. 44 of 1937), sec. 6 (b).

we were able to follow the witnesses who used the term, they meant by it the standard represented by the highest wage earned by a skilled artisan in one of the higher wage centres of the country. If this be its meaning, it is obviously a misnomer; for the level of real wages in such countries as Belgium, Germany, and Italy is only half that of the white artisan in South Africa.'[1]

The evidence presented made the Commissioners ask: 'Is a Native servant essential to a civilized existence?'[2]

In 1935 the Industrial Legislation Commission reported that numerous witnesses submitted evidence as to a necessary minimum rate for unskilled labour and that the most popular and strongly represented figure was ten shillings a day, which was declared to be the necessary minimum 'civilized standard'. 'For Johannesburg the minimum civilized rate was stated to be from 11s. to 13s. per day, whereas in Durban from 8s. to 10s. per day was suggested. At that centre it was also submitted that no European could live on less than £4 per week. On the other hand, a general minimum unskilled rate of from 3s. 6d. to 4s. per day was also proposed'.[3]

In all its recommendations the Wage Board classified different types of work and laid down detailed rates of wages for each, usually graded according to length of service.[4]

The effect of wage regulation is illustrated from the Wage Board's own account of its inquiry into the liquor and catering trades on the Witwatersrand. It reported that great difficulty had been experienced in grading both the occupations of cook and waiter and the different classes of establishment:

> 'In these circumstances', it said, 'the Board had no option but to recommend one wage common respectively to cooks and waiters, whether in first, second, or third-class establishments. To have raised wages to Grade I level would have imposed an impossible burden on all but first-grade establishments and a common wage must necessarily be lower than the top and higher than the bottom grade.'[5]

In these trades the Natives, who formed 47·6 per cent of all employees, were the lowest paid. The effect of such action on employment is obvious, for only workers whose value to the employers is equal to the statutory wage-rates will be retained. The Wage Board itself admits that statutory wage-rates of this kind affect the racial composition of the labour employed. It said:

[1] *Economic and Wage Commission* (1925), op. cit., para. 332.   [2] Ibid., para. 333.
[3] *Industrial Legislation Commission*, U.G. 37, 1935, para. 76.
[4] cf. *Report of the Wage Board*, 1929, op. cit., *passim*.
[5] *Report of Department of Labour*, 1937, op. cit., p. 63.

'It is, of course, plain that wage levels, though fixed without discrimination, do affect the race composition of employees. . . .'[1]

They did not, however, proceed to make it equally clear that establishments which could not bear the increase in labour costs would be compelled to reduce their scale of operations and of employing capacity, if not indeed to close down. It is an open question whether the total wage bill in the industry affected would be increased by such an award.

According to the evidence of Divisional Inspectors of labour, wage regulation has had little or no affect on the total volume of employment, but it has resulted in the less efficient employees being discharged and in changes in the racial composition of the labour employed.[2] In the case of the baking and confectionery industry in Pietermaritzburg comparative figures are available. This industry became subject to a wage determination on the 1st March 1931. In January 1931 there were twelve concerns in the industry employing 16 Europeans, 5 Coloured, 10 Asiatics, and 110 Native employees. In September 1934 there were eleven firms employing 29 Europeans, 3 Coloured, 9 Asiatics, and 67 Native employees. The total number employed had fallen from 141 to 108, a decrease of 33; the employment of European employees showed an increase of 13; that of Coloured a decrease of 2; Asiatic a decrease of 1; Native a decrease of 43.[3] It is clear that wage regulation has markedly affected the racial composition of employees in the industry.

(iii) The Effects of the Policy
(a) Employment in Manufacturing and Commerce

The statutory scales of wages established both by industrial councils and by the Wage Board have the effect of excluding workers whose value to the employers is less than the prescribed rates. In the words of the Industrial Legislation Commission of 1935,

'impediments to the free movement of labour from occupation to occupation explain in part the tremendous divergence of existing wage-rates from those which would probably have existed if every one were free to choose his own occupation and weigh up the advantages and disadvantages of the various types of employment. These barriers block the outflow from the large reservoir of unskilled labour into channels of employment where skill or training is a necessary factor. While it is difficult to climb the ladder, it is always easy to

[1] Ibid p. 65.
[2] *Industrial Legislation Commission*, op. cit., para. 229.
[3] Ibid., para. 214.

descend and to fall into the ranks of the unskilled masses and wage regulation itself may result in a sifting and elimination process and even to positive unemployment. In an unregulated market, the available supplies or numbers determine the wage, but, under regulated conditions, wages determine the numbers and set in motion a selective process in which all who are not worth the determined wages must make room for those who justify the payment of that wage.'[1]

In South Africa industrial legislation has served to maintain the structure of wage-rates which arose because of the scarcity of skilled workers. Their initial scarcity has been maintained by exclusive devices which have prevented the adjustment of wage-rates to the potential supply of labour and prevented a movement of wage-rates which would equalize the net advantages of labour in different occupations.[2]

Industrial legislation may not immediately reduce the absolute number of workers employed, but nevertheless it restricts capacity to employ in the occupations to which it is applied. Statistics have been cited of the industries to which the Apprenticeship Act and the Industrial Conciliation Act have been applied. It is not possible to give complete comparative figures of the number of Natives in industries directly affected by these Acts or by wage determinations. Originally, the Wage Act was intended to deal with workers who were unorganized. Consequently, one might have expected it to have been concerned primarily with Native workers. In practice this has not been the case, for until 1937 it was precluded from recommending wages upon which workers would not be able, in its opinion, to maintain 'civilized' standards, unless such rates were specially sanctioned by the Minister for Labour.

---

[1] *Industrial Legislation Commission*, op. cit., para. 23.

[2] 'European labour, once a great scarcity, is now available in increased numbers in urban areas. Moreover, these increased numbers do not consist of artisans and capable managers or supervisors only, but of every grade of labour. The labour situation has accordingly undergone a radical change. In every race, the existence of grades of labour and of difference in ability must be admitted. The same applies to Europeans in South Africa. While some are "born" craftsmen and men capable of leading others, many are only able to do manual labour and only capable of being led. The former was, until recently, a monopoly of the non-European and, indeed, was commonly referred to as "Kaffir work." Europeans in increasing numbers are, therefore, entering the ranks of unskilled labour in the towns where they have to compete with growing numbers of non-Europeans. The labour supply thus no longer consists of a small skilled European labour force superimposed upon a mass of non-European unskilled labour with a low standard of living. Economic forces have now drawn Europeans into the unskilled labour group, while some of the non-Europeans have elevated themselves into the semi-skilled and skilled groups. But notwithstanding this radical change in the structure of the labour supply, the South African wage structure has in the meantime remained essentially unaltered.' Ibid, para. 10. See also para. 19.

Since the re-drafting of the Wage Act in 1937 the Wage Board[1] has paid more attention to unskilled labourers, but it has not yet attempted to raise the wages of the lowest paid. Thus, in 1938 a determination was gazetted applying to unskilled labourers only in certain occupations in Capetown. It laid down minimum wages for labourers employed in bridge-building, excavation work, the preparation of building sites, and the demolition of buildings.[2] A determination was also made for quarrying and brick-making (Cape Peninsula), and road-making (Capetown), occupations in which the bulk of the employees are unskilled labourers.[3] Capetown, however, is the centre in which the wages of unskilled labourers have been highest, on account of distance from the sources of cheap labour: the districts with a large Native population. So that here the Wage Board has attempted to raise wages which were already higher than those prevailing for similar work in other centres.

The Wage Board has also been directed to inquire into the conditions of employment of unskilled workers in a large number of trades in Durban and Port Elizabeth.[4] Further, it has included statutory minimum rates for unskilled workers in its new recommendation for the commercial distributive trade in the principal towns in the Union. The previous determination did not lay down minimum rates for unskilled labourers in this important occupation.[5]

Once wage regulation has been instituted in some trades it is likely to give rise to demands for its extension. Employers forced to pay statutory minimum wages demand protection from the 'unfair competition' of employers paying lower rates. Thus, in Capetown the Wage Board was directed to inquire into the wages of unskilled labourers employed in demolition, clearing of sites, and other similar occupations, chiefly as a result of competition between independent contractors and builders. The latter were obliged, in terms of an industrial council agreement, to pay wages considerably above those at which unskilled labour could be obtained, consequently they wished to see competitors subjected to similar rates.[6]

---

[1] The term of office of the original Wage Board expired in August 1935. One member, Mr. A. T. Roberts had died in April 1935. The Chairman, Mr. A. W. Lucas, had already expressed his disbelief in the efficacy of wage regulation. In February, 1936, an entirely new Wage Board was appointed.

[2] Government Notice No. 1467, *Government Gazette*, No. 2565, 9 September 1938.

[3] Ibid., No. 1516, *Government Gazette*, No. 2567, 16 September 1938.

[4] *Government Gazette*, 20 October 1939.

[5] In 1937 there were 78,000 employees in the commercial distributive trade; of these 26,000 (33 per cent) were Natives. Nearly 25,000 (95 per cent) of the Natives employed were doing work classed as unskilled. *Report of the Wage Board on the Commercial Distributive Trade*, 1939. Tables I and III, pp. 11, 15.

[6] 'It is understood that the investigation was due in the first place to a complaint

On the whole, however, counteracting forces were stronger than this tendency for the extended application of wage determinations, and over the period 1932–7 there was a fall in the number of employees, including Natives, directly affected by wage determinations, their number being approximately 73,000 at the end of 1932, 74,000 at the end of 1935, and 69,000 at the end of 1937.[1] Fluctuation in the number and range of wage determinations operative was one cause of changes in the number of workers affected. This was due in part to employers and employees having preferred to establish industrial councils rather than to be subjected to wage determinations;[2] in part to a decline in the activity of the Wage Board, towards the end of the first Board's period of office;[3] and in part to judicial decisions which found many of the determinations invalid.[4]

At the end of 1938 twenty-seven wage determinations were in operation. According to statistics collected by the Department of Labour, the number of persons employed in industries subject to wage determinations was 98,000, of whom 30,000 were Natives.[5] With the exception of the important commercial distributive trade determination, the wages of unskilled labourers in most of these industries were regulated.[6] The minimum rates for unskilled varied between £1 per week and £1 4s., except in one instance (furniture manufacturing, Oudtshoorn), where the minimum was 18s.

The importance of this type of wage regulation in the market for Native labour lies in its effect not so much upon the privileged few whose wages may be raised or protected by these means as upon the many to whom opportunities for employment are thereby closed. The Wage Board, and to a limited extent industrial councils, have attempted to raise the wages of semi-skilled and unskilled workers by prescribing minimum rates of pay which in

by the Master Builders' Association of Capetown, of unfair competition from certain employers who were not subject to wage regulation.' *Report of the Wage Board*, Unskilled Work, Capetown, G.P.S. 9170–1938, p. 5.

[1] *Reports of the Department of Labour*, U.G. 37, 1933, p. 42; U.G. 4, 1937, p. 69; U.G. 30, 1938, p. 55.

[2] cf. *Industrial Legislation Commission*, op. cit., paras. 501–2.

[3] The Wage Board makes investigations only when sanctioned by the Minister.

[4] 'A total of fifty-four determinations had been made up to 31 March 1935, following investigations by the Board, but thirty-five of these had ceased to be operative, seventeen had been replaced by fresh determinations, five had been cancelled in order to make room for agreements of industrial councils, and thirteen had been declared to be, or become, invalid as a result of decisions of the Courts.' *Industrial Legislation Commission*, op. cit., para. 505.

[5] *Report of the Department of Labour* for 1938. U.G. 51, 1939, pp. 56–8.

[6] The wages of unskilled labourers in the commercial distributive trade were subsequently regulated under a new determination for that trade which came into force at the beginning of January 1940.

many cases have been substantially above those prevailing. Thereby labour costs have been raised and total employing capacity reduced below the level which might have prevailed in the absence of statutory minimum rates. The fact that the number of employed may not have fallen absolutely does not disprove the contention that employing capacity has been diminished. Other factors such as a rise in the demand for the product, or a fall in other costs, may have occasioned a countervailing increase in employment. There is no gainsaying the fact that the effect of an increase in wage-rates is to raise labour costs. It is frequently argued that this effect may be offset by improvements in the organization and efficiency of labour, but reasons why this is more likely to result from an increase in labour costs than from any other rise in costs are seldom advanced.

According to the first Chairman of the Wage Board:

'Where possible, the Board has tried by stages to raise the wages payable for work, other than that of labourers, to what may be considered a civilized wage, but that has as yet very seldom been possible.'[1]

The reason why it was not possible was that the Wage Board was required to take into consideration the ability of employers to carry on their businesses if wage-rates were raised.[2]

There is a body of opinion which considers that Native workers as a whole would benefit from the compulsory raising of their wage-rates. It is apparently founded on the belief that competition between employers is ineffective in raising wage-rates to the value of the marginal product of the worker, and that consequently there is a 'margin' which can be transferred to the worker without reducing employment or output. In the preceding chapters it was argued that the centralized control of labour on the Transvaal gold- and coal-mines has depressed the wages of labourers below the competitive level. But it was suggested that unless complete reorganization became possible, notably by the removal of legal and customary colour bars, it is not at all certain that a rise in Native wages, even on the mines, would benefit Native workers as a whole. As the scale of the gold industry is dependent upon present wage-rates, its employing capacity would

[1] F. A. W. Lucas, 'The Determination of Wages in South Africa,' *The South African Journal of Economics*, Vol. I, No. I, March 1933, p.55.

[2] cf. F. McGregor (Chairman of the Wage Board since 1936): 'Wage Regulation in South Africa,' *Race Relations*, Vol. VII, No. 1, 1940, p. 5. 'Full consideration of the many facets of what is commonly referred to as "capacity to pay" is not possible here, but this factor is certainly one of the most important of all the influences which affect the Board's proposal in general. I do admit, however, and I am speaking solely for myself, that where the lowest paid class is concerned, greater weight should be given to the "needs of the workers" and less to "the capacity of industry to pay" factor.'

be reduced, while there would also be a reduction in the employing
capacity of ancillary industries, and the Natives excluded would
be forced into less preferred occupations.

Even in the gold-mining industry there is no evidence that
capital secures an exceptional rate of reward which could be
transferred to Native labourers without diminishing the future
supply of capital and consequently reducing future output, both
in gold-mining and in ancillary industries.[1] Compulsory increases
in the wage-rates of Native labourers on the gold-mines would
restrict output unless they were accompanied by a breakdown of
the legal and customary barriers to employment which create an
artificial scarcity of many types of skilled labour. The only significant 'margin' which might be transferred to Native labourers
without reducing productivity is that which accrues to those
Europeans whose earnings are exceptionally high as a result of
the exclusion of Natives from skilled work.

There is even less likelihood that the compulsory raising of
wage-rates in manufacturing and commerce would increase the
income of Natives as a group. In these industries competition
between employers is most effective, in contrast to the situation
in the gold-mining industry, and, as we shall see in the next
chapter, in farming. There is little evidence either of combination
to depress wages among employers in manufacturing industry
and commerce, or of the ability of individual employers to influence
wage-rates appreciably. Within the towns Native labour is, on
the whole, unspecialized and mobile, which tends to prevent its
exploitation, in the sense of the payment of wages below the
competitive rate. Unless such wages are prevalent the compulsory
raising of wage-rates must restrict output because it increases
costs. The national income will be diminished and employment
restricted. Minimum wage-rates, which exclude from employment all those who cannot profitably be employed at that rate,
will not raise the lowest wages, for they increase the supply of
labour in the uncontrolled sections of the labour market, and
consequently tend to reduce wages there. There is no doubt that
wage determinations have operated in this way in South Africa.[2]

The Capetown Board of Aid investigated the circumstances of
two hundred applicants for relief with the object of discovering
to what extent their plight was due to wage regulation. It came
to the conclusion that in the majority of cases the applicants had
been dismissed because they were partially qualified workers who

[1] *Economic and Wage Commission* (1925), op. cit., para. 258. S. H. Frankel,
'Return to Capital in the Witwatersrand Gold Industry, 1887–1932.' *Economic
Journal,* March 1935, pp. 67–76.
[2] cf. W. H. Hutt, 'Logical Issues in the Study of Industrial Legislation in
the Union,' *South African Journal of Economics,* March 1935.

were unable to earn the rates of pay prescribed for the occupations they had been following. Of this group only twelve were fully qualified workers.[1]

The Industrial Legislation Commission of 1935 reviewed the effects of wage legislation. It pointed out that it is not only partly trained and inefficient employees who may lose employment as a result of wage regulation. Where minimum wages are prescribed on the basis of length of service, employers with small businesses may be forced to dismiss juniors when they become entitled to higher rates. In the commercial distributive trade, eighteen pounds a month was then the statutory minimum wage for an employee with five years' experience. Consequently, small shopkeepers who did not require more than, for example, three qualified assistants and two juniors, were sometimes forced to dismiss the latter when they became 'qualified'. In the opinion of the Commissioners wage regulation had resulted in some employers adopting this policy of 'hiring and firing', although their number was not great.[2]

Nevertheless, wage regulation of this type makes employers less willing to take on beginners, and its crippling effect on the employment of Natives is particularly severe, as they seldom have sufficient general education to make them worth the wages prescribed for qualified employees. The attempts to regulate the wages of shop assistants exemplify the difficulties which confront standardized wage regulation where workers are of very different efficiency, and where they are engaged upon different types of work. In a report upon the commercial distributive trade the Wage Board acknowledged that the wage-rates it recommended for shop assistants were impracticable in stores catering mainly for Native customers, and employing Native assistants to a large extent—though this latter consideration is not supposed to affect the Board's determinations. A minimum wage of twenty-two pounds a month was recommended for qualified male assistants (those with six years' experience)[3] in the larger towns in the Union. The Board states that it relied upon the power of the Minister to grant exemptions from the determination to make the alterations which it realized would be necessary.[4] It is obvious that friction and reduction in employment are likely to arise where wage-rates, and consequently capacity to employ, are dependent

---

[1] *Industrial Legislation Commission*, op. cit., paras. 205–7.

[2] Ibid., para. 204.

[3] Wage Board Recommendation—Commercial Distributive Trade. Government Notice No. 189, *Government Gazette*, 17 February 1939, p. 431. In the determination finally approved this rate was reduced to £21.

[4] *Report of the Wage Board on the Commercial Distributive Trade*, 1939, para. 20.

upon the ability of employers to convince officials that their business merits exemption from statutory rates.

The trend of industrial employment in the Union as a whole, and in the four principal industrial areas, is epitomized in the following table. It shows that between 1924–5 and 1936–7 the number of Natives in employment in private manufacturing industry doubled[1] while their average wages rose slightly. The

AVERAGE NUMBER OF NATIVE EMPLOYEES IN PRIVATE MANUFACTURING INDUSTRY AND THEIR AVERAGE YEARLY WAGE IN THE UNION AND THE FOUR CHIEF INDUSTRIAL AREAS, 1924–5 TO 1936–7[2]

Year	Cape Western		Port Elizabeth		Durban		Southern Transvaal		Union	
	Average Wage £	No.	Average Wage £	No.	Average Wage £	No.	Average Wage £	No.	Average Wage £	No.
1924–5	53	3,814	55	1,991	39	7,607	44	30,935	41	66,503
1929–30	59	5,285	56	2,833	43	8,559	46	38,279	45	81,233
1932–3	53	3,501	49	1,688	41	5,415	43	36,153	46	66,751
1935–6	60	5,820	52	2,760	44	10,071	44	73,602	42	122,357
1936–7	64	6,900	55	3,160	47	11,732	46	80,722	44	134,233

importance of the Southern Transvaal, which includes the Witwatersrand and Pretoria, is evident. In 1936–7 more than half the total number of Native employees were in this area, and average wages there showed much the same small rise as in the Union as a whole. In the Cape Western area, which is farthest from the Native territories, the number employed doubled, while wages rose from an average of £53 in 1924–5 to £64 in 1936–7. In Port Elizabeth and Durban the number employed rose by about 50 per cent in each case, and in the former town wages were the same in 1936–7 as in 1924–5, while in Durban they rose, although not as much as in Capetown. In particular industries, such as clothing and textiles, the number and the average wage of Natives rose relatively to the average for all industries.

Thus, despite the barriers to their employment in manufacturing

[1] The figures in the table include Native women. Their number is, however, very small. In spite of increased urbanization (see below, p. 269), in 1924–5 only 706 were employed in manufacturing establishments and in 1936–7 only 921. Thus the expansion in the employment of Native women has been much less rapid than that of men.

[2] Statistics from Annual Censuses of Industrial Establishments.

industry, Natives have shared in the expansion of employment. It is impossible to ascertain what their position might have been in the absence of the measures which have been taken to promote the employment of Europeans.

The proportion of Natives to the total number of employees in private factories rose slightly between 1924–5 and 1936–7, the percentage of Natives being 44 and 46 respectively. This slight rise took place at the end of the period. Unfortunately no statistics of industrial production were collected during the depths of the industrial depression of 1929 to 1933; that is, between the industrial censuses of 1929–30 and 1932–3. In the latter period, when industry was still relatively depressed, the number and proportion of Natives in employment had declined relatively to Europeans. Comparing the two periods, the total number of employees fell from 218,000 to 192,000, the number of Natives fell from 81,000 to 68,000, and the proportion from 44 to 40 per cent: the number of Europeans fell from 70,000 to 69,000, but the proportion rose from 38 to 42 per cent. That is to say, Europeans were retained while Natives were dismissed. To some extent this is only to be expected in view of the fact that Europeans are employed on the more skilled work and in supervision while Natives are largely employed in unskilled and casual work.

In those Government and local government undertakings, which are included in the census of industrial production, both the number and proportion of Natives employed has fallen markedly since 1924–5. In that year, out of a total of 39,000 employees, 16,000 (42 per cent) were Natives and 17,000 (45 per cent) Europeans. In 1936–7, out of 39,000 employees, 12,000 (30 per cent) were Natives and 25,000 (64 per cent) Europeans. The number and percentage of Coloured and Asiatic employees had likewise fallen.

To some extent the course of employment in private industry has been influenced by the customs tariff which has been used to implement the official 'civilized labour policy'. This action was foreshadowed as early as 1911, when a Commission on Trade and Industries[1] recommended that a policy of protecting agriculture and industrial undertakings should be adopted, and that one of the conditions on which protection should be granted should be that a 'fair proportion of white labour' be employed.

This recommendation was incorporated in the Customs Act of 1925,[2] which contains a clause, still operative, authorizing the levying of the minimum duty on any article if the protected industry concerned is reported to be maintaining 'unsatisfactory

[1] U.G. 10, 1912 (commonly known as the 'Cullinan' Commission), p. 13.
[2] Act No. 36 of 1925.

labour conditions'. The Board of Trade and Industries, in its report on the Revision of the Customs Tariff,[1] leaves no doubt as to the interpretation to be placed on 'unsatisfactory labour conditions', for it states that in framing the tariff

the Board has also had in view the use of the tariff as a means of encouraging the employment of civilized labour, tariff assistance in industries being partly conditional on good labour conditions and on the understanding that, wherever possible, a larger proportion of civilized labour be employed.

In one case the Board considered an application for a higher duty, and in spite of being very favourably impressed with the quality and price of the local article, recommended only a suspended duty, to be applied in the event of 'improved' labour conditions. The prevailing labour conditions were considered 'extremely unsatisfactory', thirteen Europeans being employed and one hundred and thirty Indians and Natives. In another case the Board even took 'the bold step of recommending the withdrawal of the existing preference' in favour of motor spirit imported in bulk, one of the reasons being that the local packing establishment employed only twenty Europeans as compared with two hundred and thirty Natives and Indians.[2]

In 1933 Divisional Inspectors of the Labour Department were advised:

It is the Minister's wish that the departmental officers should now do everything in their power to ensure that industries maintain a fair ratio as between civilized and non-civilized labour, particularly those industries which have benefited as the result of the protectionist policy of the Government.[3]

At that time the ratio of European to non-European employees, in a number of fully protected secondary industries for which data were available, was 5·7 per cent, as compared to 41·9 per cent for all industries included in the Industrial Census.[4] One is given to understand that the Government has not laid down any definition of 'a fair ratio' of civilized labour, but that 'individual industries are treated on their merits, due regard being given to the nature of each industry and the availability of suitable employees'. As the Minister has power to refuse to allow the free importation of raw material to a factory 'maintaining unsatisfactory labour conditions',[5] industrialists can thus be forced to employ

[1] *Board of Trade and Industries*, Report No 51, 1925.
[2] Ibid., pp. 10–12.
[3] Quoted *Cape Coloured Commission*, op. cit., para. 180.
[4] *Customs Tariff Commission*, 1934–5, U.G. 5, 1936, para. 37.
[5] *Cape Coloured Commission*, op. cit., paras. 182–4.

'civilized' labour, and the tariff is used to enable them to pass on
the cost.

In addition, the regulations of the Union Tender and Supplies
Board provide for approved lists of Government tenders and for
the exclusion from the approved list of South African firms which
do not maintain 'satisfactory labour conditions, including the
employment of a reasonable proportion of civilized workers'.[1]
Thus, the extent to which employers are being compelled to employ
European labour is steadily increasing.

(b) Opportunities for Natives as Entrepreneurs, Professional Workers, and Domestic Servants

Official policy has strengthened environmental and traditional
influences which might, in themselves, have retarded the emergence of Natives as skilled industrial workers. Prejudice against
social equality also prevents the employment of Natives in most
occupations, either in supervisory work, or even on an equal
footing with Europeans. In addition, it prevents Native entrepreneurs from employing Europeans, for few Europeans would
consent to take orders from Native employers, although they
might be willing to consult Native professional men, such as
medical practitioners, or to use Native contractors.

A considerable number of Native craftsmen work on their own
account, but there are very few large or even medium scale enterprises under the control or management of Natives. In 1936–7,
of over 7,000 working proprietors included in the census of
manufacturing industry, only 8 were Natives; of over 20,000
managers, accountants, and salaried staff, only 89.[2] According
to the urban Native census of 1938, there were then nearly 16,000
Native craftsmen working on their own account in urban areas.
For the most part they work independently, supplying both other
Natives and Europeans. Very often they are not as highly skilled
as fully trained European or Coloured artisans. This is probably
due partly to the difficulty which those who attend Native industrial schools experience in completing their education under the
existing organization of apprenticeship which, as we have seen,
practically excludes Natives from serving as apprentices; and
partly to the rigid classification of grades of work which prevents
unskilled labourers from acquiring skill by assisting skilled artisans.

There are a considerable number of Natives who run shops,
but almost without exception their businesses are conducted on
a very small scale. In 1936 there were estimated to be between

[1] *Official Year Book*, No. 19, 1938, p. 261.
[2] *Census of Industrial Establishments*, 1936–7, op. cit., pp. 28–9.

five and six hundred Native retail traders on the Witwatersrand.[1] Their shops are small and cater principally for the Native population which, it must be remembered, is very poor.

The Natives (Urban Areas) Act, which lays down the legal terms upon which Natives may live in urban areas, makes provision for the letting of sites to Natives within locations for trading or business purposes. Further, it gives the Minister of Native Affairs power after inquiry to compel urban authorities to regulate such leases. They may, however, only be let to Natives, and only Natives may be employed on them. The Act specifically repealed an Orange Free State law which prohibited the grant of trading licences to Coloured persons (including Natives).[2] In that province Urban Native Advisory Councils have asked for trading sites to be let to Natives, but such sites have only been made available in one location, although in several towns Natives are permitted to hawk goods.[3]

As a result of the social and legal barriers which close so many avenues of employment to Natives, teaching, and to a minor degree the administrative services in Native areas, provide the most important opportunities for employment outside the field of relatively unskilled manual work. Yet the numbers in these occupations are very low: in 1921, according to the census classification of the personal occupations of Natives, there were 9,756 in the professional group, which included teachers, ministers, chiefs, headmen, and members of other professions. There were also 1,634 interpreters and clerks of all classes. This out of a total Native population of 4,700,000.[4]

Comparative statistics of the number of Native teachers are not available. The number of teachers in state and state-aided schools for non-Europeans rose from 5,476 in 1917 to 12,225 in 1936; at the latter date 8,179 of these were Natives. In addition, there were 1,153 Native teachers in private schools for non-Europeans.[5]

Salary scales for teachers in state and state-aided schools for Natives were laid down in 1928 by the Native Affairs Commission. For both European and Native teachers they are lower than those for teachers with similar qualifications and responsibilities in schools for Europeans. The basic salaries for Native teachers in primary schools are £66 per annum for men who have had three years teacher-training after passing Standard VI, and £54 for

[1] R. E. Phillips, op. cit., p. 20.
[2] Law No. 8 of 1893.
[3] *Race Relations News*, No. 5, November 1938, p. 1.
[4] *Third Census of the Population of the Union of South Africa* (1921), Part VIII, U.G. 40, 1924, Table 24, p. 143.
[5] *Official Year Book*, No. 18, 1937, p. 382, and No. 19, 1938, p. 376.

women with similar qualifications. Extra allowances may be granted, and the range of salaries for qualified male teachers in primary schools is from £66 per annum to £150. In secondary schools the basic salaries for men with degrees and professional qualifications are supposed to be £180, rising by increments of £9 to £306, and for women with similar qualifications, £120, rising by increments of £5 to £204. In practice, however, owing to the shortage of funds provided for Native education, Native teachers have not received the increments prescribed when the scale was laid down. The pension rights of Native teachers are either non-existent or inferior to those of Europeans.[1]

Nevertheless, teaching provides some of the most attractive opportunities open to Natives, and a large proportion of the Native children who pass Standard VI train to be teachers.

Domestic service continues to be one of the most important fields of employment of Native labour and, until very recently, there has been no attempt to restrict the number of Natives entering it.

We have seen how early commentators in Natal were surprised to find Native men performing every type of domestic service, even that of nursemaid.[2] The system of employing male Natives in domestic service has continued to be a feature of life in South Africa, particularly in Natal and the Transvaal. In 1921 there were nearly 89,000 Native men and 163,000 women engaged in domestic service.[3] Unfortunately statistics of their distribution between urban and rural areas are not available. In 1929 the Committee on the Labour Resources of the Union estimated that 111,000 Native men were engaged in domestic service. According to the urban Native census of 1938 there were then some 228,000 Natives in domestic service in urban areas, of these nearly 138,000 were women and 90,000 men.[4]

The Labour Resources Committee considered that the employment of Native men as domestic servants was 'uneconomical' when 'the two major industries of the country' (farming and mining) were 'suffering from a serious labour shortage'.[5] It recognized that (given the opportunities open to Natives in other

---

[1] *Inter-Departmental Committee on Native Education*, 1935–6, op. cit., paras. 191–209.   [2] See above, p. 47.
[3] *Third Census of Population*, op. cit., Table 24, p. 143.
[4] There was much apprehension among the Native population about the reasons for this enumeration of Natives in urban areas. Many considered that information collected would be used to eject Natives from the towns. Consequently there was opposition to enumeration and it is probable that this census understates numbers.
[5] *Inter-Departmental Committee on the Labour Resources of the Union*, 1930, para. 86.

occupations) domestic service was an attractive occupation,[1] nevertheless it considered that female labour, both Native and European, should be substituted, although it did not recommend any specific measures to this end. Indeed, it recognized that there were serious obstacles to any quick transition. Tribal sentiment has been much opposed to women leaving the tribe, with the result that the supply of domestic servants from rural areas has been limited on the whole to those prepared to break away from tribal discipline, and they have not provided the most docile type of servant; while, at the same time, Native women have not been subject to control under the pass laws.

Men-servants have been subject to greater control, and some employers are said to have preferred to employ them on this account. The growing urbanization of Natives has, however, led to an increase in the number of Native women employed in domestic service.[2]

C. OFFICIAL MEASURES DIRECTLY AFFECTING THE SUPPLY OF NATIVE LABOURERS IN URBAN AREAS

The measures we have been discussing react directly upon the demand for Native labour. But they also affect the supply by reducing opportunities for advancement and consequently rendering employment less attractive than it might be. In addition to such repercussions, official attempts are being made to limit the number of Native workers in urban areas by restricting their right of entry and by making provision for the removal of Natives not in employment.

Since 1911 there has been a considerable increase in the urban Native population and Natives have tended increasingly to stay in towns for longer periods or to make them their permanent homes. This tendency is illustrated by the growth in the numbers of Native women and children in urban areas. The number and

[1] 'The native finds that he is forced to do a certain amount of work to earn enough cash for his needs. Being placed in this position, he chooses those occupations in which he can earn it in the shortest time and in the least objectionable way. Domestic service has moral objections, but once he has overcome these, it gives him the advantage of light work, very good pay and plenty of food, to which is added the attraction of living for a period of the year in an urban area. There is, therefore, never any shortage of natives willing to become house-boys, and the number engaged in this occupation is estimated at 110,000 or 13 per cent of the available native adult labour force.' Ibid., para. 85.

In calculating the 'available Native adult labour force' the Committee assumed that 'the proportion of his time, which the male native of working age devotes to the industries of the Union, apart from his own agricultural and other economic activities, is 44 per cent', and that, therefore, the total Native labour force was not 1,458,000, as it would have been on the basis of population, but 644,000. Ibid., para. 73.

[2] See *Cape Coloured Commission*, op. cit., para. 149.

sex of Natives in urban areas in 1911, 1921, and 1936 is shown in the following table:

Natives in Urban Areas, 1911, 1921, and 1936

	1911	1921	1936
Males	410,161	459,707	749,768
Females	97,981	147,293	356,874

In 1918 the severe epidemic of influenza, during which the mortality among Natives and Coloured people was particularly heavy, directed attention both to the growth of the urban Native population and to the slum conditions under which many Natives and other non-Europeans were living.[1] To improve the situation, and to protect the European community, the Government in 1923 passed the Natives (Urban Areas) Act.[2] According to the preamble, its objects included provision

> for improved conditions of residence for natives in or near urban areas and the better administration of native affairs in such areas; for the registration and better control of contracts of service with natives in certain areas and the regulation of the ingress of natives into and their residence in such areas. . . .

These ends were to be achieved through compulsory residential segregation and through making urban local authorities responsible for the accommodation and control of Natives living within their boundaries. Residential segregation was not an innovation. Residence in urban locations had previously been compulsory for Natives not living on their employers' premises, in towns in the Transvaal, the Orange Free State, and Natal, and in some towns in the Cape Province.[3] Even where it was not legally compulsory in the Cape Province, special areas were usually set aside for non-Europeans. The Act of 1923 extended the application of residential segregation in regard both to the number of towns and the number of Natives affected. By 1938 compulsory segregation had been applied to the whole or the major portions of some seventy-six towns, including nearly all the larger towns.[4]

With the exception of certain exempted classes, all Natives may now be compelled to live in the areas or buildings set aside for them. The exempted classes include domestic servants for whom approved accommodation has been provided, resident registered owners of property valued at £75 or more, in the

---

[1] *Report of the Native Affairs Department*, 1919–22, U.G. 34, 1922, p. 12.
[2] Act No. 21 of 1923.
[3] *Report of Native Affairs Department*, 1922–6, U.G. 14, 1927, p. 10.
[4] List of areas proclaimed in terms of Section 5 (1) of Act 21 of 1923, as amended, supplied by courtesy of the Department of Native Affairs, 2 December 1938.

Cape Province registered Parliamentary voters,[1] and a few other classes not numerically important. Previously even where residential segregation was compulsory all Native employees had been permitted to live on their employers' premises. Now they may be compelled to live in the official locations or, alternatively, employers may be compelled to provide approved accommodation for natives in their employment.[2] Little use has yet been made of this latter provision.

Local authorities are responsible for the accommodation of the Natives employed within their areas and may be compelled to fulfil their obligation if, in the opinion of the Minister for Native Affairs, the provision made is inadequate or unsuitable for the needs of the Natives ordinarily employed. Officials of this Department have interpreted the 'normal requirements' of urban areas to include a 'reasonable number' temporarily unemployed or in search of work, and a 'reasonable number working on their own account to serve the needs of their compatriots.'[3] Subject to the concurrence of the central government, each local authority is empowered to decide what constitutes the labour 'requirement' of its area.

Since the original Act was passed many of the larger towns, including the seven largest,[4] have embarked on housing schemes to accommodate Natives. With the exception of Bloemfontein, the municipalities themselves have undertaken the construction of barracks for single men, and also in some cases for single women, and small cottages of one, two, or three rooms. Sanitary and medical services are usually provided. The schemes also usually make provision for trading sites, recreation halls, sports grounds, and school accommodation. So far the schoolrooms which have been provided have been quite inadequate to accommodate the children living in the urban locations.

The buildings which have been erected are substantial but drab. Except in Bloemfontein, until 1937 no provision had been made in the newer locations for Natives to build their own houses should they desire to do so. In that year plans were considered for increasing the variety of accommodation. An account of these plans by a newspaper correspondent is illuminating, for it indicates the provision which has hitherto been available in towns in which segregation provisions are in force. It states that

Ambitious and far-seeing schemes for the establishment in

[1] Except voters qualifying through the occupation of premises belonging to the urban local authority.
[2] Native Laws Amendment Act, No. 46 of 1937, Sections 2 and 3.
[3] *Native Economic Commission*, 1930–32, op. cit., Annexure 15.
[4] Johannesburg, Capetown, Durban, Pretoria, Port Elizabeth, East London, and Bloemfontein.

Johannesburg, Pretoria and along the Reef of miniature 'African towns' with modern conveniences at present unknown to the bulk of urban natives are now being considered by various municipalities. . . . Provision is being made in the schemes both for detached and semi-detached cottages, and areas are also being allocated in which the better-class native will be allowed to erect his own house under supervision and with expert advice.[1]

Hitherto most of the larger municipalities have not been able to charge rentals sufficient to cover the cost of the erection, redemption, and maintenance of the buildings provided. This is in part the result of the high cost of building and the employment of skilled European workers at the usual high wage-rates. Consequently deficits have repeatedly been incurred in spite of the fact that municipalities have been able to borrow money from the central government at specially low rates. Within urban areas Native labourers may thus be a liability on the local authorities, for the latter may be compelled to subsidize their housing.[2] In this way the real wages of Native labourers may be raised through the operation of the Natives (Urban Areas) Act which would tend to increase the supply of labour in the towns.

On the other hand the segregation provisions prevent Natives from freely acquiring or occupying land in urban areas. Even within their own urban 'locations' they cannot, as a rule, buy land but may only rent sites, as in Bloemfontein, or, as in most of the newer locations, occupy buildings provided by the municipalities. This amounts to a reduction in real wages and must react on the desire of Natives to undertake employment.

Further, many locations are situated on the outskirts of towns and they are often far from the industrial and commercial districts. Consequently Natives have to travel long distances to and from work. In the larger towns the cost of transport both in money and time is often very heavy. For example, the distance from Johannesburg to the Native Locations Orlando and Pimville is ten and twelve miles. A monthly railway ticket costs 8s. 6d. and a weekly one 2s. 6d. Such compulsory additions to the cost of living reduce real wages and the attractiveness of work.

---

[1] *Cape Argus*, 5 August, 1937.

[2] It is frequently argued that the municipalities overstate the deficits they incur as a result of providing accommodation for Natives because they include redemption of capital expenditure, while they are actually acquiring the buildings for which Native tenants are paying. Municipalities cannot, however, borrow from the Government at the special low rates available for housing schemes unless they sacrifice an amount of revenue equal to the Government's sacrifice of interest. Moreover they are not permitted to make a profit from their Native Revenue Accounts, which are inspected by the Department for Native Affairs of the central government. The position would appear to be that the present tenants are sharing part of the cost of accommodating their successors.

It is difficult to determine the net effect of these provisions on the supply of labour. It is certain, however, that the disabilities imposed have not counteracted the forces causing Natives to migrate townwards. Consequently steps have been taken to restrict their right to reside within even their urban locations.

The Natives (Urban Areas) Act made it possible to extend the monthly pass system previously in force in labour districts (principally the gold- and coal-mining areas) to urban areas. In terms of the Act:

> In any urban or industrial area proclaimed under Section 12, every male Native not belonging to certain exempted classes must carry and may be required to produce on demand either a permit to seek work or a duly registered service contract, in order to establish his right to be within the area.

Fees to cover the cost of administration are levied on the employers of Native labour, except in the case of casual labourers; the latter have to take out special monthly passes for which fees are charged.[1] The monthly pass system was first introduced in order to control the movements of Native mine labourers and provide a mechanism for enforcing the fulfilment of contracts of service.[2] To make it effective it had to be made applicable to all employment within easy reach of the mines.

This system has now been applied to some seventy-six towns including all the principal towns of the Transvaal, Kimberley, Capetown, Durban, Pietermaritzburg, and Bloemfontein. All Natives, with the exception of registered voters in the Cape Province, are subject to its provisions, and it is being used to keep a tally of Natives in urban areas in order to limit their numbers. The length of time which Natives are allowed for the purpose of finding employment has been left to the discretion of the local authority. Any Native who has not found work in the time permitted has his pass endorsed and he has to move on to another district or to return home. In Johannesburg the initial period for which permits to seek work are given has been seven days, in Capetown it has been fourteen; in each case passes may be renewed at the discretion of the registering officer.

In practice it has been found difficult both to limit the entry of Natives into urban areas and to enforce the removal of unemployed Natives. During the depression of 1929 to 1933 officials in the Transkeian Territories were asked not to grant passes to Natives wanting to come to Capetown to look for work,[3] but it was found

---

[1] Act No. 46 of 1937, sec. 18 (g). [2] See above, pp. 133 et seq.
[3] Evidence, City of Capetown to Native Economic Commission, Reply to Questionnaire, 57/6.

that they soon learnt to ask for passes to other districts, and once they were within the Cape Province proper their movements were then no longer subject to control.

In 1930 the Urban Areas Act was amended, and a provision inserted whereby local authorities might restrict the entry of Natives into their areas. Few[1] towns made use of this provision and therefore[2] in 1937 the Government once more amended the Act and took upon itself the power to restrict the entry of Natives into towns and to enforce the removal of unemployed Natives. It is noteworthy that the prohibition on entrance into urban areas does not apply to Natives employed in mining (or in any other industry notified by the Minister after consultation with the urban local authority).[3]

By 1938 the restriction of entry had been applied to some two hundred towns and villages.[4] A Native may not enter them unless he has been engaged for employment, is on a temporary visit, or unless the urban local authority is prepared to permit him to seek work. In the two latter cases he has to obtain a permit from the local authority of the district he wishes to enter.

Further, under the Amending Act, urban authorities are required to render detailed returns concerning the Natives within their areas and the 'number and sexes of Natives which, in the opinion of the urban local authority, are necessary to supply the reasonable labour requirements of the urban areas.' The returns rendered by local authorities are to be collated and circulated to magistrates and commissioners in the Native areas. It is proposed that these returns should guide these officials when issuing passes to Natives.[5] Presumably a pass is to be refused to a Native desiring to go to a town in which, in the opinion of the local authority, there is 'sufficient' labour.

These provisions also have effects on the market for Native labour. Moreover they directly affect occupations such as domestic service in private households, which are exempt from statutory wage regulation. The registration of contracts affects both demand and supply. Its effects on demand are twofold. On the one hand, in so far as contracts can be enforced more

[1] Up to the end of 1936 twelve towns had been proclaimed for this purpose under sub-section (G) of section 5 of the Act. *Report of the Native Affairs Department*, 1935–6, U.G. 41, 1937, p. 34.
[2] *Notes on Conference between Municipalities and Native Affairs Department* held at Pretoria on 28th and 29th September 1937 to Discuss the Provisions of the Native Laws Amendment Act (No. 46 of 1937), p. 3.
[3] Act No. 46 of 1937, section 9.
[4] *Government Gazette*, 27 May 1938, Notice No. 115, 1936, p. 886, and Notice 210, 1938. Capetown municipality did not apply for power to restrict the entry of Natives until the central government threatened to take over the administration of the provisions of the Act, and to enforce them in Capetown.
[5] *The Forum*, July 11, 1939, p. 14.

effectively, it may tend to make the employment of Natives more attractive. The Native Labour Resources Committee considered that some employers preferred Native men servants to women because the former were subject to control through the pass law.[1] Against this must be set the irksomeness of the necessity for registering contracts and obtaining monthly passes, and the cost of the pass fees. These impositions either reduce the wages paid to the labourer or add to the cost of employing Native labour. In Capetown, where the system was new, the Native Economic Commission was informed that some employers had refused to engage Natives on account of the necessity for registering their contracts of service.[2]

The effect of these provisions on the supply of labour is also twofold.

In certain instances they may restrict the supply. This may occur either directly by preventing the Natives from living in urban areas or indirectly by making work in urban areas less attractive.

How far the present restrictions can be enforced remains to be seen. In towns in the Orange Free State and Transvaal, where pass systems have previously been in operation, the difficulty will probably not be so great as in Natal, where the pass system has not been as effective in controlling the movement of the Native population,[3] or in the Cape Province in which, outside the Transkeian Territories, the Native population has been free of such control since the pass laws fell into disuse in the 1880's.

The system of restricting the entry of Natives into urban areas is designed in part to maintain urban wage rates and is the logical corollary of a policy of fixing wage-rates above the equilibrium level of competitive conditions. In Bloemfontein where a minimum wage for unskilled labour was fixed above the prevailing level, the result was an influx of Natives,[4] and Bloemfontein was one of the few towns to request that it should be proclaimed an area into which the immigration of Natives should be prohibited.

In addition to the authority to restrict the entry of Natives into urban areas the central government now has power to enforce the removal of Natives not in employment.[5] If the Minister of Native Affairs in consultation with the Native Affairs Commission is satisfied that the number of Natives within an area is in excess of its 'reasonable labour requirements' he may require the local

[1] *Inter-Departmental Committee on the Labour Resources of the Union*, 1930, para. 91.
[2] *Native Economic Commission*, 1930–32, typescript of evidence, p. 7171 (75).
[3] Typescript of Evidence to Economic and Wage Commission (1925), p. 3846.
[4] J. R. Cooper (Manager, Native Administration Department, Bloemfontein), 'The Urban Native Problem' (unpublished).
[5] Native Laws Amendment Act, No. 46 of 1937, section 21.

authority to furnish a list of the names of Natives who, in its opinion, ought to be removed and he may determine which of the Natives specified shall be removed.[1]

Thus it may be said that the effect of the urban pass system in certain cases will be to restrict the supply of Native labour. On the other hand the supply of labour may in other conditions be increased. This will be so if the projected use of officials in Native areas is effective in spreading information regarding vacant situations and in reducing the difficulties encountered by Natives seeking employment in strange surroundings far from home.

Any scheme which breaks down ignorance of local conditions and leads to a freer flow of labour to the centres where it is most valuable will increase production. But genuine labour exchanges would offer a more direct solution to the very real problem of ignorance about prospects of employment than a pass system which restricts entry into urban areas to those Natives whom the local authority is willing to admit and those who have found employment in advance of entering an area. The system of issuing passes only to Natives who had already obtained employment was tried in British Kaffraria in the 1850's but, as we have seen, it soon proved unsatisfactory to both employers and Natives because it restricted the free movement of labour seeking employment.[2] It is doubtful whether it will prove more satisfactory to-day.

Official labour exchanges financed by the Government are provided throughout the country, but their services are not available for non-Europeans, except in Capetown and Kimberley where separate offices cater for the Cape Coloured. The provision of similar facilities for Natives might be a means of increasing the productivity of Native labour. It might reduce the unemployment which arises from the high rate of labour turnover which is due in part to the employment of migratory labourers. The Native Farm Labour Committee recommended that a labour bureau be established with branches conducted by local officers of the Department of Native Affairs. It considered that the bureau should register Natives seeking work and applications for labourers and that it should dispatch Natives to situations, but that it should not undertake active recruiting. This limitation was presumably intended to prevent official pressure being exercised to force Natives to seek employment. The Committee considered, however, that Native distrust of official agencies was so great that an official bureau might well prove ineffective.

To be successful, labour agents need to be in close touch with

[1] The cost of removal is to be borne by funds specially voted by Parliament for the purpose and the cost of making provision for the accommodation of such Natives and of settling them on the land is to be defrayed by the South African Native Trust Fund. Act No. 46 of 1937, section 21 (6) and (7).

[2] See above, p. 29 et seq.

employers as well as would-be employees. Where Native
labourers travel long distances to work it is only when they have
been engaged on standardized contracts that recruiting through
agents has functioned to the satisfaction of both employers and
employees. For, where the parties to labour contracts are scattered, it is difficult to ensure that both sides understand and keep
the terms agreed upon. If contracts are not thoroughly understood, and observed, the drafting of Natives to employers through
official channels might increase distrust and might eventually
diminish rather than increase the total supply of labour.

In recommending a bureau the Native Labour Committee was
interested primarily in increasing the supply of farm labour,
although it considered that 'legitimate applications' for labourers
from urban areas should be met. The trend of policy has been
directed increasingly to stimulating the flow of Native labour to
farming and mining and restricting the supply in urban areas. This
policy is consistent with the policy of raising sectional wage-rates.

It commands very general support, and not only from those
sections of the community which are directly benefited. Many
professed adherents of the doctrine of 'trusteeship' advocate it.
For example, the Native Affairs Commission, which, since 1936,
has repeatedly affirmed its acceptance of the principle that
Europeans in South Africa must act as trustees for the benefit of
the less advanced sections of the community,[1] has declared that
Native labour should be directed in the first place to mining and
farming and considers that manufacturing industry should not
be permitted to compete for Native labour. Its argument is that
the tariff protection enjoyed by manufacturing industry gives it a
special pull on the supply of Native labour and so enables it to
drain labour away from mining and farming, and thereby reduce
the wealth of the community.[2]

[1] The Native Affairs Commission, established under the Native Affairs Act
(No. 23 of 1920), is an advisory body consisting of not fewer than three or more
than five members, appointed by the Governor-General and presided over by
the Minister of Native Affairs. The functions of the Commission 'include the
consideration of any matter relating to the general conduct of the administration
of Native Affairs, or to legislation in so far as it may affect the native population
(other than matters of departmental administration) and the submission to the
Minister of its recommendations on any such matters.'
   In their report for 1936 (U.G. 48, 1937), the Commissioners (G. Heaton
Nicholls, W. R. Collins, J. Mould Young, E. A. Conroy, with General J. C.
Smuts, Acting Chairman), stated that 'With the policy of segregation South
Africa has accepted the principle of trusteeship of the Native races . . .'
(para. 1) . . . and 'As its guiding principle, therefore, the Commission accepts
all the implications denoted by the term "Trusteeship" as denoting the solemn
duty accepted by South Africa, to safeguard and advance the interests of the
Native people as a race. . . .' (para. 7).
[2] *Report of the Native Affairs Commission*, for the years 1937–8, U.G. 54,
1939, p. 7.

To implement its recommendation would deny to those sections of the Native population which have been able to find employment in protected industries, any share in the sectional advantage which tariff protection may give to individuals.

The policy of limiting the entry of Natives into urban areas gains support because the consequent rise in money wage-rates within urban areas is immediate and apparent, while the effect on those excluded is less obvious. The unprivileged are relegated to work on farms and in mines, or to trying to make a living from peasant farming in the Native areas, supplemented by periodic visits to the mines or seasonal work on farms. Thus the attempt to exclude migratory labourers from seeking work in towns actually reinforces the system of migratory labour in the mining industry and, to a minor degree, in farming.

The coercive action designed to prevent the growth of the urban Native population closes preferred fields of employment to Natives. It directs them into employment which they regard as inferior. This may have undesirable repercussions on the European as well as the Native community if it reduces the Natives' incentive to work and restricts their productivity.

CHAPTER XIV

OTHER FIELDS FOR NATIVE EMPLOYMENT. (II) RURAL

A. THE DEMAND FOR NATIVE LABOUR

IN South Africa one of the most outstanding characteristics of the twentieth century has been the development of the policy of fostering the farming industry. Measures to this end have had notable influence on the market for labour. On the one hand, in so far as they have promoted farming, they have raised the demand for farm labour. On the other hand, they have included far-reaching attempts to increase the supply.

The development of grain and fruit farming has led to a change in the nature and extent of the demand for labour. In the nineteenth century farming throughout the interior of South Africa was largely pastoral, consequently the demand for labour was relatively small. It was very generally met by the Natives who had been living on the land before it was taken up by Europeans. Where farming was more intensive, as in parts of the western Cape Province and Natal, the Cape Coloured people were employed and, in Natal, indentured Indians. In the latter part of the nineteenth century the mineral discoveries led not only to an extension of the demand for Native labour on the farms, by opening up new markets, but also to increased competition for labour in other employments. This led to attempts to increase the supply of Native labourers and to encourage them, through location Acts, squatters' laws, and differential taxation, to work for farmers.

In the twentieth century the development of transport and the growth of markets at home and abroad extended the possibilities of commercial farming in South Africa. Grain farming became profitable in the interior. On the Transvaal Highveld and in the greater part of the Orange Free State, maize became the staple crop instead of a side-line grown only for domestic purposes. Maize production increased from 722 million lb. in 1904, when it must be remembered conditions were still disturbed as a result of the South African War, to 1,726 million in 1911 and 5,042 million in 1936–7. The production of wheat has also greatly increased, largely as a result of the rise in the cost of importation during the War of 1914–18, and subsequent protection of the local industry. Wheat production increased from 142 million lb. in 1904 to 362 million in 1911, and 935 million in 1936–7. Other grains are grown principally for home use and their production has not changed appreciably.[1] Deciduous and citrus fruits have become important export products since the Great War.

The growth in the production of maize, wheat, and fruit, has not taken place to the exclusion of pastoral farming. Wool production has continued to increase, the number of wooled sheep, which had been nearly halved during the South African War, rising from 12 million in 1904 to 22 million in 1911, and 33 million in 1936; the wool export doubled in amount during the latter period. The production of cattle and dairy produce also rapidly expanded, again particularly after 1914.

All types of farming have been fostered by Government action. The State has made it possible for European farmers to acquire land on easy terms. It has provided special credit facilities through a State Land Bank. It has assisted irrigation, fencing, and labourers' housing; given preferential rates on state-owned railways; set up experimental farms and research institutions; provided free advice on technical questions, free vaccines and veterinary services. Expenditure has been undertaken on a generous scale for drought relief, relief from indebtedness, and locust destruction.[2] Since the depression of 1929–32 successive governments have taken more direct measures to maintain farm production. Subsidies on exports, first from the General Exchequer and subsequently financed by special boards, have been employed as an expedient designed to compensate farmers for lower external prices. Internal prices have been maintained by protection, by the prohibition of importation and by compulsory export.[3] Farm products are being increasingly withdrawn from the free play of market forces and subjected to a growing network of control boards with wide and arbitrary powers designed to enable them to regulate prices, production and marketing.[4]

[1] *Official Year Book*, No. 11, 1928–9, pp. 372, 778, 779. *Agricultural Census No. 3, 1920*, U.G. 12, 1921, p. 4, and No. 17, 1936–7, U.G. No. 18, 1939, p. 8.
[2] cf. E. Davis, 'Some Aspects of the Marketing of Farm Products in South Africa,' *The South African Journal of Economics*, Vol. I, No. 2, June 1933, p. 167. L. C. A. and C. M. Knowles, *Economic Development of the Overseas Empire*, Vol. III, Chap. VIII. H. M. Robertson, 'Schütz der Landwirtschaft in Südafrika', *Weltwirtschaftliches Archiv.*, Nov. 1935. E. H. D. Arndt, 'Die Landboukrediet en Landbouskuldvraagstuk, *The South African Journal of Economics*, Vol. I, No. 2, June 1933. *Annual Reports of the Irrigation Commission. Settlers' Relief Commission*, 1934, U.G. 25, 1935. *Farming in South Africa, passim*. This publication is a monthly journal issued by the Department of Agriculture. Since 1926 the annual reports of the Secretary for Agriculture have been published in it.
[3] J. G. Van der Horst, 'Two Conferences', *The South African Journal of Economics*, Vol. I, No. 1, March 1933. S. C. Richards, 'Subsidies, Quotas, Tariffs, and the Excess Cost of Agriculture in South Africa.' *The South African Journal of Economics*, Vol. III, No. 3, September 1935.
[4] S. C. Richards, 'The "New Despotism" in Agriculture,' *The South African*

All these measures have reacted on the demand for farm labour which has been stimulated since the beginning of the century by the many official measures diverting national resources to farming, and maintained during the last ten years by the additional official attempts to assist farmers to keep up the prices and production of their products.

B. TERMS AND CONDITIONS OF EMPLOYMENT

Evidence is scant concerning the response of wages and other conditions of employment to the rise in the demand for farm labour.[1] Throughout the country, farm-wages are largely paid in kind. In some districts, notably in the northern and eastern Transvaal, no cash wages are paid to the 'labour tenants' who do most of the farm work in return for the right to graze cattle and cultivate fields. Even elsewhere such scattered investigations as have been made, indicate that cash wages constitute a relatively small part of the real wages of Native farm labourers. This applies even where, as in the greater part of the Orange Free State and the eastern Cape Province, the bulk of the Native labour force consists of full-time permanent employees. Thus officials of the Department of Agriculture found that the average cash wages on 199 maize farms in the north-eastern Free State were £5 16s. per year of three hundred working days, approximately 9s. 6d. per month. This was estimated to constitute 28 per cent of the total wage.[2] In the eastern Cape Province Mrs. Haines found the average cash wage on ten farms on which fifty-six heads of families were employed to be 13s. 10d. per month; the modal cash wage was 10s. and represented 36 per cent of the estimated total wage.[3] Other investigations in these areas give similar accounts of cash wages.[4]

Journal of Economics, Vol. IV, No. 4, December 1936. 'Economists' Protest: The Dairy Produce and Maize Marketing Schemes', *The South African Journal of Economics*, Vo. VI, No. 1, March 1938. 'Economists' Protest: Marketing Act, 1937, Scheme relating to Marketing of Wheat', *The South African Journal of Economics*, Vol. VI, No. 2, June 1938. 'Planning and Control in Agriculture—(1) Planned Agriculture in South Africa: (P. R. Viljoen); (2) A Defence of Control in the Marketing of Agricultural Products (J. R. McLoughlin); (3) A Reply (Professor S. C. Richards).' *The South African Journal of Economics*, Vol. VI, No. 3, September 1938.

[1] The main sources of information, to which general reference should be made, are indicated in later footnotes to this section, which refer only to specific points.

[2] *Native Economic Commission*, 1930–32, op. cit. annexure 24, VIII.

[3] E. S. Haines, 'The Economic Status of the Cape Province Farm Native,' *The South African Journal of Economics*, Vol. III, No. 1, March 1936, p. 61.

[4] cf. M. Hunter, *Reaction to Conquest*, p. 509; *Farm Labour in the Orange Free State* (April 1939), South African Institute of Race Relations. Monograph No. 2, pp. 17, 18. *Native Farm Labour Committee*, 1937–9, paras. 174, 189.

Wages in kind usually consist chiefly of rations, use of arable land, and grazing rights. It is the general practice to supply rations to labourers working on farms, although on some farms in the Transvaal labour tenants do not get rations even while they are working for the landowner. The usual ration per month is about 100 lb. (half a bag) of mealie meal, or some substitute. If more than one member of a family is working the amount is increased. Meat, milk, and vegetables may be supplied spasmodically but they do not usually form a part of the regular ration. In the Cape Province, meat is fairly frequently supplied from time to time, for example monthly. It is seldom given as often as weekly.

The amount of land allotted to Native labourers for growing crops varies according to the locality and the type of farming carried on. From sample investigations which have been made it appears to be least in the eastern Cape Province, where it is often less than a morgen, and greatest in parts of the Transvaal, where as much as five or even seven morgen may be cultivated. In the Orange Free State, the usual amount allotted to the head of a household is two or three morgen. On grain farms the farmer frequently ploughs and sows the land, leaving only the cleaning and reaping to the labourer and his family.

The number of stock which labourers are allowed to graze also varies. In some cases no grazing is allowed while in others as many as twenty head of stock may be permitted. It is common, however, for the number to be restricted to five or six per family.[1]

Where full-time labourers are resident on farms, members of their families are usually expected to work for the farmer, especially in busy seasons. Where several members of a family are at work additional cash wages are paid and rations supplied. When they are employed as domestic servants cash wages are commonly from 5s. to 12s. 6d. per month for an adult woman, and cooked food is supplied of a more varied kind than the usual ration of mealie-meal. There are also opportunities for young boys and girls to earn cash wages of 4s. or 5s. per month, or in the case of older boys, 7s. 6d., and rations.

Estimates concerning the value of real wages on farms differ. Officials of the Department of Agriculture have tended to place a higher value on payments in kind than unofficial investigators. Thus Mrs. Haines estimated at 27s. 6d. per month the average cost to the farmer of the wages of heads of families on the farms she studied. In the same area the Department of Agriculture estimated the average cost at 34s., although, according to the

---

[1] *Native Farm Labour Committee*, 1937–9, paras. 71, 187. Haines, op. cit., p. 62.

Department, the average cash wage was slightly lower. Such discrepancies arise most easily in considering the value to be attached to grazing and cultivation rights. In this connexion one must remember that, in general, sale values of land in South Africa are higher than the figures which would be justified by the returns to be made from farming it. Moreover, Natives are specifically excluded from acquiring land outside 'scheduled' or 'released' areas;[1] so that very different estimates might be reached by valuing these concessions on the basis of what the Native would have to pay for equivalent land and grazing, or by assessing the cost to the farmer of forgoing the use of these small portions of his farm.

The conditions of service of labour tenants vary even more widely than those of permanent labourers resident on farms; three, four, six, or even nine months' service a year may be required. In the northern and eastern Transvaal ninety days' service has been the common period of work required; this service might be required continuously or it might take the form of two days' service a week. In Natal the most common requirement has been six months continuous service during which a cash wage of from five to fifteen shillings per month is usually paid.

The services of the kraal head are not always demanded if he has grown-up sons to work in his place; sometimes, especially at harvest time, the services of the whole family may be required free; sometimes the services of the women and children are required and are paid for by small cash wages; while sometimes the women and children are not employed by the owner of the land.[2]

In return for these services labour tenants cultivate the land allotted to them and graze cattle. The system has been retained in those districts in which farming is least intensive, namely the northern and eastern Transvaal and the upper districts of Natal, where it is usual for labour tenants to plough and plant their own fields.

Sometimes, for example, on irrigation settlements, Native labourers are employed casually or by the month. In this case cash wages are higher. Rations are similar to those supplied to resident permanent workers. These wages vary according to the nature of the work, the skill of the worker, and the locality. In the Transvaal a shilling a day is a common wage for this type of work. In the neighbourhood of industrial areas and at harvest and shearing time higher wages may be paid.

[1] See below, p. 291 et seq.
[2] *Inter-Departmental Committee on the Labour Resources of the Union*, 1930, para. 61; cf. Evidence from Pietersburg, Letaba, Rustenburg, quoted in the Addendum by Mr. Lucas to the *Native Economic Commission*, 1930–32, paras. 170, 174, and 177.

On the sugar estates in the coastal belt of Natal £2 for thirty shifts (thirty days worked) or 1s. 4d. per shift is a usual wage.[1] In Zululand wages are lower, 30s. or 35s. being paid for thirty shifts. Labourers are accommodated in compounds and cooked rations are provided. The standard of accommodation, cleanliness and food varies on different estates, but it is generally below that provided on the gold-mines.

On farms full-time workers and labour tenants usually erect their own huts from whatever materials are available. Poles, thatching grass, sods, or clay are used and their huts are usually made in one of the traditional Native styles. Occasionally a farmer assists in the provision of other materials such as doors and window frames. Although substantial dwellings may be erected, many farm-labourers live in flimsy huts or mere hovels. They frequently complain that insufficient time is allowed them for the construction of their huts. Farmers do not usually make provision for housing casual and seasonal workers who normally either stay with the permanent labourers, or find what other shelter they can.[2]

It is frequently stated that real wages on farms compare favourably with those in towns when account is taken of payments in kind and the higher cost of housing, transport, and some foodstuffs in towns.[3] In the case of the most highly paid farm workers this is probably true. On the whole, however, there is little doubt that the money value of the wages (in cash and kind) of farm-labourers is lower than that of the wages of workers in other occupations. According to estimates made by the Native Farm Labour Committee the money value of the income of Native *families* in favourable circumstances on farms is considerably (from £1 to £2 per month) below the average cash wage per *labourer* in manufacturing industry in the principal industrial areas.[4]

Moreover hours of work on farms are long and irregular in comparison with those in towns. Farm life also compares unfavourably as regards opportunities for education, recreation, and buying in small quantities even farm products like meat.

On the other hand, farm work is a means of continuing to live on land which may have been occupied for generations by the family's ancestors. It is a means of obtaining grazing for highly

---

[1] A shift is a whole day's work.
[2] *Native Farm Labour Committee*, 1937–9, paras. 235–44.
[3] cf. *Native Economic Commission*, 1930–32, para. 270. 'Generally speaking, the opinion of qualified witnesses is that in value, the privileges of a Native labour tenant are worth more to him than the wages he would normally receive in town.'
[4] *Native Farm Labour Committee*, 1937–9, paras. 147, 176, 191, 208.

prized cattle. It also provides more opportunities for the women and children to supplement the family income. It may provide greater security. For example, many farmers assist their labourers when they fall ill or if their crops fail. But against this must be set the insecurity which arises under the Native Service Contract Act (1932). In terms of this Act the whole family is liable to eviction if one member fails to render the service required. Thus if a young son who is liable to work on a farm goes off to work elsewhere, the livelihood of the whole family is jeopardized. In the case of the labour tenants the head of a family may be independent if he has sons to work for him or when he has finished his period of service. This is very highly valued and may outweigh the persistence of conditions which are miserable in other respects.

The attractions of farm work have much less weight with the younger Natives on farms. Their position compares very unfavourably with that of the young urban worker. Restrictions on grazing prevent them from accumulating stock, while they are expected to work in return for payment in kind made, not to themselves, but to the family, or for much lower cash wages than they could obtain in towns. Consequently there is a tendency for young farm Natives to migrate and there are many complaints that they evade their obligations to the farmers on whose land their parents live.

Evidence as to the trend of the wages of farm-labourers is conflicting. In parts of the eastern Cape Province where wages have long been paid partly in cash and partly in kind, the cash wages of permanent workers appear to have changed little during the last fifty years. In other parts of the country cash wages have superseded payment in stock, which adds to the difficulty of making comparisons. In some districts, for example in the Orange Free State, payment in kind is said to have been reduced. Grazing rights are more restricted than formerly and, where rations are provided, milk is now said to be more rarely supplied.

The latter reduction is probably due to increased opportunities for marketing fresh milk. Where cream or butter is produced on farms the separated milk is frequently available for labourers.[1]

Although the actual amount of grazing allowed may have fallen, it does not follow that its value to the labourer is less, for cattle remain the chief investment of the rural Native and restrictions on his right to own or rent land have made grazing rights more valuable.

[1] *Farm Labour in the Orange Free State*, op. cit., p. 18. *Native Farm Labour Committee*, 1937–9, para. 226.

C. THE SUPPLY OF NATIVE LABOUR

The great majority of farm-labourers are Natives. Throughout the country very few Europeans are employed as farm-labourers, although the European owner of a farm and his sons may work alongside their Cape Coloured or Native employees. In the western Cape Province, Cape Coloured labourers form the bulk of the labour force, but for the province as a whole Native farm workers outnumber Coloured. In Natal some Indians are engaged in farming, but they number only seventeen thousand as compared with the hundred and fifty-five thousand Native workers on farms. In the Transvaal and the Orange Free State the number of non-Native farm labourers is negligible.[1]

Many Natives employed by farmers are not, however, full-time employees. They work for the farmer for a part of the year, and during the remainder they cultivate their fields, tend their cattle, or seek work elsewhere. The seasonal nature of much of the work, and the system of maintaining a reservoir of labour living on the land but not employed all the year round, makes it difficult to distinguish between the farm labourer and the independent cultivator. Consequently reliable statistics are not available of the extent of employment in farming. In other industries work is more continuous so that although migratory labourers may be employed, each for a few months at a time, some idea of the relative volume of employment can be obtained.

A further difficulty in the collection of statistics has been lack of precision in the use of the term 'squatter.' It may be used to describe tenants giving no service, labour tenants, or even full-time regular workers receiving part of their wages in the form of land for cultivation and grazing rights. Evasion of the legislation which taxes cash tenancy or makes it illegal also leads to tenants who are not genuinely employed, even for a part of the year, being described as labour tenants.[2] Again, neither European farmers nor Native peasants can be relied upon to furnish accurate returns. The European, who is usually called upon to supply particulars concerning the Natives who live on his land, often does not have sufficient knowledge to supply accurate information and does not regard accuracy as important; while the Native frequently mistrusts the purposes for which it is required and eludes enumeration. For all these reasons it is difficult to judge changes in the supply of farm labour.

According to official returns the number of Native farm

[1] Agricultural Census, No. 17, U.G. 18, 1939, p. 19, Table 3.
[2] cf. *Native Economic Commission*, 1930–32. Addendum by Mr. Lucas, para. 87; E. S. Haines, 'The Economic Status of the Cape Province Farm Native,' *The South African Journal of Economics*, Vol III, No. 1, March 1935, p. 59.

labourers has increased from 368,000 (301,000 male and 67,000 female) in 1921, to 476,000 (361,000 male and 115,000 female) in 1930, and to 658,000 (464,000 male and 194,000 female) in 1937.[1] The figures are not, however, comparable. For 1930 they include those Natives 'regularly employed in farming operations' (including labour tenants) who were actually working at the end of August. For 1937 they include those reported to have been 'regularly employed' during the year September 1936 to August 1937. All labour-tenants were regarded as 'regularly employed', but casual labourers such as shearers and fruit-packers were excluded. These latter figures, therefore, do not indicate either the average number of farm workers nor the actual number employed at the date of the agricultural census.

The greater part of the farm labour supply is drawn from Natives living more or less permanently on the farms on which they work. In the year 1936–7 nearly 588,000, or over 89 per cent of the 658,000 'regular' farm workers were resident on the farms on which they were employed. To supplement this supply, migratory labourers are employed. Labour migration takes various forms and much of it is seasonal. In the Transvaal, the old system of having two farms (one of the Highveld and one on the Lowveld, for winter grazing and shooting), has led in some cases to farmers using farms in the Lowveld as reservoirs of labour, labour tenants on such farms being required to render their service on another farm belonging to the same owner.[2] In Zululand the same practice is common among sugar planters. There is also considerable voluntary migration, particularly of seasonal labour, to farms which are near Native territories. Thus farmers in the Orange Free State and eastern Cape Province draw seasonal labour from Basutoland and the Transkeian Territories. The sugar industry of Natal is largely dependent on recruited seasonal labour. Its seasonal demands extend over about eight months. roughly from February to September. At the height of the harvest season between forty and fifty thousand[3] Natives are employed; about one-third are usually recruited,[4] the bulk of the recruits coming from the Transkeian Territories. It has been found that it is only through recruiting that a dependable supply of labour can be obtained.[5] Labour is usually recruited

[1] *Third Census of the Population of the Union of South Africa* (1921), op. cit., Table 24, p. 143; *Agricultural Census* No. 13, 1929–30, U.G. 12, 1932, p. 94, Table 17; *Agricultural Census*, No. 17, U.G. 18, 1939, p. 19, Table 3.

[2] *Inter-Departmental Committee on Labour Resources*, 1930, paras. 103–5.

[3] *Official Year Book*, 1938, No. 19, p. 777.

[4] *Native Economic Commission*, 1930–32, op. cit., para. 877.

[5] A witness told the Native Economic Commission that, when the greater part of his labour force had been voluntary, an outbreak of malaria together with exceptionally early rains, which had made the Natives return home to

for 180 shifts. Consequently, as on the gold-mines, recruiting can be used to counteract seasonal fluctuations in supply. Tobacco plantations, too, have a seasonal demand for labour, some of which is met by labour migration; for example, tobacco plantations in the western Transvaal attract seasonal labourers from the Bechuanaland Protectorate.

Work on farms often serves as a stepping-stone to the industrial centres. Natives from within the Union, from the British Protectorates and from farther afield take service on farms on their way to seek employment in the towns. Natives from the Transkeian Territories and Basutoland often take employment on Free State farms on the way to the mines and industries in the Transvaal. Transvaal farmers also employ (in addition to their labour tenants) Natives from Bechuanaland Protectorate, from Portuguese East Africa, from Central Africa[1] and Rhodesia, some of whom are making their way to the industrial centres, while some remain content with farm work.

In spite of the fact that the importation of Portuguese Native labour has been desired by farmers as well as mining companies,[2] the Mozambique Convention of 1928 attempted to restrict the inflow of Portuguese labour. It confined the employment, without special sanction, of Portuguese Natives to gold- and coal-mining in the Transvaal. Nevertheless they continued to be employed, especially on farms and plantations in the eastern Transvaal and Zululand, and little attempt was made to prevent it, though both the Union and Portuguese authorities knew what was taking place.[3]

This restriction was relaxed in 1934 when the Mozambique Convention was revised. One of the reasons for the relaxation of the prohibition upon the employment of Portuguese labour outside the Transvaal mining industry was to enable the sugar planters in Zululand to use this labour, which is 'malaria-tolerant'. The seriousness and spread of malaria in the sugar areas of Zululand had led to a decline in the supply of labourers from the Transkei and for the same reason the Basutoland Administration prohibited recruiting for the sugar industry.

plough, had resulted in an acute shortage of labour in September. He had determined that henceforth he would recruit half his labour force. *Native Economic Commission*, 1930–32. Typescript of evidence, p. 6206.

[1] It was estimated that in 1932 there were 20,000 Nyasaland Natives in the Union and 90 per cent of the Natives leaving Nyasaland went on foot as they had no money for railway fares. *Report of Committee on Emigrant Labour*—Nyasaland, 1935, paras. 18, 54.

[2] cf. *Report of Department of Native Affairs*, 1922–6, U.G. 14, 1927, p. 14.

[3] *Departmental Committee on Labour in Zululand, Transkei*, etc., 1935, para. 25. cf. *Report of Transvaal Chamber of Mines* for 1930, p. 16: 'A considerable number of "clandestine" natives are still entering the Union from Mozambique.'

In spite of the large and apparently constantly increasing number of Natives employed on farms there have been continual complaints of 'shortage' of Native labourers.[1] This implies that at the prevailing rates of wages it would pay farmers to employ more labourers and, as in the case of the gold-mining industry, it suggests that competition has been prevented from driving wage-rates up to the point at which demand and supply are in equilibrium.

In farming, wage-rates below the competitive level are not enforced by formal agreement. Farmers are not highly organized for collective bargaining. Nevertheless there appears to be a measure of tacit monopsony (monopolistic buying) in the market for farm labour. Farmers themselves report that they have refrained from offering better terms lest their action should arouse the displeasure of their neighbours.[2]

Supply conditions are particularly favourable to the monopsonistic buyer, for much of the labour employed on farms is extremely immobile. Farm-labourers are confronted with the choice between accepting the terms offered, and they may bind the whole family, or embarking on a costly and uncertain move.

The mobility of labour is further curtailed by pass laws and other restrictions on movement, and by the limited alternative avenues of employment open to Natives.

Nevertheless there is a widespread belief that there has been a considerable movement of Native labour away from farms. Statistics of the number of farm-labourers do not bear this out, but they cannot be relied upon, and the number of Natives in urban areas has most certainly increased. Farmers, particularly in the Orange Free State, complain that able-bodied Natives have left the farms and that only very young boys and old men are available for farm work. In this province, a very severe drought in 1933 led to many labourers leaving farms, which were then unable to support them, and some farmers have been unable to attract labourers back.

It may be significant that the 'shortage' of farm labour is reported to be most acute in the Orange Free State where, as we shall see in the next section, legislation has been most successful

---

[1] *Transvaal Labour Commission* [Cd. 1896], 1904, Majority Report, paras. 23, 39; *South African Native Affairs Commission*, 1903–1905, para. 382; *Inter-Departmental Committee on the Labour Resources of the Union*, 1930, paras. 14–21; *Native Farm Labour Committee*, 1937–9, paras. 16–29.

[2] 'Witnesses disclosed wide divergences of treatment in almost every respect dealing with their labour, even on adjoining farms in the same district. Each employer seems to take his own line with the restraining influence that he fears that if he gives terms which others regard as too liberal he may suffer in popularity.' *Native Farm Labour Committee*, op. cit., para. 462.

in altering the status of the rural population from peasant farmers to farm labourers.

D. OFFICIAL ATTEMPTS TO INCREASE THE SUPPLY OF NATIVE LABOUR

Complaints of 'shortage' of farm labour have led to various measures to increase the supply. Despite the recommendation of the Cape Labour Commission in 1894, that employers could do more by improving conditions of work and their relation with farm workers than anything the Government could carry out;[1] official measures have been directed more to restricting the opportunities and movements of Native labourers than to encouraging farmers to offer more attractive terms and conditions of service.

In particular, attempts have been made to restrict the right of Natives to buy or rent land, thereby reducing their alternative opportunities of making a living. Latterly attempts have also been made to regulate the system of labour tenancy. Labour tenants are not continuously employed, so efforts have been made to increase the supply of labour by restricting the number allowed upon any one farm and by extending the period for which they must work.

On the other hand, at least for the time being, Native farm-labourers have lost their privileged position as taxpayers. In 1925 Native taxation in the different provinces was made uniform and differential taxation in the Cape Province and the Transvaal between farm labourers and other Natives came to an end. This marked the abandonment of attempts to make work on farms more attractive and to stem the drift away from them by exempting farm labourers from direct taxation.

Restrictions on the right of Natives to buy or rent land were no innovation. In the Orange Free State, with the exception of the Thaba Nchu area, Natives had never been allowed to own land. In the Transvaal their right to buy land individually had been in doubt until 1905 when it was established by the courts.[2] In the Cape Province and Natal they were free to buy land. In both these provinces, however, as also in the Orange Free State and the Transvaal, their right to occupy European-owned land was limited by law, but it had proved impossible to enforce these laws.

When discussing the scarcity of farm labour, the South African Native Affairs Commission of 1903–5 recommended the strict

[1] cf. above, p. 147.
[2] *Ex parte* Tsewu 1905. Transvaal Supreme Court 130. Under the Republican government Natives had not been permitted to own land personally, but they had been permitted to purchase it, ownership being vested in a European official in trust for the purchaser.

enforcement of the laws designed to check 'squatting' (the renting of land by Natives), as a means of assisting farmers to obtain labour.

In 1909 the Cape Colony followed up this advice, and the Location Act was once more amended. Under the new Act no one was to establish a private location without a licence. A fee of ten shillings per annum was payable for every 'labour tenant' and one of two pounds per annum for 'ordinary tenants'.[1] Moreover, in the case of 'ordinary tenants' the consent of the Divisional Council and the Governor-General had to be obtained before a licence was issued. The Act did not apply to Natives who were the sole owners of property, the lessees of property held under separate title, or the lessees of portions of farms for which an annual rent of not less than thirty-six pounds was paid.

It was intended to discourage the renting of land to small-scale cultivators, and has apparently been successful, for between 1907 and 1931 the number of private locations in the Cape Province fell from 1,100, with a population of over 35,000, to 138, with a population of under 7,000.[2] This fall may, however, have been due, at least in part, to the increased opportunities open to European farmers of using their land for other purposes, and to the expansion of opportunities for Natives to make a living in other occupations.

In 1913, three years after the Union had been formed, the Central Government passed a much more general measure: the Natives' Land Act. It was destined to have important reactions on the market for labour. It prohibited a Native from acquiring,[3] whether by purchase or hire, from a person other than a Native, any land outside areas scheduled in the Act as Native areas. Within the scheduled areas non-Natives were similarly prevented from acquiring land. The continuation or renewal of existing arrangements regarding the leasing or hiring of land was permitted under the Act, except in the Orange Free State, where the renting of land by Natives, whether for cash or on the share-cropping system, became illegal.[4]

The Act did not have the effect of confining the rural Native population to the scheduled areas, nor was this intended. It was, indeed, specifically laid down that nothing in this or any other Act was to be construed as 'restricting the number of Natives

---

[1] A 'labour tenant' was defined as any Native male adult resident in a private location and 'bona fide required by the location proprietor for the due working of his private property', but not necessarily continuously employed. 'Ordinary tenants' were tenants who were not labour tenants or servants.

[2] H. Rogers, Native Administration in the Union of South Africa, p. 154.

[3] Without the approval of the Governor-General.

[4] Natives' Land Act., 1913, Sections 7 and 8.

who, as farm-labourers, may reside on any farm in the Transvaal'.[1] A farm-labourer was defined as a Native residing on a farm and *bona fide*, but not necessarily continuously, employed for at least ninety days service per calendar year.[2]

Although some displacement of population resulted, the general effect of the prohibition on renting land in the Orange Free State was to cause Native tenants to become, in name at least, labourers and labour tenants. In this province particularly, the Act caused great hardship to Native tenants, for they had either to agree to work on the terms offered by their landlords or remove themselves and their cattle elsewhere.[3] Moreover, land was hard to come by, as most Native tenants had few resources beyond their stock. The scheduled areas in which Natives might acquire land were already very fully occupied,[4] and no provision was made for enabling evicted tenants to acquire land either by lease or purchase. Despite this Act, there was no net reduction in the rural Native population even of the Orange Free State. On the contrary, between 1911 and 1921 the rural non-European (mostly Native) population of this province increased by 24·44 per cent.[5]

In the Transvaal and Natal,[6] new arrangements for leasing or renting land became illegal, but the renewal of existing arrangements was permitted. This restriction tended to tie tenants to their landlords. The renting of land to Natives went on, and new leases were also entered into despite their illegality, for it continued to be the most profitable use to which much land could be put,[7] and the prohibition on renting land in the Orange Free State, and on new leases in the Transvaal and Natal, was difficult to enforce where there was collusion between landlord and tenant. Consequently in the Transvaal and Natal this provision did not have much effect on the supply of Native labour, except in so far as it reduced the mobility of Native tenants.

[1] Ibid., Section 6.   [2] Ibid., Section 10.
[3] cf. MacMillan, *Complex South Africa*, p. 126. S. T. Plaatje, *Native Life in South Africa, passim*.
Giving evidence to the Select Committee on Native Bills Sir Herbert Sloley said: 'When I was in Basutoland in 1913 when the Land Act came into operation, I saw myself that many squatters were driven with their families, and their belongings and stock, across the Border. They were removed from the Free State and trekked into Basutoland, which was rather a burden on an already overcrowded territory. These people's little homes were broken up, and it was rather a pathetic sight to see them trekking with their possessions.' *Select Committee on Native Bills*, S.C. 10, 1927, p. 311.
[4] *Natives' Land Commission, Beaumont Minute*, U.G. 25, 1913, para. 95.
[5] The actual increase was from 301,757 to 365,494. *Report of the Third Census*, U.G. 37, 1924, p. 47. Table XXVI.
[6] In 1917 the restrictions imposed by the Natives' Land Act were found to be inapplicable to the Cape. Thomson and Stilwell *versus* Kama. Appellate Division of the Supreme Court.
[7] *Select Committee on Native Bills*, 1927, op. cit. p. 118. Evidence Transvaal Land Owners' Association.

In 1932, to meet evasion of the Natives' Land Act, the onus of proof that the landowner was an actual party to the occupation of his land by Natives was transferred from the Crown. The landowner is now presumed to be a party to an agreement or transaction unless the contrary is proved.[1]

Additional steps have since been taken to limit the right of Natives to occupy land owned by Europeans. The policy of segregation has been carried several stages farther by the National-ist-Labour Coalition which came into power in 1924 and the Nationalist–South-African-Party Coalition of 1933. In 1926 the Prime Minister, General Hertzog, introduced legislation for this purpose which was finally passed in an amended form in 1936.

Meanwhile, in 1932, the Native Service Contract Act was passed, one of its objects being to reduce the number of Native peasant farmers occupying land owned by Europeans in the Transvaal and Natal.[2] To achieve this a tax of five pounds per annum for every able-bodied adult male Native (other than a chief, headman, minister, evangelist, or marriage officer or teacher) was to be levied in areas which were to be proclaimed. Natives giving service for a prescribed period of not less than three months, viz. labour tenants, were not subject to the tax.

In practice no districts were proclaimed under this Act, but the principle of levying prohibitive taxation has been embodied in the Native Land and Trust Act passed in 1936. The latter Act gave effect to the 1913 promise that the Union would be finally divided into areas in which Natives and non-Natives respectively would be allowed to acquire land. It also followed up the restrictions imposed by the 1913 Act, and earlier measures, in regard to the occupation by Natives of land outside areas reserved for Native occupation. Like them, it was designed to reduce the number of Native peasants living on European-owned land.

Chapter IV of the Act, which comes into force upon proclama-tion by the Governor-General, is applicable to European areas or European-held land in 'released areas', and can be applied piecemeal both as to areas and the provisions to be applied. According to it a Native may not reside on proclaimed land unless he is the registered owner, a servant of the owner, registered as

---

[1] Native Service Contract Act, No. 24 of 1932.

[2] Introducing the 2nd reading of the Act the Minister of Justice (Mr. Pirow) said the Act was designed 'to put an end as far as possible to the position which is more and more deeply eating like a cancer both into the Transvaal and Natal, viz. native farming, as it is called by the public. Large land companies, and also individual owners, very often establish private native locations on their lands in conflict with the law and by evading the law, and very often even in terms of the law. . . .' *Hansard*, 4 February, 1932, col. 641.

a labour tenant, registered as a squatter, or otherwise exempted from the prohibitions contained in the chapter.

To check cash tenancy and share-farming, a progressive scale of fees, amounting in the tenth and subsequent years to £5 per annum for each 'squatter', is to be levied on European land-holders in proclaimed areas. Moreover, the number of labour tenants permitted on any farm may be limited by Labour Tenant Control Boards[1] to what they consider the 'requirements' of the farmer. For determining this number, it is to be assumed that every labour tenant renders at least six months' service a year, and that, unless otherwise proved, five labour tenants are sufficient for any one farm.[2] Displaced tenants will have to become full-time servants or labour tenants (if permitted by the Control Board), or leave the area.

In contrast to the Natives Land Act of 1913, the Act makes some provision for displaced Natives, for it lays down that the authorities must 'make such provision as may be necessary and adequate in the opinion of the Minister' for accommodating them in a scheduled Native area or a released area.[3] This condition is likely to delay the general application of this chapter of the Act.

It has been applied to the Leydenburg District of the Transvaal, where one hundred and eighty days (which may be spread over a longer period than six months) has been proclaimed as the minimum period of service for labour tenants.[4] In this district ninety days has been the usual period and the effect of the application of this provision of the Act was to confront labour tenants with the choice between supplying twice as much labour as previously or removing elsewhere.[5]

A considerable movement of Natives from this district immediately took place, with the result that farmers there became alarmed and asked for these provisions to be extended to the whole Transvaal, presumably to prevent Natives from obtaining better terms elsewhere. Meanwhile the difficulty experienced by the authorities in fulfilling their obligation to accommodate displaced tenants in the Native areas led to the suspension of the penal sanction for the enforcement of the measure. [6]

The attempt to regulate the system of labour tenancy and to

[1] These boards are to consist of the Secretary for Native Affairs and two landowners engaged in farming in the district. In the Cape Province Divisional Councils and, where no Divisional Council exists, the magistrate, are to perform the functions of these Boards.
[2] The Native Land and Trust Act, 1936, Sections 29, 30.
[3] Ibid., Section 38.
[4] Proclamation No. 264 dated 14 December 1937. Government Notice 196, 24 December 1937. Government Notice No. 342, 4 March 1938.
[5] J. D. Rheinallt Jones, *Memorandum*, Institute of Race Relations.
[6] *Race Relations News*, No. 5, November 1938, p. 3.

increase the period of labour service arises from a widespread belief that under the system labour is 'wastefully distributed' and land is not used to the greatest advantage. In parts of the country where farming has become more intensive the system has given place to one of full-time labourers. The fact that it continues in some areas shows that despite its disadvantages it still suits some farmers and some Natives. On the one hand, where farmers hold large tracts of undeveloped land it is often most convenient for them to pay labour in land and grazing rights. Labour tenants, on the other hand, are able to raise crops, pasture their cattle, and enjoy a measure of independence. Farmers would not continue to maintain labour tenants if they considered that they could obtain labour more cheaply in other ways. Similarly, Natives would move elsewhere if they knew of preferable alternatives. Except in so far as labour tenancy continues because of ignorance of alternative opportunities which would be broken down by its prohibition, its compulsory abolition is not in the interests of many farmers and Natives.

Nevertheless the system has serious drawbacks. Farmers complain that labour tenants are inefficient and take no interest in their work. This is not surprising, for ability and enterprise are not specially rewarded. There is no incentive to labour tenants to improve their position, for there is little possibility of earning higher wages, or of accumulating capital to buy or rent land and establish themselves as independent farmers. The remedy for inefficient service and 'wasteful' use of land and labour is to be found in devising adequate incentives and increasing opportunities rather than in limiting them and making conditions of service more onerous.

Efforts have also been made to prevent farm Natives from seeking work on the mines or in towns. We have seen that, in terms of the Natives (Urban Areas) Act and its amendments, Natives have been legally prohibited from freely seeking work in the great majority of urban areas in the Union. There is no doubt that this provision is in part intended to increase the supply of labour to farmers. Its success depends upon the possibility of enforcing it.

The movements of Natives are controlled under pass laws, which vary in stringency in the different provinces. In the Transvaal and the Orange Free State all Natives travelling outside proclaimed Native areas are required to carry passes issued by authorized persons for periods not longer than thirty days. These passes have to indicate the purpose for which they are issued and the destination of the bearer. In Natal and in the Transkeian Territories Natives are officially required to obtain passes on entry or before departure. In practice, however, in these territories the administration of the pass law has been lax. In the rest of the Cape Province Natives have not been required to carry passes. Under the Natives (Urban Areas) Act, however, they are required to obtain permits before entering towns which are closed in terms of the Act, and within urban areas they are required to produce on demand copies of their contracts of service with their employers.

In Natal and the Transvaal, additional steps have been taken to prevent labour tenants from breaking their contracts and seeking work elsewhere. Where, as is frequent in the Transvaal, labour tenants receive no cash wages, they or their dependants have to go elsewhere to earn the money required for taxes, for clothing, for the food they buy to supplement their crops, and perhaps for school fees. Increasing opportunities for employment, combined with growing wants, lead them to find work in towns, and they may in consequence fail to provide the farm service required of them. Young Natives, in particular, for whom labour tenancy has few attractions, frequently find their way to towns, where they obtain cash wages, independence, and the excitements of town life.

It must be remembered that the terms on which labour tenants occupy land are often extremely vague and uncertain. Some employers do not explain their conditions of employment, while very few make written contracts. To remedy this situation and to prevent the evasion of contracts, the Native Service Contract Act (1932) has made it an offence to employ a male Native domiciled outside a location in the Transvaal or Natal, unless he produces a labour contract between himself and the owner of the land on which he is domiciled, or a signed statement that he is not obliged to render any service during the period in question. Further, passes to seek work in towns may not be issued to any Native who does not produce permission from the landowner on whose land he resides.

In order to counteract the growing tendency for young Natives to evade labour obligations incurred on their behalf by their parents or guardians, the employment of Natives under eighteen is forbidden without the written consent of the guardian, and in addition, in the case of male Natives, the consent of the owner of the land on which the guardian is living. Authority is also given to the guardian of any Native, male or female, on his or her behalf to enter into a labour service contract with the owner of the land on which the guardian is domiciled. Penalties for breaches of the masters and servants laws, which apply to labour tenants, have also been increased, and servants who appear to be not more than eighteen years old are now liable to be sentenced to be whipped for offences under them.

The Act also makes provision for the registration, at the option of either party, of labour service and other contracts. Little use has yet been made of this provision. Labour contracts, whether oral or written, are limited to three years.[1] In the absence of any stipulation as to the duration of a contract, it is deemed to have been entered into for one year, subject to the right of either party to terminate it at the end of any year, provided three months' notice has been given. Ignorance of this provision is alleged to have resulted in the service of Natives being prolonged for at least an additional year.

In order to prevent other industries from attracting farm-labourers, attempts have also been made to restrict their competition. To this end, in many farming areas the recruiting of labourers, either for the mines or for Government undertakings, is not permitted. Such restrictions tend to preserve the immobility of labour which recruiting is designed to overcome. Immobility is one of the most important conditions making possible the exploitation of labour, in the sense of enabling employers to pay a wage below the potential value of the worker. The Committee on Labour Resources (1930) drew attention to this effect of restrictions on recruiting. It reported:

> There is always a danger that the conservation of labour for the benefit of local employers may tend to depress wages unfairly, and affect conditions of employment unfavourably.[2]

Official policy has been directed towards conserving and increasing the supply of Native labour to farmers rather than towards developing the mobility of labour and assisting it to those occupations in which its productivity and value are greatest. This policy ignores the possibility that the productivity of Native labour may be greater in other occupations, and that it may be further diminished if labourers are condemned to occupations which they regard as inferior and their incentive to work is thereby reduced.

---

[1] Under the Masters and Servants Laws contracts exceeding one year had to be in writing. Written contracts might be made for periods up to five years.
[2] *Report of the Inter-Departmental Committee on the Labour Resources of the Union*, 1930, para. 107.

CHAPTER XV

THE SIGNIFICANCE OF THE NATIVE RESERVES

A. EFFECT ON THE SUPPLY OF NATIVE LABOUR

PRIOR to the adoption of the policy of 'segregation' by the Government of the Union of South Africa, the essence of a Native reserve consisted in the protection of Native land-holders. Originally territories occupied by Natives were set aside for their sole use lest they might otherwise sell their land to European settlers or speculators without realizing the consequences of such action, since the Native conception of land rights differed from the European. Thus, the reservation of land was designed to protect Natives from undesirable results of sudden impact with a legal and economic system with which they were unfamiliar. For the same reason the Clay-Martin-Mills Report of the Economic and Wage Commission in 1925 urged that the present reserves should be safeguarded and extended. Their value lay largely in serving as a temporary expedient to ease the transition from primitive to industrial conditions,[1] a transition which these Commissioners regarded as inevitable.[2]

Thus a system of Native reserves does not necessarily imply a desire to maintain separate European and Native economies. It may simply be designed to protect, perhaps temporarily, certain groups. Indeed, in Natal the policy of segregation proposed by the Voortrekker Volksraad had been definitely opposed by the British authorities and the reserves which the latter set aside were deliberately scattered between areas designed for European settlement. It was hoped thereby to hasten the introduction of European civilization among the Natives and to provide the European colonists with an accessible supply of labour, while at the same time guaranteeing a certain degree of security to the Native land-holders. Similarly, in the Cape Colony, in British Kaffraria, European settlers were deliberately placed between the Native reserves in order to break up their cohesion. Moreover, in the Cape Colony there were no legal or administrative obstacles preventing Natives from buying land outside their reserves. It

---

[1] 'The function of the reserve is to ease the transition, a temporary function for, perhaps, a majority of the native population, and to provide a shelter for that slowly diminishing minority who cannot, or will not, be assimilated to the economic system of western civilization.' *Economic and Wage Commission* (1925), U.G. 14, 1926, para. 284.

[2] Ibid., paras. 274-9.

was not until the Native Land and Trust Act was passed in 1936 that Natives in the Cape were prohibited from buying land from Europeans outside the areas set aside for their use. Similarly, in Natal, before 1913, there was no legislation preventing Natives from buying land outside their reserves, although from the beginning of the twentieth century they were in practice prevented from buying Crown land.[1]

In itself, the reservation of land places those Natives who are entitled to use it, and who wish to acquire it, in a privileged position, since the cost of acquiring the right to settle upon it is less than if Europeans were free to compete. In so far as it may withhold land from more productive uses, however, it restricts the national income in the same way as any other measure which diverts resources. The direct effect on the supply of labour is that reserves may provide those Natives entitled to occupy them with land on easier terms than would otherwise be available, and will consequently affect the urgency of their need to seek employment. In these circumstances reserves provide a privileged source of income and thereby give those entitled to use them additional bargaining power when seeking employment. Describing this effect of Native reserves, the Clay-Martin-Mills Report (Economic and Wage Commission, 1925) said:

'Reserves, if adequate, serve two purposes: they provide the most apt safeguard against unjust economic exploitation of the native, and they provide the best means of maintaining his morale in the difficult transition from primitive simplicity to the complexity of modern economic civilization. Adequate reserves protect the native against exploitation, because they give him an alternative to employment on unjust terms. While it is untrue to say that the native, who leaves, for example, the Transkei to work on the mines, seeks employment there as a subsidiary source of income merely, it is the case that the rights he possesses in the land of his tribe enable him to resist an unjust contract and to exact something like the full economic value of his services. The reserve thus meets the same need in the life of the native in European employment as the strong trade union meets in the life of the European wage-earner, and meets it in a manner that is consonant with his traditions, and is, in a way, automatic. In addition, it fulfils the purposes which a reserve of capital fills in the European's life, helping to tide him

[1] For restrictions on the right of Natives to buy land, see above, pp. 290-93. Whenever Natives have had the opportunity to buy land they have availed themselves of it. By 1936 they owned approximately 118,000 morgen in the Cape Province, 180,000 in Natal, 611,000 in the Transvaal, and 55,000 in the Orange Free State, excluding the land in the Native reserves. In both the Transvaal and the Orange Free State much less land had been reserved for the use of Natives than in the Cape Province and Natal. Mrs. Rheinallt Jones, 'Some considerations which arise from the administration of the Native Trust and Land Act, 1936.' *Race Relations*, Vol. V, No. 3, August 1938, p. 53.

over interruptions in employment, whether due to trade depression, sickness, or other causes, and providing support in infancy and old age.'[1]

There is no reason to criticize the general tenor of this judgment. Yet, in South Africa it is often contended that an effect of the reservation of land for the use of Natives is to reduce wage-rates outside the reserves. Thus, for example, when discussing the effect of reserves and the recruiting system on the economic status of the urban Native in a useful and generally admirable survey of *Some Economic Problems of the Bantu in South Africa*, Mr. D. Hobart Houghton has said (p. 36):

> 'The recruiting system has had important economic and social consequences. It does not create a permanent class of town dwellers, but is in effect the temporary transference of reserve Natives to the industrial centres to work for a period of nine months or more, after which they are returned to their homes in the Native territories. These recruited labourers are not wholly dependent upon their possessions in the reserves. They go to the mines to obtain cash to augment their farming income. They can, therefore, accept wages that are less than sufficient to support a man and his family dependent entirely upon their urban earnings.'[2]

And later (p. 57), he says, that in addition to urban and recruited Natives

> 'there are a large number who, while they have come to town of their own accord, still have economic interests in the reserves and intend to return there eventually. These exert a depressing effect upon urban wages in much the same way as recruited labourers, for like them they are not wholly dependent on their urban earnings.'

The contrary is surely the case. The reserves give their inhabitants *additional* bargaining power. In South Africa, as elsewhere, those wage-rates which are not fixed by statutory regulation are determined by bargaining between employers and employees. The presence of reserves tends to withdraw some labourers from the market, especially at the lower wage-rates, by providing them with an alternative source of income, even though it may be a small one, and thus to raise wage-rates. As Professor Plant has written:

> The importance of the reserves (like the 'pin money' of the semi-independent young lady) lies in the additional power which they give to such natives to pick and choose their work instead of being obliged to accept an early offer. The possession of land in a reserve increases rather than reduces the bargaining power of the natives,

[1] Op. cit., para. 281.
[2] *South African Institute of Race Relations.* Monograph Series, No. 1.

THE NATIVE RESERVES

setting a lower limit to the terms which an employer can offer, not
excluding the central, 'monopsonist' labour department of the
Chamber of Mines, despite all the skill displayed by its recruiting
staff. A good harvest in the reserves does *not* enable the mining
companies to cut wages. On the contrary. It is consequently quite
erroneous to argue that the inadequacy of the wages of urbanized
natives is explained by a general readiness of those from the reserves
to accept less than the full cost of subsistence. Wage offers have no
such direct relation to the cost of living in a particular condition,
but are determined by the desire of natives for income, the nature
of their other sources of income, and the attractiveness of other
offers of employment.[1]

It is sometimes alleged that the supply of migratory labour
from the reserves restricts the opportunities for Natives outside
the reserves, and particularly for urban Natives, because, in view
of the supply of migratory labourers, it does not pay employers
to train Native workers or to organize their labour force in such
a way as to make the most effective use of Native labourers. The
remedy often proposed is to restrict the entry of Natives into
urban areas in order to curtail the supply of labour and consequently to force employers to pay more attention to the organization of labour. Official attempts are now being made to put this
policy into operation. Its effect is, however, to raise costs and
therefore to restrict productivity. There is no reason for assuming
that it will stimulate such an increase in efficiency as to reduce
costs below their former level and so enable production to expand.
It leaves untouched the problem of those excluded from the towns.
A population can only become better off by increasing the production of wealth; on this ground the Native Economic Commission
wisely recommended that

> the main attack on the urban wage problem be launched in the
> reserves, where it can at the same time help to solve the much larger
> problem of the augmentation of the National Income.[2]

[1] Arnold Plant, 'An African Survey,' *Economica*, Vol. VI (New Series),
No. 22, May 1939; cf. the statement of the President of the Transvaal Chamber
of Mines on the contrasting effects of good harvests and drought on the supply
of Native labour to the gold-mines: 'The number of British South Africa
Natives engaged during 1939 was rather less than in 1938. Both years were
good from the point of view of native crops, and therefore unfavourable for
recruiting, and the extent to which the output was maintained was distinctly
satisfactory. This was achieved through the great expansion in the scale of
operations of the native recruiting corporation in recent years, and the corporation's persistent propaganda in the native territories.
These factors enabled full advantage to be taken of the drought conditions
which appeared in the Transkei and Basutoland in December 1939, for the first
time for several years. In January and February 1940 the number of B.S.A.
natives obtained reached the record total of 70,172. This compares with
53,150 and 52,857 for the same months in 1938 and 1939. . . .' *Cape Argus*,
19 March 1940.
[2] *Native Economic Commission*, 1930–32, op. cit., para. 563.

B. THE PRODUCTIVITY OF FARMING

Within the Native reserves of the Union of South Africa there is plenty of scope for increasing the productivity of both labour and land.[1] The reserves were set aside at different times during the course of the colonization of South Africa by Europeans. In 1913 the Natives' Land Act was passed.[2] It specified in a schedule the land set aside for the use of Natives and prohibited Natives from acquiring land from non-Natives outside these scheduled areas, unless its acquisition was specially sanctioned by the Governor-General. At the same time it reinforced the prohibition against Europeans acquiring land from Natives within the scheduled areas. These areas comprised the then existing reserves, together with some of the land which Natives held in private ownership. In 1917 the restrictions imposed on Natives by this Act were found to be *ultra vires* in the Cape Province on the ground that they might prevent Natives acquiring the property qualification required for suffrage.[3] In the other provinces the Natives Land Act stabilized the position with regard to the owner-ship of land. It was designed to be a temporary measure, and it therefore made provision for the appointment of a commission which was to demarcate areas within which Europeans and Natives respectively might be permitted to acquire land. The allocation of land suggested by the Commission which was appointed—the Beaumont Commission—failed to satisfy either Europeans or Natives, and was not adopted by the Government. Subsequent recommendations by local committees appointed to reconsider its suggestions were also shelved until 1936. In that year the Native Land and Trust Act[4] made provision for additional land to be set aside for the use of Natives. Meanwhile, there had been some relaxation of the Natives Land Act (1913), and in certain cases Natives had been permitted to acquire land by consent of the Governor-General. The scheduled areas reserved for the use of Natives in 1913 comprised approximately 10,410,000 morgen, distributed as follows:

				Morgen[5]
Cape Province (including Transkeian
Territories) .	.	.	.	6,107,000
Natal	.	.	.	2,997,000
Transvaal	.	.	.	1,232,000
Orange Free State		.	.	74,290
Total	.	.	.	10,410,290

[1] This is also true of the British Protectorates of Basutoland, Bechuanaland, and Swaziland.   [2] Act No. 27 of 1913.
[3] Thompson and Stilwell *versus* Kama, 1917, Appellate Division of the Supreme Court.   [4] The Native Land and Trust Act, No. 18, 1936.
[5] 1 morgen = 2·12 British acres.

The total area reserved was 7·3 per cent of the area of the Union.[1]

In 1936 the Native Land and Trust Act demarcated further areas, termed 'released areas', within which Natives may acquire land. This Act also established a Native Trust and vested in it all the land which had previously been set aside for the use of Natives and, in addition, nearly all the other Crown land in scheduled or released areas.[2] The Trust is empowered to acquire additional land for Native settlement. The maximum of additional land which may be acquired is seven and a quarter million morgen, including land acquired after 1936 by individual Natives.[3] The land which may be acquired is allocated between the four provinces according to a fixed schedule.

In 1936 the Minister of Native Affairs estimated that between £10 million and £15 million would be required for the purchase and development of the seven and a quarter million morgen which the Trust might acquire. The Prime Minister then gave an assurance that funds amounting to £10 million would be made available within the succeeding five years, and that further funds would be made available if necessary.[4] In April 1939 the Minister of Native Affairs informed the House of Assembly that £4 million had so far been spent on the purchase of land and that the House would be asked to vote a further million for that purpose during the following year.[5]

If the total seven and a quarter million morgen is acquired for the use of Natives, the total area of land held by them in the Union may in the future amount to about 18,610,000 morgen.[6]

Much of this land is already occupied by Natives. Consequently the effect of its acquisition on the distribution and means of livelihood

[1] Statistics as given in the Reports and Proceedings of the Joint Committees (i.e. of both the Senate and the House of Assembly) on Natives and Coloured Persons, 1930–34, p. 60.

[2] All Crown land in released areas except that reserved for public purposes, or in the actual and legal occupation of Europeans.

[3] Land outside scheduled and released areas which is owned by Natives may be acquired by Natives.   [4] *Hansard*, 30 April 1936, columns 2752, 2829.

[5] *Cape Times*, 27 April 1939.

[6] Total Morgenage of Land Possible for Native Occupation in the Union:

1913 Scheduled Amendments . . .	10,410,000
Permitted Acquisitions by 1936 Act . . .	7,250,000
Owned by Natives within Released Areas and therefore, if retained by present owners, extra to the morgenage named in the Act (approx.)	650,000
Owned by Natives in European Areas and therefore, if retained by present owners, extra to the morgenage named in the Act (approx.)	300,000
	18,610,000

Mrs. Rheinallt Jones, 'Some considerations which arise from the administration of the Native Land and Trust Act, 1936,' *Race Relations*, Vol. V, No. 3, August 1930.

of the Native population is not likely to be as great as might be suggested by a comparison of the area of land previously set aside for Natives in the scheduled areas with the newly released land.

The density of population in Native rural areas is in striking contrast to the sparsity of population in European rural areas. Thus, in the Transkeian Territories the average density of the rural population in 1921 varied between 39·59 per square mile in East Griqualand, a mountainous district, and 78·85 in the Transkei; whereas the density of the rural population of the Union as a whole is 11·09. Statistical comparisons of density of population which do not take into account differences in the nature of the land are misleading. Many of the Native areas, particularly in the Cape Province, are situated in regions which are fertile and well watered according to South African standards. Nevertheless, the great density of the rural population in Native rural areas is in striking contrast to contiguous and comparable areas in European occupation.

The Native reserves do not offer large rewards or diversity of occupation to enterprising Natives. They are almost entirely rural. In 1921 the total urban population (both Native and European) of the Transkeian Territories was 7,523, as compared with the rural population of 1,203,647. Farming is almost the only occupation, but even in farming opportunities are restricted by the lack of rail transport, the system of land tenure, and the poor farming methods and equipment. Consequently specialized marketing services have not developed and the more enterprising have difficulty in securing higher prices for a superior product.

Throughout the Native reserves the land is deteriorating in fertility as a result of overcrowding and of customary methods of farming.[1] The yield of plots worked by trained Native agricultural demonstrators has been from three to six times as great as that from neighbouring plots worked by customary and more conservative methods.[2]

[1] *The Native Economic Commission*, 1930–32, para. 69, reported: 'We have now throughout the Reserves a state of affairs in which, with few exceptions, the carrying capacity of the soil for both human beings and animals is definitely on the downgrade; a state of affairs which, unless soon remedied, will within one or at the outside two decades create in the Union an appalling problem of Native poverty.'

The White Paper on Land Policy under the Native Land and Trust Act, 1936, said: 'Speaking generally, it is notorious that the existing Native locations and Reserves are congested, denuded, overstocked, eroded, and for the most part, in a deplorable condition.'

[2] 'On 1,524 acres of ground worked by the (agricultural) demonstrators in the Transkei in 1929–30, 8,350 bags of mealies were reaped, or 11 bags to the morgen. On adjoining plots worked by the owners, from 1,904 acres of ground 3,993 bags were reaped, or approximately 4 bags to the morgen. In one of the Kuruman Reserves under the adverse conditions prevailing there, the demonstrators succeeded in obtaining an average yield of 3 bags of mealies

Accurate statistics of agricultural and pastoral production are difficult to collect, and in the case of Native production the difficulties have proved so great that the census method has been abandoned and, except in the case of Natives living on farms in European occupation, estimates are now relied on for particulars of livestock and crops.[1] Several estimates of the production of Native families within the reserves have been made, and they all show the income from the sale of produce to be very small. For the period preceding the depression of 1929–32 the then Director of Native Agriculture estimated the income from the sale of produce for a family unit of five in the Transkei to be £4 1s. per annum. The late Mr. S. G. Butler, then principal of the Tsolo Agricultural School, estimated it at £2 12s. 6d.[2] The value of farm products exported from the Transkei in 1929 was approximately 8s. 4d. per head of population, the chief exports being wool, mohair, kaffir-corn, maize, hides, and skins.[3] In certain reserves in the Northern Transvaal the income from the sale of produce was estimated to be a little over £6 for a similar family unit, but grain production fell far short of consumption. The extent to which grain was purchased to supplement domestic production resulted in there being practically no income from the sale of farm produce for the purchase of other food, and clothes, or for the payment of taxes and school fees. As a consequence of low productivity within the reserves Natives seek work in industrial centres or on farms in order to obtain part of the means they require to pay taxes[4] and to buy those commodities which they do not themselves produce.

per acre, while on neighbouring plots, worked according to native methods, the yield averaged under ½ bag per acre.' (These figures, however, do not show the relative costs of production.) (1 morgen = 2·12 British acres.)

Board of Trade and Industries Report No. 219. Establishment of Industries in Native Territories; cf. *Report of Native Economic Commission*, 1930–32, para. 286.

[1] *Report on the Agricultural and Pastoral Production of the Union of South Africa*, U.G. 54, 1936, p. 5.

[2] *Native Economic Commission*, 1930–32, Annexure 14.

[3] S. H. Fazan, Memorandum entitled: 'A Report on a visit made to the Union of South Africa for the purpose of comparing the methods of land tenure in the native reserves there with the system obtaining in Kikuyu Province. *Kenya Land Commission*, 1934, Vol. I, pp. 1081–2.

[4] The extent to which taxes are paid outside the home district of the tax-payer is an indication of the reliance upon wage earning to secure the means to pay taxes. The proportion of the 'general tax' (poll tax £1 per adult male Native) for 1929 collected outside the home district of the taxpayer, is shown in the following table:

	Total Tax Collected	Collected outside Home District
Cape Province	£431,000	£205,000
Natal	£315,000	£129,000
Orange Free State	£108,000	£26,000
Transvaal	£330,000	£149,000

Native Economic Commission, 1930–32, Annexure 25.

There is reason to believe that systems of land tenure within
the reserves have tended to hinder the more enterprising Natives
from adopting improved farming technique. They have also
prevented the growth of large-scale farming. During the latter
part of the nineteenth century in the Cape Colony individual title
to arable land was regarded as an essential condition for the
improvement of agriculture. It was also supported by some
Europeans on the ground that it would increase the number of
Native labourers by forcing permanently into the labour market
those Natives who did not secure allotments. That is to say, it
was thought that individual tenure would lead to greater specialization of labour among the Native population, some becoming
self-supporting peasant farmers and some becoming whole-time
industrial workers. In practice it has not in general had this result.

In 1930–32 the Native Economic Commission made careful
inquiries to find out whether the grant of individual title had
resulted in improved methods of farming. It reported:

> The opinion of witnesses best qualified to judge is that while the
> possession of the title gives the Native a large measure of personal
> satisfaction, there is very little difference to be noticed in the way in
> which land is worked as between surveyed and unsurveyed districts.
> The work of the demonstrators has in this respect borne much more
> fruit. The nett economic effect up to the present would seem to be
> that the Natives paid out a large sum of money in survey fees, while
> any increase in production has been negligible, and high land values
> have been created.[1]

This is no doubt in part because individual tenure was confined
to arable allotments and the allotments were themselves comparatively small, the usual size being three to five morgen.
Further, in practice there was not much difference between the
system of tenure in surveyed and unsurveyed districts. In a
valuable report upon the Transkeian system of land tenure, Mr.
S. H. Fazan comments:

> 'One usually reads about it as a system of private small holdings;
> it is really, in respect of about four-fifths of its area in the surveyed,
> and two-thirds of its area in the unsurveyed districts, a particularly
> stark system of commonage.'[2]

In the surveyed districts[3] the arable land has been allocated
according to the principle of 'one man, one lot', the sub-division
of allotments being prevented by restrictions on inheritance and

---

[1] *Native Economic Commission*, 1930–32, op. cit., para. 148.

[2] S. H. Fazan, op. cit., p. 1072.

[3] The total area of the seven surveyed districts is 3,458 square miles, and is
distributed approximately as follows: Arable, 637 square miles; Village and
kraal sites, 62 square miles; Commonage, 2,759 square miles. S. H. Fazan,
op. cit., p. 1072.

transfer. In unsurveyed districts, both within the Cape Province proper and the Transkeian Territories, the same broad principles apply, but allotments are distributed on the basis of 'one wife, one lot', instead of 'one man, one lot'.[1] In both surveyed and unsurveyed districts, however, there are many married men who have no arable allotments. In the former the number of garden lots is restricted to those originally surveyed. Lots become available only through inheritance, voluntary transfer, or forfeiture. In unsurveyed districts it is possible to add to the number of arable allotments, but only at the expense of reducing the commonage. The additions which have been made have not been sufficient to accommodate all those who desire to live and farm in the reserves. Consequently throughout the reserves in the Cape Province, including the Transkeian Territories, Natives who have not acquired allotments have 'squatted' on the commonage, with the incidental effect of reducing the amount of grazing land. In the Glen Grey district, in 1922, there were as many married and unmarried men living on and cultivating the commonage as there were men possessing garden lots.[2] In the division of Kingwilliamstown and other parts of the Ciskei, Mr. Vos, who made an official investigation into the system of individual tenure in the Native reserves, considered there were probably more men living on the commonage than there were owners of garden lots. In the Transkei, he considered, the same situation was rapidly arising.[3] The introduction of individual title to land and the limitation of the number of allotments has evidently not had the effect of forcing permanently and continuously into the labour market those Natives who have not secured title to land in the surveyed districts, nor registered allotments in the unsurveyed.

The Native Economic Commission was of the opinion that individual tenure failed to achieve its purpose partly because it had not been accompanied by instruction in improved methods of farming, but it considered that a more important cause of failure was the size of the allotments which, in its opinion, were too small to encourage enterprising Natives to become whole-time farmers.[4] It recommended that the rule of 'one man, one lot' be

---

[1] S. H. Fazan, op. cit., p. 1072. H. Rogers, *Native Administration in the Union of South Africa*, pp. 121–3. In unsurveyed districts land is apportioned by the headman, subject to confirmation by the Native Commissioner, and both homestead and arable allotments are roughly demarcated and registered.

[2] *Report on Native Location Surveys*, U.G. 42, 1922, p. 7.

[3] Ibid., p. 8.

[4] 'If the idea was to secure the added interest of private ownership of land, this should have been consistently applied. The granting of a title deed and the beaconing off of plots is not enough to secure economic progress. There is no magic in individual title to overcome the inertia of custom. Survey introduced the setting for progress, but instructions in better methods was required to enable advantage to be taken of it. Most of the Natives did not know how

relaxed and that individuals in the surveyed areas should be allowed to acquire up to fifty morgen of land in order that enterprising individuals might find an outlet for their abilities in farming within the reserves.[1] Mr. Fazan, in his report, likewise criticized the system of universal small holdings on the one hand because, he said, 'it acts as a check on enterprise and limits the will to improve and expand', and also because the holdings were too small to give landless Natives employment as farm-labourers or to provide sustenance for elderly or unfit relatives. He considered that the system tended to produce uniformity of crops and thus to make the population more vulnerable to a failure of food crops in times of drought than if more subsidiary crops were grown.[2] It was largely to combat this uniformity of crops that the early Native administrators had advocated the grant of individual title to arable land, but the system introduced has so far largely failed to achieve this objective.

In Native locations in Natal and the Transvaal the distribution of land has been for the most part left in the hands of the Native chiefs. The Magistrates in Natal have had the final say, in case of disputes, but they have rarely been called upon to mediate. Consequently, the system of land tenure has continued on tribal lines, although the area available for distribution by the chiefs has been curtailed.

Under the Native Land and Trust Act, 1936, the South African Native Trust was constituted 'for the settlement, support, benefit, and material and moral welfare of the Natives of the Union'. The policy of land settlement to be followed by the Trust has been described in a White Paper which lays down the principle that

> a primary factor to be borne in mind in the acquisition of land by the Trust is that of affording relief, in so far as possible, to the existing locations so as to enable the necessary remedial measures to be instituted, and to afford them an opportunity to recover.[3]

Much of the land in the released areas is already occupied by Natives, who, like those in the reserves, go out to work to supplement their meagre incomes from the land. On land purchased by the Trust which is not already occupied by Natives, settlement is to be on a tribal basis, but under strict supervision. Land is

to set about improving their holdings. Many were satisfied if they got from them what they got before. But our chief criticism is that the holdings were not big enough to make agriculture a whole-time job for those who had the energy, the desire, and the skill so to make it, and the system made no provison for development to meet the needs of such men.' *Native Economic Commission*, op. cit., para. 149.

[1] Ibid., para. 145.   [2] S. H. Fazan, op. cit., p. 1085.
[3] White Paper, February 1937. Statement of Land Policy under the Native Land and Trust Act, 1936, p. 8.

to be acquired for specific tribes in order to provide necessary extensions to existing tribal locations and to provide accommodation for tribes and communities which have been been assigned locations.[1]

In exceptional cases only will the purchase of land by Natives be permitted; according to the White Paper:

> While, as has already been indicated, it is contemplated that Trust land will in the ordinary course be made available for native settlement only under a form of leasehold tenure and will be occupied by them under supervision and control, it is realized that in exceptional cases Natives, whether tribes, communities, or individuals, should be permitted actually to purchase land from the Trust or be assisted by the Trust to acquire land in released areas from private owners.[2]

In spite of the recommendations of the Native Economic Commission, present land policy does not appear designed to stimulate the growth of a class of Native farmers who will be in a position to make a living from the land without supplementing their incomes by going to work. Indeed, Mrs. Rheinallt Jones, who has for years made a special study of Native land-holding, has written:

> In point of fact present policy appears to be to oust Native tenant farmers to make room for tribal leaseholdings.[3]

Much stricter control of the occupation of land than that previously exercised is contemplated, both within the existing reserves and in the newly acquired areas; and the survey of all locations with a view to the definition of residential, arable, and rotational grazing areas, the acquisition of additional land, the fencing of land, the limitation of stock, and many other measures for reclamation, development, supervision, and control are being undertaken.[4] The effect of these measures upon the supply of labour will depend upon the extent to which they increase productivity, and upon the attractiveness of sources of income alternative to working under European supervision outside the reserves.

[1] Ibid, p. 6. [2] Ibid., p. 7.
[3] Mrs. Rheinallt Jones: 'Some Considerations which arise from the Administration of the Native Trust and Land Act, 1936,' *Race Relations*, Vol. V, No. 3, August 1938, p. 57. Mrs. Rheinallt Jones's judgment has since been confirmed by the Native Affairs Commission, which has been entrusted with the selection of the land to be purchased by the Native Trust. It has reported: 'The only clear principle which the Commission has been able to enunciate, when addressing the native people in reply to demands of individuals to be allowed to buy land from the Trust, is that the Native Trust exists to serve the interests of the whole of the native people; and that the 7¼ million morgen of land set aside by Parliament for the natives was intended to serve the needs of all the people and not a comparatively small section of advanced natives. . . . The broad rule, therefore, which the Commission has followed, is that the communal claims of the mass of the native people must have first consideration. . . .' U.G. 54, 1939, pp. 10–11. [4] White Paper, February 1937, op. cit., p. 5.

In the past, tribal tenure of land has not proved conducive to improved methods of farming, nor has individual tenure of garden lots, combined with communal grazing, produced any better results. The authorities responsible for administering the Native Trust apparently consider that expert layout and supervision will overcome the difficulties which have previously arisen where tribal settlements have occupied restricted areas.[1]

The Native Economic Commission considered that the system of endeavouring to give each man a holding, an essential feature of tribal tenure, could only be maintained at the cost of progress and would entail the continuance of a very low standard of life, for opportunities were few for raising the standard of life by specialization within the reserves, and in European areas opportunities were being increasingly restricted.[2] There seems no reason to criticize this judgment.

Under present conditions and those contemplated by the Trust there does not appear to be much scope for the progressive Native farmer. This is borne out by the attitude of those responsible for the planning and administration of attempts to assist farming in South Africa. In recent years the attempts to assist farming, which have long been a major part of government policy, have taken the form of establishing control boards with very wide powers. The protection which these control boards are expected to give is, however, designed to assist the European farmer and not the Native. The Secretary of an important control board in a considered statement of policy has said:

> 'The consensus of opinion in this country is that the White race and its civilization cannot be preserved unless the white man owns and farms the land. Furthermore, his proximity to Native influence makes it necessary that while so owning and farming the land he must achieve a standard of living commensurate with the requirements of the civilization which he must preserve. That achievement is not possible in South Africa unless the burden is assumed by the nation as a whole.'[3]

He argues:

> 'In practically all secondary industries and in mining, the labour of the white man is protected against the cheaper labour of the Native. But in agriculture, particularly in the livestock industry, the White man competes with the Native on very difficult terms. Take, for instance, the competition of livestock from the adjoining

[1] cf. Mrs. Rheinallt Jones, op. cit., p. 56.
[2] *Native Economic Commission*, 1930–32, paras. 143, 144.
[3] J. R. McLoughlin, General Secretary of the Livestock and Meat Industries Control Board, 'A Defence of Control in the Marketing of Agricultural Products,' *The South African Journal of Economics*, Vol. VI, No. 3, September 1938, p. 295.

Territories and one finds that the Native there, as in many portions of the Union, has free communal lands, and has virtually no direct cost of production. It should be quite obvious that this White agriculturist is up against one of the most serious problems that faces a White standard of civilization.[1]

Similarly the former Secretary for Agriculture, Colonel G. N. Williams, has foreseen that in time, as a result of technical guidance and education, the Native areas may, at least in good seasons, produce for sale and

in the interests of the farming community, it will be necessary to institute measures to prevent such surplus, with its lower cost of production by Native peasants, being dumped on the market, thereby depressing prices.'[2]

The Marketing Act provides the means for carrying out the policy of preventing Native farmers from competing with Europeans. It provides the framework within which the control boards for the different farm products function, and it is significant that no person other than a European may vote on any proposed scheme of control,[3] although such a scheme may control the production, sale, and processing of all producers, including Natives. At the same time different provisions may be applied to different areas in order to discourage or encourage different types of production. It is possible for European control boards representing the supposed interests of European farmers to determine the prices at which Native farmers may sell their products, and the amount they may sell at those prices.

The effect of discrimination in prices on Native output may be little. But if their receipts are arbitrarily reduced, the effect must be to increase their need to go out to work.

The desire to prevent Native farmers from competing with European is confirmed by the Board of Trade and Industries which, in its report on the establishment of industries in the Native territories, recommends, for example, that cotton-growing and the production of oil-producing beans and seeds be considered on the ground that they would not come into competition with vested interests and existing production in other areas.[4]

C. OTHER OPPORTUNITIES FOR EMPLOYMENT

Within the reserves opportunities are few for making a living in other ways than by farming. Industries have not as yet

---

[1] Ibid., pp. 299–300.   [2] *The Forum*, 10 October 1938, p. 18.
[3] Marketing Act, No. 26 of 1937, Section 21 (4).
[4] *Board of Trade and Industries*, Report No. 219, 'Establishment of Industries in Native Territories', November 1936, para. 12.

developed. They have been handicapped among other things by poor transport facilities, and the low purchasing power of the population. A certain amount of employment is available in domestic service in the villages and towns in which live the European officials, professional men and traders. Natives are also employed as teachers, clerks, interpreters, assistants in trading stores and on public works, such as the roads and land reclamation. Nevertheless most Natives who desire to supplement their income or to earn their living in some way other than by small peasant cultivation leave the reserves.

Within the Native areas there is little scope for the full-time specialized artisan. Some specialized crafts, such as that of blacksmith, were a feature of Bantu culture before contact with Europeans, while some men and women acquired more skill at particular occupations such as metal-work, weaving, making pottery, or thatching. Such specialists exchanged their products for others, the rates of exchange being stabilized according to customary standards. Nowadays the services of men who are expert, for example, in building sod and sun-dried brick huts, are, usually hired, payment being made in cash or stock. Specialists, however, do not occupy themselves exclusively in working for hire but have their own lands and cattle and merely supplement their income by specialization. The demand for the services of the Bantu craftsman is being restricted because European factory-made goods, tin plates, basins, buckets, knives, spoons, and clothing, are largely replacing Native-made articles,[1] and in some cases European craftsmen have supplanted the Native.[2]

The low standard of housing and living conditions means that there is little effective demand for the trained artisan's services,[3] and the tradition of the self-sufficient family group as the productive unit makes it difficult for him to establish himself as a specialist.[4]

In many schools special attention has been paid to the industrial training of Natives since the days of Sir George Grey, but the results of this policy have disappointed educationalists. The

[1] Hunter, op. cit., pp. 96–102. Schapera, 'Economic Conditions in a Bechuanaland Native Reserve,' S.A. Journal of Science, Vol. XXX, pp. 640–44. Board of Trade and Industries, Report No. 219. 'Establishment of Industries in Native Territories,' November 1936, para. 26. Schapera, 'Work and Wealth,' The Bantu-Speaking Tribes of South Africa, pp. 153, 170–72.

[2] For example, in British Bechuanaland, where Native iron workers were almost the only specialized workers bartering goods outside the family circle, iron goods are now purchased from traders, and repairs to wagons and ploughs and similar work is done by European blacksmiths. Schapera, 'Economic Conditions in a Bechuanaland Native Reserve', South African Journal of Science, Vol. XXX, October 1933, p. 641.

[3] Native Economic Commission, 1930–32, para. 142.

[4] cf. Inter-Departmental Committee on Native Education, U.G. No. 29, 1936, para. 594.

Inter-Departmental Committee on Native Education reported in
1936 that:

> It cannot be claimed that this policy has even to-day produced
> any very adequate or satisfactory results.

The following table for the Cape Province, the only one for
which figures are available, shows that little increase in the
industrial training of Natives in schools has been made over a
period of fifty years.

Year	Black-smith-ing	Book-bind-ing	Carp-entry	Mason-ry	Print-ing	Shoe-making and Leather Work	Wagon Making	Tailor-ing	Total
1882	6[1]	1	119	—	8	24	16	—	174
1905	—	5	188	23	15	12	9	—	252
1912	2	5	162	26	16	22	11	4	248
1922	3	—	118	20	12	13	7	15	188
1932	21	2	192	35	10	28	4	27	319

As we have seen, training through apprenticeship in European
areas is in practice barred to Natives. The Inter-Departmental
Committee considered that in view of the opposition to competition from Native artisans in European areas and the conditions in the reserves the expansion of industrial education for
Natives would be purposeless.[2]

Within the reserves there is a certain amount of rather hap-
hazard trade in Native handmade curios and other articles, but
excluding a few mission schools, one of which sells goods to the
value of £700 a year, there is little regular production for the
European market and it is only by chance that tourists in the
reserves can obtain Native-made articles. There is little doubt
that there is a potential demand for goods such as hand-woven
cloths, beadwork, rugs, Native pots and furniture, and that there
has been little systematic attempt to supply it.[3] The market,
however, is limited; it is largely confined to luxury articles and
there is little likelihood of Native home industries competing
successfully with most factory-made goods. Home industries
may be developed to supplement peasant farming, but they are
unlikely generally to provide an alternative livelihood.

[1] Ibid., para. 581, p. 115.
[2] Ibid., paras. 575–6, 600.
[3] *Board of Trade and Industries*, Report No. 219. 'Establishment of Industries
in Native Territories,' November 1936, para. 26.

Commerce has offered a limited field of employment, Natives being employed in trading stores as assistants and sometimes as managers.[1] Few Natives conduct their own businesses in the reserves. In the Transkeian Territories until 1934 new licences for trading sites were not granted within five miles of an existing store. This rule gave European traders a considerable degree of monopoly, for few Natives have had the means to buy out the established traders, who were all Europeans. The five-mile rule was modified in 1934 to allow Native traders to establish stores outside a radius of two miles from existing trading sites.[2] During 1936 licences were approved for four Native traders, six Native butchers, and one Native baker.[3]

The general absence of differentiation of occupation has combined with the traditional social organization, according to which hospitality is readily accorded, to mask unemployment or partial employment among Natives. It was not until the depression of 1929 to 1932 reduced the opportunities open to Natives from the reserves to supplement their incomes by working outside them that general attention was directed to the poverty of the reserves. In 1932 the Transkeian Territories General Council called the attention of the central government to 'the sad plight of the Natives' in these territories and asked it to consider the encouragement of industries to give increased employment to Natives.[4]

At length, in September 1936, the Board of Trade and Industries turned its attention to the possibility of developing industries in the Transkeian Territories and Bechuanaland. Despite the lifting of trade depression, its report is a melancholy document which confirmed the Native Economic Commission's findings concerning the severity and extent of poverty and the lack of opportunity within the reserves.

When discussing the possibilities of starting industries the Board stated that cheap labour was the only attraction which the reserves offered, but it considered that industries established on that basis

> would be given an unfair competitive advantage *vis-à-vis* Union
> manufacturers producing the same or similar articles, and who have

---

[1] *Native Economic Commission*, 1930–32, paras. 942–53.

[2] Proclamation, No. 244 of 1931.

[3] *Report of the Department of Native Affairs*, 1935–6, U.G. 44, 1937, p. 73.

[4] The following year the Department of Native Affairs was informed that the Minister of Commerce and Industries 'took a sympathetic view of the General Council's desire to establish industries to afford employment for Natives in the Territories. However, he trusted that such industries could be developed without detriment to existing industries in the Union, which not only efficiently serve the demands made upon them, but which also provide employment for very large numbers of natives.' *Board of Trade and Industries*, Report No. 219, op. cit., p. 5.

to comply with provisions of our wage legislation or are compelled, through competition, to pay higher wages.[1]

It maintained that official assistance would be required to establish industries. On both grounds it ruled out of consideration those likely to compete with existing enterprises in other parts of the country. It recommended that if government assistance was given, factories should not be permitted to produce commodities already manufactured in the Union, in order that they should not compete with existing concerns but should open up new fields of employment. Further, it considered that they should offer a ready market for Native produce. It relaxed these limiting conditions somewhat in order to recommend that a boot-and shoe-making industry should be established. In the opinion of the Board, such an industry would be likely to compete only in the cheaper types of footwear and its competition would probably be ineffective outside the reserves, on account of the inferior hides of Native cattle. Even so, the Board reported that it would be 'both possible and advisable to restrict the sale of the products to Native Territories.'[2]

Throughout its report the Board is careful to emphasize that none of the suggestions made are likely to interfere with the supply of labour from these territories.[3] Migratory labour is evidently designed, in its opinion, to remain the chief source of money income for the population of the Native reserves. The Native Affairs Commission, an official advisory body, has also indicated that it does not contemplate the development of the Native areas in such a way as to make their inhabitants independent of migratory labour. In determining the policy of land settlement it has stated that 'having regard to the fact, already emphasized, that the whole economic structure of the Union depends upon the maintenance of the reserve subsistence for the families of workers employed in European industry, this rule (preference of tribal settlement) could not be departed from without grave maladjustment.'[4]

Labour migration is an important factor both in the industrial organization of South Africa and in the economy of the Native reserves, yet there is little accurate information as to the proportion of time which Natives domiciled in the reserves spend working outside their home districts. In 1930 the Inter-Departmental Committee on Labour Resources estimated that reserve Natives spend about a third of their time out working.[5] Mr. E. C.

[1] Ibid., para. 40.   [2] Ibid., paras. 54 and 55.   [3] Ibid., paras. 16–29.
[4] *Report of the Native Affairs Commission for the Years* 1937–1938, U.G. 54, 1939, p. 11.
[5] *Inter-Departmental Committee on the Labour Resources of the Union*, 1930, para. 75.

Thompson, District Superintendent of the Native Recruiting Corporation in the Transkei, told the Native Economic Commission 'that practically every available fit labourer enters upon a term of employment with a period of two years.'[1] It was estimated that in the Herschel District 75 per cent of the adult males are away for at least six months in every year.[2] Writing of labour migration in Pondoland, the last of the Transkeian Territories to come under European rule, Miss Hunter says:

> 'Nowadays in Pondoland practically every man goes at least once during his life to a labour centre to work for Europeans. Many go again and again. Most men go to the gold-mines or to the sugar estates in Natal; a few to East London, Capetown, Durban, and Maritzburg. A few women also go to European towns to work as domestic servants, and a small number of women and men are employed as servants by Europeans living in Pondoland and on public works.'[3]

In Natal and the Transvaal, Natives have likewise to leave their home districts to obtain money for taxes and for the purchase of European goods. The British Protectorates of Basutoland, Bechuanaland, and Swaziland are in a similar position to the Native reserves within the Union in regard to low productivity and dependence on labour migration.[4] The Basutoland Census of 1936 collected statistics of the number of absentees at labour centres which indicated that nearly half the adult male population were away at work.[5] In a Bechuanaland reserve Professor Schapera found that approximately 40 per cent of the adult male population were away at work every year.[6]

Natives seek work in European areas for many and varied reasons; for money to pay taxes and to buy European goods to supplement local produce; to avoid irksome parental and tribal discipline; to experience for themselves the attractions and adventures about which they hear from those who return; to acquire the prestige which results from a visit to the European

[1] *Native Economic Commission,* 1930–32, Addendum by Mr. Lucas, para. 64.
[2] MacMillan, *Complex South Africa,* p. 178.
[3] M. Hunter, op. cit., p. 108.
[4] *Report on the Financial and Economic Position of the Bechuanaland Protectorate,* 1933 [Cmd. 4368]; *Report on Financial and Economic Situation of Swaziland,* 1932 [Cmd. 4114] pp. 21–4; *International Labour Conference,* 1935, Report IV, 'The Recruiting of Labour in Colonies and in Other Territories with Analogous Labour Conditions', pp. 35–6.
[5] *Basutoland Government Publication.* Census 1936, Tables V and VI.

	Males	Females
Absentees at Labour Centres	78,604	22,669
Population enumerated	238,705	320,568
Age Group, 15–50—population	90,201	161,145

[6] Schapera, 'Economic Conditions in a Bechuanaland Native Reserve', *S. A. Journal of Science,* Vol. XXX October, 1933, p. 652.

areas. The predominant motive, however, is for means to pay taxes and to buy manufactured goods.[1]

Debt is probably the most general immediate motive causing Natives to go out to work for Europeans. They frequently borrow to meet urgent wants and only seek employment when pressed to pay off their debts, or when further credit is refused. No statistics are available of the indebtedness of Natives coming from their reserves, but it is known to be a powerful force, and is widely cited by Natives as the reason for their emigration.

Labour migration is at the same time a result and a cause of the low productivity of Native farming.[2] It is often said that according to the system of division of labour usual among the Bantu, the men played no part in agriculture and therefore their absence at outside work has little effect.[3] But the introduction of the plough has increased the share of agricultural work undertaken by the men and their absence is a severe handicap, especially at the ploughing season. Among some Bantu tribes, women are not permitted to handle cattle and consequently a woman whose husband or sons are away has to depend upon relatives to plough for her.[4] The greater the proportion of men who are away the more difficult it becomes to get the ploughing done in time to get the benefit of early rains.[5] Even when the men are able to get back in time for the ploughing season agriculture is impeded, for they are not able to help with the preparatory work.[6] Similarly

[1] 'The principal motive for its existence is unquestionably economic; the people go out primarily in order to earn money. Their main local source of income is the sale of their produce, which does not yield enough, especially at the present time (1933), to enable them both to provide for all their needs and to pay their taxes. Were it not for the necessity of paying their taxes regularly in cash, most of them might perhaps go out once only. As it is, they have to go out more often.' Ibid., pp. 651–2.

In the Bechuanaland Protectorate (and perhaps elsewhere) there are additional incentives arising from the power of the chiefs. In several of the Bechuanaland reserves it is the practice of the chief to send men who fail to pay their taxes to work on the Rand gold-mines. To avoid this alternative and also to avoid compulsory work for no wages, which the chiefs have the right to call for, many prefer to seek work for which they will get rewarded individually. Ibid.

[2] cf. Mrs. Rheinallt Jones: 'Some Considerations which arise from the Administration of the Native Trust and Land Act, 1936', Race Relations, Vol. V, No. 3, August 1938, p. 56.

[3] cf. J. F. W. Grosskopf: 'Vestiging en Trek van die Suid-Afrikaans naturelle-bevolking', The South African Journal of Economics, Vol. 1, No. 3, September 1933, p. 273.

[4] In some parts, e.g. Pondoland, the taboo on women working with cattle has made ploughing the work of the men; in others, e.g. Bechuanaland Protectorate, the taboo has broken down, possibly as a result of labour migration, and ploughing is also done by the women and young boys. Hunter, op. cit., pp. 74–5. Information on the Bechuanaland Protectorate supplied by Professor Schapera.

[5] Schapera, 'Labour Migration from a Bechuanaland Native Reserve', Journal of the African Society, Vol. XXXIII, No. 130, p. 53.

[6] 'The absence of males from their homes during the greater part of the year is

less care is given to cattle than formerly, for in the absence of the men the cattle are now left almost entirely to the care of the young boys who lack the supervision which was customary.

Labour migration lowers the standard of farming and hampers development in the Native areas, for many of the Natives who periodically leave the reserves fail to acquire skill in farming. They also lose interest. Similarly their application to other types of work is intermittent, and as a result their productivity in all occupations remains low.

invariably reflected in the cultural operations of the land and the resultant low yields. Even while the responsible male times his visit home to coincide with the ploughing and seeding season, agriculture suffers. It allows of no preparatory cultivation nor does it enable him to take advantage of favourable rainfalls. It necessitates leaving to the women and juniors the major part of the work. There can be no organized system of working. The standard of agriculture, therefore, is low and there can be no development.' Mr. Germond, Lecturer in Agriculture at the South African Native College at Fort Hare, quoted in *Native Economic Commission*, 1930-32, Addendum by Mr. Lucas, para. 259.

CHAPTER XVI

THE POLICY OF RACIAL SEGREGATION AND DISCRIMINATION

IT will be clear from the discussion in the preceding chapters of the development of the market for Native labour that racial discrimination has in South Africa become a dominant force, strengthened by legal enactment and administrative device. Racial and cultural differences inevitably impeded to some degree the fluidity of the labour market. Custom, tradition, and other environmental influences, even though not re-enforced by authoritarian regulation, would have manifested themselves in one form or another in racial preferences in human relations, given the diversity of racial and cultural groups which obtains in South Africa. It is not possible to decide the precise degree to which official intervention in the labour market has determined the existing pattern of Native employment. Much may be said for the view that the redoubling in recent years of legislative and administrative action to regulate economic co-operation between Europeans and Natives provides a fair measure of the tendency for new opportunities for such co-operation to emerge. That in itself is probably not a complete explanation of government intervention in this field; an almost equally strong case could be made for the view that with the quickening of economic life the growing competition in the labour market has evoked and rendered more articulate and insistent a demand for discrimination based on race and colour.

In a mixed community, racial differentiation and discrimination may take an infinite variety of forms, ranging between two extreme types of society. At the one end there might emerge a community from which every form of distinction, social or legal, between persons of different racial origin was entirely absent—a classless and casteless society. At the other, it is possible to conceive of a group of completely separated communities, co-operating neither in production nor in trade—an insulated system of non-coöperant, non-competing entities.

Each of these extreme types, social identity and social segregation, has its advocates in South Africa among both Europeans and Natives, yet the majority of both races regards neither one nor the other as immediately practicable. Even among professed adherents of the policy of social and legal identity there are few who would not advocate the retention, at least for a time, of a system of reserving land for the use of the Native population.

Similarly, at the other extreme, few would advocate the immediate and complete withdrawal of Native labourers from employment under European supervision.

There is, however, no general agreement among either concerning the nature and extent of desirable differentiation or discrimination. Social identity is opposed by the majority of the European population. It is also opposed by those Natives who hope to continue the development of a primarily Bantu culture. Nevertheless, Europeans still seek to employ and trade with Natives, while Natives on their part seek to increase their incomes by selling their goods and services to Europeans.

Official policy has not followed a consistent course. Beginning with an attempt to prevent contact and to keep the Europeans and Native communities separate for reasons of defence, it was soon modified to allow trading and to enable Natives to work for European colonists. For a time, in the Cape Colony and Natal, contact was officially encouraged in order to promote co-operation between the races. Latterly the policy of 'segregation' has gained ground. It does not, however, seek to recreate completely independent communities. The dependence of the European community upon the supply of Native labour is at least to some extent realized. The 'segregationists' seek rather to regulate the direction and extent of co-operation.

At present it would appear that the development of a caste system is officially encouraged. The Natives are to supply the unskilled labour; they are to provide a common base upon which each of the other racial groups, European, Cape Coloured, and Asiatic, is to form a separate economic and social unit, advancement being possible only within the group into which members of the different races are born.

To this end the use of labour and land is being increasingly circumscribed. The reservation of land for the use of Natives has become a justification for the imposition of countervailing, if not greater, disabilities. At the end of the nineteenth century Cecil Rhodes justified the imposition of a 'labour tax' as a *quid pro quo*. Since then the existence of reserves has been made the excuse for every type of discrimination and for the policy of 'segregation' itself; for in South Africa 'segregation' is in reality nothing more than a policy of discrimination, partial exclusion, and attempted exploitation.[1]

Outlining his Native policy in 1925 General Hertzog said:

'I am convinced that not only for the European, but for the Native

[1] I use the term exploitation in the sense of the payment of wages below the value of the marginal product of the worker.

also, the best thing with regard to the possession of land is to separate
the native from the European.[1]

In his view Natives should be employed in Native areas and
European employees should be the exception. In European areas
the regulation of the labour market, he said,

> must be extended to a certain extent in favour of Europeans, so that
> within his own areas he will always have the assurance of obtaining
> employment, as will be the case with the natives in the natives' areas
> generally.[2]

The intention was that the employment of Natives in European
areas should be limited, but not prohibited.[3]

From 1924, when his party assumed office in alliance with the
'white' Labour Party, increased attempts have been made to
promote the employment of Europeans, with consequent reactions
on the market for Native labour. The measures adopted have
been studied and their significance appraised in the preceding
chapters.

The repercussion of social and legal discrimination between
the various races upon the market for Native labour has been
extremely complex. Both demand and supply have been affected.
It must be repeated that it is impossible to isolate the spontaneous
preferences of employers from those arising from official measures.
Thus, except in the Cape Province, Natives have not been
admitted to trade unions organized by European craftsmen. At
the same time growth of Native trade unions has been slow.
Their slow growth cannot be dissociated from statutory measures
such as the Native Labour Regulation Act, which in effect
make most strikes of Native labourers a criminal offence. Native
trade unions have not been officially recognized for purposes of
collective bargaining,[4] whereas European trade unions have been
encouraged to develop by official recognition.

The spontaneous preferences of employers for one race rather
than another have certainly been affected in some degree by
legislative and administrative measures which exert a dual effect
upon them. In many cases the effects of different provisions of

[1] Report of General Hertzog's speech outlining his Native Policy to the
Native Conference in Pretoria, 3 December, 1925. *Cape Times* 4th December
1925.
[2] Ibid.
[3] 'It appears to me that there can be nothing more reasonable under the
circumstances than that the activities of the natives in connexion with certain
occupations within the white man's area shall be limited.' General Hertzog,
ibid.
[4] In April 1939 the Minister of Labour announced that Native trade unions
were to be officially 'recognized'. 'Recognition' is, however, not statutory and
does not bring them within the terms of the Industrial Conciliation Act for
purposes of collective bargaining.

the same law are contradictory. Thus measures such as the
Native Labour Regulation Act make the employment of Natives
more attractive, in so far as they make breach of contract a
criminal offence, but they also impose obligations on employers.
In such cases it is inevitably difficult to determine the net effect.

Again, measures like the statutory provision for the compensation of workmen for accidents lay down lower scales of payment
for Native than for other employees, with the probable effect of
increasing the preference of employers for Native workers.

Other measures, like the colour bar, the apprenticeship system,
and the statutory regulation of wages, limit the field of employment of Native labour and reduce the incentive of employers so
to adjust their customary organization of labour as to make full
use of the capacities of Natives.

In view of the comparatively short periods for which many
Natives seek employment and the restrictions on the use which
may be made of them it has not paid employers to devote much
attention to devising methods of increasing their efficiency. In
1914 the Economic Commission reported that it shared the opinion
expressed by one witness that 'native labour in South Africa is so
cheap that it has come to be looked upon as a thing which can be
used extravagantly'. In its view 'insufficient attention has been
given to the organization of Native labour, upon which industrial
prosperity in South Africa so largely depends'.[1] In 1925 the
Economic and Wage Commission (Clay-Martin-Mills Report)
was of the same opinion. 'There is', it said, 'much evidence that
native and other labour might be used more economically on
work of a more exacting character.'[2]

Each commission might well have laid rather more stress upon
the unlikelihood that attempts to train Native workers for more
skilled work would have been profitable, in view of the short
period of labour contract and the colour bar then prevailing on
the mines.

Since 1925 the structure of industry has become more rigid,
largely as the result of the multiplication of statutory and administrative decrees. Limitations on the employment of Natives are
both more numerous and more effective: the incentive to employers to train them for special work is thereby increasingly
weakened.

There is another aspect of this same point which affects the
supply of Native labour. If it does not pay employers to train
Natives for special work, the supply is also affected, for we must
take account of not only their numbers but also of their 'efficiency',

[1] *Economic Commission*, 1914, op. cit., para. 55.
[2] *Economic and Wage Commission* (1925), op. cit., para. 143.

that is, of their ability and willingness to work. It is almost certain that the denial of opportunity to rise will reduce the willingness of at least some of the Natives to go to work under European employers; the lack of incentive to employers to train them for higher wages and posts certainly results in a reduction in the ability of Natives to undertake skilled work, for which indeed there is little scope. In the absence of restrictions the supply of Native labour would be greater at least in the sense that there would be more skilled Natives, and that with the increased opportunity more Natives would be willing to work. It cannot be said with certainty that in such conditions employers would wish to maintain as large a force of unskilled Native labour: it might well pay them to reorganize their productive methods.

The effect of government policy upon willingness to work deserves some further consideration. The barriers which race at present imposes on social and political intercourse in South Africa affect both incentive and opportunities to increase income. The effect is probably greatest in the case of non-Europeans, regarded as they are by the great majority of the politically dominant Europeans as socially 'untouchable', no matter what their ability, cultural attainments, or wealth. This attitude must react upon the behaviour of those among them whose ambition it is to enter the European community. The Native who has assimilated Western European culture is excluded from social intercourse with almost all Europeans of a similar cultural level. His tastes are different from those of the majority of the Native population, consequently existing facilities for the entertainment and leisure of Natives may not suit him. He is not permitted to enter the majority of places of entertainment, which are reserved for Europeans. Sporting and other clubs and societies are almost exclusively organized on racial lines and non-Europeans have not yet provided for themselves or, until recently,[1] obtained from local or government authorities facilities comparable with those enjoyed by Europeans.

Probably more immediately important than these social barriers are the limitations on the right of Natives to buy land in both rural and urban areas, the strict control exercised over the allocation of land, and the consequent high prices of the small amount which is available for Natives to buy. Unless a missionary spirit of service to his own people compensates for restricted opportunities, there is little incentive for the enterprising Native to attempt to combat the obstacles which confront him. It may well be that in these circumstances many Natives

[1] Since the passing of the Native (Urban Areas) Act sporting and social facilities are being increased in urban locations.

*

will decide that the effort of working for wages is not worth making, beyond the extent required for the payment of taxes and the satisfaction of elementary wants.

Discriminatory measures which make more onerous the terms on which Natives are employed will also reduce their willingness to work. In the eighties of the last century there were frequent complaints that the pass laws restricted the supply of Native labour from the Transkeian Territories because Natives feared lest they might be apprehended if they entered the Colony to seek work. To-day the control over the migration of Natives is being increased. Thereby the advantages of employment and the mobility of labour are both reduced.[1] In the same way, if Natives believe that the Masters and Servants Acts, and similar laws, discriminate against them, they will seek to avoid those fields of employment in which these laws are most frequently invoked.

It is impossible to determine the net effect on the national income of all these measures. That those which restrict the employment of Natives reduce national productivity is certain. They have been adopted in order to promote the employment of Europeans and to assist them to maintain 'civilized standards'. In the short run they may be effective, but only at the expense of raising costs and limiting production. They may temporarily protect a privileged few from the difficulties of adjustment required by a changing world. They can do this only by impeding progress and growth in the wealth of the community taken as a whole, and the Native population in particular.

It may be argued that they create employment for Europeans and thereby add to national productivity by assisting the development of unused resources. If they have any such effect it is offset because these measures prevent the development and full use of one of South Africa's greatest resources, the labour of her Native population. Moreover, they raise costs and the South African economy is especially vulnerable to cost-raising devices on account of its exceptional dependance upon exports. It is not a closed community within which employment may be self-generating. In South Africa the retention of export markets is essential for the maintenance of the national income, and on this account cost-raising devices are particularly dangerous.

[1] In 1928 a Native Councillor said that the Travelling Pass System was vexatious and irritating, and that rather than submit to it many Natives preferred to seek work at the coast towns where it was not in operation. Report of a conference between representatives of the Union Government, the Transvaal Chamber of Mines and the Transkeian Territories and Pondoland General Councils, held in the Chamber of Mines Building, Johannesburg, on Friday 30 November 1928, submitted in evidence to the Native Economic Commission, 1930–32.

Are not all such restrictive measures short-sighted? They involve the creation and maintenance in South Africa of a caste system dependent upon authoritarian action. In the economic environment of the twentieth century a caste system can be maintained only by the exercise of force. It is a highly unstable condition, promising racial and social strife. It is damaging to the national income. It is based on a short view of European advantage, preferring the convenience of the present generation of the European population to the prospects for prosperity and peace of their descendants.

BIBLIOGRAPHY

AGAR-HAMILTON, J. A. I. 1928. The Native Policy of the Voor-trekkers. An essay in the history of the interior of South Africa, 1836–58. Capetown: Maskew Miller, Ltd.

AGAR-HAMILTON, J. A. I. 1937. The Road to the North, South Africa, 1852–86. Longmans.

AMPHLETT, G. T. 1914. History of the Standard Bank of South Africa, Ltd, 1862–1913. Glasgow: Maclehose.

ANGOVE, J. 1910. In the Early Days: Reminiscences of Pioneer Life on the South African Diamond Fields. Handel House: Kimberley and Johannesburg.

ARNDT, E. H. D. June 1933. Die Landboukrediet en Landbouskuld-vraagstrik, S. Afr. J. Econ., Vol. I.

AXELSON, C. (unpublished thesis, Natal University College). The History of Taxation in Natal prior to the Union.

AYLWARD, A. 1878. The Transvaal of To-day. War, witchcraft, sport, and spoils in South Africa. Blackwood & Sons.

BAINES, T. 1877. The Gold Regions of South Eastern Africa. Edward Stanford.

BARROW, J. 1804 (2nd edn. 1806). Travels into the Interior of Southern Africa.

BLOMMAERT, W. Het Invoeren van de Slavernij aan die Kaap. Argief-Jaarboek vir Suid-Afrikaanse Geskiedenis, Part I.

BROOKS, H. 1876. Natal, a history and description of the Colony. L. Keene & Co.

BROWNE, G. ST. J. ORDE-. 1933. The African Labourer. Oxford University Press.

BROWNE, ROSS E. Working Costs of the Witwatersrand.

BROWNLEE, C. 1896. Reminiscences of Kafir Life and History, and other Papers. Lovedale Press.

BROWNLEE, F. 1923. The Transkeian Native Territories: historical records. Lovedale: Mission Press.

BUSSCHAU, W. J. 1936. The Theory of Gold Supply. Oxford University Press.

CAMPBELL, PERSIA C. 1923. Chinese Coolie Emigration to Countries within the British Empire. P. S. King & Son.

CASALIS, J. E. 1859 (English translation, 1861). The Basutos.

DAVIS, E. June 1933. Some Aspects of the Marketing of Farm Products in South Africa. S. Afr. J. Econ.

DE CHAVONNES and his Council, and of Van Imhoff on the Cape, 1918. Van Riebeeck Society, I.

DEHÉRAIN, H. 1909. Le Cap de bonne-espérance au XVIIe siècle (Études sui l'Afrique, 2me sêr.).

DE KIEWIET, C. W. 1929. British Colonial Policy and the South African Republics, 1848–72. Longmans.

DODD, A. D. 1938. Native Vocational Training. A study of conditions in South Africa, 1652–1936. Lovedale Press.

DU PLESSIS, J. 1911. A History of Christian Missions in South Africa. Longmans.

EYBERS, G. W. (ed.). 1918. Select Constitutional Documents illustrating South African History, 1795–1910. Routledge.

FAZAN, S. H. 1934. A survey of the system of land tenure in the Transkeian Territories, etc. *In.* 'Kenya Land Commission, Evidence and Memoranda,' Col. 91, Vol. I, 1071–99. H.M.S.O.

FITZPATRICK, J. P. 1899. The Transvaal from Within. A private record of public affairs. Heinemann.

FLEMING, F. (Francis Patrick Flemyng). 1853. Kaffraria and its Inhabitants.

FRANKEL, S. H. March 1935. Return to Capital in the Witwatersrand Gold Industry, 1887–1932. Economic Journal.

FRERE, SIR BARTLE. 1882. Laws affecting relations between civilized and savage life. Journal of the Anthrop. Inst., Vol. XI.

GILBERT, D. W. August 1933. The economic effects of the gold discoveries upon South Africa. Q. Jnl. Econ.

GLANVILLE, E. 1876. The Industrial Progress of the Natives of South Africa. Society of Arts, pp. 448–56.

GOLDMANN, C. S. 1895–6. South African Mines; their position, results, and developments; together with an account of Diamond, Land, Finance, etc. 3 vols. Effingham, Wilson & Co.

GRAHAM, — and LATEGAN, P. N. The Coals of the Witbank District.

GROSSKOPF, J. F. W. 1933. Vestiging en trek van die Suid-Afrikaanse naturelle-bevolking onder newere ekonomiese voorwaardes. S. Afr. J. Econ., I, 261–80.

HAINES, E. S. 1935. Economic Status of the Cape Province Farm Native. S. Afr. J. Econ., III, 57–79.

HALL, H. 1859. Manual of South African Geography. Capetown.

HEADLAM, C. (ed.). 1933. Milner Papers, Vol. II, 1899–1905. Cassell & Company, Ltd.

HODGSON, M. L. 1924. The Hottentots in South Africa to 1828: a problem in labour and administration. S. Afr. J. Sci., 21, 594–621.

HOLDEN, W. C. 1855. History of the Colony of Natal, South Africa. Alexander Heylin.

HOLDEN, W. C. 1866. The Past and Future of the Kaffir Races. Richards, Glanville.

HUNTER, MONICA. 1936. Reaction to Conquest. Oxford University Press.

HUTT, W. H. March 1935. Logical Issues in the Study of Industrial Legislation in the Union. S. Afr. J. Econ.

HUTT, W. H. 1930. The Theory of Collective Bargaining. P. S. King.

HUTT, W. H. 1939. The Theory of Idle Resources. Cape.

JONES, J. D. RHEINALLT. 1935. Economic maladjustments and the civilized labour policy. Race Relations, 2, 134–40.

JONES, (MRS.) RHEINALLT. 1938. Some considerations which arise from the administration of the Native Land and Trust Act, 1936. Race Relations, 5, 51–60.

KNOWLES, L. C. A. and C. M. 1936. The Economic Development of the British Overseas Empire, Vol. III, Chap. VIII, The Union of South Africa. Routledge.

LESLIE, R. 1930. Coloured Labour and Trade Unionism in Capetown. J. Econ. Soc. S. Afr., 3, No. 6, 53–63.

LICHTENSTEIN, M. H. C. Travels in Southern Africa in the Years 1803–6. 1811–12. Van Riebeeck Society, X, XI.

LIVINGSTONE, D. 1857. Missionary Travels and Researches in South Africa. Murray.

LORAM, C. T. 1917. The Education of the South African Native. Longmans.

LUCAS, F. H. W. March 1933. The Determination of Wages in South Africa. S. Afr. J. Econ.

McGREGOR, F. 1940. Wage Regulation in South Africa. Race Relations, Vol. VII, No. 1.

MACLEAN, J. (ed.). 1858. A Compendium of Kafir Law and Customs. Mount Coke: Wesleyan Mission Press.

McLOUGHLIN, J. R. September 1938. A Defence of Control in the Marketing of Agricultural Products. S. Afr. J. Econ., Vol. VI.

MACMILLAN, W. M. 1929. Bantu, Boer, and Briton: the making of the South African Native Problem. Faber & Gwyer.

MACMILLAN, W. M. 1927. The Cape Colour Question. A historical survey. Faber & Gwyer.

MACMILLAN, W. M. 1930. Complex South Africa. An economic footnote to history. Faber & Faber.

MACMILLAN, W. M. 1936. The frontier and the Kaffir wars, 1792–1836. The Cambridge History of the British Empire, Vol. VIII, pp. 295–317.

McPHEE, J. 1930. Coal in the Transvaal. Proc. Empire Mining and Metallurgical Congress. Part III, pp. 680–703.

MALAN, F. S. 1936. The Union of South Africa. Cambridge History of the British Empire, Vol. VIII, pp. 641–61.

MARAIS, J. S. 1937. The Cape Coloured People, 1652–1937. Longmans.

MATTHEWS, J. W. 1887. Incwadi Yami, or Twenty Years Personal Experience of South Africa. Sampson Low & Co.

Medical Research, Publications of the South African Institute of. Vol. V, 1932.

MENTZEL, O. F. Life at the Cape in Mid-Eighteenth Century. Being the biography of R. S. Allemann. Trans. from the German by Margaret Greenlees. 1919. The Van Riebeeck Society, II.

MERRIMAN, J. X. 1876. Memorandum on Immigration and Water Supply.

MORTON, —. 1877. South African Diamond Fields. Proceedings of the American Geographical Society. 1877.

MURRAY, I. (unpublished thesis, University of Capetown). Early Railway Development in the Cape Colony.

NOBLE, J. 1875. Descriptive Handbook of the Cape Colony. Capetown.

ORENSTEIN, A. J. 1939. Diet of Natives on the Witwatersrand Gold Mines. Race Relations, Vol. V, No. 1.

PAISH, F. W. November 1938. Causes of Changes in Gold Supply. *Economica*, Vol. V (New Series).

PAULING, G. 1926. Chronicles of a Contractor. Being the Autobiography of the late George Pauling. Edited by David Buchan, with an Introduction by J. O. P. Bland. Constable & Co., Ltd.

PAYTON, C. A. 1872. The Diamond Diggings of South Africa. A personal and practical account . . . with a brief notice of the new Gold Fields. Horace Cox.

PEACE, WALTER. 1883. Our Colony of Natal. Published by permission of the Natal Government (Second Edition, 1884). E. Stanford.

PEARSALL, C. W. December 1937. Some Aspects of the Development of Secondary Industry in South Africa. S. Afr. J. Econ.

PHILLIPS, R. E. 1938. The Bantu in the City. A study of cultural adjustment on the Witwatersrand. Lovedale Press.

PLAATJE, S. T. 1916. Native Life in South Africa, before and since the European War and the Boer Rebellion. P. S. King.

PLANT, A. May 1939. An African survey. Economica.

RICHARDS, S. C. March 1938. Economists' Protest: The Dairy Produce and Maize Marketing Schemes. S. Afr. J. Econ.

RICHARDS, S. C. June 1938. Economists' Protest: Marketing Act, 1937, Scheme relating to Marketing of Wheat. S. Afr. J. Econ.

RICHARDS, S. C. December 1936. The 'New Despotism' in Agriculture. S. Afr. J. Econ.

RICHARDS, S. C. September 1935. Subsidies, Quotas, Tariffs, and the Excess Cost of Agriculture in South Africa. S. Afr. J. Econ.

RICHARDS, S. C. September 1938. Planning and Control in Agriculture. A Reply. S. Afr. J. Econ.

ROBERTSON, H. M. December 1937. The Cape of Good Hope and Systematic Colonization. S. Afr. J. Econ.

ROBERTSON, H. M. 1934-5. 150 Years of Economic Contact between Black and White. S. Afr. J. Econ. 2, 403-25; 3, 3-25.

ROBERTSON, H. M. November 1935. Schütz der Landwirtschaft in Südafrika. Weltwirtschaftliches Archiv.

ROBINSON, JOAN. 1933. Economics of Imperfect Competition. Macmillan.

ROGERS, H. 1933. Native Administration in the Union of South Africa. Johannesburg: University of the Witwatersrand Press.

SAUER, H. 1937. Ex Africa . . . Bles.

SCHAPERA, I. (ed.). 1937. The Bantu-speaking Tribes of South Africa: an ethnological survey. Routledge.

SCHAPERA, I. 1933. Economic Conditions in a Bechuanaland Native Reserve. J. Afr. Soc. Lond., 30, 633-55.

SCHAPERA, I. 1930. The Khoisan Peoples of South Africa. Bushmen and Hottentots. Routledge.

SCHAPERA, I. 1933-4. Labour Migration from a Bechuanaland Reserve. J. Afr. Soc. Lond., 32, 386-97; 33, 49-58.

SCHAPERA, I. (ed.). 1934. Western Civilization and the Natives of South Africa. Routledge.

SHANNON, H. A. June 1937. Urbanization, 1904–36. S. Afr. J. Econ., 5, 164–90.

SMITH, ADAM. Wealth of Nations, 1776 (ed. Edwin Cannan, 1904).

South African Journal of Economics, 1935–8.

SPENDER, J. A. 1923. Campbell-Bannerman, Vol. II. Hodder and Stoughton.

THEAL, G. McC. 1908. Records of the Cape Colony, from 1793 to 1827, copied . . . from the Manuscript Documents in the Public Record Office, London, Vols. V, VII. Printed for the Government of Cape Colony.

The Times History of the War in South Africa, 1899–1902, Vol. VI. 1909. Sampson Low.

TROLLOPE, A. 1878. South Africa. Chapman & Hall.

VAN DER HORST, J. G. March 1933. Two Conferences. S. Afr. J. Econ.

VAN DER POEL, J. 1933. Railway and Customs Policies in South Africa, 1885–1910.

VENTER, P. J. June 1934. Die Inbockstelsel. Die Huisgenoot, June 1, 1934.

WALKER, E. A. 1935. A History of South Africa (2nd revised, enlarged edn.). Longmans.

WALKER, IVAN L. November 1935. The Civilized Labour Policy and the Displacement of Non-European Labour. Race Relations, Vol. II, No. 5.

WILLIAMS, GARDNER F. 1902. The Diamond Mines of South Africa: some account of their rise and development. Macmillan.

WILSON, D. M. Behind the Scenes in the Transvaal.

WYNDHAM, H. A. 1936. The formation of the Union, 1901–10. Cambridge History of the British Empire, Vol. VIII, pp. 613–40.

INDEX

Tax, 152; and Portuguese labour, 288; and recruiting, 191, 212; and segregation, 267, 270; and trading licences, 314; and urban areas, 270, 274

Native Bills, Select Committee on (1927), 292

Native Conference (1925), 321

Native Economic Commission (1932), 152, 172, 183–4, 210–14, 218, 243, 271–7, 283–6, 304–18; and wages, 206, 210, 212, 228, 246, 254, 281

Native Farm Labour Committee. *See under* Farming

Native Grievances Inquiry (1913–14): and advances, 194–5; and allotment of labour, 196; and colour-bar, 184; and labour supply, 203; and long-period contracts, 194; and maximum average, 209; and mixed locations', 187; and piece-work, 193, 209–10; and recruiting, 194; and wages, 193–4, 206, 208–9

Native Labour Commissioner, 134; Committee, 277; in Zululand (Report on), 197

Native Land, Natives' Land. *See under* Land

Native Laws Amendment Act (1937), 271, 274–6

Native Laws and Customs Commissioner (1883), 124

Native Recruiting Corporation, 187–8, 193–4, 196–200, 203, 208, 211–12, 224, 301, 316

Native Revenue Accounts, 272

Native Service Contract Act (1932), 285, 293, 296

Native Tax (Consolidated) Bill, 151

Native Trust (South Africa), 113, 276, 303, 308–9

Native Trust and Land Act (1936), 299, 304, 317

Natives (Urban Areas) Act (1923), 245, 267, 270–73, 323; (amended, 1930) 274, 295–6, 323

Nyasaland, 194, 217, 221, 288

Orange Free State: allotments, 282; 'apprenticeship', 56–8; and Basutos, 24, 43, 56, 105, 145, 287–8; colour-bar, 179, 267; diamond-mines, 216–17, 228; European labour, 249–50; European-owned land, 54, 111–13, 290; exports, 54–5; farming, 54–7, 63, 98–9, 145–7, 160, 279–81, 286–9; Griquas, 56; hut-tax, 112; labour distribution and supply, 56–8, 110, 153, 289; labour tax, 54, 57; locations, 143, 270; Masters and

Servants Law, 37; and mining industries, 216–17; and Natal, 92; Native-owned land, 290, 299; pass system, 124, 143, 275, 295; population, 54–6, 292; railways, 92, 140; registration of Natives, 111; reserves, 112, 302; segregation, 270; 'slavery', 57–8; squatters, 153; taxation, 110–13, 305; and Tembus, 106; and the Transkei, 287–8; transport, 54, 92; and Transvaal, 44; Trollope in, 63, 96; Voortrekkers, 42–4, 53; wages, 147, 244, 275, 281, (in kind), 235; wool, 54–5

Pass system, and colour-bar, 37; Commission on Native Affairs (1865) and, 33; Commission on Native Laws (1883) and, 124; Department of Labour and, 246; District Pass, 133–4; Employer's Pass, 134; fees, 275; and Fingoes, 32, 34, 91; and Hottentots, 9, 276; Industrial Conciliation Act (1924) and, 250; industrial councils and, 247; and 'labour districts', 180, and labour-supply, 34, 124, 274–6; laws, 123–4, 133, 144, 161, 177; 269; and mobility of labour, 289; Monthly Passes, 273–5; and 'Native Foreigners', 32–4; penalties, 30; restrictions, 273–4; statistics, 91, 137, 153; and stock-theft, 34; and Thembu, 32, 123; Town Pass, 143; and Wage Boards, 252–3; and women, 269. *See also* Cape Colony, Coal-mines, Contracts, Gold-mines, Natal, Orange Free State, Transvaal, Transkei

Peddie, 15, 16, 27–9, 39, 91, 117, 145

Piece-work, 193, 208–10, 227

Pondo, 23, 36, 42, 105, 109, 149, 153, 316–17

'Poor Whites', 173–85, 236

Population: Bloemfontein (1852), 54; Durban (1881), 86; Kimberley (1877), 86; Kingwilliamstown (1875), 104; Port Elizabeth (1865–91), 86, 94. *See also under* Cape Colony, Cape Town, Natal, Orange Free State, Transkei, Transvaal, Union of South Africa

Portuguese East African Natives: and coal mines, 228–9; and contracts, 194, 211, 214, 218; Convention of 1928, 220, 223; and diamond-mines, 219; on farms, 90, 288; Lord Milner and, 219; and *modus vivendi*, 219; on public works, 90–1; on railways, 91, 140; recruiting, 135, 164, 192, 196–7, 211, 214,